# CARNIVORES
of the
# WORLD

SECOND EDITION

# CARNIVORES
## of the
# WORLD

SECOND EDITION

Luke Hunter & Priscilla Barrett

PRINCETON UNIVERSITY PRESS

Princeton and Oxford

# For Sophie

Published in the United States, Canada, and the Philippine Islands by
Princeton University Press,
41 William Street, Princeton, New Jersey 08540

First published in 2011 in the UK as *A Field Guide to Carnivores of the World*
by New Holland Publishers (UK) Ltd

This edition published in the United Kingdom 2018 by Bloomsbury Wildlife. Bloomsbury Wildlife,
Bloomsbury, and the Diana logo are trademarks of Bloomsbury Publishing Plc.

Skull and footprint illustrations (pages 200–248) by Sally McClarty
Maps by Lisanne Petracca

Luke Hunter has asserted his right under the Copyright, Designs and Patents Act, 1988, to be
identified as Author of this work

For legal purposes the Acknowledgements on p. 251
constitute an extension of this copyright page

A catalogue record for this book is available from the British Library
Library of Congress Control Number: 2018947081
Paper ISBN 9780691182957

Design by Rod Teasdale
Typeset in Adobe Garamond Pro
Printed and bound in China by C&C Offset Printing Co., Ltd

To find out more about our authors and books visit www.bloomsbury.com
and sign up for our newsletters

# CONTENTS

## INTRODUCTION

Carnivore Families........................................... 7

Conservation of Carnivores............................ 11

Structure of the Species Accounts........................... 13

## SPECIES ACCOUNTS

FELIDAE
Cats............................................... 14

HYAENIDAE
Hyaenas...................................... 52

HERPESTIDAE
Mongooses ...................................... 56

EUPLERIDAE
Fosa and Allies.................................... 74

PRIONODONTIDAE
Linsangs ...................................... 78

VIVERRIDAE
Civets, Genets and Oyans ............................. 78

NANDINIIDAE
African Palm-civet................................ 96

CANIDAE
Dogs ............................................ 98

URSIDAE
Bears ...................................... 130

PROCYONIDAE
Raccoons, Coatis and Allies............................ 142

AILURIDAE
Red Panda .................................... 148

MEPHITIDAE
Skunks and Stink-badgers .................... 150

MUSTELIDAE
Badgers, Martens, Weasels and Otters.............. 158

SKULLS ......................................... 200

FOOTPRINTS ..................................... 233

Glossary ........................................ 249

Acknowledgements ................................ 251

Index ......................................... 252

# INTRODUCTION

This book describes all of the world's terrestrial carnivores, 250 species that are united in a shared ancestry of subsisting mainly on meat. Many other species, humans included, eat meat, but this does not make them carnivores in scientific nomenclature. That label belongs exclusively to the members of the order Carnivora, which, despite remarkable variation in size and shape, all descend from a small civet-like carnivorous ancestor that lived more than 60 million years ago. Some modern carnivores eat little meat or, as in the case of the Giant Panda (page 130), none at all, but all members of the Carnivora trace their ancestry back to the same predatory origins, and retain many of the physical, behavioural and ecological adaptations common to their truly carnivorous relatives.

The Carnivora is the fifth-largest mammalian order (of twenty-nine extant orders), occurs on every large landmass including Antarctica, and inhabits every major habitat on Earth, from the hyper-arid interior of the Sahara Desert to Arctic ice sheets. The world's smallest carnivore, the tiny Least Weasel (page 184), can squeeze through a wedding ring and weighs 10,000 times less than the largest terrestrial species, the Polar Bear (page 140). The order Carnivora includes some of the world's most iconic,

magnificent and admired species – and, regrettably, some of the most endangered.

This book covers the world's thirteen terrestrial carnivore families. It does not include three chiefly marine carnivore families, the sea-lions (family Otariidae, sixteen species), seals (family Phocidae, nineteen species) and the Walrus (family Odobenidae). While these three families have, at times, been classified as a separate order, the Pinnipedia, there is no dispute today that they belong within the Carnivora. Although they do not appear here, the pinnipeds are covered in many excellent field guides to marine mammals.

Carnivores are separated into two major suborders, reflecting a divergence early in the order's evolution an estimated 45–50 million years ago (although given the paucity of fossil remains, possibly considerably earlier). Suborder Feliformia contains the 'cat-like' families Felidae, Hyaenidae, Herpestidae, Eupleridae, Prionodontidae, Viverridae and Nandiniidae. Suborder Caniformia comprises the 'dog-like' families Canidae, Ursidae, Procyonidae, Ailuridae, Mephitidae and Mustelidae, as well as the three pinniped families.

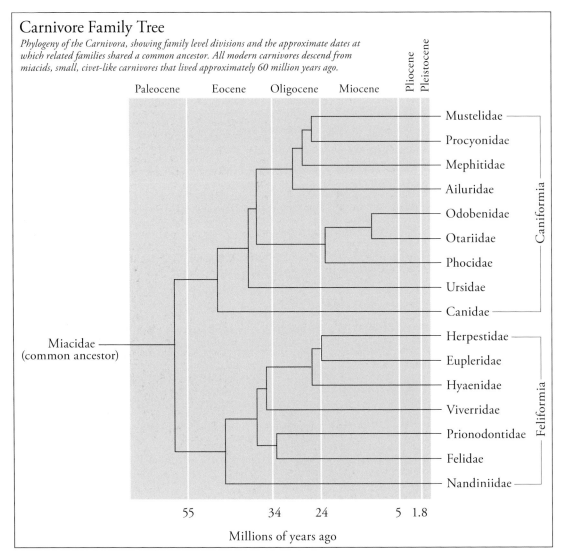

## Carnivore Family Tree

*Phylogeny of the Carnivora, showing family level divisions and the approximate dates at which related families shared a common ancestor. All modern carnivores descend from miacids, small, civet-like carnivores that lived approximately 60 million years ago.*

## How many species of carnivores?

This book's first edition covered 244 species of terrestrial carnivores. In the intervening years, at least a further nine species have been described, while others have been subsumed, bringing the total in this edition to 250. The changes are mostly the product of increasingly powerful genetic comparisons between populations. Some pairs of species long assumed to be different, based mainly on appearance, turned out to be the same (e.g. Grandidier's and Broad-striped vontsiras, page 76), while others that were thought to be the same turned out to be hidden, or cryptic, species, so similar in appearance to another, usually very closely related, species that only molecular techniques revealed the underlying differences (e.g. tigrinas, page 30; and Japanese and Siberian weasels, page 180).

In principle, these newly discovered genetic distinctions reflect other meaningful biological differences, for example, in morphology, behaviour or ecology, and especially in the defining characteristic of species, reproductive isolation; species cannot produce fertile offspring with a second species. Although that principle mostly holds true in the Carnivora, exceptions exist. Few would question that Coyotes (page 102) and Grey Wolves (page 100) are separate species, yet very fluid hybridisation between them in eastern North America (see page 104) reveals the challenges in delineating the boundaries between species. Our classification of organisms as species is a momentary snapshot in time on the extremely complex and ongoing evolutionary process of speciation, and exactly what defines a species is debated vigorously – even among biologists. This book takes a conservative approach to adopting new species and includes only those supported by multiple lines of published evidence (e.g. molecular, morphological, ecological and biogeographic) and that are widely accepted (e.g. by the International Union for Conservation of Nature Species Survival Commission (IUCN SSC) Specialist Groups devoted to carnivores). Additions, as well as cases where species have been subsumed and some that remain unresolved, are summarised below in the section 'Carnivore Families'.

# CARNIVORE FAMILIES

### Suborder FELIFORMIA, 7 families, 121 species

## FAMILY FELIDAE CATS, 40 species
**Size range** Rusty-spotted Cat and Black-footed Cat (1–2.5kg) to Tiger (75–261kg)

The cat family arose approximately 30 million years ago in what is now Eurasia, and today occurs globally except in Antarctica and Australasia. A single subfamily, the Felinae, comprises all extant species (the famous sabretooth cats belong in a second, now extinct, subfamily, Machairodontinae). Some authorities group the genera *Panthera* and *Neofelis* into a separate subfamily, Pantherinae ('big cats'). Recent and comprehensive analyses based largely on genetics use the term 'lineages' to denote closely related groups of cats – effectively the same as 'subfamily' used for other carnivore families (highlighting some confusing subjectivity in naming conventions). For consistency, lineage is used here. The eight lineages within the Felidae are:

- *Felis* lineage, wildcats and allies (6 species).
- *Prionailurus* lineage, Pallas's Cat, leopard cats and allies (6 species).
- *Puma* lineage, Jaguarundi, Puma and Cheetah.
- *Lynx* lineage, lynxes and Bobcat (4 species).
- *Leopardus* lineage, Ocelot and allies (8 species).
- *Caracal* lineage, Caracal, African Golden Cat and Serval.
- *Pardofelis* lineage, Marbled Cat, Asian Golden Cat and Bay Cat.
- *Panthera* lineage, 'big cats' (7 species).

Forty wild cat species are currently recognised. Since this book's first edition, new analyses have resulted in the division of three species into six (wildcats, page 14; leopard cats, page 20; tigrinas, page 30). There is preliminary genetic evidence that both the Marbled Cat (page 24) and Flat-headed Cat (page 22) may warrant being split into separate continental and Sunda species, as is the case for clouded leopards and leopard cats.

Cats are hypercarnivores that subsist almost entirely on animal prey, which is generally killed by a suffocating bite to the throat in the case of large prey, or by crushing the skull of small prey. Most

*Domestic cat*
The domestic cat, Felis silvestris catus, *descends from the wildcats (page 14), with which it is still able to interbreed. They are considered the same species, but some authorities argue that the genetic differences selected by human-mediated breeding warrant the domestic cat being considered a separate full species,* Felis catus.
Worldwide, the number of domestic cats, including feral and semi-wild populations, is crudely estimated to exceed 600 million.

cats are solitary, territorial and nocturno-crepuscular. The Lion (page 46) is the only cat that lives in large, permanent, complex social groups, although male Cheetahs (page 40) form small, enduring coalitions, and free-living domestic cats in colonies sometimes form small, stable social groups.

## FAMILY HYAENIDAE HYAENAS, 4 species
**Size range** Aardwolf (7.7–14kg) to Spotted Hyaena (49–86kg)

The hyaena family arose at least 23 million years ago in Eurasia and reached an evolutionary peak 6–12 million years ago, when as many as twenty-four different species existed. Despite their dog-like appearance, hyaenas belong in the Feliformia and thus are more closely related to cats and their allies than to dogs. There are four extant species. All of them evolved in Africa, which remains the stronghold of modern hyaena distribution, with one species, the Striped Hyaena (page 52), also found in the Middle East through to India. The family is divided into two main subfamilies:

- Protelinae, a clade of relatively gracile, dog-like hyaenas with a single extant member, the Aardwolf, which diverged from the rest of the family around 10.6 million years ago.
- Hyaeninae, or bone-cracking hyaenas, a group that contains the other three modern species.

Hyaenas are hypercarnivores with a prodigious digestive ability that probably arose early in the family's evolution. In the Aardwolf (page 52), this capacity evolved to deal with noxious defensive terpenes secreted by termites, which are its primary prey. The bone-cracking hyaenas are capable of digesting all parts of animal prey except the hooves, the hair and the keratin sheaths of ungulate horns, and they tolerate the extremely high bacterial loads present in rotting carrion.

All hyaena species live in enduring social groups that take their simplest form in the Aardwolf's monogamous, cooperatively breeding pairs. Striped Hyaenas also live in monogamous pairs, but small groups comprising female and multiple males have recently been documented; the full range of their sociality is still poorly known. Brown Hyaenas (page 54) form small family groups that share a territory, but otherwise spend most of their time alone. The most complex social patterns are displayed by the Spotted Hyaena (page 54), which lives in large clans with a unique matrilineal social structure. Females are larger than, and dominant to, males, and usually live their entire lives in the same clan; female cubs inherit their mother's rank and outrank immigrant males, even adults. This is not known in any other carnivore, and in fact it most closely resembles the societies of primates such as baboons.

## FAMILY HERPESTIDAE MONGOOSES, 34 species
**Size range** Common Dwarf Mongoose (210–340g) to White-tailed Mongoose (1.8–5.2kg)

Mongooses were formerly classified within the Viverridae, but are now recognised in their own family, the Herpestidae. Within the Feliformia, the family is most closely related to the Eupleridae (which emerged as an early Herpestidae offshoot) and the Hyaenidae. The mongoose family is subdivided into two large subfamilies:

- Herpestinae, solitary mongooses (23 species).
- Mungotinae, social mongooses (11 species).

This major division is thought to reflect a divergence early in mongoose evolution, in which the opening up of forested habitats favoured sociality in an ancestral group-living species that ultimately gave rise to the modern social species.

Mongooses occur in Africa, the Middle East and South Asia, with one species, the Egyptian Mongoose (page 60), present in Portugal and Spain. Members of this family are primarily carnivorous and eat mainly small vertebrates and invertebrates; fruit and vegetable matter is eaten to a limited degree by some species. Reflecting the subfamily classification, mongooses are either largely solitary (although some Herpestinae have semi-social tendencies, for example denning together) or live in complex social groups. Social patterns are best understood in dwarf mongooses (page 68), Banded Mongoose (page 70) and Meerkat (page 66); the rest of the Mungotinae are believed to be similarly social, although they are not nearly as well studied.

## FAMILY EUPLERIDAE EUPLERIDS, 7 species
**Size range** Narrow-striped Boky (450–740g) to Fosa (6.2–8.6kg)

Members of the Eupleridae have historically been classified as cats, mongooses or civets, but it is now known that the family arose from a single mongoose-like ancestor that colonised Madagascar from mainland Africa an estimated 16.5–24 million years ago. Subsequent rapid adaptive radiation on Madagascar led to the seven living species, now grouped in two subfamilies:

- Euplerinae, 'civet-like' species; Fanaloka, Fosa and Falanouc.
- Galidiinae, 'mongoose-like' species; vontsiras and Boky (4 species).

Since this book's first edition, genetic analyses have led to the reclassification of two *Galidictis* species as a single species, the Broad-striped Vontsira. Similarly, there is now stronger evidence that two recently proposed species are invalid; the Western or Giant Falanouc (*Eupleres major*) is considered the same species as the Falanouc (page 74), and Durrell's Vontsira (*Salanoia durrelli*) is considered the same species as the Brown-tailed Vontsira (page 76).

Euplerids eat mostly animal prey; their feeding habits range from almost exclusive insectivory/vermivory in the Falanouc to the mammal-dominated diet of the Fosa (page 74). Most species are thought to be chiefly solitary, although both temporary and enduring sociality has been observed in five species. Most euplerids are poorly studied.

## FAMILY PRIONODONTIDAE LINSANGS, 2 species
**Size range** Banded Linsang (590–800g) to Spotted Linsang (550g–1.2kg)

The Prionodontidae is an ancient carnivoran family originally classified among the Viverridae and once thought to be most closely related to African oyans (page 96; formerly also called linsangs), which are morphologically and ecologically very similar. In fact, recent molecular analysis reveals that linsangs represent an early sister group to the Felidae, with a shared common ancestor around 42 million years ago. Linsangs are only distantly related to oyans (family Viverridae), a remarkable case of evolutionary convergence.

Linsangs are restricted to Southeast Asia, where they inhabit evergreen and moist forested habitats. They are highly arboreal and hypercarnivorous nocturnal hunters of small prey. They are solitary, but little detail is known of their social and spatial organisation.

## FAMILY VIVERRIDAE CIVETS, GENETS AND OYANS, 33 species
**Size range** Leighton's Oyan (500–700g) to Binturong (9–20kg)

The Viverridae is an ancient lineage of the Feliformia thought to have arisen at least 34 million years ago in Eurasia, followed by later colonisation of Africa. It is subdivided into four subfamilies:

- Viverrinae, large terrestrial civets (6 species).
- Genettinae, genets and oyans (16 species).
- Paradoxurinae, palm civets and Binturong (7 species).
- Hemigalinae, Otter Civet and allies (4 species).

The species limits within the Viverridae are mostly well defined, although the critically endangered Malabar Civet (page 86) is possibly the same species as the Large-spotted Civet (page 86), and the classification of genets is controversial, with as many as 17 species proposed in the genus *Genetta* (14 are recognised in this book).

Viverrids are restricted to Africa and South Asia; the Small-spotted Genet (page 92) also occurs in Europe, although this is possibly as a result of human introduction. They are largely solitary and nocturnal. Many species are semi-arboreal to highly arboreal and have protractile claws, as in felids. Viverrids are primarily carnivorous, with a diet dominated by small vertebrates and invertebrates, or, in the case of the Paradoxurinae, largely frugivorous.

## FAMILY NANDINIIDAE AFRICAN PALM-CIVET, 1 species
**Size** African Palm-civet (1.2–3kg)

The African Palm-civet (page 96) is a primitive species retaining some unique ancestral features (mainly in the structure of the skull and carnassials) that no longer occur in any other modern carnivore. It was formerly classified in the Viverridae as an African member of the otherwise entirely Asian palm civet family Paradoxurinae, giving rise to its erroneous common name. Molecular data confirm that it represents an ancient sister species to all other feliform carnivores; it shared a common ancestor with all other Feliformia an estimated 36–54 million years ago.

Morphologically and ecologically, the African Palm-civet probably closely resembles the earliest feliform carnivores. Endemic to equatorial Africa, it inhabits forest and woodland savannahs. It is mainly frugivorous, and also takes vertebrate and invertebrate prey. It is arboreal, nocturnal and mainly solitary, with defined and defended territories.

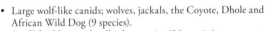

## Suborder CANIFORMIA, 9 families, 164 species (including pinnipeds, 36 species)

## FAMILY CANIDAE DOGS, 35 species
**Size range** Fennec and Blanford's Fox (0.8–1.9kg) to Grey Wolf (18–79.4kg)

The Canidae is thought to be the most ancient living caniform family, whose origins began more than 40 million years ago in North America. This remained the centre of canid evolution until around 6 million years ago, when the formation of the Beringian land bridge connected Asia to North America, allowing canids to flood into Eurasia. Canids similarly colonised South America with the emergence of the Isthmus of Panama 3 million years ago. All modern canids are considered members of the subfamily Caninae (there are two extinct subfamilies), which is further divided into two distinct lineages that diverged 5–9 million years ago:

- Large wolf-like canids; wolves, jackals, the Coyote, Dhole and African Wild Dog (9 species).
- Small fox-like canids; all other species (26 species).

Canid species are largely well defined, although hybridisation between Grey Wolves (page 100) and Coyotes (page 102) in eastern North America has fuelled an ongoing debate about the number of species; these forms (including the Red Wolf, treated as a species in the first edition) are covered here in a special section on canid hybrids (page 104). Since this book's first edition, Golden Jackal (page 106) populations in Africa have been identified as a distinct species most closely related to the Grey Wolf and now reclassified as the African Wolf (page 106).

The Canidae is the most widespread family within the Carnivora, with at least one species found on every continent except Antarctica (colonisation of Australia by the Dingo was

*Domestic dog*
*The domestic dog descends from the Grey Wolf (page 100), with which it is still able to interbreed, and is either regarded as the Grey Wolf subspecies* Canis lupus familiaris *or as the parataxon* Canis familiaris *(meaning that while technically the same species as the Grey Wolf by phylogenetic criteria, it is sufficiently distinct to be recognised as though it is a separate species). The number of domestic dogs worldwide, including feral and stray populations, is crudely estimated at almost a billion.*

assisted by humans 3,500–4,000 years ago; page 98). It is also the most social family. All canids form enduring social relationships centred around a monogamous male–female pair that cooperates to raise pups; in some cases, yearling offspring remain with their parents to act as 'helpers' in raising subsequent litters. In most foxes and jackals, the mated pair remains the basic social unit, while it forms the nucleus for larger, more complicated social groups in many other canids such as Grey Wolves, African Wild Dogs (page 110) and Dholes (page 108). Within this range, canid sociality is extremely flexible, with some species shifting across a continuum from monogamous pairs to pack living, depending on the availability of resources. Canids are obligate carnivores that eat mainly animal prey; fruits and vegetables are additionally consumed by some species.

## FAMILY URSIDAE BEARS, 8 species
**Size range** Sun Bear (25–80kg) to Polar Bear (150–800kg)

The bear family arose early in carnivoran evolution and, together with the Canidae, is thought to be one of the most ancient families within the Canifornia. The earliest putative species are approximately 33–37 million years old, although their similarity to early canids (with which bears share an ancient common ancestor) obscures precise dating of the family's origins. Today's eight species of bear are divided into the following three subfamilies:

• Ailuropodinae, Giant Panda.
• Tremarctinae, Andean Bear.
• Ursinae, 'typical bears'; all other species (6 species).

The Giant Panda (page 131) and Andean Bear (page 134) are the most ancient and distinctive species. The inter-relationships of the other six species (the 'typical bears') are poorly understood, except it is clear that Polar Bears evolved recently and rapidly from a population of Brown Bears (page 138) isolated during the mid-Pleistocene, perhaps only 200,000 years ago.

Bears occur mainly in Eurasia and North America, with one species, the Andean Bear, found in northern South America. Most species are omnivorous, shifting their diet seasonally depending on food availability to focus on the energetically richest diet; the family's extremes are represented by the completely herbivorous Giant Panda, and the Polar Bear, which subsists largely on seals.

Bears are distinctive among carnivores in weathering severe winters by going into hibernation, essentially a strategy to survive the leanest period of the year. During hibernation, bears do not eat, drink, urinate or defecate, but they use as many as 4,000 calories daily by burning fat reserves. Hibernating American Black Bears (page 136) reduce oxygen consumption and metabolic rate by half, breathe only once every 45 seconds and reduce their heart rate to as low as eight beats per minute.

In concert with hibernation, breeding females undergo delayed implantation, or embryonic diapause, in which development of the embryo is postponed shortly after conception, which typically occurs in the northern spring–summer. This allows recently impregnated females to gain sufficient fat for winter hibernation without having to nourish developing embryos. It is also likely to reduce the period in which hibernating females nourish embryos, although birth still occurs about midway through the fast while in the den. Both of these features probably arose early in ursid evolution. All modern bears display some degree of delayed implantation, although only species (or populations) that experience harsh winters hibernate. Populations that enter hibernation undergo a period of hyperphagia before denning, in which individuals spend up to 20 hours each day foraging for

high-quality food (especially hard mast) to lay down fat reserves.

Bears are largely cathemeral and solitary, and occupy stable ranges generally without strict territorial defence. The range size of the Polar Bear is the largest recorded among carnivores, and among the largest recorded in mammals.

## FAMILY PROCYONIDAE RACCOONS, COATIS AND ALLIES, 13 species
**Size range** Ringtail (0.8–1.1kg) to Northern Raccoon (1.7–28kg)

The Procyonidae arose approximately 27–30 million years ago as an offshoot from the lineage that gave rise to the Mustelidae, hence these two families are considered the other's closest relative within the Canifornia. The earliest procyonids evolved in Europe, from which they colonised Asia and North America; the family died out in Eurasia and today occurs only in North and South America. Divisions within the family, including the exact number of species, remain controversial. The olingo genus *Bassaricyon* (page 146) was revised in 2013 to include four species, and the Mountain Coati (page 144) may prove to consist of two distinct species.

Procyonids are among the least carnivorous of carnivores, with most species having broadly omnivorous diets. The Northern Raccoon (page 142) is one of the most omnivorous mammal species on Earth, while the Kinkajou (page 148) eats fruit almost exclusively. Procyonids are largely nocturnal, and vary between being solitary to highly social, and from being terrestrial to almost exclusively arboreal.

## FAMILY AILURIDAE RED PANDA, 1 species
**Size** Red Panda (3–3.6kg)

The Red Panda (page 148) is the only member of a unique family, the Ailuridae, and has an uncertain phylogenetic position. It belongs in the Canifornia, where it is thought to be most closely related to procyonids, but there is also evidence for grouping it closely to mustelids, mephitids and ursids. It was formerly grouped with the Giant Panda in a separate family due mainly to a similar diet of bamboo and associated adaptations (the Red Panda was actually discovered and named first, making a misnomer of the Giant Panda's common name). Although this classification is no longer accepted and the Giant Panda is unequivocally a bear, the Red Panda's closest relatives remain uncertain.

Red Pandas are restricted to forests of southeast China and bordering countries. Their diet is almost exclusively bamboo. They are cathemeral and solitary, and occupy stable ranges.

## FAMILY MEPHITIDAE SKUNKS AND STINK-BADGERS, 11 species
**Size range** Pygmy Spotted Skunk (130–230g) to Striped Skunk (0.6–5.5kg)

Skunks and stink-badgers were formerly classified in the mustelid family, but are now recognised in their own family as an early offshoot of a branch of carnivore evolution that also gave rise to the mustelids, procyonids and Red Panda. They are further subdivided into two subfamilies:

• Mephitinae, true skunks (9 species).
• Myadinae, stink-badgers (2 species).

Many skunk species are poorly defined, and genetic analysis is likely to identify more hidden species or subsume species, particularly among the spotted skunks (genus *Spilogale*). Since this book's first edition, an analysis of the hog-nosed skunks (genus *Conepatus*) has combined Humboldt's Hog-nosed Skunk with Molina's Hog-nosed Skunk as a single species (page 152), and there is preliminary evidence that the Striped Hog-nosed Skunk (page 152) may comprise two species, in Meso-America and South America respectively.

True skunks are restricted to North and South America, and stink-badgers are endemic to insular Southeast Asia. All members of the family have enlarged muscular anal scent glands that spray potent fluid in self-defence, and all have associated black-and-white aposematic coloration. Mephitids are omnivorous, with invertebrates and small vertebrates dominating the diet. They are largely solitary with little evidence of territoriality; many species can reach high densities, congregate at food patches and have extensively overlapping ranges.

## FAMILY MUSTELIDAE BADGERS, MARTENS, WEASELS AND OTTERS, 60–62 species
**Size range** Least Weasel (25–300g) to Sea Otter (14.5–45kg)

The Mustelidae is the largest family of the Carnivora, and arose in Eurasia at least 24 million years ago. Subdivision within this large family is complicated and undergoes regular revision as new molecular and fossil discoveries are made. Eight subfamilies are generally recognised, the composition of which has been better defined with new evidence since this book's first edition:

- Taxidiinae, American Badger.
- Mellivorinae, Honey Badger.
- Melinae, Eurasian and hog badgers (6 or 7 species).
- Helictidinae, ferret badgers (4 or 5 species).
- Guloninae, martens, Tayra, Fisher and Wolverine (11 species).
- Ictonychinae, grisons, zorillas and allies (7 species).
- Mustelinae, American Mink, true weasels and polecats (17 species).
- Lutrinae, otters (13 species)

The total number of species in Mustelidae is unresolved; however, evidence for at least five additional species has accumulated since 2011. The European Badger (page 162) is now considered to be three or possibly four discrete species based on new molecular data supporting earlier morphology-based divisions. Recent genetic analysis show that populations of the Siberian Weasel (page 180) in Japan actually comprise two distinct species, including the newly delineated Japanese Weasel (page 180). Similarly, populations of American Marten on the North American Pacific coast are now classed as a separate species, the Pacific Marten (page 166). There are others that await further study. Based on only two samples but including compelling genetic evidence, the very unusual Cuc Phuong Ferret Badger (page 172) has recently been described. Less convincing and lacking genetic analysis are the Egyptian Weasel (*Mustela subpalmata*), Sichuan Weasel (*M. russelliana*) and Tonkin Weasel (*M. tonkinensis*), which are treated in this book as populations of the Least Weasel (page 184).

From their Eurasian origins, mustelids underwent repeated colonisations into the Americas and Africa. Today, the family occurs globally, with species on every continent except Antarctica and Australasia (although Least Weasels and Stoats, page 184, have been introduced to New Zealand by humans). Most modern species are variations on the family's earliest evolutionary form, a solitary long-bodied terrestrial hunter of small mammals. However, as befits such a large and diverse family, mustelids have evolved to adopt a wide variety of lifestyles, from aquatic and social in the case of otters, to semi-arboreal in the martens.

In common with their close relatives, the Mephitidae, most mustelids have anal glands that produce strongly smelling secretions. These glands are best developed in the Striped Weasel (page 176), Libyan Weasel (page 176), Zorilla (page 176) and Marbled Polecat (page 174), which are able to spray secretions defensively.

The Mustelidae is remarkable for the prevalence of delayed implantation, in which development of the embryo in the womb is temporarily postponed, in some cases for as long as 11 months. This adaptation allows both mating and birth to occur during optimal summer–spring periods, when finding mates and raising young is most benign. Thus, a breeding female American Badger (page 158) typically conceives in the summer and gives birth the following spring. Approximately a third of mustelids are thought to display some degree of delayed implantation; this compares to less than 0.05 per cent of mammals overall (it is also prevalent among bears).

# CONSERVATION OF CARNIVORES

Carnivores are rare. Their positions at the tops of intricate food pyramids dictate that they are naturally far less common than the species on which they prey. Every Tiger (page 44) needs to kill about fifty medium or large ungulates a year to survive. In naturally functioning ecosystems, this represents about 10 per cent of available prey; that is, a population of 500 prey animals is required to sustain a single Tiger for a year. Therefore, a tiny population of ten Tigers requires 5,000 prey animals (not accounting for the needs of coexisting carnivores such as Leopards, page 48, and Dholes, page 108); in turn, these require large expanses of habitat for their survival. The outcome of these calculations has been labelled the large carnivore problem: predators require large tracts of suitable habitat with abundant prey populations. The problem is most acute for top-level carnivores such as big cats, hyaenas, wolves, African Wild Dogs, bears, Fosas and Wolverines (page 164), but *natural* vulnerability to extinction is an inherent feature of the entire order Carnivora.

The primary threat to most carnivores is the combined loss of habitat and prey. More than two-thirds of Earth's terrestrial land area is now devoted to supporting humans, with the remaining natural habitat disappearing at an estimated rate of 1 per cent per year. Where people replace forests, woodlands and grasslands with cities, agriculture and livestock, most carnivores decline or disappear. Even maintaining habitat is valueless if there is no food for carnivores. Tracts of relatively intact but 'empty forest' across Asia, Latin America and central Africa are worthless to carnivores because people have hunted out their prey.

Compounding the relentless depletion of resources on which carnivores depend – *indirect* threats, in conservation nomenclature – are the reasons why humans kill them directly. People have hunted carnivores for millennia and for many reasons, but the two most critical modern motives contributing to carnivore declines are the killing of carnivores as a perceived or real threat to livestock (and, less so, human life), and the hunting of carnivores because their body parts are considered valuable. The former affects large carnivores wherever they encounter people and their herds; subsistence yak shepherds in Central Asia trap Snow Leopards (page 42) for essentially the same reasons that commercial cattle ranchers in the western United States clash with reintroduced Grey Wolves, page 100.

The killing of carnivores for their parts occurs globally, but is particularly problematic in Asia, where the consumption and use of wildlife for traditional medicine has a history of thousands of years. The primary threat to the Tiger today is intense poaching pressure to feed this trade, which is growing rapidly as a burgeoning Chinese middle class covets certain parts of the species (and many other species too). Not surprisingly, these two drivers are often interleaved; Mongolian herders make extra money by selling the furs of sheep-killing Grey Wolves (or any they can shoot, for that matter), and the claws, fat and other sought-after parts of Lions poisoned by African pastoralists are often sold or traded.

Although not nearly as widespread, ancillary anthropogenic threats to carnivores can be very damaging to populations at a local level. Recreational hunting, whether by big-game hunters for trophies or by trappers for fur-bearing carnivores, can provoke declines where they are poorly regulated or in concert with other factors, for example natural fluctuations in prey numbers.

Infectious disease is a natural part of wildlife populations worldwide, but it can be particularly problematic to carnivores when introduced by humans and their domestic animals. Wild canids are especially vulnerable to rabies and canine distemper transmitted by domestic dogs, and outbreaks have devastated populations of Ethiopian Wolves (page 108) and African Wild Dogs (page 110). Similarly, recurrent outbreaks of plague are the primary factor impeding the recovery of endangered Black-footed Ferrets (page 178). Finally, hybridisation with domestic animals threatens some carnivores. The European Wildcat (page 14) and Dingo (page 98) are unlikely to remain genetically distinct due to interbreeding with feral domestic cats and dogs, respectively.

Four modern carnivore species are extinct, all as a direct result of human impacts – primarily hunting for trade (the last record is given in parenthesis):

- Falkland Island Wolf *Dusicyon australis* (1876).
- Sea Mink *Neovison macrodon* (1894).
- Japanese Sea Lion *Zalophus japonicus* (1951).
- Caribbean Monk Seal *Monachus tropicalis* (1952).

Seventy-four[1] carnivores, including ten pinnipeds, are threatened with extinction according to the IUCN Red List (page 13). Three species – Malabar Civet (page 86), Pygmy Raccoon (page 142) and European Mink (page 182) – are listed as Critically Endangered, with an extremely high risk of extinction in the wild. Twenty-eight species (including seven pinnipeds) are Endangered, with a very high risk of extinction. Forty-three species (including three pinnipeds) are Vulnerable, with a high risk of extinction.

The persistence of most carnivores relies on large expanses of wilderness relatively free from human influences. Any meaningful effort to conserve carnivores must set aside vast protected areas and ensure that they are truly protected; this does not necessarily entail excluding people, but it does mean vigorously limiting their worst impacts, such as clearing habitat, hunting wildlife and introducing livestock and disease. Worldwide, there are hundreds of globally significant parks that protect carnivores. However, as human populations continue to grow, the pressure for their land and resources intensifies, while the opportunity for expanding or creating more protected areas dwindles. Accordingly, parks alone will not be sufficient to guarantee the survival of many carnivore species.

Equally as important, attention must be devoted to the human-modified landscapes that now dominate the globe and that, historically, have been omitted from conservation planning. Despite their demanding ecological requirements, many carnivores are able to survive in modified habitats – a habitat need not necessarily be pristine for carnivores to maintain a presence. Even those carnivores that are most difficult to conserve, such as wolves, bears and big cats, can inhabit landscapes where people and their livestock dominate, provided the reasons for intolerance and retaliatory killing are addressed. The key is in fostering mechanisms for coexistence, typically through reducing the problems that carnivores create (e.g. by improving livestock husbandry to reduce vulnerability to predators), or by making carnivores valuable to people who bear the burden of living with them (e.g. through tourism). Many communities that live with carnivores today are experimenting with a combination of both.

1 Excluding four taxa that are not considered species in this book, Red Wolf (*Canis 'rufus'*, CR, page 104), Western Falanouc (*Eupleres major*, EN, page 74), Grandidier's Vontsira (*Galidictis grandidieri*, EN, page 76) and Eastern Mountain Coati (*Nasuella meridensis*, EN, page 144).

## Measurements

*Animals are usually measured laid out on their side with the tail extended in a straight line behind the body. Values are provided for total head–body length (HB), tail length (T), shoulder height (SH) and weight (W). Where possible, measurements are given for both sexes, especially for species with marked sexual dimorphism.*

Tail (T)          Head–Body (HB)

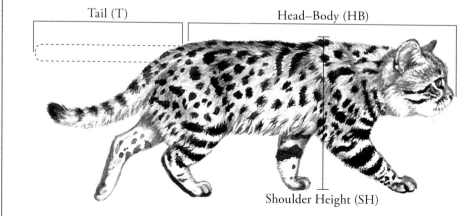

Shoulder Height (SH)

# STRUCTURE OF THE SPECIES ACCOUNTS

Every species account in the following section is written in a standardised format, starting with the most widely accepted common name, scientific name and other common names in usage. Standard measurements as explained opposite are provided under the names. The species is then introduced in a brief description, noting the main features useful for identification, including regional and seasonal variation. Key points on classification and phylogeny, especially recent changes, are also included here. Where other species are mentioned in the account, their common name is followed by a page reference to their own entry in the guide.

The accompanying plates depict every species, with a range of forms shown for more variable species. Variants are labelled where they represent discrete regional or morphological types, for example melanistic Jaguar (page 38) and the various forms of Arctic Fox (page 114). Labels do not appear where the depicted forms represent a sample of the variation present in a species regardless of geography, season or population, such as in the Bobcat (page 36), African Wild Dog (page 110) and Sun Bear (page 132).

Distribution maps appear for every species using data provided by the IUCN Red List Unit (http://maps.iucnredlist.org). Red List mapping data are categorised according to the level of certainty: Extant, where presence is certain or very likely; Possibly Extant, where presence is expected but there are no recent data; and Possibly Extinct, where presence is unlikely but there are no recent data. Distribution maps in this book combine Extant and Possibly Extant categories (and thus show a somewhat optimistic scenario for many species).

The species accounts summarise current knowledge in four major categories as described below. Much of this information is lacking for many carnivores, illustrating the inequity between the few well-studied species and the many that are poorly studied or virtually unknown. Observations or features indicative of a specific region or population are noted with the site name in parenthesis; where multiple figures are available (e.g. for territory size), a range is provided from the typical habitats or conditions in which the species occurs, with preference given to the most recent data generated from modern scientific techniques. Certain site names are abbreviated, for example of protected area types: BR (biosphere reserve), CA (conservation area), GR (game reserve), HR (hunting reserve), NP (national park), NR (nature reserve), PA (protected area), TR (tiger reserve), WR (wildlife refuge or wildlife reserve) and WS (wildlife sanctuary). The four major categories of information in the species accounts are:

- **Feeding Ecology** Diet, including primary prey species, other food items, and whether humans, livestock or crops are eaten; hunting strategies and behaviour, including when foraging occurs and whether it is social or solitary; estimates of hunting success; other notable features of feeding ecology, including whether the species scavenges or caches food.
- **Social and Spatial Behaviour** Degree of sociality, monogamy and territoriality; features of dispersal behaviour; estimates of range size and population density (adults/km² except where stated otherwise).
- **Reproduction and Demography** Degree of seasonality; length of gestation; litter size; breeding patterns; inter-litter interval; development of young, including age of weaning and dispersal; age at sexual maturity or first breeding; mortality rates (for cubs and adults where known) and main natural causes of death; lifespan for wild individuals (where known) and/or in captivity.

- **Status and Threats** Summary of the species' status and the main threats, with CITES and IUCN Red List information (see below).

## CITES

The Convention on International Trade in Endangered Species (CITES) is an agreement between governments (currently 183) to control international trade in wild animals and plants. It covers the importing and exporting of live wildlife and its parts, including furs, hunting trophies and souvenirs. The species covered by CITES are listed in three appendices, according to the degree of protection they need (see below). Carnivores not listed are not considered threatened, or international trade is not considered a possible threat: species lacking a CITES designation in this book have not been listed (but may be threatened by factors other than trade). CITES assessments are usually made for a species across its range, but locally endangered populations or subspecies are often listed separately. The three appendices in CITES are:

- Appendix I covers species threatened with extinction. Trade in these species is legally permitted only in exceptional circumstances.
- Appendix II covers species not necessarily threatened with extinction, but in which trade must be controlled in order to avoid utilisation that may threaten their survival.
- Appendix III covers species that are protected in at least one country which has asked other CITES signatories for assistance in controlling trade. For more information, see www.cites.org.

## IUCN RED LIST

The International Union for Conservation of Nature (IUCN) is the largest professional global conservation organisation. It produces the Red List of Threatened Species, a comprehensive and expert-driven process that assesses the status of wildlife species and classifies them according to the degree of threat and likelihood of extinction. Assessment is a complex process based on multiple criteria, including population size, number of subpopulations, number of breeding individuals, degree of various threats, and so on.

Each Red List category has a precise definition and criteria (for details, see www.iucnredlist.org). From most threatened to least threatened, the categories are: Extinct (EX), Extinct in the Wild (EW), Critically Endangered (CR), Endangered (EN), Vulnerable (VU), Near Threatened (NT) and Least Concern (LC). CR, EN and VU categories apply to species that are threatened with extinction, to differing degrees; popular usage of the term 'endangered' actually applies to the species in these three categories. Where the data are not available for a full assessment, species are classified as Data Deficient (DD), which does not mean they are *not* threatened. Those species not yet assessed by the Red List are Not Evaluated (NE). Red List assessments are usually made at the species level, but populations or subspecies that are more endangered are often evaluated separately. The Red List additionally provides an estimate of population trend – categorised as Decreasing, Stable, Increasing or Unknown– which is also included here. Note that population trend applies to the species overall; the trend for individual populations, regions or subspecies is not estimated in most cases, and can differ significantly from the global trend.

# CHINESE MOUNTAIN CAT *Felis bieti*

## CHINESE DESERT CAT, CHINESE STEPPE CAT

HB 68.5–84cm; T 32–35cm; W 6.5–9kg

Light yellow-grey in winter, darkening to tawny or grey-brown in summer, with very faint markings or none at all except for a dark dorsal line. Tail bushy, conspicuously banded, with a dark tip. Ears tufted. Limited genetic data suggest this is a subspecies of African Wildcat, but classification is still disputed. **Distribution and Habitat** Known only from Qinghai, Sichuan and Gansu provinces, C China. Records from elsewhere in China and Tibet are equivocal. Inhabits alpine grassland, meadows, shrubland and forest edges at 2,500–5,000m. May also occur in true montane forest, semi-desert and cold desert, but this is unconfirmed. **Feeding Ecology** Virtually unstudied in the wild. A single study on diet showed that small mammals such as voles, mole rats, hamsters and pikas make up 90% of the diet. Also eats birds, including records of pigeons, partridges and pheasants. **Social and Spatial Behaviour** Unknown. Probably solitary. Dens in rock outcrops, burrows under tree roots and dense thickets. **Reproduction and Demography** A handful of records suggest seasonal breeding, which is likely given C China's harsh winters. Male–female pairs are mostly observed January–March, which is the likely breeding season, with kittens born around May. MORTALITY and LIFESPAN Unknown. **Status and Threats** Very restricted distribution, and thought to be naturally rare. Killed for its fur, which is mostly for local use, but hunting is widespread and pelts are common in fur markets. Large-scale government-mandated poisoning of rodents and lagomorphs prevalent in C China is likely to constitute a serious threat both by reducing prey populations and secondary poisoning. CITES Appendix II; Red List VU, population trend Decreasing.

# EUROPEAN WILDCAT *Felis silvestris,* AFRICAN WILDCAT *Felis lybica*

HB ♀ 40.6–64cm, ♂ 44–75cm; T 21.5–37.5cm;
W ♀ 2–5.8kg, ♂ 2–7.7kg

Considered conspecific until 2017, now classified as 2 distinct species that diverged ~1 million years ago. The domestic cat first arose from the African Wildcat in the Fertile Crescent more than 9,000 years ago, with later genetic contributions in Egypt, and possibly also from the European Wildcat in SE Europe. Domestic cats hybridise with both wildcats and the wild species likely interbreed where distributions abut around the Caspian Sea. Wildcats closely resemble the domestic cat, although wild individuals are generally larger, taller and more robust. African Wildcat: in Africa/Middle East, sandy grey to pale beige with banded legs and red-backed ears; in Asia ('Asiatic Wildcat', possibly a distinct subspecies, *F. l. ornata*), typically spotted on an isabelline background with noticeable ear-tufts. European Wildcat looks like a heavily built striped tabby with a bushy tail, white chin and white throat. Piebald, ginger and black variants are usually the result of hybridisation with domestic cats.

**Distribution and Habitat** European Wildcat: W Europe from N Scotland to the W Caspian. African Wildcat: Africa (except C Africa and the Sahara), the Middle East, and much of W and S Asia to C China. Very broad habitat tolerance, from sea-level to 3,000m. European Wildcats inhabit mainly temperate forest, woodland, scrub and associated habitats. African Wildcats occur in virtually all habitats with cover, excluding dense forest and open desert interiors. Both species avoid very open habitat, including high montane areas and deep snow. Both readily occupy agricultural lands, fields with cover and plantations, but avoid intensively farmed habitat with little cover. **Feeding Ecology** Through almost their entire ranges, diet of both species is dominated by small rodents such as mice, rats, voles, jirds, gerbils and jerboas; a notable exception is European Wildcat in Scotland, where European Hares and European Rabbits comprise up to 70% of prey. Other important prey includes small birds, especially ground foragers such as doves, pigeons, partridges, sandgrouse, guinea fowl, quails and weavers. Reptiles, including large venomous snakes (e.g. Puff Adders and cobras), amphibians and arthropods are also eaten. Readily kills poultry and (rarely) very young domestic goats and lambs. Drinks daily when water is available; African Wildcat often occurs far from water in the Kalahari, Namib and Sahara, suggesting it is water-independent. Hunts mostly on the ground, and is chiefly nocturno-crepuscular; when protected, may be active during the day, especially in cold winters. Scavenges, and sometimes caches food by covering it with debris, soil and leaf litter. **Social and Spatial Behaviour** Solitary and territorial. Displays typically feline territorial behaviours such as marking with urine and faeces, but extent of territorial defence probably varies widely between different habitats. Range size also varies widely, typically (but not universally) with larger male ranges overlapping multiple female ranges. Range estimates include 1.7–2.75km² (♀s) to 13.7km² (1 ♂; Portugal), 1.75km² (average for both sexes; E Scotland with abundant lagomorphs), 3.5km² (♀s, average) to 7.7km² (♂s, average; S Kalahari), 8–10km² (both sexes; W Scotland with scarce prey), 11.7km² (average for both sexes; Saudi Arabia) and 51.2km² (1 ♀; United Arab Emirates). Density 0.7–10/km². **Reproduction and Demography** Breeds seasonally in areas with extreme seasonality, i.e. most of European Wildcat range, and the Sahara, mating winter–early spring and giving birth spring–early summer. Elsewhere, kittens may be born year-round, although birth peaks often coincide with prey flushes during or after the rainy season, e.g. E and South Africa. Gestation 56–68 days. Litter size typically 2–4, rarely to 8. Weaning at 3–4 months, independent at 5–10 months. Sexually mature at 9–12 months, but wild individuals probably first breed at 18–22 months. MORTALITY Poorly documented; most mortality in studied populations is due to human factors. Known predators include large cats, Golden Eagle, Honey Badger (page 158; of kittens) and domestic dogs. Approximately 20 Meerkats (page 66) killed a 6-week-old African Wildcat kitten after pulling it from a burrow in the Kalahari, South Africa. Starvation of kittens and subadults contributes to low survival in harsh winters. LIFESPAN 11 years in the wild, 15 in captivity. **Status and Threats** Both species are widely distributed, adaptable and tolerant of human activity such as agriculture and forestry, which often elevates rodent populations. Not endangered in any traditional sense, but both hybridise with domestic cats (producing fertile hybrids), especially in W Europe; in Scotland, up to 88% of wild-living European Wildcats may be hybrids. Only remote populations are thought to entirely lack hybrids, although hybridisation in many rural areas is not as extensive as once assumed. Other important threats include persecution for killing poultry and for perceived killing of game species (Europe) and small stock, hunting for fur (mainly C Asia), domestic cat diseases and roadkills. Both species: CITES Appendix II; Red List LC, population trend Decreasing.

■ Chinese Mountain Cat

■ European Wildcat
■ African Wildcat

**Plate 1**

CHINESE
MOUNTAIN CAT

AFRICAN
WILDCAT

Asiatic
form

African
form

EUROPEAN
WILDCAT

# BLACK-FOOTED CAT *Felis nigripes*

### SMALL-SPOTTED CAT
HB ♀ 35.3–41.5cm, ♂ 36.7–52cm; T 12–20cm;
W ♀ 1–1.6kg, ♂ 1.5–2.58kg

One of the smallest cats. Light tawny to buff-grey with ginger to black markings. Northern individuals are generally paler, with the darkest, most strongly marked animals found in Eastern Cape, South Africa, but there is wide variation within populations. **Distribution and Habitat** Endemic to southern Africa and restricted to open, short grass habitat, dry savannah, Karoo scrub and semi-desert. Independent of drinking water, but does not occur in open hyper-arid desert interiors. **Feeding Ecology** Specialises in rodents <100g and ground-roosting birds to the size of Black Bustard. Heaviest prey is Cape Hare; attacks on newborn Springbok lambs are unsuccessful. Reptiles, amphibians, eggs and invertebrates are also eaten. Nocturno-crepuscular, hunting up to 70% of the night with 3 strategies: rapid bounding through cover to flush birds; painstaking weaving around cover searching for prey; and waiting in ambush at rodent burrows. Succeeds in 60% of hunts (Benfontein NR, South Africa), with 10–14 rodents or birds caught per night, averaging a kill every 50 minutes. Surplus food is cached in shallow diggings or hollow termitaria; scavenges. **Social and Spatial Behaviour** Solitary and territorial, with very frequent urine-marking and vocalising. Male ranges encompass up to 4 female ranges. Males guard oestrous females and fight intruding males. Ranges average 8.6km² (♀s) and 16.1km² (♂s). Density estimates up to 16.7/100km² (high-quality habitat; typically at much lower densities). **Reproduction and Demography** Seasonal (South Africa). Birth peaks coincide with spring–summer rains and prey flushes. Oestrus 36 hours; gestation 63–68 days. Litter size 1–4. Kittens weaned by 2 months and independent at 3–4 months. Sexual maturity at 7 months (♀s) and 9 months (♂s). MORTALITY Poorly known; predators include Black-backed Jackal (page 112), Caracal (page 26), domestic dogs and large owls. LIFESPAN 8 years in the wild, 16 in captivity. **Status and Threats** Probably naturally uncommon. Threatened by agricultural expansion into semi-arid areas and associated overgrazing, burning and insecticides, which impact rodent and insect populations. Hundreds of Black-footed Cats are killed annually during control activities intended for jackals in South Africa. CITES Appendix I; Red List VU, population trend Decreasing.

# SAND CAT *Felis margarita*

HB ♀ 39–52cm, ♂ 42–57cm; T 23.2–31cm;
W ♀ 1.35–3.1kg, ♂ 2–3.4kg

Very small, strikingly pale cat with indistinct markings on the body, resolving to dark stripes on the legs and tail. W African cats are smaller, paler and more strongly marked than eastern individuals, which are typically darker grey in tone. Flat, broad head topped by oversized ears. Feet densely covered in dark fur, probably for traction and insulation on loose hot sand. **Distribution and Habitat** N Africa, the Middle East and C Asia. A desert specialist, capable of occupying true desert with rainfall of <20mm/year. Inhabits a variety of sandy and stony desert habitats with cover, and arid shrub-covered steppes. Absent from heavily vegetated valleys in these habitats. **Feeding Ecology** Eats mainly small rodents, including gerbils, spiny mice, jirds and jerboas, plus occasional kills of young hares, small birds, reptiles (including venomous snakes) and invertebrates. Independent of drinking water. Foraging is mainly nocturnal. Capable of very rapid digging to excavate burrowing prey, and sometimes caches food with a covering of sand. **Social and Spatial Behaviour** Solitary. Poorly known but preliminary radio-tracking data from Morocco indicates exceptionally large home ranges likely to average ~200km² for both sexes; over 9–10 months, 1 female covered 760km² and 3 males covered 150km² to >500km². A fourth male, possibly a disperser, covered 1,500km² over 9 months. Nightly straight-line movements average 5.4km, up to 21km. **Reproduction and Demography** Breeding appears seasonal in the Sahara. Mating November–February; births January–April. Oestrus 5–6 days; gestation 59–67 days. Litter size 1–6, rarely >4, average 2.7 (captivity). Weaning at around 5 weeks, and independence from 4 months. Sexually mature at 7–14 months (captivity). MORTALITY Unknown, but likely vulnerable to African Wolf (page 106) and large raptors. LIFESPAN 16 (♂) to 19 (♀) years in captivity, significantly less in the wild. **Status and Threats** Probably naturally rare, but its habitat is so remote that it is somewhat insulated from human activities. Threats include expansion of cultivation, and feral domestic cats and dogs, which result in predation, competition and possible disease transmission. Killed around human settlements in traps for canids. CITES Appendix II; Red List LC, population trend Unknown.

# JUNGLE CAT *Felis chaus*

### SWAMP CAT, REED CAT
HB ♀ 56–85cm, ♂ 65–94cm; T 20–31cm;
W ♀ 2.6–9kg, ♂ 5–12.2kg

Leggy cat with a short tail. Uniformly coloured, with indistinct body markings that become more obvious on the limbs. Temperate animals tend to be darker and more richly marked than tropical individuals. Melanism reported from India and Pakistan. **Distribution and Habitat** Temperate and tropical S Asia, extending into Egypt along the Nile Valley. Prefers dense reed-beds, long grass and scrub habitats in swamps, and wetland and coastal areas, but also inhabits dry and evergreen forests. Tolerates cultivated marshy landscapes, including sugar-cane fields and rice paddies. **Feeding Ecology** Small mammals (<1kg) comprise primary prey, especially small rodents, Muskrat, squirrels and hares; Coypu (5–9kg), and neonates of gazelle and Chital occasionally recorded. Birds make up second-most important prey category, especially waterfowl, francolins, pheasants, peafowl and jungle fowl. Also eats small reptiles and amphibians, and has been observed diving into shallow water for fish. Recorded eating large quantities of Russian Silverberry fruits during winter (Tajikistan). Readily preys on domestic poultry, and sometimes scavenges from the kills of larger carnivores and people's furbearer traps. **Social and Spatial Behaviour** Poorly known. Solitary. Typical feline scent-marking and vocalisation suggest maintenance of exclusive core areas. Larger male home ranges likely overlap several smaller female ranges. There are no density estimates, but it is frequently the most common felid where it is found. **Reproduction and Demography** Thought to be weakly seasonal. Most observed mating November–February. Kittens born December–June. Gestation 63–66 days. Litters average 2–3, exceptionally to 6. Kittens independent at 8–9 months. Sexually mature at 11 months (♀s) and 12–18 months (♂s). MORTALITY Unknown. LIFESPAN 20 years in captivity. Domestic dogs are a confirmed predator in India. **Status and Threats** Common in many parts of its range and tolerates agricultural landscapes with cover. Destruction and development of wetland habitats are a particular threat in arid areas, e.g. Egypt. Persecuted for poultry raiding, trapped heavily around Coypu fur farms (former USSR) and hunted for fur in its northern range. CITES Appendix II; Red List LC, population trend Decreasing.

■ Black-footed Cat ■ Sand Cat    ■ Jungle Cat

**Plate 2**

**BLACK-FOOTED CAT**

Dark form

Pale form

**SAND CAT**

Dark form

**JUNGLE CAT**

Pale form

# PALLAS'S CAT *Otocolobus manul*

### MANUL, STEPPE CAT

HB ♀ 46–53cm, ♂ 54–57cm; T 23–29cm;
W ♀ 2.5–5kg, ♂ 3.3–5.3kg

Stocky, heavily furred small cat, silvery grey to rufous-grey with faint striping on the body. Long winter coat has a pale, frosted appearance; spring–summer coat is darker, with more obvious stripes and often a reddish tinge. Face has dark cheek stripes, and the crown is distinctively marked with small spots. Bushy tail is banded with narrow stripes and ends in a dark tip. Coloration provides excellent camouflage in open rocky habitat: Pallas's Cat is poorly adapted for running, and when threatened freezes and flattens itself to the ground, conferring very effective concealment. **Distribution and Habitat** C Asia, from the Caspian Sea through N Iran, Afghanistan, Pakistan and N India to C China, Mongolia and S Russia. Confirmed by camera-trap from Bhutan and Nepal in 2012. Lives at 450–5,073m in cold, arid habitats with cover, especially dry grassland steppes with stone outcrops and stony semi-desert. Prefers valleys and rocky areas, and avoids completely open habitat. Although well adapted for extreme cold, usually avoids areas with deep snow. **Feeding Ecology** Hunts mainly small rodents and lagomorphs. Pikas are especially important prey, typically comprising more than 50% of the diet; voles, mice, hamsters, gerbils, ground squirrels and marmots are also important. Occasional prey includes hares, hedgehogs, small birds, lizards and invertebrates. There is 1 verified record of predation on newborn Argali lamb (Mongolia). Hunts by 3 distinct techniques: 'stalking', by carefully creeping around cover; 'moving and flushing', used mainly in long summer undergrowth; and waiting in ambush at rodent burrows. Not known to kill any livestock or poultry. Recorded scavenging from carcasses. **Social and Spatial Behaviour** Solitary. Both sexes maintain enduring home ranges, with large overlapping male ranges encompassing multiple smaller female ranges that overlap minimally with each other. Likely to be territorial, at least in the breeding season; breeding males often have injuries consistent with fighting. Female territories 7.4–125.2km², averaging 23.1km², compared with male territories of 21–207km², averaging 98.8km² (Hustain Nuruu NP, Mongolia). Density estimates 2–8/100km². **Reproduction and Demography** Highly seasonal. Mating December–March; births late March–May. Oestrus very short at 24–48 hours; gestation 66–75 days. Litters average 3–4, exceptionally to 8 (captivity). Kittens independent at 4–5 months. Sexual maturity at 9–10 months for both sexes. MORTALITY 68% of kittens do not survive to disperse, 50% of adults (>1 year old) survive to age 3 (Hustain Nuruu NP). Most mortality occurs in winter in October–April. Known predators include large eagles, Red Fox (page 114) and domestic dogs. LIFESPAN 11.5 years in captivity. **Status and Threats** Lives in remote areas but at low densities. Poorly adapted to avoid predators, and depends on fairly specific habitats, making it naturally vulnerable to threats. Hunted for fur in much of its range, and domestic dogs often constitute a key predator; human factors (including dogs) account for 56% of deaths in C Mongolia. State-sanctioned rodent-poisoning campaigns in China, Mongolia and Russia are a serious threat to Pallas's Cat prey. Captives, especially kittens, are very vulnerable to toxoplasmosis (assumed contracted in captivity), which is often fatal. Legally hunted without limits in Mongolia. CITES Appendix II; Red List NT, population trend Decreasing.

# FISHING CAT *Prionailurus viverrinus*

HB ♀ 57–74.3cm, ♂ 66–115cm; T 24–40cm;
W ♀ 5.1–6.8kg, ♂ 8.5–16kg

Robust cat with a powerful, blocky head and short, thick tail. Olive-grey fur covered in dark spots that often coalesce into stripes on the nape, shoulders and back. Feet partially webbed, with large claws that are protractile but protrude partially from the claw-sheaths. Fur is not waterproof, as sometimes claimed. **Distribution and Habitat** Southeast Asia from NE Bangladesh and NE India to S Thailand, and isolated populations in Nepal, extreme SE Pakistan (confirmed Chotiari wetlands, Sindh province, 2015), SW India and Sri Lanka. No confirmed records from Java since 2000, and its presence in Sumatra has never been established. Closely associated with wetland habitats, including marshes, riverine woodland, dense Terai grassland (Nepal) and mangroves. Sometimes found in degraded habitats around aquaculture ponds and rice paddies, but generally intolerant of wetland modification. **Feeding Ecology** Paws and claws are adapted for aquatic foraging and a diet dominated by fish. Capable swimmer that submerges itself in pursuit of prey, and hunts along the water's edge or in shallows, where it scoops up fish with its paws. Despite its aquatic adaptations, its dentition is more generalised, indicating a broader diet. Also kills small mammals, birds (including ducks and coots hunted in the water), reptiles, amphibians and invertebrates. Occasionally kills prey to the size of Chital fawns. Sometimes kills livestock, mainly very young goats and poultry; there are credible but unconfirmed records of kills of neonate calves. Reports of killing children are extremely unlikely. Scavenges. **Social and Spatial Behaviour** Poorly known. Solitary. Range sizes 2–6.8km² (4 ♀s) and 4–13.5km² (2 ♂s; mostly agri-aquacultural habitat, Thailand) and 4–6km² (2 ♀s) and 22km² (1 ♂; Terai grassland, Chitwan NP, Nepal). Scats are apparently deposited in latrines. **Reproduction and Demography** Unknown from the wild. In captivity, gestation 63–70 days, litter size 1–4. Sexual maturity in 1 captive female occurred at 15 months. MORTALITY Poorly known; of 11 known deaths during a Thai study, 5 were caused by people, the rest to unknown causes. LIFESPAN 12 years in captivity. **Status and Threats** Until recently, considered widespread and relatively common, but accelerated development of wetlands and floodplains throughout Asia, especially for aquaculture, is a pervasive threat and a key factor in rapid and widespread declines. Illegal persecution, mostly as a perceived threat to poultry and aquaculture, exacerbates declines. Now rare in Java, Laos and Vietnam, and has lost significant range in India and Thailand. May no longer occur in Pakistan. Main strongholds appear to be S Thailand, Sri Lanka and isolated areas of Bangladesh, NE India and Nepal. CITES Appendix II; Red List VU, population trend Decreasing.

Pallas's Cat

Fishing Cat

**Plate 3**

**PALLAS'S CAT**

Defensive
hiding

Fishing

**FISHING CAT**

# MAINLAND LEOPARD CAT
*Prionailurus bengalensis*

# SUNDA LEOPARD CAT
*Prionailurus javanensis*

**INDOCHINESE LEOPARD CAT** (*P. bengalensis*)
HB ♀ 38.8–65.5cm, ♂ 43–75cm; T 17.2–31.5cm;
W ♀ 0.55–4.5kg, ♂ 0.74–7.1kg
Considered conspecific until 2017, now classified as 2 species that diverged an estimated >900,000 years ago and are morphologically and genetically distinct. A hybrid zone occurs on the Thai–Malay peninsula, provisionally classified as *P. bengalensis*, with genetic and morphological characteristics of both. Preliminary molecular analysis suggests 2 Sunda subspecies, *P. j. javanensis* in Java and Bali, and *P. j. sumatranus* in Sumatra, Borneo and the Philippines; and 2 highly variable subspecies on continental Asia, divided into a southern subspecies, *P. b. bengalensis*, occurring from Afghanistan and India to approximately E China, and a northern subspecies, the Amur Leopard Cat (*P. b. euptilurus*), of the Russian Far East, NE China, the Korean Peninsula, Taiwan, and Japan's Tsushima and Iriomotejima islands. Sunda Leopard Cats are the smaller and generally less variably coloured and patterned of the 2 species, typically with small, solid dark spots and dabs on a muted background colour that varies widely from drab ginger-brown to very dark brown. Mainland Leopard Cats vary along a south–north cline; southernmost individuals are small and richly coloured, becoming larger and generally plainer in the north. Individuals in mainland tropical Asia have rich yellow to tawny-brown or ginger-brown fur, and bold markings varying from large solid spots and rosettes to blotches with dark tawny or reddish centres. Amur Leopard Cats in temperate Russia, Korean Peninsula and China are very pale ginger-grey to silver-grey in winter, with long, dense fur that moults to a darker summer coat of russet-brown to dark grey-brown. Complete melanism has not been recorded in either species, although there are occasional records of pseudomelanistic individuals with extensive enlarging and coalescing of the dark markings.

## Distribution and Habitat
Sunda Leopard Cat: Sumatra, Java, Bali, Borneo, and the Philippine islands of Palawan, Panay, Negros and Cebu. Possibly introduced by humans to some or all of its Philippines' range. It may occur on the Malay Peninsula south of the Kra Isthmus (currently regarded as *P. bengalensis*). Mainland Leopard Cat: very widely distributed in tropical and temperate mainland Asia, from the Russian Far East, China, Taiwan, Japan (Tsushima and Iriomotejima islands) throughout Southeast Asia to S India, N Pakistan, E Afghanistan and extreme S Tajikistan. Both species inhabit all forest types, woodland, scrub, shrublands, marshes, wetlands and mangroves, from sea-level to at least 3,000m (4,250m recorded for Mainland Leopard Cat, Arunachal Pradesh, India). Amur Leopard Cats inhabit vegetated valleys in cold temperate forest with winter snowfall, limited to areas with shallow snow. Both species largely avoid open grasslands, steppes and rocky areas lacking vegetation. Leopard cats inhabit human-modified habitats provided there is cover, including in secondary forest, sugar-cane fields, rice paddies and plantations of oil palm, coffee, rubber and tea. They occur very close to human habitation, including in suitable habitat patches in major metropolises, e.g. Miyun Reservoir and Yeyahu NR, Beijing.

## Feeding Ecology
Leopard cats hunt a wide variety of small vertebrates, chiefly small rodents (especially mice, rats and squirrels), tree shrews, shrews, birds, snakes and lizards. Both species are surprisingly aquatic, and forage in shallow water for freshwater crabs, amphibians and invertebrates. Records of larger prey, e.g. langurs, hares, Lesser Mouse Deer and Wild Boar, were probably scavenged. Amur Leopard Cats in Russia reputedly kill unguarded neonate (<1-week-old) ungulates, including Siberian Roe Deer, Sika Deer and Long-tailed Goral. Introduced Black Rats, skinks, snakes, frogs and a large cricket species are the main prey of Iriomotejima cats. Harmless to hoofstock, but they take domestic poultry and are easily baited with chickens. Hunting activity is variable, ranging from strictly nocturnal at some sites to cathemeral.

## Social and Spatial Behaviour
Solitary and apparently weakly territorial. Male ranges generally overlap numerous smaller female ranges (although range size differs little between sexes in some populations, e.g. Phu Khieo WS, Thailand). Overlap between same-sex adults is considerable at range edges, and usually minimal in exclusive core areas (which overlap significantly in Phu Khieo). Range size 1.4–37.1km$^2$ (♀s) and 2.8–28.9km$^2$ (♂s). Leopard cats are often the most abundant felid in most of the respective range. Density estimates 17–22/100km$^2$ (subtropical–temperate Himalayan forest, Khangchendzonga BR, India), 34/100km$^2$ (Iriomotejima), 37.5/100km$^2$ (Tabin WR, Sabah).

## Reproduction and Demography
Breeding varies from highly seasonal in Russia to aseasonal in the tropics; Sunda Leopard Cats are assumed to be entirely aseasonal. Captive individuals are able to have 2 litters a year, although a single litter is probably typical in the wild. Gestation 60–70 days. Litter size 1–4. Sexual maturity at 8–12 months (captivity). MORTALITY Estimated annual adult mortality varies from 8% (remote sanctuary, Phu Khieo) to 47% (accessible protected area, Khao Yai NP, Thailand). Probably vulnerable to a wide variety of predators; records confirmed for Leopards (page 48), Reticulated Pythons and domestic dogs. Humans are the main source of mortality in many areas, mainly from hunting, persecution and roadkills (especially on Iriomotejima and Tsushima). LIFESPAN 13 years in captivity.

## Status and Threats
Both species are widespread, adaptable and reach high densities in suitable natural and anthropogenic habitats. The Mainland Leopard Cat is legally killed for fur and is heavily hunted in its temperate range, especially in China, where densities are naturally low. High fur harvests are likely to produce declines. In tropical and subtropical Asia, both species are widely killed for fur and meat, in retaliation for poultry predation, and are targeted for the pet trade. Many island populations are small and threatened by rapid development; populations are declining on Tsushima (Mainland Leopard Cat), and Panay, Negros and Cebu (Sunda Leopard Cat). Mainland Leopard Cat: CITES Appendix I – Bangladesh, India, Thailand, Appendix II – elsewhere; Red List LC (CR on Iriomotejima), population trend Stable. Sunda Leopard Cat: CITES Appendix II; Red List LC (VU in the Philippines), population trend Stable.

■ Mainland Leopard Cat

■ Sunda Leopard Cat

Plate 4

MAINLAND
LEOPARD CAT

Amur
form

Iriomote
form

Swimming

Spotted
form

SUNDA
LEOPARD CAT

# RUSTY-SPOTTED CAT
## *Prionailurus rubiginosus*

HB 35–48cm; T 15–29.8cm; W ♀ 1–1.1kg, ♂ 1.5–1.6kg

One of the smallest cats, the size of a slight, very small domestic cat. Rufous-brown or grey-brown with rows of reddish to dark brown spots that sometimes form complete stripes on the nape, shoulders and upper flanks. White or pale cream underparts. Tail solid rust-brown, sometimes with faint bands. **Distribution and Habitat** Endemic to India, Sri Lanka and SW Nepal (confirmed by photographs from Bardia NP, 2012, and Suklaphanta NP, 2016). Putative range abuts extreme SE and NE Pakistan, where it may occur marginally. Once regarded as a moist forest specialist, now revealed through camera-trapping to have a much wider distribution and habitat range, including dry forest, bamboo forest, wooded grassland, arid shrubland, scrubland and vegetated rocky habitats. Recorded to 2,100m. Occurs in modified habitats, including cropland such as maize and rice (which harbour abundant rodents and amphibians), tea plantations and occasionally in abandoned dwellings in villages. **Feeding Ecology** Poorly known. Has a reputation for being especially fierce and taking outsized prey, based on observations in unnatural settings; an 8-month-old individual in captivity almost killed a tame gazelle lamb several times its size by a throttling throat bite before people intervened; such attacks in the wild are highly unlikely. The known diet is mainly small vertebrates such as shrews, Indian Gerbil, bandicoot rats and mice, especially the Little Indian Field Mouse; small birds, hatchlings, reptiles, amphibians and invertebrates are also eaten. It sometimes kills free-ranging domestic poultry, mainly chicks; it rarely, if ever, enters coops or dwellings for poultry. Most sightings of foraging cats are on the ground, but it is a highly agile climber and possibly hunts both on the ground and arboreally. An adult caught a shrew after a 50m ground chase that began while the cat was apparently foraging in the low branches of a tree. Chiefly nocturnal. **Social and Spatial Behaviour** Unknown. **Reproduction and Demography** Unknown from the wild. In captivity, reproduction is aseasonal; 2 wild litters, 1 each from India and Sri Lanka, both found in February. Gestation 66–79 days, usually 67–71 days. Litter size 1–3. MORTALITY Unknown but likely vulnerable to predation by many larger carnivores; a mother with 2 young kittens was observed losing one to an Indian Cobra (Sri Lanka). LIFESPAN 12 years in captivity. **Status and Threats** Regarded as rare. Recent observations have dramatically expanded the known range, although it is not considered common anywhere. Found fairly often in association with human settlements; given its tiny size and potential utility in controlling rodents, it can prosper provided it is tolerated by people. However, it is often killed for skins and meat, by domestic dogs and as a perceived threat to poultry. Unintentional mortality likely results from very widespread use of insecticides and rodenticides in rural S Asia. The cats are sometimes mistakenly persecuted as Leopard cubs (Sri Lanka). CITES Appendix I – India, Appendix II – elsewhere; Red List NT, population trend Decreasing.

# FLAT-HEADED CAT
## *Prionailurus planiceps*

HB ♀ 44.6–52.1cm; ♂ 41–61cm; T 12.8–16.9cm; W ♀ 1.5–1.9kg, ♂ 1.5–2.2kg

Very small, unusual cat with a short tubular body; stubby tail; compact, foreshortened face with a flattened forehead; large, closely set eyes; and small ears. Feet partially webbed and claws protrude partially from reduced claw-sheaths; the claws are protractile. Body is dark roan-brown, becoming rusty brown on the head, with white to whitish-grey underparts. Face is bright white on muzzle, cheeks and under the eyes, with contrasting dark rusty-brown forehead, cheek and eyebrow stripes. Body is largely unmarked except for light dappling and banding on the underparts, chest and lower limbs; the tail is sometimes faintly banded. **Distribution and Habitat** Peninsular Malaysia (possibly also just across the border into S Thailand), Borneo and Sumatra. Very strongly associated with low-elevation moist forested habitats; >70% of records are within 3km of large rivers or water sources, and >80% occur below 100m. Inhabits primary and secondary forest, peat-swamp forest, mangrove and coastal scrub forest. Reports from oil palm and rubber plantations suggest some tolerance of habitat modification, but records from such habitats are dubious or very uncommon. **Feeding Ecology** Very poorly known, but the unique morphology, behaviour and habitat preferences of the species suggest specialisation for hunting aquatic prey in shallow water and along muddy riverbanks. Captive animals are attracted to water, readily submerging themselves and feeling for food in pools with spread paws, similar to raccoons. Stomach contents of dead wild individuals contained fish and crustaceans. Captives adeptly kill rodents with a typically felid nape bite; wild individuals almost certainly take small mammals, reptiles and amphibians. They are sometimes killed in traps set at poultry coops, suggesting they take domestic fowl. Chiefly nocturnal based on camera-trap images. **Social and Spatial Behaviour** Flat-headed Cats have never been radio-collared and socio-spatial behaviour is unknown. Always the least common felid in camera-trap surveys, even when targeted, suggesting naturally very low densities. **Reproduction and Demography** Unknown from the wild. Gestation 56 days (captivity). Litter size 1–2 (based on only 3 captive births). MORTALITY Unknown. Presumably vulnerable to a wide array of predators; occasionally killed by people and dogs, and on roads. LIFESPAN 14 years in captivity. **Status and Threats** Known from ~110 physical records and sightings; despite extensive camera-trapping efforts, 44 of 46 known photos come from just 4 sites in Borneo, with a single image each from Peninsular Malaysia and Sumatra. The species' relatively restricted distribution and very close association with moist, forested habitats makes it particularly vulnerable to habitat loss. As of 2009, an estimated 54–68% of suitable Flat-headed Cat habitat had been converted by people, especially clearing and draining of forest wetlands for croplands and forestry. Overfishing and freshwater pollution from agriculture and mining are likely to exacerbate declines driven by habitat loss, and hunting by people may exert strong local effects; Flat-headed Cat skins often occur in longhouses in Sarawak. Live animals (usually kittens) occasionally appear in the pet trade. Many authorities now consider the Flat-headed Cat to be Southeast Asia's most threatened small felid. CITES Appendix I; Red List EN, population trend Decreasing.

Rusty-spotted Cat

Flat-headed Cat

**Plate 5**

Hunting bird in flight

**RUSTY-SPOTTED
CAT**

Feeling for prey

**FLAT-HEADED
CAT**

## MARBLED CAT *Pardofelis marmorata*

HB 45–62cm; T 35.6–53.5cm; W 2.5–5kg
Resembles a small clouded leopard, with thick grey-buff to red-brown fur, patterned with large, dark-bordered blotches that become small dabs on the limbs. Tubular bushy tail proportionally very long, sometimes exceeding the head–body length and distinctive in the field. During relaxed walking, the tail is held horizontally in a continuous straight line from the body. Melanism occurs very rarely. **Distribution and Habitat** Southeast Asia, south of the Himalayas in Sikkim, India, to SW China, and through Indochina, Borneo and Sumatra. It may occur in E Nepal, although there are no unequivocal records. Restricted to forested habitats, chiefly undisturbed evergreen, deciduous and tropical forests. Can occupy secondary and logged forests, although it is unknown whether modified habitat is suboptimal. **Feeding Ecology** Except for 1 radio-collared female tracked for a month in Thailand, the species has never been studied by telemetry in the wild. Diet is likely to be dominated by small vertebrates. Highly agile climber and has been observed hunting in trees, perhaps for arboreal mammals such as squirrels, as well as birds. From limited camera-trapping in protected areas, thought to be mostly diurnal. **Social and Spatial Behaviour** Virtually unknown. Occasional sightings of adult pairs have fostered speculation that it forms long-term pair bonds, but it is more likely to be solitary. A collared Thai female used a range of 5.3km² in 1 month. Density estimates 5/100km² (upland forest, Dampa TR, India), 7.1/100km² (upland forest, Tawau Hills Park, Borneo), 8.8/100km² (upland forest, Htamanthi WS, Myanmar), 10.45/100km² (selectively logged lowland forest, Tabin WR, Borneo), 19.6/100km² (protected lowland forest, Danum Valley CA, Borneo). **Reproduction and Demography** Very poorly known. Gestation 66–82 days (captivity). Litters average 2 kittens (based on only 2 captive births). Females sexually mature at 21–22 months (captivity). MORTALITY Unknown. LIFESPAN 12 years in captivity. **Status and Threats** Reaches high densities in protected forest but seems highly forest-dependent and is very vulnerable to habitat loss. Hunting is very prevalent throughout its range and likely exacerbates declines in concert with deforestation. CITES Appendix I; Red List NT, population trend Decreasing.

## BAY CAT *Catopuma badia*

HB 53.3–67cm; T 32–39.1cm; W (1 emaciated ♀) 2kg
Resembles a small, slender Asiatic Golden Cat with a proportionally smaller, rounded head and stubby, rounded ears. Occurs in 2 morphs: rich, rusty red; and grey with variable red undertones, especially along the transition from the upper body colour to the paler underparts. Unmarked except for stripes on the forehead and cheeks, and faint spotting along the transition between the upper body colour and pale underparts. Bright white underside to the tail with a dark dorsal tip that is distinctive in the field. **Distribution and Habitat** Endemic to Borneo. Closely associated with densely forested habitats, with most historical records in primary, riverine, swamp and mangrove forests. Tolerates moist plantation forests with a dense understorey, and has been camera-trapped from recently logged secondary forest, suggesting some tolerance for habitat modification. **Feeding Ecology** Unknown, but presumably small vertebrates make up major food items. Two Bay Cats were trapped in 2003 when they entered an animal dealer's pheasant aviaries, suggesting that the species may attack domestic poultry. **Social and Spatial Behaviour** Unknown. Rarely photographed during camera-trapping surveys, suggesting that it occurs at very low densities, e.g. Bay Cats were photographed 25 times at 4 sites in eastern Sabah over 4 years, compared with 259 images of Sunda Clouded Leopards (page 42) and more than 1,000 images of Sunda Leopard Cats. **Reproduction and Demography** Unknown. **Status and Threats** Apparent extreme rarity of the species and its dependence on forest raise concerns for its conservation prospects. Forest conversion, especially to oil palm plantations, is regarded as a serious threat. The species' rarity and value are known to animal dealers, elevating illegal trapping pressure. CITES Appendix II; Red List EN, population trend Decreasing.

## ASIATIC GOLDEN CAT
### *Catopuma temminckii*

TEMMINCK'S GOLDEN CAT
HB ♀ 66–94cm, ♂ 75–105cm; T 42.5–58cm;
W ♀ 8.5kg, ♂ 12–15.8kg
Usually rich russet-brown, but varying from pale tawny to dark greyish brown. Largely unmarked except for the face and faint spotting on the chest and belly. A richly spotted 'ocelot' morph is recorded from Bhutan, China and Myanmar. Melanism occurs. Except in black individuals, the underside of the tail is always conspicuously bright white with a dark upper tip. **Distribution and Habitat** Sub-Himalayan Nepal, NE India and Bhutan to S China, Southeast Asia and Sumatra. Found in a variety of moist and dry forests, usually below 3,000m, but higher on Himalayan slopes, e.g. 3,738m (Bhutan) to 4,369m (Myanmar). Has been sighted or killed near human settlements, including in open agricultural areas, and appears to be more tolerant of open habitat than clouded leopards (page 42), Marbled Cat and Bay Cat; even so, it is never far from cover. **Feeding Ecology** Poorly known. Confirmed prey includes mice, rats, Berdmore's Ground Squirrel, mouse deer, Dusky Leaf Monkey (~6.5kg), snakes, lizards and birds. Powerfully built and reputed to kill medium-sized ungulates, including muntjacs and livestock to the size of neonate cattle and buffalo calves (which is unlikely). Confirmed records of livestock kills are mostly from hunters shooting the cat over depredated carcasses, in which it may have been the predator or possibly only a scavenger. Sometimes raids poultry. Nocturno-crepuscular, but diurnal activity is recorded under protection. **Social and Spatial Behaviour** Poorly known. Solitary. Only range sizes known are 32.6km² (1 ♀) and 47.7km² (1 ♂) from Phu Khieo WS, Thailand. **Reproduction and Demography** Unknown from the wild. In captivity, reproduction aseasonal, gestation 78–80 days and litter size 1–3 (typically 1). Sexual maturity in captive animals at 18–24 months. MORTALITY Unknown. LIFESPAN 17 years in captivity. **Status and Threats** Threatened by forest loss and illegal hunting, which are widespread throughout its range, but status and degree of threat are poorly known. Skins of Asiatic Golden Cats are traded heavily in China and Myanmar, where hunting pressure is regarded as high. CITES Appendix I; Red List NT, population trend Decreasing.

■ Marbled Cat

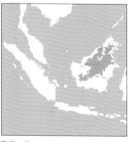
■ Bay Cat

■ Asiatic Golden Cat

**Plate 6**

MARBLED
CAT

BAY
CAT

Red form

Grey form

'Ocelot' form

ASIATIC
GOLDEN CAT

Typical form

# SERVAL *Leptailurus serval*

HB ♀ 63–82cm, ♂ 59–92cm; T 20–38cm;
W ♀ 6–12.5kg, ♂ 7.9–18kg
Dappled with bold spots, coalescing into blotches on the extremities and nape. A buff-coloured morph with a faint freckled appearance ('Servaline') occurs in W and C Africa. Melanism is recorded chiefly in Equatorial highlands and forest-savanna ecotone. **Distribution and Habitat** Africa. Inhabits mainly woodland savannah, grassland, forest and alpine moorland to 3,850m, usually associated with rivers, marshes and floodplains. Absent from rainforest and desert. Tolerates agricultural areas with cover. **Feeding Ecology** Specialises in hunting small mammals in long grass or shrubby habitats, with rodents and shrews comprising 80–93.5% of the diet. Small grassland birds are the next most important prey, and it sometimes hunts large birds, including flamingos and storks. Ancillary prey includes genets, mongooses, hares, juvenile antelopes, small reptiles and arthropods. Livestock depredation is unusual, but it occasionally kills poultry and untended young goats. Hunting is mostly crepuscular, becoming nocturnal near humans. Rarely scavenges. **Social and Spatial Behaviour** Solitary and territorial, although same-sex adults appear relatively tolerant. Home ranges overlap considerably. Range size 15.8–19.8km² (♀s) and 31.5km² (1 ♂) in KwaZulu-Natal, South Africa. Density estimates 9.9/100km² (Luambe NP, Zambia, with full carnivore complement) and 41/100km² (optimum protected habitat, Ngorongoro Crater, Tanzania), to 76/100km² (Secunda CTL fuel plant, South Africa, a fenced industrial complex with extensive moist grassland, very high rodent abundance and no other carnivores). **Reproduction and Demography** Breeding appears weakly seasonal; births peak November–March (southern Africa) and August–November (Ngorongoro Crater). Gestation 65–75 days. Litters average 2–3, exceptionally to 6. Kittens independent at 6–8 months. MORTALITY Known predators include Lion (page 46), Leopard (page 48), Nile Crocodile and domestic dogs. Predation by Martial Eagle on kittens recorded. LIFESPAN 11 years (♀s) in the wild, 20 in captivity. **Status and Threats** Conversion of wetland and grassland by draining, burning and overgrazing by livestock is a significant threat. Popular in the local fur trade in NE Africa and W African Sahel belt, and for fetish and traditional use in South Africa. Sport-hunted with few restrictions in Tanzania and southern Africa. May benefit from conversion of forest/woodland to grassland; expanding or recolonising range in Gabon, C Namibia, and C and NW South Africa. CITES Appendix II; Red List LC (global), CR (N Africa), population trend Stable.

# CARACAL *Caracal caracal*

HB ♀ 61–103cm, ♂ 62.1–108cm; T 18–34cm;
W ♀ 6.2–15.9kg, ♂ 7.2–26kg
Uniformly coloured, pale sandy brown to brick red, unmarked except for faintly spotted undersides. Ears have conspicuous silvery-black backs and long black tufts. Melanistic cases are actually dark chocolate brown. Formerly classified as a lynx, but they are not closely related. **Distribution and Habitat** Africa (except for true desert and rainforest), the Middle East and SW Asia. Prefers dry woodland savannah, dry forest, grassland, coastal scrub, semi-desert and arid mountainous habitat. Sometimes inhabits evergreen and montane forests, exceptionally to 3,300m. Tolerates agricultural landscapes with cover. **Feeding Ecology** Formidable hunter, recorded killing adult Bushbuck, Springbok and Impalas, but most prey weighs <5kg; small rodents, hyraxes, hares, Springhare and birds are the most important. An estimated 2,920–3,285 rodents are eaten by each adult annually (Sariska TR, India). Reptiles comprise 12–17% of the diet (West Coast NP, South Africa); amphibians, fish and invertebrates are occasionally consumed. Readily kills small untended livestock, which comprises up to 55% of the diet in farming areas in southern Africa. Occasionally hoists kills into trees, and readily scavenges. **Social and Spatial Behaviour** Solitary. Adults maintain enduring home ranges with exclusive core areas and overlap at the edges. Female territories 3.9–26.7km² (South Africa) to an average of 57km² (Israel), compared with male territories of 5.1–65km² (South Africa) to an average of 220km² (Israel). An adult Kalahari male used 308km², and an adult Saudi male used 865km² (Harrat-al-Harrah PA). Density poorly known; 15/100km² (protected area with abundant rodents and no large carnivores, Postberg NR, South Africa). **Reproduction and Demography** Breeds year-round, but births peak October–February (South Africa), and November–May (E Africa). Gestation 68–81 days. Litters average 2–3, exceptionally to 6. Kittens independent at 9–10 months. MORTALITY Most known mortality is anthropogenic; occasionally killed by larger carnivores, including domestic dogs in rural areas; Black-backed Jackals (page 112) recorded killing kittens. Infanticide by males documented rarely. LIFESPAN 19 years in captivity. **Status and Threats** Habitat degradation, loss of prey and human hunting are significant threats in C, W and N Africa, and Asia, where Caracals are rare. An estimated 50–100 Caracals are trafficked annually from Somalia to the Gulf States for the pet trade. Persecuted intensely on livestock land in E and southern Africa, but resilient and difficult to extirpate there. Sport-hunted with few restrictions in E and southern Africa. CITES Appendix I – Asia, Appendix II – elsewhere; Red List LC, population trend Unknown.

# AFRICAN GOLDEN CAT *Caracal aurata*

HB 61.6–101cm; T 16.3–37cm; W ♀ 5.3–8.2kg, ♂ 8–16kg
Two distinct colour morphs, red-brown and grey, ranging from heavily spotted to plain in either. There is some intergradation between morphs, and melanism occurs. Does not change colour as is sometimes claimed. **Distribution and Habitat** Endemic to equatorial Africa. Strongly associated with undisturbed moist forests to 3,600m, including alpine bamboo forest, dense coastal forest and riverine forest strips in woodland savannah. Occurs in banana plantations inside forest, and in abandoned logged areas with secondary undergrowth. Avoids open and dry habitats. **Feeding Ecology** Eats a wide variety of small prey typically weighing 1.5–3.6kg; birds, shrews, rodents and small forest duikers are the most important. Actively hunts forest monkeys, but hunting is mainly terrestrial; scavenging of eagle kills on the forest floor may account for most primate occurrences in the diet. Reported to raid poultry in villages and to scavenge from wire snares. **Social and Spatial Behaviour** Unstudied and very poorly known. Solitary. Adults urine-mark and leave faeces exposed on trails, suggesting territorial behaviour. **Reproduction and Demography** Gestation 75 days. Litter size 1–2. Kittens weaned at around 6 weeks (captivity). Sexual maturity in captive animals 11 months (♀s) and 18 months (♂s). MORTALITY Poorly known; Leopard (page 48) is a confirmed predator. LIFESPAN 12 years in captivity. **Status and Threats** Thought to be naturally rare. Forest-dependent; many W and E African moist forests are now heavily degraded and converted to savannah. Bushmeat hunting in W and C Africa heavily impacts prey species, and African Golden Cats are killed frequently in some areas for bushmeat and fetish markets. CITES Appendix II; Red List VU, population trend Decreasing.

■ Serval

■ Caracal ■ African Golden Cat

**Plate 7**

SERVAL

Typical form

Servaline form

CARACAL

AFRICAN
GOLDEN CAT

Red
form

Grey form

# MARGAY *Leopardus wiedii*

### TREE OCELOT

HB ♀ 47.7–62cm, ♂ 49–79.2cm; T 30–52cm;
W ♀ 2.3–3.5kg, ♂ 2.3–4.9kg

Lightly built, resembling a small, lean Ocelot, but with a proportionally much longer tail, rounded head and distinctive large eyes. Melanism is very rare, with only two apparent records from camera-trap photos in Colombia (2013) and Costa Rica (2014). **Distribution and Habitat** From N Mexico throughout Central and South America to N Argentina, E Paraguay and N Uruguay. One specimen from S Texas around 1850 is the only US record, possibly a former captive given that the arid habitat is very atypical for the species. Forest-dependent, typically to 1,500m, exceptionally to 3,000m in the Andes; more closely associated with forest habitats than any other Neotropical cat. Avoids converted landscapes except for dense plantations, e.g. of coffee, cocoa, eucalyptus and pine. **Feeding Ecology** Most prey weighs <200g, and mainly comprises small rodents, shrews and mouse opossums. Larger prey includes Southern Opossum, cavies, agoutis, pacas and Brazilian Rabbits. Birds, including chachalacas and guans, herptiles, invertebrates and small amounts of fruit are eaten. Forages terrestrially and arboreally: a spectacularly acrobatic climber able to hunt the most agile prey, including small primates, although foraging is likely to be mainly ground-based. Occasionally kills domestic poultry. Mainly nocturnal, with peak activity 2100–0500. **Social and Spatial Behaviour** Poorly known, with very limited telemetry data. Solitary. Range sizes 0.9–20km² (♀s) and 1.2–15.9km² (♂s). Based on camera-trapping, reaches lower densities than Ocelot, although there are few estimates; 12 cats/100km² estimated for protected montane pine–oak forest, C Mexico. **Reproduction and Demography** Unknown from the wild. In captivity, known for surprisingly low reproductive rates, with protracted gestation and small litters. Aseasonal (captivity). Gestation 76–84 days. Litter size usually 1, rarely 2. MORTALITY Poorly known. LIFESPAN 24 years in captivity. **Status and Threats** Strongly forest-dependent and responds poorly to forest conversion, its main threat. Formerly heavily hunted for fur (at least 125,547 skins were legally exported 1976–85), from which it may be slow to recover given its low reproductive potential. Localised illegal hunting and persecution for killing poultry is likely to have significant effects on populations in areas where there is existing pressure on habitat. CITES Appendix I; Red List NT, population trend Decreasing.

## OCELOT *Leopardus pardalis*

HB ♀ 69–90.9cm, ♂ 67.5–101.5cm; T 25.5–44.5cm;
W ♀ 6.6–11.3kg, ♂ 7–18.6kg

Latin America's third-largest cat. Powerfully built, with stocky limbs and a relatively short tail that rarely reaches the ground. Fur is creamy buff, tawny, cinnamon, red-brown or grey, with white underparts, and very richly marked with highly variable combinations of open and solid black blotches, streaks and rosettes with russet-brown centres. Simple solid spots or blotches usually cover the lower legs, and the tail has partial or complete black rings and a black tip. Melanism is unknown. **Distribution and Habitat** N Mexico to S Peru, N Argentina and SE Brazil, including on Trinidad and Isla de Margarita, Venezuela. Two relict populations occur in extreme SE Texas, numbering 50–80. Five individuals (4 males, 1 unidentified) documented in extreme S Arizona 2009–15; it is unknown if a resident breeding population occurs. Absent from Chile and now thought extinct in Uruguay. Inhabits a wide range of habitats but always with dense cover, from arid scrub to all kinds of dry and moist forest, usually below 3,000m. Tolerant of modified habitat provided there is dense vegetation and prey, e.g. agricultural landscapes with extensive brush, such as fallow cultivation or rice fields with forest edges. Avoids very open habitat but readily hunts in pasture and grasslands close to cover, especially at night. **Feeding Ecology** A flexible generalist with a wide diet, capable of killing large prey such as sloths, tamanduas, howler monkeys, Crab-eating Raccoons (page 142), coatis, and juvenile peccaries and deer, but mostly eating small rodents and mid-sized vertebrates, e.g. agoutis, pacas, squirrels, opossums, armadillos and iguanas. Other relatively common prey includes rabbits, tree porcupines, tamarins and squirrel monkeys, as well as birds such as large guans, macaws and seriemas. Readily consumes aquatic and semi-aquatic prey, including fish, amphibians and crustaceans, indicative of the species' ability to inhabit inundated habitats. Incidental prey includes bats, lizards, snakes, small turtles, caimans (presumably hatchlings) and arthropods. Sometimes kills poultry, otherwise not considered dangerous to stock. Foraging is chiefly nocturno-crepuscular and terrestrial, although Ocelots are adept climbers that sometimes hunt in trees, e.g. a young Mantled Howler Monkey (Isla Barro Colorado, Panama). Scavenges, including from refuse piles left by people fishing, and sometimes caches large carcasses by covering with debris. **Social and Spatial Behaviour** Solitary and territorial. Male ranges (average 5.2–90.5km²) overlap multiple female ranges (average 1.3–75km²). Ranges are smallest in the Brazilian Pantanal and largest in *cerrado* savannah (Emas NP, Brazil). Ocelots appear to reach higher densities than all smaller sympatric felids, reaching very high numbers in good habitat; density estimates include 2.3–3.8/100km² (tropical pine forest, Belize), 13–19/100km² (Atlantic forest, Brazil), 26/100km² (tropical rainforest, Belize) and 52/100km² (dry Chaco–Chiquitano forest, Bolivia). **Reproduction and Demography** Unexpectedly low reproductive rates, with a fairly long gestation, very small litters and long inter-litter intervals; lifetime reproductive output per female is similar to much larger felids. Aseasonal. Gestation 79–82 days. Litter size 1–2, exceptionally 3 (only known in captivity). Kittens independent at 17–22 months. MORTALITY Annual mortality (Texas) is 8% (resident adults) to 47% (dispersers). Predators include large cats, Coyote (page 102) and domestic dogs; confirmed, rare records by Boa Constrictor and American Alligator. LIFESPAN 20 years in captivity. **Status and Threats** Widespread and often abundant, but reliant on dense habitat and has a low reproductive potential. Vulnerable to habitat loss, illegal hunting and persecution for depredation; all are prevalent over much of the range. Texan Ocelots die mainly from anthropogenic factors, especially as roadkills. CITES Appendix I; Red List LC, population trend Decreasing.

■ Margay

■ Ocelot

**Plate 8**

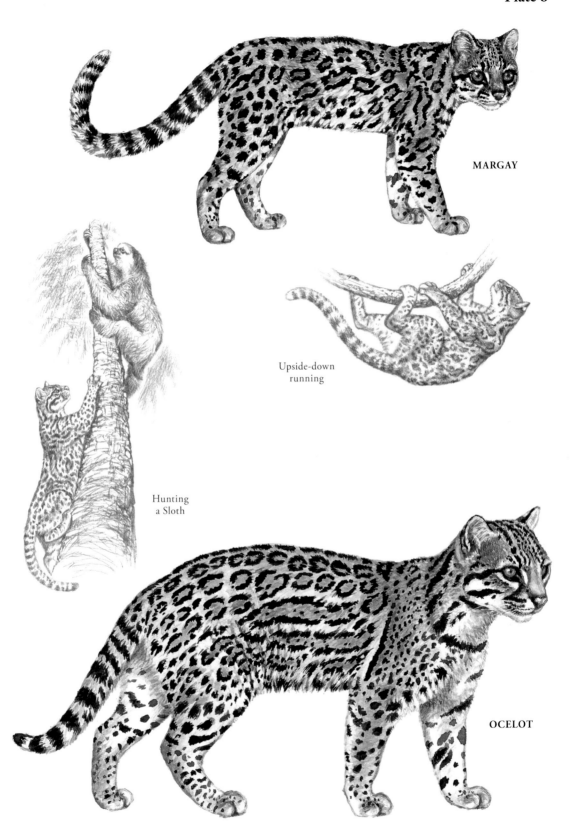

MARGAY

Upside-down
running

Hunting
a Sloth

OCELOT

# NORTHERN TIGRINA
*Leopardus tigrinus*

# SOUTHERN TIGRINA
*Leopardus guttulus*

ONCILLA, LITTLE-SPOTTED CAT, TIGER CAT
HB ♀ 43–51.4cm, ♂ 38–59.1cm; T 20.4–42cm;
W ♀ 1.5–3.2kg, ♂ 1.8–3.5kg
Considered a single species until 2013, tigrinas are now thought to represent a complex of closely related 'cryptic' species, between which the phylogenetic and geographic borders are poorly understood. Currently regarded as 2 distinct but very similar species that diverged at least 100,000 years ago, based mainly on genetic data. Two additional species have been proposed but lack sufficient evidence to be widely accepted: *L. pardinoides* in NW South America; and *L. oncilla*, an isolated population in Central America. The 2 tigrina species show no genetic evidence of recent interbreeding. However, Southern Tigrinas hybridise with Geoffroy's Cats in the wild; Northern Tigrinas do not hybridise with Geoffroy's Cats yet they show evidence of past, historical hybridisation with the Colocolo (page 32). Northern and Southern tigrinas are extremely similar in appearance. Very small, slender, lightly built cats about the size of a young, lean domestic cat. Fur colour pale to dark buff or ochre, marked with orderly rows of black or dark brown dabs, blotches or small rosettes with a coffee-brown or reddish centre. Northern Tigrinas apparently tend towards lighter colouring with smaller rosettes than Southern Tigrinas, but wide variation occurs in both species, and distinct morphological differences have yet to be established. Melanism occurs in both species. **Distribution and Habitat** Northern Tigrina: N South America, from Venezuela and Colombia through E Peru and NE Bolivia to C Brazil, with a disjunct population in the Cordillera Central of Costa Rica and extreme W Panama. Southern Tigrina: SE and S Brazil, SE Bolivia, E Paraguay and probably extreme NE Argentina. The boundary between the two appears to be C Brazil. Both inhabit a broad range of habitats, including all types of forest, woodlands, wet and dry savannahs, arid scrublands and coastal *restinga* (scrub on sandy beaches), from sea-level to at least 3,200m. Northern Tigrina recorded at 3,626m (Costa Rica) to 4,800m (Colombia). In Central America, Northern Tigrinas are restricted to oak-dominated cloud and elfin forests above 1,000m. Tigrinas are apparently very rare or absent from Amazon Basin lowland rainforest. Both species tolerate habitats close to people, including rangelands, plantations, agricultural mosaics and peri-urban areas even near large cities, provided there is dense cover. **Feeding Ecology** Prey typically weighs <1kg and mainly comprises rodents, shrews, small opossums, birds, eggs, reptiles and invertebrates. Mid-sized diurnal lizards (ameivas and small iguanas) dominate the diet in semi-arid *caatinga*, NE Brazil, where rodent densities are low. Thought to forage mainly terrestrially and nocturno-crepuscularly depending on prey activity (and possibly the presence of Ocelots, page 28,

which might depress their density), e.g. Northern Tigrinas are more diurnal in *caatinga*, reflecting reliance on diurnal reptiles. Tigrinas rarely take poultry. **Social and Spatial Behaviour** Solitary. Range size 0.9–25km² (♀s) and 4.8–17.1km² (♂s). Density estimates 0.01/100km² (lowland Amazon forest) to 1–5/100km². **Reproduction and Demography** Unknown from the wild. Gestation 62–76 days. Litter size typically 1, rarely 2. MORTALITY Poorly known. Single records each of deaths to Ocelot predation and heartworm disease. Domestic dogs are likely to be a significant predator in anthropogenic landscapes. LIFESPAN 17 years in captivity. **Status and Threats** Both species appear to be naturally rare, elevating their vulnerability to threats, but their status is poorly known. They have become locally extinct where dense submontane forest has been converted for agriculture (Costa Rica and the Andes). Formerly heavily hunted for fur trade; some hunting for local fur demand still occurs. Localised killing for furs, by dogs, in retaliation for killing poultry and on roads probably impacts populations close to people. Both species: CITES Appendix I; Red List VU, population trend Decreasing.

# GEOFFROY'S CAT *Leopardus geoffroyi*

HB ♀ 43–74cm, ♂ 44–88cm; T 23–40cm;
W ♀ 2.6–4.9kg, ♂ 3.2–7.8kg
Largest of the South American temperate zone small felids, reaching the size of a large domestic cat. Yellow-brown to silver-grey with small, solid dab-like spots, becoming elongated blotches on nape, chest and lower limbs; southern, temperate animals are typically paler. Melanism is common in Uruguay, SE Brazil and E Argentina, but rare elsewhere. Hybridises with Southern Tigrina in S Brazil. **Distribution and Habitat** C Bolivia to Uruguay and S Brazil, and most of Argentina. Inhabits subtropical and temperate brushland, forest, semi-arid scrub, pampas grassland and marshland, from sea-level to 3,300m in the Andes. Absent from tropical and temperate rainforest. Tolerant of disturbed habitats, including ranchland and conifer plantations. **Feeding Ecology** Eats small rodents such as grass mice, rice rats and cavies, as well as small birds and herptiles. Occasionally takes Six-banded Armadillo, tree porcupines and small opossums. Introduced European Hare dominates the diet in Patagonia. Large waterbirds, including cormorants, ibis, coots, ducks, Chilean Flamingo and Coscoroba Swan are primary prey in coastal lagoon habitat (Mar Chiquita, Argentina). Mostly nocturno-crepsucular and terrestrial, but swims readily, taking Coypu, marsh rats, frogs and fish at the water's edge. Occasionally recorded caching large kills, e.g. hares, in trees and burrows. Raids domestic poultry; sheep are probably scavenged. **Social and Spatial Behaviour** Solitary. Deposits faeces in trees, creating arboreal middens. Range sizes average 1.5–5.1km² (♀s) and 2.2–9.2km² (♂s). Density estimates 4/100km² (Argentine pampas during a prey shortage) to 45–58/100km² (Argentine ranchlands); 139/100km² estimated for protected Argentine scrubland may be an overestimate. **Reproduction and Demography** Seasonal in temperate southern range (possibly elsewhere), with most births December–May. Gestation 62–78 days. Litter size 1–3. MORTALITY Starvation and high parasite loads elevate mortality during droughts. Puma (page 38) is a known predator. LIFESPAN 14 years in captivity. **Status and Threats** Widespread and abundant in good habitat, including some anthropogenic landscapes, but the species has disappeared where habitat is converted to agricultural monocultures. Often killed by vehicles, domestic dogs and for attacking poultry. CITES Appendix I; Red List LC, population trend Stable.

■ Northern Tigrina
■ Southern Tigrina

■ Geoffroy's Cat

**Plate 9**

NORTHERN
TIGRINA

SOUTHERN
TIGRINA

Geoffroy's Cat
in tree midden

GEOFFROY'S
CAT

# GUIÑA *Leopardus guigna*

### GUIGNA, KODKOD
HB ♀ 37.4–51cm; ♂ 41.8–49cm; T 19.5–25cm;
W ♀ 1.3–2.1kg, ♂ 1.7–3kg

Tiny cat, grey-brown to russet-brown with small, dark dab-like spots coalescing into irregular lines on the back and nape. Face distinctively marked with dark stripes under the eyes bordering the muzzle, resembling that of a Puma (page 38) kitten. Melanism is common, sometimes with rich brown (rather than black) extremities on which the markings are obvious. **Distribution and Habitat** C and S Chile, including Chiloé Island, and marginally in adjacent Argentina. Strongly associated with dense temperate habitats, especially evergreen forest, montane forest, thicket and scrubland. Avoids open land and plantations with little understorey, but uses secondary forest and exotic plantations, as well as forested ravines and coastal forest strips in cleared habitat. **Feeding Ecology** Hunts small rodents and marsupials, e.g. Monito del Monte, ground-foraging birds such as tapaculos, ovenbirds, thrushes and lapwings, and small reptiles and insects. Fishes for cavity-nesting bird chicks, e.g. rayaditos and wrens, in artificial nestboxes (and very likely natural cavities). Regularly kills free-range domestic poultry in fragmented human-dominated landscapes, e.g. Chiloé Island, and is considered a pest. Reports of goat killing and hunting in groups are implausible. Cathemeral. **Social and Spatial Behaviour** Solitary. Ranges overlap considerably, including in core areas, suggesting limited territoriality. Range size 0.6–2.5km² (♀s) and 1.6–4.4km² (♂s). Density estimates from radio-telemetry, counting adults and subadults, 1–3.3/km². **Reproduction and Demography** Unknown from the wild; cold winters possibly drive seasonal breeding. Gestation 72–78 days. Litter size 1–3. MORTALITY Poorly known; where studied, humans are the main cause of death. LIFESPAN 11 years in captivity. **Status and Threats** Very restricted distribution and dependent on dense habitat. Forest loss from agriculture and pine plantations has reduced its range to many small, fragmented populations, which are further threatened by illegal killing, mainly over poultry depredation. CITES Appendix II; Red List VU, population trend Decreasing.

# COLOCOLO *Leopardus colocolo*

### PAMPAS CAT
HB 42.3–79cm; T 23–33cm; W 1.7–3.7kg

Highly variable, ranging from smoky grey to dark rusty brown, with little or no spotting to rich russet-coloured blotches on the body. Based on morphology, the species clusters into 3 major groups: 'Colocolo' in Chile, W side of the Andes; 'Pampas Cat' in Colombia to S Chile, E side of the Andes; and 'Pantanal Cat' in Brazil, Paraguay and Uruguay. They are mistakenly sometimes considered separate species; all forms intergrade, and genetic data indicate only moderate differences. Melanism is recorded from Brazil and Peru. **Distribution and Habitat** S Colombia to S Chile, extending into C Brazil, Paraguay and Uruguay. Occupies more habitat types than any other Latin American felid, including pampas and *cerrado* grassland, woodland savannah, marshland, open forest, cloud forest, semi-arid desert and Andean steppes to 5,000m. Does not occur in rainforest. Tolerates plantations and agricultural habitat

with cover, e.g. maize cropland. **Feeding Ecology** Focuses mainly on small mammals, especially tuco-tucos, mountain viscachas, chinchilla rats, leaf-eared mice, rats and introduced European Hare. Other notable prey includes flamingos (probably chicks), tinamous, Magellanic Penguin chicks, small reptiles, eggs and beetles. Kills domestic poultry. Foraging is generally terrestrial and nocturnal, but varies with the region; almost entirely diurnal in the Brazilian *cerrado*, perhaps due to the presence of nocturnal large cats. Scavenges from carcasses, including those of livestock, Vicuña and Guanaco. **Social and Spatial Behaviour** Solitary. Range size 3.7–37km², averaging 19km² in Emas NP, Brazilian *cerrado*) and 4.7–55.3km² (Argentina–Bolivia border region). Density estimates 11.3–17.6/100km², (Argentine espinal forest-grasslands) and 20–78/100km² (3 surveys in Argentine high Andes, upper figures are possibly an overestimate). **Reproduction and Demography** Unknown from the wild. Gestation 80–85 days. Litter size 1–3. MORTALITY Poorly known. Apparently frequently killed by domestic dogs in some locations, e.g. NW Argentina. LIFESPAN 16.5 years in captivity. **Status and Threats** Widely distributed, with a broad habitat tolerance, and often fairly rare in camera-trap surveys compared to sympatric felids. Killed for raiding poultry and vulnerable to shepherds' dogs, especially in open Andean habitats. In rural areas, killed for religious ceremonial uses in which the skin or a stuffed cat is believed to confer fertility and productivity on domestic livestock and crops. CITES Appendix II; Red List NT, population trend Decreasing.

# ANDEAN CAT *Leopardus jacobita*

### ANDEAN MOUNTAIN CAT
HB 58–75cm; T 38–46cm; W 4.6–5.8kg

Silver-grey marked with russet blotches on the body that darken to rich grey-brown on the face, limbs and tail. Tail very thick and bushy, with distinctive thick banding that becomes paired brown or russet rings, often with mid-brown centres, towards the tip. **Distribution and Habitat** S Peru to NW Argentina; restricted to high Andean habitats mostly at 3,000–5,100m. Has been recorded from the Patagonian steppe at 1,800m (Mendoza, Argentina) and 600–700m (Neuquén, Argentina). Occurs only in semi-arid to arid treeless habitats with rocky slopes and cliffs, and associated shrubland and grassland. **Feeding Ecology** Specialises in high-altitude rodents, especially 2 species of mountain viscacha, as well as mice, leaf-eared mice and chinchilla rats; cavies, European Hare and tinamous are also recorded prey. Mostly nocturnal, with crepuscular activity peaks in high-altitude areas reflecting activity patterns of viscachas. Sometimes scavenges from the carcasses of dead ungulates. **Social and Spatial Behaviour** Solitary. Range size 20–65km² (Argentina–Bolivia border region), and 47.1km² for a female in the Bolivian altiplano monitored for 4 months. Density estimates 7–12/100km² (Argentine high Andes). **Reproduction and Demography** Poorly known. Kittens have been observed October–April, suggesting seasonal breeding with spring/summer births. Litter size 1–2. MORTALITY and LIFESPAN Poorly known. People and dogs are the primary known sources of mortality. **Status and Threats** Status virtually unknown. During surveys, evidence of Andean Cat is found far less frequently than that of Colocolo and other carnivores, suggesting the species is naturally rare. It has a very restricted distribution and narrow habitat preference, which is vulnerable to livestock grazing and agriculture. This may also impact on prey numbers, especially combined with hunting of prey, particularly viscachas, which is considered a serious threat. Killed for religious beliefs (see Colocolo) and for suspected poultry and livestock killing; sometimes killed by herders and their dogs, e.g. Neuquén Province, Argentina, even though it does not prey on stock. CITES Appendix I; Red List EN, population trend Decreasing.

■ Guiña ■ Colocolo      ■ Andean Cat

**Plate 10**

GUIŃA

Colocolo
form

Pantanal
form

**COLOCOLO**

Pampas
form

**ANDEAN
CAT**

# EURASIAN LYNX *Lynx lynx*

HB ♀ 85–130cm, ♂ 76–148cm; T 12–24cm;
W ♀ 13–21kg, ♂ 11.7–29kg
Largest lynx. Colour varies from silver-grey and tawny to red-brown, with highly variable spotting, including unspotted, small coin-like spots, large dab-like spots and elongated brown rosettes. Coloration varies considerably between and within populations. **Distribution and Habitat** Fenno-Scandinavia, Russia (75% of range), China and temperate C Asia, with scattered populations in E and W Europe. Inhabits mainly forest, montane areas with cover, cold semi-desert, tundra, open woodland and scrub. Occurs to 4,700m in the Himalayas, exceptionally to 5,500m. **Feeding Ecology** In contrast to other lynx, hunts mainly small to medium-sized ungulates. The most important prey across much of its range is European and Siberian roe deer, followed by Chamois, musk deer and juveniles of Red Deer, Sika Deer, Moose, ibex and Wild Boar. Ungulates are especially important prey in winter, when snow elevates vulnerability to predation: exceptional kills of adult Red Deer occur in deep snow. Hares, small rodents, squirrels, marmots and birds increase in importance during spring and summer. In far northern forests, where ungulates are less common, Mountain Hares and European Hares are the most important prey year-round. Kills livestock and poultry, including frequent predation on semi-domestic Reindeer in Finland, Norway and Sweden. Mainly nocturno-crepuscular, but may be cathemeral, especially in winter and during the breeding season. Scavenges, and sometimes caches large carcasses with a covering of ground debris. **Social and Spatial Behaviour** Solitary. Male ranges are larger than female ranges, and overlap more extensively. Both sexes demarcate territorial boundaries with urine, scent and faecal marks, but ranges are generally too large to permit exclusivity, except among females with small kittens. Range sizes increase from south to north, reflecting prey availability; 98–1,850km² (♀s) and 180–3,000km² (♂s). Average range size in W and C Europe 106–264km² (both sexes combined), compared with 307–1,515km² in Scandinavia. Largest recorded ranges are in Norway. Density estimates include 0.25/100km² (S Norway) to 1.9–3.2/100km² (Poland). **Reproduction and Demography** Seasonal. Mates February–mid-April; births May–June. Oestrus 3–5 days; gestation 67–74 days. Litter size 1–4, very rarely 5, typically 2. Independent at 9–11 months, with dispersal occurring before the mother's next litter. Females first breed at 22–24 months, males at 3 years. **MORTALITY** Kitten mortality usually at least 50%; 59–60% of Swiss kittens die before independence. Natural adult mortality low, only 2% annually in Scandinavia, but anthropogenic factors increase that by a factor of eight; 44–60% of subadults die during dispersal (Switzerland). Predation occurs occasionally by Grey Wolf (page 100), Tiger (page 44) and Wolverine (page 164; on young animals). **LIFESPAN** 18 (♀) and 20 (♂) years in the wild, 25 in captivity. **Status and Threats** Considered secure, with large areas of its massive range still intact, especially in Russia (where the population is estimated at 30,000–35,000), Mongolia and China. Extirpated from most of W and C Europe, where remaining populations are small and isolated, but recovering and expanding in W Europe, e.g. the Alps. No longer legally hunted for fur except in Russia (~1,000 lynx/year), although illegal trade is widespread in its Russo-Asian range. Sport hunting is legal in much of the range; the highest quotas are in Russia, Estonia, Finland, Latvia, Norway and Sweden. CITES Appendix II; Red List LC, population trend Stable.

# IBERIAN LYNX *Lynx pardinus*

### SPANISH LYNX, PARDEL LYNX

HB ♀ 68.2–75.4cm, ♂ 68.2–82cm; T 12.5–16cm;
W ♀ 8.7–10kg, ♂ 7–15.9kg
Tawny grey to reddish brown, with solid spotting or blotches that sometimes break up into freckling. Both sexes have a prominent white facial mane with black streaks, and the ears have long black tufts. Tail ends in a black tip. **Distribution and Habitat** Restricted to 3 populations on the southern Iberian Peninsula: the largest, a meta-population comprising a main population with 2 satellite reintroduced populations, Sierra Morena mountains, S Spain; a population in Doñana NP (S Spain); and a small, reintroduced population in Vale do Guadiana NP, SE Portugal. Occurs in dense mosaics of forest, thicket, brushland and Mediterranean scrub, with open pastures and edges favoured for hunting. Shuns agricultural land and exotic plantations, but uses pine plantations for dispersal. **Feeding Ecology** Highly reliant on European Rabbit, which comprises 75–93% of the diet, depending on the location and season. Cannot live in areas without abundant rabbits, and requires an estimated 277/year for a female without kittens, up to 379/year for a male. Incidental prey includes small rodents, hares and birds, including ducks, geese, partridges, magpies and pigeons. Juvenile Red Deer and Fallow Deer are sometimes killed during autumn and winter. Kills other carnivores, including Red Fox (page 114), Egyptian Mongoose (page 60), Common Genet (page 92) and feral domestic cats, but these are rarely eaten and probably mainly killed as competitors for rabbit prey. Kills rabbits by biting the skull; larger prey such as deer are killed by suffocation. Does not kill livestock or poultry, due largely to very limited opportunity in its remaining range. Covers larger kills with leaf litter and debris to consume over a number of days. **Social and Spatial Behaviour** Solitary and territorial. Each male range overlaps 1 and sometimes 2 female ranges, with intra-sexual overlap at the edges and exclusive core areas. Territorial fights are occasionally fatal. Range size 8.5–24.6km², averaging 12.6km² (♀s), and 8.5–25km², averaging 16.9km² (♂s). Density estimates 10–20/100km² with moderate rabbit densities to 72–88/100km² in highly protected enclaves with extremely abundant rabbits. **Reproduction and Demography** Seasonal. Mating usually January–February, with births peaking March and occasional births April–June. Litter size 2–4, averaging 3. Kittens independent at 7–8 months, remaining in their natal range until dispersal at 18–20 months. Females can breed at 2 years, but usually first give birth in the wild at 3 years, and breed until age 9. **MORTALITY** Kitten mortality around 33%; 2 kittens usually survive from most litters of 3. Adult mortality around 10% for resident animals insulated from human factors, but anthropogenic mortality is now the major cause of Iberian Lynx deaths. **LIFESPAN** 10 years in the wild, 14 in captivity. **Status and Threats** The world's most endangered felid in terms of total population, which numbers approximately 400 adults in 2 isolated populations in Spain, plus 10 adults reintroduced to SE Portugal (2014–15; kittens documented 2016). Decline driven by extensive habitat conversion of forest to exotic plantations, combined with disease epidemics in rabbits and direct human killing of lynxes. A massive conservation effort has produced recovery from fewer than 150 adults in 2002, and they were downlisted from Critically Endangered in 2015. Anthropogenic killing has declined but remains a serious threat, responsible for 75% of lynx deaths, mostly by illegal trapping, shooting and roadkills. CITES Appendix I; Red List EN, population trend Increasing.

■ Eurasian Lynx

■ Iberian Lynx

**Plate 11**

EURASIAN
LYNX

IBERIAN
LYNX

# BOBCAT *Lynx rufus*

BAY LYNX, RED LYNX

HB ♀ 50.8–95.2cm, ♂ 60.3–105cm; T 9–19.8cm;
W ♀ 3.6–15.7kg, ♂ 4.5–18.3kg

Various shades of grey to rusty brown, with markings ranging from very minimal spotting to large, Ocelot-like blotches. Bobtail has 3–6 dark half-stripes and a vivid white underside and tip, distinguishing the species from Canada Lynx. Melanism occurs occasionally, recorded mostly from SE USA. **Distribution and Habitat** Southern Canada, USA and N Mexico. Very wide habitat tolerance, including all forest types, brushland, scrub, prairies, semi-desert and mountainous terrain. Tolerant of farmland, agricultural land and peri-urban landscapes provided there is cover. **Feeding Ecology** Recorded killing adult deer weighing up to 68kg, but typical prey is hare-sized or smaller. Lagomorphs are key prey throughout its range, especially Snowshoe Hare, Eastern Cottontail, jackrabbits and Marsh Rabbit. White-tailed Deer, Mule Deer and Pronghorn are taken primarily as fawns, but northern Bobcats kill more adults, especially in winter. Other prey includes rodents to the size of porcupines, smaller carnivores, opossums, birds, herptiles, fish, arthropods and eggs. Kills sheep, goats and poultry, although problems are usually localised. Rarely kills small pets in peri-urban areas (small dogs and domestic cats are not recorded in the diet). Forages mostly on the ground. Generally nocturnal with crepuscular activity peaks. Sometimes caches carcasses with a covering of dirt or snow to consume over time, e.g. up to 14 days for an adult deer kill. Eats carrion: road- and winter-killed deer are important food sources, especially in northern winters. **Social and Spatial Behaviour** Solitary and territorial. Range size and overlap decrease with increasing prey availability. Territorial fights are occasionally fatal. Average range size 1–2km² (Alabama; California; Louisiana; Oregon) to 86km² (Adirondacks, New York) for females, and 2–11km² (Alabama; California; Louisiana; Oregon) to 325km² (Adirondacks) for males. Ranges contract during prey peaks, especially of hares and rabbits. Nightly movements are as large as 20km. Density estimates include 4–6/100km² (Minnesota), 20–28/100km² (Arizona, Nevada), exceptionally to >100/100km² (e.g. coastal California, when protected from hunting). **Reproduction and Demography** Weakly seasonal. Births occur year-round, but peak spring–summer, strongly so in northern areas. Gestation 62–70 days. Litter size averages 2–3, exceptionally to 6. Weaning at 2–3 months. Kittens independent at 8–10 months. Females can breed at 9–12 months, but usually first give birth after 24 months. MORTALITY Kitten mortality fluctuates extensively, depending mainly on prey numbers, e.g. 29–82% mortality in Wyoming in different years. Adult mortality 20–33% for unharvested populations to 33–81% for hunted populations. Mostly killed by humans, as well as by winter starvation, predation by Puma (page 38), Coyote (page 102) and domestic dogs, and episodic disease outbreaks in dense populations. LIFESPAN 16 years in the wild, 32.2 in captivity. **Status and Threats** Widespread, resilient to human pressures and secure in most of its range, with >1 million estimated for the US alone. None the less, some populations are exposed to intense hunting pressure and Bobcats are vulnerable to overharvesting. Around 40,000–50,000 are legally killed in the USA and Canada annually, mainly for skins; globally, it is the most heavily traded felid species for fur. Persecuted for supposed livestock depredation, e.g. Mexico, and 2,000–2,500 are killed annually in legal control in the USA. CITES Appendix II; Red List LC, population trend Stable.

# CANADA LYNX *Lynx canadensis*

CANADIAN LYNX

HB ♀ 76.2–96.5cm, ♂ 73.7–107cm; T 5–12.7cm;
W ♀ 5–11.8kg, ♂ 6.3–17.3kg

Uniformly coloured, typically buff-grey with silver or bluish frosting in winter, and brownish in summer, unspotted or lightly spotted on the limbs. Tail shorter than Bobcat's, with a completely black tip. Lynx–Bobcat hybrids occasionally occur where the 2 species overlap in Maine, Minnesota and New Brunswick. **Distribution and Habitat** Most of Canada south of the treeline and some US border states, south to Utah. Reintroduced successfully to S Colorado and unsuccessfully to New York. Closely tied to dense boreal and coniferous forests; rarely uses open habitat. **Feeding Ecology** Strongly dependent on Snowshoe Hare, which comprises 35–97% of the diet locally and seasonally. Northern hare populations cycle every 8–11 years, sometimes spectacularly, from 2,300/km² to 12/km². Lynx numbers are closely linked, lagging 1–2 years behind. Lynx switch prey during declines and during summer. Southern populations (which experience weak or non-existent hare cycles) have more diverse diets year-round, although Snowshoe Hare remains the primary prey. Other important prey includes American Red Squirrel, other rodents, small birds, and game birds like grouse and ptarmigans. Ungulate lambs, especially of Caribou, are sometimes killed, but most ungulates are scavenged. Rarely kills livestock or poultry. Hunting is mainly crepuscular, nocturnal and chiefly terrestrial. Occasionally caches prey by covering it with snow or leaves. **Social and Spatial Behaviour** Solitary and probably territorial, but spatial behaviour varies extensively depending on Snowshoe Hare availability. Southern populations with stable but low densities of hares tend to maintain large, enduring home ranges with high overlap between neighbours. Northern populations maintain smaller and possibly more exclusive ranges during hare peaks, but ranges expand during declines, sometimes leading to nomadism. Average range size estimates include: 39–133km² (♀s) and 69–277km² (♂s) in southern populations; 13–18km² (♀s) and 14–44km² (♂s) in northern populations with high hare numbers; and up to 63–506km² (♀s) and 44–266km² (♂s) in northern populations with few hares. Density estimates include 2–4/100km² during low hare density to 10–45/100km² during peaks. **Reproduction and Demography** Seasonal. Mating March–May; births May–early July. Gestation 63–70 days. Litter size 1–8, with more females breeding and larger litters produced during hare peaks. Independent at 10–17 months. Females breed as early as 10 months during high hare years, but usually first breed at 22–23 months. MORTALITY Kitten survival is linked closely to hare numbers, reaching 60–95% mortality in poor years. Estimates of adult mortality include: 11–27% and up to >60% during hare shortages for unharvested populations; and 45–95% for harvested populations. Starvation and trapping by humans are responsible for most deaths. LIFESPAN 16 years in the wild, 26.9 in captivity. **Status and Threats** Generally widespread and secure, especially in Canada. Extirpated from most of its US distribution, and its range appears to be retreating north with forestry and climatic warming; suitable habitat has receded ~175km northwards in C Canada since the 1970s. On average, at least 11,000 Canada Lynx are legally harvested annually, most in Canada and Alaska; they are vulnerable to overharvesting during Snowshoe Hare declines. CITES Appendix II; Red List LC, population trend Stable.

■ Bobcat

■ Canada Lynx

Plate 12

BOBCAT

CANADA LYNX

# JAGUARUNDI *Herpailurus yagouaroundi*

**EYRA**

HB ♀ 53–73.5cm, ♂ 48.8–83.2cm; T 27.5–59cm;
W ♀ 3.5–7kg, ♂ 3–7.6kg

Uniformly coloured with 2 distinct, highly variable morphs: red-brown (often with a bright white muzzle and chin), varying from light tawny to brick red; and grey, varying from pale slate grey to deep black-grey (often with a paler neck and head). Litters can include kittens of both colours. Body and head elongated and lean, with a long, slender tail, giving the impression of a mustelid in the field. **Distribution and Habitat** C Argentina to N Mexico, and formerly in the Rio Grande Valley, Texas, USA, but not confirmed there since 1986. Occurs from sea-level to 2,000m (occasionally to 3,200m) in all types of forest, scrub, chaparral, brush, dense grassland and pasture. Does well in human-modified or recovering habitat with cover and high rodent densities, e.g. pasture grassland, old fields and secondary forest. **Feeding Ecology** Makes kills to the size of an armadillo, but most prey weighs less than 1kg. Principal prey includes rats, mice and birds, especially ground-dwellers like tinamous and quail. Also eats small primates (rarely), cavies, rabbits, opossums, reptiles, fish and arthropods. Brocket deer are recorded in scats, but probably from scavenging. Occasionally raids poultry coops. Appears to be primarily crepuscular/diurnal; a capable climber, but most hunting takes place on the ground. **Social and Spatial Behaviour** Solitary. Exhibits typical felid marking behaviour and is presumably territorial, although radio-tracked individuals overlap extensively. Based on relatively few studies, range size is similar for females and males, or slightly larger for the latter: 12.1km² (♀s) and 16.2km² (♂s; Tamaulipas, Mexico); 1.4–18km² (♀s) and 8.5–25.3km² (♂s; Brazil). Ranges for 3 monitored Belizean cats were 20km² (1 ♀) and 88–100km² (2 ♂s), the latter an unusually high figure probably indicating dispersers. **Reproduction and Demography** Poorly known; possibly weakly seasonal, although reports are contradictory. In captivity, gestation 72–75 days, and litters number 1–4 (average 1.8–2.3). Weaning begins at around 5–6 weeks. Sexual maturity at 17–26 months. MORTALITY Poorly known. Recorded predators include Puma, and domestic dogs near villages. LIFESPAN 10.5 years in captivity. **Status and Threats** Tolerant of human activity and seldom hunted for its unicolour fur. Persecuted for killing poultry, and common roadkill in some areas, but most populations are secure. Widespread and relatively common in South America. Endangered in Central America; considered Critically Endangered in the USA, but likely extinct there. CITES Appendix I – Central and North America, Appendix II – elsewhere; Red List LC, population trend Decreasing.

# PUMA *Puma concolor*

**COUGAR, MOUNTAIN LION, PANTHER (FLORIDA)**

HB ♀ 95–141cm, ♂ 107–168cm; T 57–92cm;
W ♀ 22.7–57kg, ♂ 39–80kg (exceptionally to 125kg)

Uniformly coloured, ranging from light grey through tawny brown to brick red, with creamy-white underparts. Temperate Pumas tend to be larger, with paler, greyish coloration, while tropical individuals are smaller with richer reddish tones. Tail tip and backs of the ears are dark brown to black, and the white muzzle is bordered by black. Long tubular tail is distinctive in the field. Cubs have rich, dark brown spots that usually fade within the first year. **Distribution and Habitat** Relatively widely distributed in SW Canada, W USA and South America. More restricted in Mexico and Central America, and extirpated from E USA except for 100–120 in S Florida ('Florida Panther'). Presence in El Salvador is uncertain, with no recent records. Very wide habitat tolerance provided there is vegetation or rocky terrain, including temperate and tropical forests, woodland, coastal and desert scrublands, and rocky desert, from sea-level to >4,000m (exceptionally to 5,800m in the Andes, S Peru). Mostly shuns open areas, but readily passes though marginal habitat. Lives close to humans provided cover and prey are available. **Feeding Ecology** Very broad diet encompassing arthropods to adult male Elk. Large kills are more common in temperate populations, where deer, Moose, Elk and wild sheep form the principal prey; Guanaco is a key prey species in Chile. Tropical Pumas focus more on smaller prey such as brocket deer, peccaries, Capybara, paca, agoutis and armadillos. Locally, the diet may be dominated by feral livestock, e.g. pigs (Florida) and wild horses (Nevada). Kills reptiles to the size of adult caimans and alligators, and birds such as Wild Turkey, various geese and rhea. Readily kills livestock, and sometimes takes domestic pets in peri-urban areas. Humans are rarely killed, 26 recorded fatalities (including 2 from rabies infection) in North America in 1890–2018. Hunting is mainly nocturno-crepuscular. Typically discards entrails of large kills before covering them in dirt or leaf litter, consuming the carcasses over a period of 3 days to 4 weeks (winter). Scavenges, although this usually represents a small amount of its intake. **Social and Spatial Behaviour** Broadly solitary and territorial, but with considerable overlap in ranges, and greater sociality in some populations, e.g. Greater Yellowstone Ecosystem resident adults have frequent non-agonistic interactions among non-related animals, including prolonged associations and sharing large carcasses for up to 5 days. Territorial fights are sometimes fatal, particularly in disturbed populations (such as those heavily hunted). Home range is 25–1,500km², averaging 33km² (Venezuela) to 685km² (Utah) for females, and 60km² (Venezuela) to 826km² (Utah) for males. Pumas are superb dispersers: 6–32km (♀s) and 24–208km (♂s; Florida), to 12–99km (♀s) and 12–1,067km (♂s; Black Hills, South Dakota). In 2011, a South Dakota male was killed by a vehicle in Connecticut ~2,800km away. Density estimates: 0.3/100km² (e.g. Utah; Texas) to 1–3/100km² (Alberta; California; Utah; Wyoming), 3–4.4/100km² (Pantanal, Brazil), 2.4–4.9/100km² (rainforest, Belize), exceptionally to 7/100km² (Vancouver Island). **Reproduction and Demography** Weakly seasonal. Births occur year-round, but typically peak in summer (Yellowstone NP; Canada) or spring (Florida). Oestrus lasts 1–16 days; gestation averages 92 days (range 82–98 days). Litter size averages 2–3 kittens, exceptionally to 6. Weaning at around 4–5 months. Cubs independent at around 18 months (range 10–24 months). Females first give birth at 18 months (typically >24 months) and males first breed at around 3 years. MORTALITY 36–58% of cubs die in their first year. Estimates of adult mortality include 9% (♂s) to 18% (♀s) in New Mexico, and 3% (♀s) to 61% (♂s) in NW Montana. Mostly killed by humans (legal hunting, roadkills, illegal killing); principal natural causes of death for adults are starvation, disease and hunting accidents. LIFESPAN 16 years in the wild, 20 in captivity. **Status and Threats** Tolerant of human activity, but extirpated from around 40% of its Latin American range and most of its eastern North American range. Habitat loss, combined with intense persecution in livestock areas, are the major threats, especially in Latin America. Legal sport hunting kills 2,500–3,500 Pumas per year in the USA, triggering population declines in some states. Road accidents are a major threat in Florida, e.g. 63% of 381 known deaths in 2000–17. Argentina is the only range state still paying bounties in Pumas, producing extremely excessive harvests of ~2,000 annually. CITES Appendix I – Nicaragua through Panama, Appendix II – elsewhere; legally hunted in Argentina, Canada, Mexico, Peru and USA (all states except California and Florida); Red List LC, population trend Decreasing.

■ Jaguarundi    ■ Puma

**Plate 13**

Red form

**JAGUARUNDI**

Grey form

Temperate
form

**PUMA**

Tropical
form

Cubs

# CHEETAH *Acinonyx jubatus*

HB ♀ 105–140cm, ♂ 108–152cm; T 60–89cm;
SH ♀ 67–89cm, ♂ 74–94cm; W ♀ 21–51kg, ♂ 29–64kg
Yellow-blond fading to white underparts, with black coin-like spots and unique facial tear streaks. Saharan Cheetahs have very short, pale fur, ranging from brown-spotted beige to near white with faint cinnamon spots. So-called King Cheetahs are a recessive colour morph and may be born to normally spotted parents. Cubs have a fluffy smoky-grey mantle that dwindles by 4–5 months to a short mane on the shoulders, which is inconspicuous in most adults but often obvious in Asiatic Cheetahs. Mantle's function is unclear, but it probably assists with camouflage and thermoregulation; mimicry of Honey Badger (page 158) to deter predators, as is often claimed, is doubtful. Claws dog-like and lack fleshy claw-sheaths present in other cats, but are partially protractile. Claws appear in tracks, except for the sharp, strongly curved dewclaw, which is used for prey capture.

### Distribution and Habitat
Relatively widely distributed in southern and E Africa, rare in W Africa, and extinct in N Africa except S Algeria and possibly W and NE Libya. Extinct in Asia except for ~50 in Iran. Favours woodland–savannah mosaics and open grassland, becoming sparser in dense humid woodland, e.g. Zambian miombo, and absent from rainforest. Tolerates arid habitats, including the deserts of C Iran (which experience winter snowfall), and the Namib and Sahara, but transient in the driest areas. Recorded to 3,500m (Mt Kenya, Kenya).

### Feeding Ecology
Usually hunts ungulates weighing 10–60kg, particularly gazelles, Impala, Steenbok and duikers, occasionally specialising in prey up to size of Nyala (62–108kg); also juveniles of larger ungulates, including oryx, wildebeest, zebra and (rarely) buffalo and giraffe. Male coalitions take large prey, e.g. adult hartebeest, oryx and wildebeest. Asiatic Cheetahs eat mainly Urial and Persian Ibex following the widespread extirpation of gazelles. Hares are important prey in certain habitats, e.g. S Kalahari, and especially to recently independent young adults and in prey-depleted landscapes, e.g. Iran. Kills small untended livestock, but is easily deterred by people or dogs, and is not recorded killing humans. Hunting mostly diurnal to maximise visibility and avoid nocturnal competitors. Following a short and careful stalk, pursues prey for up to 500m at a maximum recorded speed of 105km/h. Prey is bowled over or pulled off balance using the dewclaw, and usually killed by suffocation. Around 30% (Serengeti NP, Tanzania) to 43.4% (S Kalahari, South Africa) of chases are successful, more so for small prey: 73–93% for hares (Kalahari and Serengeti NP), 86–100% for juvenile gazelles (Serengeti NP). Rarely defends kills, losing up to 13% (Serengeti NP), chiefly to Spotted Hyaena (page 54) and Lion (page 46). Very rarely scavenges and seldom returns to carcasses previously fed upon.

### Social and Spatial Behaviour
Unusual social system in which females are solitary and non-territorial, while male sociality and territoriality vary widely. Females occupy large home ranges that are not defended. Where prey is scarce or migratory, female ranges reach 1,500km² (average 833km²; Serengeti NP) to 6,353.7km² (average 1,400–1,836km²; Namibia). Areas with resident or abundant prey produce smaller ranges (e.g. 185–246km²; Kruger NP, South

■ Cheetah

Africa), although females are non-territorial regardless. Dispersing females usually settle near their natal range, so that neighbouring females are often related. Males typically disperse further to avoid breeding with female relatives, and live in permanent coalitions of 2–4, usually littermates; around a third of Serengeti coalitions include an unrelated member. Coalitions defend territories where profitable, repelling rival males in fights that may be fatal. Serengeti coalitions target small areas with high female overlap averaging 37km². Males in woodland habitats with resident females establish medium-sized territories, e.g. Kruger NP, 126km² (3 ♂ coalition) to 195km² (single ♂). Coalitions defend territories more successfully than loners, and single males are often nomadic 'floaters' with much larger home ranges, averaging 777km² (Serengeti NP) to 1,829km² (Namibia). A pair of Iranian males (likely nomadic) used 1,737km² in 5 months of radio-tracking. Coalitions sometimes also float on large ranges (average 1,608.4km²; Namibia) as an alternative to territorial defence. Cheetahs naturally occur at low densities: 0.16/100km² (Iran), 0.25–2/100km² (Namibian farmland) and 0.5–2.30/100km² (Kruger NP), to 2.5/100km² (Serengeti NP). Seasonal densities exceptionally reach 20/100km² when Cheetahs congregate temporarily in localised areas (Serengeti NP).

### Reproduction and Demography
Cheetahs have a reputation for poor reproduction arising from the difficulties of breeding them in captivity, but wild Cheetahs are prolific. Aseasonal, although Asiatic Cheetahs apparently mate in winter (January–February) and give birth in spring (April–May). Gestation 90–98 days. Litter size typically 3–6, rarely to 8; litter of 9 from Kenya may have included an adoption. Inter-litter interval averages 20.1 months (Serengeti NP). Weaning begins at 6–8 weeks and is complete by 4–5 months. Cubs independent at 12–20 months (average 17–18 months) and disperse as a sibling group; females leave the group before sexual maturity, while males remain together. Females can conceive at 21–24 months; first give birth around 29 months (Serengeti NP) and can reproduce to 12 years. Males are sexually mature at 12 months, although they rarely breed before 3 years. MORTALITY 71% (S Kalahari) to 95% (Serengeti short grass plains) of cubs die before independence, most killed by other carnivores. Losses in the denning period are the highest. In Serengeti NP, 20% of cubs that emerge at >8 weeks survive to adulthood, but the short grass habitat here is likely particularly unfavourable for survival; mortality is lower everywhere else where data exist. Other post-emergence estimates include 38% (Phinda GR, South Africa), 43% (Nairobi NP, Kenya), 50% (Kruger NP) and 73% (S Kalahari). Adults occasionally killed by Lion, Leopard (page 48) and Spotted Hyaena; males killed in territorial fights, and some adults killed in hunting accidents. Despite high genetic homogeneity, wild Cheetahs suffer little disease. LIFESPAN Maximum 13.5 (average 6.2) years for Serengeti females, 11 (average 5.3) for males; 21 in captivity.

### Status and Threats
Reduced to approximately 7,100 adults and subadults in 33 known populations occupying 9% of the historic global range. More than 50% of Cheetahs occur in a single transboundary population across 6 southern African countries. Most of the range (77%) is non-protected where declines are poorly understood, but likely sufficient to justify upgrading the Cheetah's status to Endangered. Widely persecuted by livestock farmers despite causing relatively minor damage, and profoundly affected by reduction of prey in pastoral areas. Human hunting of prey is critical in the Sahel, N Africa and Iran, where Cheetahs are naturally very rare. Limited hunting for skins occurs, e.g. Sahel and NE Africa, where there is also a significant trade in live cubs and adults, mainly to the Arabian Peninsula. High genetic homogeneity has had little impact on wild populations. CITES Appendix I, permitting trade of approximately 200 hunting trophies (Namibia and Zimbabwe) and live animals; Red List VU (global), CR (Asia), population trend Decreasing.

**Plate 14**

**CHEETAH**

Saharan
form

Typical
form

Cub

King Cheetah

# SNOW LEOPARD *Panthera uncia*

**Ounce**

HB ♀ 86–117cm, ♂ 104–125cm; T 78–105cm; SH to 60cm;
W ♀ 21–53kg, ♂ 25–55kg

Dark cream to smoky grey with large, dark grey or black open blotches, and smaller solid markings on the head and legs. Muscular tail proportionally the longest of any felid, used for balance during hunts and wrapped around the body to insulate it against extreme cold. The species is unmistakable, but C Asian Leopards (page 48) in long, pale winter coat are sometimes mistaken for it (chiefly in fur markets). **Distribution and Habitat** Found in 12 countries in C Asia throughout the world's highest mountain ranges, including the Altai, Himalayas, Karakoram, Hindu Kush, Pamirs and Tien Shan. 2017 surveys in N Myanmar failed to confirm its presence. Uniquely adapted to high and steep rugged terrain, and copes well with deep snow. Also uses meadows, steppes, wide valleys and open montane desert, but mainly to move between rocky habitats. Occurs mostly at 3,000–5,500m except at northern range limits, where it is found at 900–2,400m, e.g. in Mongolia's Gobi. **Feeding Ecology** Dependent on mountain ungulates, especially Asiatic (Siberian) Ibex, Blue Sheep and Argali, which are the main prey in much of its range. Other prey includes Markhor, Urial, Himalayan Tahr, musk deer, and occasionally gazelles, and juveniles of Eurasian Wild Boar, Wild Yak and Asiatic Wild Ass. Large kills are supplemented by small prey, especially during the summer, when herbivores disperse to higher elevations. Marmots are the most important of smaller prey; also opportunistically takes rabbits, hares, pikas, and game birds such as Tibetan Snowcock and partridges. Kills domestic animals, especially sheep and goats, but also cattle, yaks, camels, horses and dogs; depredation can reach significant levels locally and seasonally when wild prey is scarce. No recorded fatal attacks on humans. Stalks in typical felid fashion before rushing prey at close range; superbly agile over extraordinarily steep and rugged terrain. Large prey is usually killed by a suffocating throat bite. Eats carrion and has been observed displacing Dholes (page 108) from carcasses (Hemis NP, India). **Social and Spatial Behaviour** Solitary. Maintains stable ranges that are regularly marked, but extent of territorial defence is unknown. Ranges are very large; published estimates from ground-based radio-telemetry are probably gross underestimates, e.g. a Mongolian female's calculated range went from 58km² to at least 1,590km² (and possibly >4,500km²) when fitted with a satellite collar. Range size 87.2–193.2km² (♀s) and 114.3–394.1km² (♂s; Tost Mountains, Mongolia), assuming Snow Leopards closely follow the edges of mountain ranges; increases to 202.3–548.5km² (♀s) and 264.9–1,283km² (♂s) if associated steppe areas are included, but Snow Leopards mostly avoid steppe habitat. Species is extremely difficult to count, but density estimates from camera-trapping vary from 0.15/100km² (Sarychat, Kyrgyzstan) to 4.5/100km² in prey-rich habitat (Hemis NP, India). **Reproduction and Demography** Poorly known from the wild; likely to be a seasonal breeder given that it experiences extreme winters. Calling and scent-marking peaks January–March, which would coincide with spring births; captive births peak May. Gestation 90–105 days. Litter size averages 2–3 cubs, exceptionally

to 5. Weaning at 2–3 months. Age at independence 18–24 months (2 individuals; Mongolia). **MORTALITY** Estimated at 17% (adults) to 23% (subadults; Tost Mountains, Mongolia). Causes are poorly known; winter starvation, especially of young animals, is likely to be an important factor. **LIFESPAN** 20 years in captivity. **Status and Threats** Somewhat insulated from human activities given that it lives in such remote, inhospitable areas, but it is naturally rare, and human populations and their livestock are increasing in its habitat. Widely killed for livestock depredation, often compounded by prey loss from human hunting and competition with livestock. Furs and especially body parts have commercial value, chiefly in China. CITES Appendix I; Red List VU, population trend Decreasing.

# MAINLAND CLOUDED LEOPARD
*Neofelis nebulosa*

# SUNDA CLOUDED LEOPARD
*Neofelis diardi*

HB ♀ 68.6–94cm, ♂ 81.3–108cm; T 60–92cm;
W ♀ 10–11.5kg, ♂ 17.7–25kg

Classified as a single species until 2006, but now separated into 2 species: the insular Sunda Clouded Leopard; and the continental Mainland Clouded Leopard. Sunda Clouded Leopards are generally darker, with smaller cloud markings. Clouded leopards display an exceptionally large gape and elongated canine teeth, the reasons for which are unclear. **Distribution and Habitat** Mainland Clouded Leopard: continental Indochina. Sunda Clouded Leopard: Borneo and Sumatra. Both species are closely associated with dense evergreen tropical forest, but they also occur in secondary and logged forests, swamp forest, dry woodland and mangroves. Radio-collared individuals used grassland patches in open forest mosaics for hunting. **Feeding Ecology** Poorly known; confirmed prey includes primates from slow lorises to adult male Proboscis Monkey, hog deer, muntjacs, Bornean Bearded Pig, Malayan Pangolin, Asiatic Brush-tailed Porcupine, small rodents, civets and birds. Predation on orangutans by Sunda Clouded Leopard is unconfirmed. Unambiguous kills of deer and pigs revealed a deep killing bite to the nape, an unusual technique for large prey and perhaps related to the unique dentition. Recorded occasionally killing small livestock and poultry. Clouded leopards probably hunt mostly on the ground, but they are highly agile and arboreal; there are 4 published observations of clouded leopards attacking Proboscis Monkeys in trees. A female (Danum Valley, Borneo) cached an adult male Maroon Leaf Langur in a tree, where she fed on the carcass; it is unknown how frequently hauling occurs. **Social and Spatial Behaviour** Solitary. Only 8 animals have ever been radio-collared, in Borneo, Nepal and Thailand. Both species likely follow typical felid pattern of overlapping territories with exclusive core areas. Limited data suggest sexes have similar territory sizes: 34–40km² (♀s) and 35.5–43.5km² (♂s). Density estimates: 0.8–2.6/100km² for Sunda Clouded Leopard (Sabah, Sumatra), and 0.6–3/100km² (Htamanthi WS, Myanmar) to 5.1/100km² (Dampa TR, India) for Mainland Clouded Leopard. **Reproduction and Demography** Probably aseasonal. Gestation 85–95 days (rarely to 109 days). Litters average 2–3 (range 1–5). Weaning begins at around 7–10 weeks. Sexual maturity at 20–30 months. **MORTALITY** Humans are responsible for most deaths in studied areas; otherwise mortality is unknown. **LIFESPAN** 17 years in captivity. **Status and Threats** Often assumed to be more resilient than Tigers (page 44) and Leopards (page 48), but surveyed populations do not reach comparably high densities and both species are closely associated with forest habitat, which is under intense pressure for rubber and palm plantations or agriculture. Illegally hunted for skins, bones and meat. Both species: CITES Appendix I; Red List VU, population trend Decreasing.

■ Snow Leopard

■ Mainland Clouded Leopard
■ Sunda Clouded Leopard

**Plate 15**

SNOW LEOPARD

MAINLAND
CLOUDED
LEOPARD

SUNDA CLOUDED LEOPARD

# TIGER *Panthera tigris*

HB ♀ 146–177cm, ♂ 189–300cm; T 72–109cm; SH 80–110cm; W ♀ 75–177kg, ♂ 100–261kg

Background colour varies from pale yellow to rich red, with white or cream underparts. Generally darker and more richly striped in tropical S Asia, and paler and more lightly striped in temperate areas. White Tigers are not albino, and arise from a recessive mutation that produces blue eyes and chocolate-coloured stripes on a white background. There is only 1 record from the wild (Madhya Pradesh, India) since 1951, a male cub from which all captive white Tigers are descended (and, hence, are extremely inbred). An intermediate form, called 'golden tabby' or 'strawberry', is known only from captivity. True melanism is unknown, although pseudo-melanism occurs rarely, with extensive coalesced striping producing an almost entirely black appearance. Size varies very widely: Sumatran Tigers are the smallest, with males up to 140kg, while individuals from the Indian subcontinent and Russia are the largest. Largest wild male on record, from Nepal, weighed 261kg (up to 325kg recorded from captivity). Traditionally classified into 9 subspecies (three – Bali, Javan and Caspian – are now extinct) based mainly on morphology; incorporating comprehensive data, including genetic analyses, this was recently revised to 2 subspecies, the insular *P. t. sondaica*, now present only in Sumatra, and the continental *P. t. tigris*. Based on modest differences insufficient for subspecific divisions, continental Tigers are further grouped into a northern clade (Amur Tigers and the extinct Caspian Tiger) and a southern clade (all other mainland populations; Bengal Tiger).

## Distribution and Habitat

Restricted to 7% of its historic range, from W India to the Himalayas, through Indochina to Malaysia, Sumatra, the Russian Far East and extreme NE China. Extinct in Bali (1940s), C Asia (1968), Java (1980s), SC China (by ~2000) and Cambodia/Vietnam/Laos (by ~2015). Occurs mainly in various temperate and tropical forests, forest–grassland mosaics and associated dense cover such as Terai grassland, thickets, scrub, marshes, mangroves and reed beds. Reaches the highest densities on the Indian subcontinent in dry and mesic forests, and the Terai. Typically avoids human-modified habitats such as agricultural land, palm plantations and monocultures. Occurs exceptionally up to 4,201m (Himalayas, Bhutan), but typically below 2,000m.

## Feeding Ecology

Adults can kill almost anything they encounter, with the exception of adult rhinos and elephants, but the diet is dominated by various deer species and wild pigs. Typically focuses on ≤5 species of locally common prey such as Sambar, Red Deer, Chital, hog deer, Sika Deer, muntjacs and Wild Boar. Capable of killing adult Gaur and Water Buffalo weighing up to 1,000kg, but most kills of these species are subadults and juveniles. Smaller prey taken relatively often includes primates, porcupines, small carnivores and hares. Readily kills other predators, although they are not always eaten; Leopard (page 48), Dhole (page 108), Brown Bear (page 138) and Asiatic Black Bear (page 134) are recorded prey. Preys on livestock, mainly when untended in forest. Amur Tigers regularly kill domestic dogs, particularly when these are accompanying hunters in forest, and during severe winters that force the Tigers into villages. Tigers probably kill more people than any other large carnivore (mainly in India), in part because human populations in Asia are so dense and often utilise Tiger habitat intensively; true 'man-eaters' that focus on humans as prey are rare. Hunting is mainly nocturno-crepuscular. Scavenges and appropriates kills of other carnivores.

■ Tiger

## Social and Spatial Behaviour

Solitary and territorial. Adults establish exclusive territories where possible, but total exclusivity is rare. Territorial overlap is least in high-density populations with abundant prey and small ranges, e.g. Nepal, India. Territorial fights are rare, but sometimes fatal when they occur, more frequently in males than females. Recorded territory size varies from 10km² (♀s; Chitwan NP, Nepal) to 2,058km² (♂s; Russia). Range size for Terai and productive forest in Nepal or India 10–51km² (♀s) and 24–243km² (♂s), compared with 181–761km² (♀s) and 434–2,058km² (♂s) in Russia. Females mostly settle near their natal range, while males disperse more widely. Dispersal distances at Chitwan NP average 9.7km for females (maximum 33km) and 33km for males (maximum 65km), compared with 14km for females (maximum 72km) and 103km for males (maximum 195km) in Russia. Densities of populations, even in high-quality habitat, are often depressed due to human hunting of prey (even if Tigers are not hunted). Density estimates vary from 0.2–2.6/100km² in lowland tropical forest where poaching is prevalent (Laos; Malaysia; Myanmar; Sumatra) and 0.5–1.4/100km² (temperate forest, Russia), to 11.5–19/100km² in well-protected forest and Terai (India).

## Reproduction and Demography

Aseasonal over most of the range; more than 50% of Amur Tiger cubs are born late summer, August–October, and winter births are rare. Oestrus 2–5 days; gestation 95–107 days, averaging 103–105. Litter size 2–5, averaging 2–3. Weaning at around 3–5 months. Inter-litter interval 20–24 months, averaging 21 months. Cubs independent at 17–24 months. Females often inherit part of their mother's range, while males disperse more widely. Sexual maturity at 2.5–3 years (both sexes): earliest breeding 3 years for females (average 3.4 years in Chitwan NP) and 3.4 years for males (average 4.8 years, Chitwan NP). Reproduction by females is possible until at least age 15.5. MORTALITY 34% (Chitwan NP) to 41–47% (Russia) of cubs die in their first year, most related to anthropogenic causes and infanticide. Estimates of adult mortality include 23% (both sexes combined; Nagarahole NP, India) and 19% (♀s) to 37% (♂s; Russia). Humans are the main cause of death for most populations, and adults also die in territorial fights. Accidents (e.g. a male fell through a frozen river in Russia) occur, but are uncommon. LIFESPAN 16 years for females and 12 for males in the wild; 26 in captivity.

## Status and Threats

The most endangered large cat, having suffered a calamitous decline in the twentieth century that continues today, with approximately 3,900 individuals in 9 range countries. An estimated 70% of the world's Tigers (and most breeding females) now live in around 0.5% of their historic range. Combined with loss of habitat to forestry, commercial palm plantations and agriculture, Tigers are particularly threatened by intense illegal hunting to supply the traditional Asian medicinal trade. This is compounded by widespread hunting of their prey to feed a massive demand for bushmeat, especially in Southeast Asia. Given strong protection, Tiger populations recover rapidly, e.g. densities increased from 0.8/100km² to 1.4/100km² between 2013 and 2016 in Parsa NP, Nepal, but unfortunately there are few areas where sufficient protection is taking place. CITES Appendix I; Red List EN (globally), CR (China, Russia, Sumatra), population trend Decreasing.

**Plate 16**

TIGER

White
form

Bengal
Tiger

Sumatran
Tiger

Amur
Tiger

# LION *Panthera leo*

HB ♀ 158–192cm; ♂ 172–250cm; T 60–100cm; SH 100–128cm; W ♀ 110–168kg, ♂ 150–272kg

Typically tawny or sandy with pale underparts, but varying from ash grey or cream to ginger and (rarely) dark brown. Backs of the ears and tail tip are a contrasting black or dark brown. White Lions from Kruger NP region, South Africa, are leucistic (not albino), with pigmented eyes, nose and pads; they can be born to normally coloured parents. Mane colour ranges from platinum to black, and the length is highly variable. 'Maneless' males occur most often where it is extremely hot, e.g. Tsavo NP, Kenya, and in most Sahelian populations. Cubs are born with dark brown rosettes that fade with age, retained as vestigial spotting in some adults. Mane growth begins at 6–8 months. Recent molecular studies show a clear separation into a northern subspecies, *P. l. leo* (W and C Africa, and India), and southern subspecies, *P. l. melanochaita* (E and southern Africa). Northern Lions are 10–20% smaller than E and southern African individuals, and males typically have reduced manes; Indian Lions often have a distinctive belly fold (occasionally present in African Lions).

## Distribution and Habitat

Patchy distribution south of the Sahara, chiefly in and around protected areas, with the largest populations in E and southern Africa. Outside Africa, there is only 1 population, in Gujarat, India. Naturally absent only from true desert and equatorial rainforest. Optimum habitat is mesic open woodland and grassland savannah. Inhabits dry deciduous teak forest in India. Recorded to 4,200–4,300m (Bale Mountains, Ethiopia; Mt Kilimanjaro, Tanzania).

## Feeding Ecology

Opportunistic, killing virtually everything it encounters, but prefers large herbivores weighing 60–550kg; cannot persist without large prey. In any given population, the diet is dominated by 3–5 ungulates such as wildebeest, zebra, buffalo, giraffe, Gemsbok, Impala, Nyala, Kob, Thomson's Gazelle, Chital, Sambar and Warthog. Smallest preferred prey species documented is Springbok (27–48kg), in Etosha NP, Namibia. Smaller prey, especially Warthog, often dominates during the lean dry season where large prey is migratory, e.g. Chobe NP, Botswana and Serengeti NP, Tanzania. Only healthy mature elephants are invulnerable to Lion predation; large prides kill young or unwell adults, as well as adult rhinos and Hippopotamuses. Kills untended livestock and occasionally preys on humans; isolated pockets of persistent man-eating still occur, e.g. SE Tanzania and N Mozambique. Hunting is mainly nocturno-crepuscular. Although females make most kills, males are capable hunters that increase the hunting success of very large prey, e.g. buffalo and giraffe. Success estimates include 15% (Etosha NP), 23% (Serengeti NP) and 38.5% (Kalahari). Readily scavenges, comprising 5.5% of intake in Etosha NP to almost 40% in Serengeti NP. Frequently appropriates kills from other carnivores.

## Social and Spatial Behaviour

The only communally living cat. Prides comprise 1–20 (usually 3–6) related lionesses, their offspring and 1–9 (usually 2–4) immigrant

■ Lion

males unrelated to breeding females. Pride size is correlated with prey biomass, smaller in arid areas and exceptionally reaching 45–50 under ideal conditions. Female membership of the pride is mostly stable, but the entire pride is together rarely: small subgroups come and go within pride range in a continuous 'fission–fusion' pattern. Females defend their range against other prides and strange males. Coalition males are usually related to each other, but smaller coalitions (2–3) often include unrelated members. Females generally stay with the pride for life, but occasionally disperse following a male takeover or to avoid mating with male relatives. Young males are evicted or leave at 25–48 months, entering a nomadic stage lasting 2–3 years before attempting to acquire their own pride. Coalition members are highly cooperative and remain together for life, defending their territory and females from male intruders. Following a takeover, new males usually kill or evict all unrelated cubs younger than 12–18 months to hasten the lionesses' return to oestrus. Coalition tenure is generally 2–4 years. Serengeti pride territories average 65km² (woodland) to 184km² (grassland), reaching a maximum of 500km². Arid areas produce much larger ranges: to 2,800km² (Kalahari), 1,055–1,745km² (Kaudom GR, Namibia) and 2,721–6,542km² (Kunene, NW Namibia). Two Kunene male coalitions (possibly nomads) had ranges of 13,365–17,221km². Density estimates: 0.05–0.62/100km² (Kunene), 1.5–2/100km² (Kalahari), 6–12/100km² (Kruger NP), 12–14/100km² (Gir PA, India), to 38/100km² (Lake Manyara NP, Tanzania).

## Reproduction and Demography

Aseasonal, although births often peak with seasonal birth events of ungulates. Oestrus averages 4–5 days; gestation 98–115 days (mean 110). Litter size typically 2–4, up to 7. Lionesses often give birth synchronously and communally care for cubs; females suckle all cubs, but carry only their own. Weaning begins at around 6–8 weeks, but suckling may continue to 8 months. Cubs can hunt independently at around 18 months, but rarely disperse before 2 years. Inter-litter interval 20–24 months. Lionesses can conceive at 30–36 months, but typically first give birth at around 42–48 months and cease reproducing after age 15. Males are sexually mature at 26–28 months, but rarely breed before 4 years. MORTALITY 16% (Kruger NP, with abundant resident prey) to 63% (Serengeti NP, with mainly migratory prey) of cubs die in their first year, mostly from infanticide, predation and starvation; mortality in the second year typically drops significantly, from 10% (Kruger NP) to 20% (Serengeti NP). Apart from human-caused mortality, adult Lions die mostly in fights with other Lions (especially males), from injuries while hunting large prey and from starvation when old or debilitated. Disease is uncommon, but episodes are occasionally severe; more than 1,000 Lions (40% of the population) died during the 1993–94 canine distemper outbreak, Serengeti NP. LIFESPAN 19 years for females, 16 (but rarely over 12) for males in the wild; 30 in captivity.

## Status and Threats

Conservation-dependent, inhabiting <16% of historic African range, with 1 isolated population of 400 in India. Globally, the total population declined by 43% in 1993–2014; numbers in 4 southern African countries (Botswana, Namibia, South Africa and Zimbabwe) and India collectively increased by 12%, while populations in the rest of the range declined by 60%. Excluding southern Africa/India, the Lion's status is Endangered. Eradication by humans, coupled with combined loss of habitat and prey from agriculture and livestock herding, has driven declines. Intense persecution by herders (mainly outside protected areas) and poaching for bushmeat (mostly inside protected areas) are the primary ongoing threats. Highly vulnerable to poisoned baits, and to snares set for bushmeat; a majority of protected populations are significantly depleted due to poaching, mainly of prey but also ancillary poaching of Lions. Legal sport hunting takes place in 10 African countries. Lions are very sensitive to overharvest, and hunting triggers population declines under excessive quotas or where they are already suffering anthropogenic mortality, such as from snares. Excluding canned hunts of captive-bred lions in South Africa, approximately 220–240 wild Lions (mainly males) are hunted annually. CITES Appendix I – Asia, Appendix II – Africa; Red List VU (global), EN (India), CR (W Africa), population trend Decreasing.

**Plate 17**

**LION**

African Lion
southern subspecies

Male

Female

Cubs

Asiatic
Lion

Male

# LEOPARD *Panthera pardus*

## PANTHER

HB ♀ 95–123cm, ♂ 91–191cm; T 51–101cm; SH 55–82cm;
W ♀ 17–42kg, ♂ 20–90kg

Background colour varies from pale cream, through various shades of orange, to dark rufous-brown with white underparts, covered with rosettes, each a cluster of small black spots around a normally unspotted centre that is darker than the body colour. Forest Leopards tend to be dark, while those in arid areas are pale. Melanistic individuals ('black panthers') occur mainly in humid lowland and upland forests; they are most common in tropical Southeast Asia, e.g. outnumbering spotted Leopards in Malaysia, and are rarely recorded in Africa. Size varies widely, correlated with changes in climate and prey availability. The smallest Leopards, from arid mountainous areas in the Middle East, are about half the weight of African woodland-savanna individuals. Leopards from an isolated population in coastal Cape Mountains, South Africa, are also small, averaging 21kg (♀s) to 31kg (♂s). The largest Leopards are recorded from E and southern African woodland and N Iran.

## Distribution and Habitat

Widely distributed in southern, E and C Africa, significantly reduced in W Africa and most of Asia, and relict in N Africa, the Middle East and Russia. Very wide habitat tolerance, ranging from Russian boreal forests with winter lows of –30°C, to desert with summer highs of 70°C. Reaches the highest densities in mesic woodland, grassland savanna and forest, and fairly common in mountains, scrub and semi-desert. Absent from open interiors of true desert, but occupies watercourses and rocky massifs in very arid areas. Tolerates human-modified landscapes provided cover and prey are available, e.g. coffee plantations and sugar-cane fields. Recorded exceptionally to 5,638m (Mt Kilimanjaro, Tanzania).

## Feeding Ecology

Extremely catholic, with prey ranging from arthropods to adult male Elands (maximum weight 900kg), but prefers medium-sized ungulates weighing 15–80kg. Typical prey includes Steenbok, duikers, Impala, gazelles, Nyala, muntjacs, Chital, Siberian Roe Deer, Bushpig and Warthog, and young individuals of larger animals such as Gaur, wildebeest, oryx, hartebeest, Greater Kudu, Sambar and Wild Boar. Additionally, primates, hares, rodents, small carnivores and large birds are often important. Preys on livestock, occasionally entering corrals and settlements, and readily kills domestic dogs. Sometimes preys on humans. A consummate stalk-ambush hunter, approaching prey to as close as 4–5m before a final explosive rush. Hunting is mainly nocturno-crepuscular, and most daylight hunts are unsuccessful. Hunting success estimates include 15.6% (Kalahari), 20.1% (Phinda GR, South Africa) and 38.1% (NE Namibia). Kalahari Leopards average 111 (♂s) to 243 (♀s) kills annually, with females making more smaller kills. Leopards hoist carcasses weighing up to 91kg into trees to avoid kleptoparasitism, primarily from Spotted Hyaenas (page 54), and occasionally also cache in caves, burrows and kopjes. They typically pluck fur before feeding, usually starting at the underbelly or hind legs. They readily scavenge.

## Social and Spatial Behaviour

Solitary and territorial. Adults defend a core area against same-sex conspecifics, but tolerate considerable overlap at the edges, with mutual avoidance and alternating use of shared areas. Territorial fights are uncommon, but may result in fatalities in both females and males. Males associate with familiar females and cubs for as long as 24 hours, but never form permanent family groups. Recorded territory size 5.6km² (♀s; Tsavo NP, Kenya) to 2,750.1km² (♂s; Kalahari). Mean range size for mesic woodland, savanna and rainforest across the species' distribution averages 9–27km² (♀s) and 52–136km² (♂s). Ranges are much larger in arid habitats, averaging 188.4km² (♀s) and 451.2km² (♂s) in N Namibia, and 488.7km² (♀s) and 2,321.5km² (♂s) in Kalahari. A collared male in arid rocky habitat, C Iran, used 626km² in 10 months. Density estimates: 0.5/100km² (Etosha NP, Namibia), 1–1.4/100km² (Primorsky Krai, Russia), 1.3/100km² (Kalahari), 4.6–12/100km² (Gabon rainforest) and 11.1/100km² (Phinda and Mkhuze GRs, South Africa), to 12/100km² (Sabi Sands GR, South Africa). In African woodland savanna, average density under protection is almost 5 times as high as outside protected areas.

## Reproduction and Demography

Poorly known in its northern range (China, N Korea, Russia), where extreme winters might give rise to seasonality; otherwise aseasonal. Oestrus 7–14 days; gestation 90–106 days. Litter size normally 1–4, rarely to 6 (captivity). Weaning begins at around 8–10 weeks and suckling typically ceases before 4 months. Inter-litter interval averages 16–25 months. Cubs independent at 12–18 months; earliest age at which cubs survive independently is 7 months. Female dispersers often inherit part of their mother's range, while males disperse more widely. Both sexes are sexually mature at 24–28 months; females first give birth at 30–36 months, and can reproduce to 16 years (19 in captivity). Males first breed at around 42–48 months. MORTALITY 50% (Kruger NP) to 62% (Sabi Sands GR) of cubs die in their first year; where well-studied (savanna Africa), most deaths are by male Leopards, followed by Lions (page 46), less so Spotted Hyaenas. Estimates of adult mortality include 18.5% (Kruger NP) to 25.2% (Phinda GR, South Africa). Aside from deaths attributable to humans, adults are killed primarily in territorial fights and by other predators, chiefly Lions and occasionally Tigers (page 44), Spotted Hyaenas, African Wild Dog (page 110) and Dhole (page 108) packs, baboon troops (rarely) and large crocodiles. Hunting accidents and deaths from disease are uncommon. LIFESPAN 19 years for females, 14 for males in the wild; 23 in captivity.

## Status and Threats

Surprisingly tolerant of human activity and persists where other large carnivores cannot. Even so, extirpated from approximately 75% of global historic range (48–67% of African range and 83–87% of Eurasian range). Arabian (*P. p. nimr*), Amur (*P. p. orientalis*), Indochinese (*P. p. delacouri*) and North Chinese (*P. p. japonensis*) subspecies each inhabit <5% of historic range and should all be regarded as Critically Endangered. Loss of habitat and prey, closely followed by intense persecution in livestock areas, are the chief threats. Heavily hunted in S Asia for skins and parts supplying the Chinese medicinal trade, and killed for skins, canines and claws in W and C Africa. Bushmeat hunting, especially in tropical forest, competes directly with principal prey species and may drive extinctions even in intact forest. Legal sport hunting takes place in 9 African countries; Namibia (78–123 killed annually, 2012–15), Tanzania (163–205 killed) and Zimbabwe (136–163 killed) account for the highest offtake. Excessive quotas contribute to population declines, leading some countries to ban (Botswana) or suspend (South Africa, Zambia) hunting. CITES Appendix I; Red List VU (global), EN (Sri Lanka, C Asia), CR (Java, Middle East, Russia), population trend Decreasing.

■ Leopard

**Plate 18**

LEOPARD

African
savannah
form

Melanistic
form

African
forest
form

Arabian
subspecies

Amur
subspecies

# JAGUAR *Panthera onca*

HB ♀ 116–219cm, ♂ 110.5–270cm; T 44–80cm; SH 68–75cm; W ♀ 36–100kg, ♂ 36–158kg

The world's third largest cat. Background colour varies from pale yellow through ginger to rufous-golden brown, with white or cream underparts. Large block-like markings or rosettes usually enclose smaller black spots (usually lacking in the similar Leopard; page 48). Melanism occurs, with the same pattern of markings apparent in oblique light; black individuals are most common in humid lowland rainforest. Size varies very widely; the smallest Jaguars occur in Central America and are about half the size of the largest individuals from wet woodland savannah habitats of Brazil and Venezuela.

## Distribution and Habitat

N Mexico to N Argentina. Widely distributed in much of N and C South America, more fragmented in Mexico, Central America, E Brazil, Argentina and S Bolivia. Resident breeding populations no longer occur in the USA, but individuals intermittently appear in Arizona and New Mexico from N Mexico. Broad habitat tolerance; while capable of occupying dry open savannah or desert habitats, the species is more commonly associated with the dense cover of tropical and subtropical lowland forest, typically below 2,000m (exceptionally to 2,700m in the Andes, 3,000m in Mexico). Strongly associated with water, and thrives in well-watered habitats, including flooded savannah (Brazilian Pantanal and Colombian/Venezuelan Llanos), swamps, riverine thicket and scrub, and mangroves. Excellent swimmer, capable of crossing large rivers >2km wide.

## Feeding Ecology

Diverse diet, with at least 85 recorded prey species. Like all large cats, focuses on common large-bodied prey, but the natural absence of herds of large deer and wild cattle in South America results in the hunting of smaller animals more often than is the case for other big cats. Capybara and Collared and White-lipped Peccaries are frequently the most important prey species where they occur. Reptiles form a larger part of the diet than in any other large cat, especially caimans, as well as iguanas, freshwater turtles and tortoises, nesting marine turtles and large boas such as anacondas. Can subsist on abundant small prey such as armadillos, pacas, brocket deer and/or coatis. Other relatively common prey includes White-tailed Deer, agoutis, marsupials and sloths. Occasionally kills very large prey, including tapirs and Marsh Deer; Jaguars in the Brazilian Pantanal are recorded killing Amazon River Dolphins as they fish in shallow water. Readily kills domestic livestock; in ranching-dominated habitats such as the Pantanal and Llanos, introduced cattle form the major prey species. Less often, takes domestic pigs and dogs from villages. Almost never hunts humans; most recorded attacks result from extreme provocation, for example during Jaguar hunts, and verified unprovoked attacks are extremely rare. Jaguars have proportionally the strongest bite of all large cats, and kill either by biting with massive force at the back of the skull or with a typically feline suffocating throat bite. Hunting is mainly nocturno-crepuscular and terrestrial, although Jaguars readily hunt prey, e.g. Capybara and caimans, in water. Often scavenges, including from cattle carcasses; the deaths of these cattle are often erroneously blamed on the cat.

## Social and Spatial Behaviour

Solitary and territorial, but exclusive range use appears limited to small core areas; overlap between adults in some populations is extensive, possibly due to marked seasonal changes in the distribution of water and hence prey. Pantanal females establish largely exclusive ranges during the wet season, but overlap considerably in the dry season, while males overlap extensively in both. Similarly, Cockscomb Basin WS (Belize) males overlap extensively. Adults engage in typically territorial behaviours such as roaring, scrapes and urine-marking, perhaps serving to foster avoidance rather than demarcate exclusivity. Aggressive interaction between adults appears to be rare, although there are records of fatal fights. Range size estimates include 28–40km² (♂s) in Belize; 38km² (average, ♀s) to 63km² (average, ♂s) in S Pantanal, Brazil; 47–83km² (♀s) to 93–108km² (♂s) in Venezuela, and 31–98km² (♀s) to 73–268km² (♂s) in N Pantanal, Brazil. A male in arid lowland desert and pine–oak woodland in Arizona used at least 1,359km² in 2004–07. Home range sizes in inundated habitat, e.g. Pantanal, often contract in the wet season, when flooded areas limit space available to prey. Density estimates: 1.1/100km² (Iguaçu NP, Brazil), 2.5/100km² (Atlantic forest, Brazil), 3.5/100km² (Corcovado NP, Costa Rica) and 8.8/100km² (Cockscomb Basin WS), to 6–11/100km² (Pantanal).

## Reproduction and Demography

Aseasonal. Oestrus 6–17 days; gestation 91–111 days (average around 101–105 days). Litter size 1–4, averaging 2 (captivity). Weaning begins at around 10 weeks, and suckling typically ceases by 4–5 months. Cubs independent at 16–24 months. Dispersal poorly known, but appears to be typically feline, in which females settle close to their natal range while males disperse more widely. Both sexes are sexually mature at 24–30 months; females first give birth at 3–3.5 years and can reproduce to 15 years. It is not known when wild males first breed. MORTALITY Rates are poorly known. Adult Jaguars have no predators and are killed principally by humans and rarely by other Jaguars. Humans remove very significant numbers from some populations, e.g. an estimated 230 Jaguars killed in 1989–2014 by people living adjacent to Cerro Hoya and Darién NPs, Panama; and 539 Jaguars killed in 2001–15 in rural localities across Venezuela. Predators of cubs are poorly known; infanticide by male Jaguars is recorded, and there is a record of an adult female killing an unrelated cub. LIFESPAN Poorly known from the wild, but unlikely to exceed 15–16 years; 22 in captivity.

## Status and Threats

Extirpated from an estimated 49% of its historic range and extinct in El Salvador, Uruguay and the USA. Despite this, much of its remaining range is potentially still continuous, in part because the massive forested basins of South America have remained mostly inaccessible until recently. Habitat conversion for forestry, livestock and agriculture is the main threat, combined with intense persecution from ranchers and pastoralists in livestock areas, despite the fact that many cattle losses blamed on Jaguar predation occur from other factors. Widespread and intensive hunting of prey is likely to impact Jaguar populations in many areas, and emerging evidence indicates that the species is hunted to supply the Chinese medicinal trade, although impacts of both are poorly quantified. Sport hunting is illegal, but poorly enforced, in all range countries. CITES Appendix I; Red List NT, population trend Decreasing.

■ Jaguar

**Plate 19**

JAGUAR

Central
American
form

Melanistic
form

Brazilian
Pantanal
form

# AARDWOLF *Proteles cristata*

HB 55–80cm; T 19–30cm; SH 43–50cm; W 7.7–14kg

Smallest hyaena, superficially resembling Striped Hyaena but half its size and lightly built, with a narrow head and slender black muzzle. Jackal-sized in the field, but can appear much larger by erecting its dorsal mane when threatened. **Distribution and Habitat** Two disjunct populations in southern and E to NE Africa. Favours open habitat, including semi-desert, grassland and woodland savannah, and does not require standing water, which it obtains from its diet. Avoids true desert, dense woodland and forest. **Feeding Ecology** Feeds almost exclusively on Snouted Harvester Termites, lapping up as many as 300,000 (1.2kg) per night from dense feeding processions on the soil surface. Very occasionally and opportunistically consumes beetles, ants, sun spiders and scorpions. Cold winters and high rainfall force Snouted Harvester Termites below ground, driving Aardwolves to switch to less social termite species that require more energy to find and consume. Under winter food stress, adults can lose 25% of their weight and cubs are vulnerable to starvation. Foraging is generally nocturnal, but may shift diurnally in winter. Reflecting the diet, the species has a very long, paddle-shaped tongue, copious sticky saliva and small, almost nonfunctional, peg-like cheek-teeth (it has retained the large canines, which are used for territorial defence and against predators). Does not take livestock or carrion; there is 1 very unusual verified record of an Aardwolf killing 2 captive geese and partially eating one. **Social and Spatial Behaviour** Monogamous (although extra-pair matings are common) and territorial. Forms breeding pairs that endure for 2–5 years. Pairs cooperatively maintain stable territories, with very frequent scent-marking by both sexes, and share cub-raising duties, chiefly guarding the den against predators. Adults and independent cubs usually forage alone, but family members occasionally congregate at termite colonies. Territories 1–6km², depending on density of termite colonies. **Reproduction and Demography** Seasonal. Mating June–July. Cubs born October–December (Eastern Cape, South Africa). Oestrus 3 days; gestation 90 days. Litter size 2–4, exceptionally 5 in captivity. Cubs weaned at 12–16 weeks, by which time they begin to forage alone. Cubs are fully independent at 6–7 months, and most disperse before the following year's litter is born. MORTALITY Survival is tied to termite abundance; cub mortality is typically around 30%, but rose to 55% during a drought in one study. Adult mortality poorly known. Occasionally killed by all large carnivores, but the chief predator (of cubs) is Black-backed Jackal (page 112). LIFESPAN Unknown in the wild, 15 years in captivity. **Status and Threats** Generally widespread and secure. Snouted Harvester Termites thrive in disturbed grassland habitats, including livestock areas, which are suitable for Aardwolves under enlightened management. Agricultural poisoning (usually for locusts) results in termite die-offs that trigger Aardwolf declines. Despite never eating meat, Aardwolves are erroneously persecuted for livestock losses. Hundreds are killed annually as 'by-catch' in jackal-control efforts in southern Africa. CITES Appendix III – Botswana; Red List LC, population trend Stable.

# STRIPED HYAENA *Hyaena hyaena*

HB 98–119cm; T 26–47cm; SH 60–74cm;
W ♀ 23–34kg, ♂ 26–41kg

The only hyaena whose range extends into Eurasia. Ash- to straw-coloured, with black stripes on the body and legs, and a distinctive black throat patch. Tail typically lacks a black tip. Longest dorsal mane of any hyaena, which is erected defensively and becomes long and luxuriant in northern individuals in winter. **Distribution and Habitat** W, N and E Africa, the Middle East to the Caucasus, and C Asia to India. Favours open semi-arid habitats with cover, especially dry woodland savannah, dry forest, semi-desert and mountainous terrain to 3,300m. Absent from dense woodland, tropical forest and interiors of true desert. Inhabits modified habitats with cover, including agricultural and peri-urban landscapes, e.g. *Casuarina* plantations, coastal Odisha, India. **Feeding Ecology** Principally a scavenger of dead wild and domestic ungulates. Scavenges the remains of kills made by large carnivores, and is often found close to livestock herds looking for dead animals. Hunting ability poorly understood. Reputed to hunt large prey and widely blamed for killing livestock, but there is little evidence for this. Opportunistically catches small mammals and birds, and capable of opening the carapaces of large land turtles and tortoises. Also eats a wide variety of vegetables, fruits and invertebrates; seasonally, these items may surpass carrion in importance in the diet. During mass nesting events of Olive Ridley Turtles, hyaenas are recorded excavating the nests for eggs (Rushikulya sea turtle rookery, India). Raids fruit and vegetable crops in some areas, where it is treated as a pest, e.g. Israel. Typically forages alone, but may congregate loosely at food patches, including refuse dumps. Foraging is mostly nocturnal, especially where it lives close to humans. Provided it is not persecuted, it is sometimes more crepuscular in winter or during overcast and rainy weather. Often brings prey remains back to the den, which is used by many generations, sometimes creating massive bone accumulations. **Social and Spatial Behaviour** The least-studied hyaena and poorly known. Inhabits an enduring home range, which is scent-marked regularly, but there is little evidence for territorial defence. In C Asia, reportedly forms monogamous breeding pairs that may endure for more than a season; cubs of previous litters sometimes remain with a pair, suggesting helpers (as for canids). In C Kenya, forms 'proto-social' groups with 1 female and up to 3 adult males that may or may not be related. Group members occupy a shared range, and meet for social interaction and resting. Range size in C Kenya 36–101km² (♀s) and 52–115km² (♂s), with little overlap between females but high overlap among males. Density estimates 2–3/100km² (E Africa), 8.5/100km² (Negev Desert, Israel). **Reproduction and Demography** Aseasonal. Oestrus reportedly only 1 day; gestation 90–91 days. Litter size typically 1–4, exceptionally 5 (captivity). Cubs begin to eat meat at around 1 month, but are suckled for 6–12 months. Females are sexually mature at 1 year and may give birth at 15–18 months, but usually first breed at around 24–27 months. MORTALITY Poorly known; 47% of adults in C Kenya survived a further 3 years from when first identified. LIFESPAN Unknown in the wild, 23–24 years in captivity. **Status and Threats** Although widespread, occurs naturally at low densities and much of its remaining range is fragmented into isolated populations. Often intensely persecuted for its perceived effect on livestock and widespread superstitions related to grave robbing (which occurs), witchcraft and folk medicine. Frequently killed on roads when searching for roadkilled carrion. CITES Appendix III – Pakistan; Red List NT, population trend Decreasing.

■ Aardwolf

■ Striped Hyaena

**Plate 20**

Scent-marking

**AARDWOLF**

Central Asian
form, winter

Defensive posture

**STRIPED
HYAENA**

# BROWN HYAENA *Parahyaena brunnea*

HB 110–136cm; T 18–27cm; SH 71.5–82cm;
W ♀ 28–47.5kg, ♂ 35–49.5kg
Medium-sized hyaena covered in coarse, shaggy, dark brown fur that fades to blond on the neck and shoulders. Dark stripes on a light background cover the legs. Males are only slightly larger than females. **Distribution and Habitat** Endemic to southern Africa. Independent of water and inhabits various arid to semi-arid habitats, from open desert to woodland savannah. Can occupy pastoral habitats close to people, e.g. Johannesburg's outer suburbs. **Feeding Ecology** Scavenger that feeds mainly on the carcasses of dead mammals. Opportunistically takes small vertebrate prey up to the size of antelope lambs, but kills comprise only 6–16% of the diet. Coastal Namibian individuals live almost exclusively on Cape Fur Seals, which are mostly scavenged, although young pups are actively hunted. Also eats vegetables, fruits, invertebrates, eggs and human refuse. Predation on small livestock occasionally occurs. Foraging is solitary, although it congregates at large carcasses, seal colonies and refuse dumps. Mostly forages at night, but more diurnal in cool conditions when protected. Covers prodigious distances when foraging, e.g. 34–89km/24 hours in Namibia. Caches food and brings remains back to maternity dens to provision cubs. **Social and Spatial Behaviour** Forms small clans of 4–14 members centred around 1–5 related females that share a territory and raise cubs cooperatively. Unrelated adult males immigrate either permanently or as nomads that visit only for breeding. Clan members typically forage alone, but meet at carcasses and maternity dens. Territories overlap, but core areas are defended from intruders with ritualised aggression and extremely frequent 'pasting' with the anal gland. A single territory has up to 20,000 paste sites, which each adult marks up to 29,000 times annually. Individuals identify clan members from pastes. Average clan territory size estimates include 170km² (C Kalahari), 350km² (coastal Namibia, with seal colonies) to 1,900km² (inland Namibia, with unpredictable food sources). Typically occurs naturally at low densities, 1–2.9/100km² to 14–19/100km² (fenced reserve with abundant scavenging ; Kwandwe GR, South Africa). **Reproduction and Demography** Aseasonal. Oestrus 1 week; gestation 90 days. Litter size 1–5, typically 2–3. Cubs begin eating meat at 4 months and are suckled for 12–16 months. Females give birth alone, but often raise cubs in communal dens with other females. Females first breed at 35–36 months, and breed until at least 10 years. MORTALITY Moderate in protected populations: 89% of emerged Kalahari cubs reach independence and most adults die in old age. Starvation (in old age), and predation by Lion (page 46) and Spotted Hyaena are the main natural causes. LIFESPAN At least 12 years in the wild, 13 in captivity. **Status and Threats** Widespread but naturally rare, and dependent on large areas with sufficient carrion. Commercial livestock and game-farming areas, e.g. in Botswana, support densities comparable to protected areas, but the species is heavily persecuted (despite livestock depredation being infrequent) and threatened by habitat conversion to agriculture. Red List NT, population trend Stable.

# SPOTTED HYAENA *Crocuta crocuta*

HB 115–160cm; T 21–31.5cm; SH ♀ 73.5–88.5cm, ♂ 70–87cm;
W ♀ 56–86kg, ♂ 49–79kg
Largest hyaena, heavily built with very strong forequarters, and covered with dark spots that tend to fade with age. Young cubs are dark chocolate brown, developing adult coloration by 4–5 months. Females are slightly larger and heavier than males. **Distribution and Habitat** Endemic to Africa south of the Sahara, where it occurs in all woodland-savannah habitats. Largely absent from true forest, but lives in montane forest to 4,000m (Abedares, Kenya) and penetrates rainforest–savannah mosaics along roads in C Africa. Cannot survive in hyper-arid desert interiors, but occurs deep in deserts along watercourses and massifs. **Feeding Ecology** Highly efficient scavenger and formidable predator whose own kills comprise 60–95% of the diet. Individuals can overpower adult wildebeest, and small groups kill Gemsbok, zebras and African Buffalo. Scavenged and killed ungulates dominate the diet, but it eats virtually anything organic, including small mammals, birds, reptiles, fish, crabs, snails, insects, eggs, vegetables, fruits and human refuse. Readily kills livestock and domestic dogs, but very rarely humans. Appropriates kills from Leopards (page 48), Cheetahs (page 40) and African Wild Dogs (page 110), often shadowing them when hunting. Large groups displace Lions (page 46) from kills, provided they have numerical superiority and adult male Lions are absent. Foraging is alone or in groups: clan members often hunt cooperatively or congregate on large carcasses. Usually nocturnal, especially near humans, but forages diurnally where it is protected. Rarely caches food; sometimes carries remains to dens, but does not provision cubs. **Social and Spatial Behaviour** Forms clans of 10–80, averaging 29 across sub-Saharan Africa; the largest recorded clan averaged 113 (maximum 126), during a period in which Lions were heavily reduced by anthropogenic killing (Masai Mara NR, Kenya). Clans comprise inter-related females with their cubs, and unrelated immigrant adult males. Clan members occupy shared territory but are rarely all together; individuals move alone or in small subgroups that meet up frequently with ritualised greetings. Clans defend territories from intruders, but 'commuters' passing through as they track migratory herds in E Africa are tolerated. Clan ranges vary from 20km² where resident prey is abundant, e.g. Ngorongoro Crater, Tanzania, to >1,500km² in the Kalahari Desert. Density estimates: 0.6–0.8/100km² (Kalahari and Namib deserts), 7–20/100km² (Kruger NP, South Africa) and 60–80/100km² (Masai Mara–Serengeti ecosystem), to 170/100km² (Ngorongoro Crater). **Reproduction and Demography** Aseasonal. Oestrus 1–3 days; gestation 110 days. Litter size 1–3, usually 2. Cubs have a very prolonged suckling period of 13–24 months. Females usually give birth alone and suckle only their cubs, but bring them to communal dens to raise; up to 30 cubs of 20 litters were counted at a single den complex. Females are sexually mature at 24 months, but first breed at 3–6 years. MORTALITY Cub mortality in first year 40–73%, mainly from Lions, humans, starvation when mothers are killed, occasional infanticide and siblicide (rarely). Annual adult mortality averages 13–15% in protected areas, from Lions, humans and occasional disease outbreaks (rabies and canine distemper). Annual mortality of all age classes is <10% in Liuwa Plain NP, Zambia, with abundant prey, very few Lions and little conflict with people. LIFESPAN Around 12–16 years, exceptionally to 20 in the wild; 41 in captivity. **Status and Threats** Relatively resilient and reasonably secure in southern and E Africa, but it has undergone significant declines everywhere outside protected areas due to very pervasive persecution by humans. Spotted Hyaenas are killed as livestock predators, and for superstitious beliefs mainly related to traditional medicine. They are highly vulnerable to snares due to their habit of scavenging: snaring kills 400 adults a year in the Serengeti ecosystem. Red List LC, population trend Decreasing.

■ Brown Hyaena

■ Spotted Hyaena

**Plate 21**

Cubs at den

BROWN HYAENA

Greeting

SPOTTED
HYAENA

Cub

# SMALL INDIAN MONGOOSE
## Herpestes (Urva) auropunctatus

HB 19.2–44.6cm; T 19.2–29cm; W 305–662g
The 9 Asian *Herpestes* mongooses (plates 22 and 23) form a closely related group, possibly descended from a unique Asian common ancestor; they are sometimes classified together in the genus *Urva*. Small Indian Mongoose is the smallest. Fur is grizzled and its colour varies widely, including pale yellow-grey, buff and rufous-brown, with pale buff around the mouth, chin and throat. **Distribution and Habitat** Southern Asia, from E Iraq to Myanmar; replaced by Small Asian Mongoose in SE Asia. Widely introduced, including to Bosnia-Herzegovina, Croatia, Fiji, Hawaii, Jamaica, Japan, Mauritius and many Caribbean islands. Occurs in virtually all habitats with cover, including those close to humans. **Feeding Ecology** Highly opportunistic and omnivorous, eating small vertebrates to the size of rats, a wide variety of insects, arachnids, crabs and fruits. Kills poultry. Significant pest in its introduced range, where it has caused extinction of many endemic species, e.g. Hawaii. Foraging is diurnal and solitary. Scavenges from carrion, handouts and human refuse. **Social and Spatial Behaviour** Solitary. Males apparently form coalitions in some introduced populations, e.g. Hawaii, possibly due to super-abundant food allowing greater sociality. Males have larger ranges that overlap multiple female ranges. Range size 0.014–1km². Density estimates 34/km² (dry season) to 55/km² (wet season) in Puerto Rico; recorded sometimes up to 300/km² in introduced populations. **Reproduction and Demography** Breeding year-round, but birth peaks vary among populations. Gestation approximately 49 days. Litter size 1–5, averaging 2. Females have up to 3 litters a year. MORTALITY and LIFESPAN Unknown. **Status and Threats** Common and adaptable. In some areas of its native range it is heavily hunted for meat and fur, but it is resilient to exploitation. Super-abundant in much of its introduced range. CITES Appendix III – India; Red List LC, population trend Unknown.

# SMALL ASIAN MONGOOSE
## Herpestes (Urva) javanicus

JAVAN MONGOOSE
HB 30.2–41.5cm; T 21–31.5cm; W 0.45–1kg
Very small mongoose, uniformly grizzled rufous-brown to dark brown. Formerly classified with Small Indian Mongoose, but molecular data indicate they are 2 valid species with a putative dividing line around the Salween River, Myanmar. Many records of this species actually concern Small Indian Mongoose outside the former's Southeast Asian range. **Distribution and Habitat** Thailand, Indochina to Peninsular Malaysia, Sumatra and Java; possibly extreme E Myanmar. Inhabits lowland dry and wet forests, scrubland, brush and grassland below 1,800m. Occurs near humans, including in rice fields and cultivated areas. **Feeding Ecology** Poorly known; assumed to resemble Small Indian Mongoose, eating mainly small vertebrates and invertebrates. Bold

and aggressive predator capable of killing large rodents and snakes. Raids domestic poultry. Foraging is diurnal and solitary. **Social and Spatial Behaviour** Assumed to be solitary. **Reproduction and Demography** Thought to be aseasonal. Gestation approximately 7 weeks. Litter size 2–4. MORTALITY and LIFESPAN Unknown. **Status and Threats** Widespread, common and tolerant of anthropogenic habitats. Reaches high densities in suitable habitat; trapped as a pest in some areas. CITES Appendix III – India, Pakistan; Red List LC, population trend Unknown.

# SHORT-TAILED MONGOOSE
## Herpestes (Urva) brachyurus

HB 35–49cm; T 19.3–24.5cm; W 2–3kg
Medium-sized mongoose, dark olive-brown with tawny speckling, especially on the head, neck and tail, and solid tawny around the mouth and chin. Short tail is bluntly conical in profile. Hose's Mongoose (*H. hosei*), is an aberrant Short-tailed Mongoose specimen (confirmed by genetic analysis) and not a valid species. **Distribution and Habitat** Borneo, Sumatra and Peninsular Malaysia; records from Singapore and the Philippines are dubious. Occurs primarily in intact lowland rainforest, usually close to streams and watercourses. Tolerates regenerating forest, and plantations close to forest with ground cover. **Feeding Ecology** Believed to eat small vertebrates, invertebrates, eggs and some fruits; has been captured in traps baited with chicken pieces and salted fish. Foraging is solitary and strictly diurno-crepuscular. **Social and Spatial Behaviour** Based on the only radio-collaring study (5 animals, Krau WR, Malaysia), it is solitary and occupies mostly exclusive ranges. Male ranges overlap up to two female ranges, while female ranges overlap very little. Range size 1.15–1.5km² (♀s) and 2.24–2.5km² (♂s). **Reproduction and Demography** Unknown. **Status and Threats** Widespread and locally common in Borneo, uncommon and localised in Peninsular Malaysia; status poorly known in Sumatra. Appears relatively intolerant of habitat conversion, and much of its range is exposed to intense forest loss and hunting pressure. Eaten in some parts of Sarawak. Red List NT, population trend Decreasing.

# INDIAN GREY MONGOOSE
## Herpestes (Urva) edwardsii

COMMON GREY MONGOOSE
HB 35.5–46cm; T 32–45cm; W 0.9–2kg
Small to medium-sized mongoose with grizzled tawny-grey to pale grey fur. Lower legs are usually darker than the body, ranging from rufous-brown to black. Tail never has a dark tip, but may be rufous in some individuals. **Distribution and Habitat** Indian subcontinent, from Bangladesh to Pakistan, including Sri Lanka, and SE Iraq, S Iran, Kuwait, Bahrain and Persian Gulf coast of Saudi Arabia. Occurs in dry forest, scrub and grassland. Common in cultivated areas and near rural villages. **Feeding Ecology** Mainly carnivorous, eating small mammals, reptiles, birds, eggs and invertebrates. Aggressive predator of snakes, including large venomous species; resistant to haemorrhagic snake venom, and hence is the species commonly kept in India and Pakistan for staged mongoose–cobra fights. Apparently eats some fruits and vegetables. Foraging is solitary and diurno-crepuscular. Readily scavenges from carrion and human refuse. **Social and Spatial Behaviour** Poorly known. Solitary. The only range estimate is for an adult male tracked for 3 months, 0.16km² (Nilgiri Biosphere Reserve, India). **Reproduction and Demography** Breeding year-round; births peak May–June and October–December. Gestation approximately 56–68 days. Litter size 2–4. Females have up to 3 litters per year. MORTALITY and LIFESPAN Unknown. **Status and Threats** Widespread, common and able to live close to humans. Killed for meat and hair used in shaving and paint brushes. CITES Appendix III – India, Pakistan; Red List LC. Population trend Stable.

- ■ Small Indian Mongoose
- ■ Small Asian Mongoose

- ■ Short-tailed Mongoose
- ■ Indian Grey Mongoose

**Plate 22**

SMALL INDIAN
MONGOOSE

SMALL ASIAN
MONGOOSE

SHORT-TAILED
MONGOOSE

INDIAN GREY
MONGOOSE

# COLLARED MONGOOSE
*Herpestes (Urva) semitorquatus*

HB 40–46cm; T 25.8–30.3cm; W 2–4kg
Large, slender-legged mongoose, usually with dark reddish-brown fur, dark brown legs and a cream tail. Throat tawny yellow, becoming cream along the lower jaw. Body colour is occasionally light red to orange (including all recent records from Sumatra). Sometimes wrongly considered the same species as Short-tailed Mongoose (page 56). **Distribution and Habitat** Borneo, Sumatra (formerly disputed, confirmed by camera-trapping since 2011) and possibly the Philippines. Occurs in lowland rainforest, disturbed forest and plantations to 1,200m. **Feeding Ecology** Unknown. Camera-trap records indicate foraging is diurnal. **Social and Spatial Behaviour** Unknown. Camera-trap images suggest it is solitary. **Reproduction and Demography** Unknown. **Status and Threats** Poorly known. Rare in camera-trap surveys and known only from lowland areas that are under intense pressure from forestry and hunting; presence in better protected upland areas is uncertain. Red List NT, population trend Decreasing.

# BROWN MONGOOSE
*Herpestes (Urva) fuscus*

INDIAN BROWN MONGOOSE
HB 33–48cm; T 20–33.6cm; W 1.1–2.7kg
Large, stocky mongoose, uniformly grizzled dark brown with a slightly paler head and tawny chin and throat. Tail bushy with a tapering conical profile. **Distribution and Habitat** Endemic to Western Ghats, SW India, and W Sri Lanka; introduced to Viti Levu, Fiji. Inhabits mainly dense rainforest and adjacent habitats, including dense grassland, as well as anthropogenic habitats such as tea and coffee plantations. **Feeding Ecology** Unknown. Assumed to feed on a variety of invertebrates and small vertebrates. Recorded around refuse dumps near research camps, and eats groundnuts (but not bananas or boiled chicken) left as bait during rodent surveys. Scavenges from large mammal carcasses. Camera-trap surveys suggest foraging is nocturnal. **Social and Spatial Behaviour** Unknown. Camera-trap surveys record mostly lone individuals. **Reproduction and Demography** Unknown. **Status and Threats** Considered naturally rare, with a very restricted distribution that is under considerable pressure from forest conversion to agriculture and pasture, but is more adaptable to modified habitats than previously thought. CITES Appendix III – India; Red List LC, population trend Stable.

# CRAB-EATING MONGOOSE
*Herpestes (Urva) urva*

HB 44–55.8cm; T 26–35cm; W 3–4kg
Large, fairly stocky mongoose, grizzled pale grey to dark greyish brown, with dark legs and a pale tail ranging from tawny to white.

Mouth and chin white, extending as a distinctive neck stripe. **Distribution and Habitat** S China, Taiwan, Nepal, Bhutan, NE India, E Bangladesh and continental Southeast Asia to Peninsular Malaysia. Inhabits forest, forest–swamp mosaics, scrubland and wetland to 2,000m. Occurs in degraded forest, rice fields and cultivated areas, and near human settlements. **Feeding Ecology** Eats mainly water-associated prey, particularly aquatic insects, crustaceans, rodents, earthworms, reptiles and amphibians. Birds, fish, arachnids, snails and fruits are eaten in small amounts. Occasionally raids poultry and urban fish ponds. Forages diurnally, usually near water; capable swimmer and dives for prey, at least in controlled conditions such as garden ponds. Hair of a Formosan Rock Macaque found in a scat suggests that it scavenges. **Social and Spatial Behaviour** Poorly known. Mostly solitary but observed groups of 2–4 suggest possible sociality. **Reproduction and Demography** Poorly known. Gestation thought to be 50–63 days. Litter size 2–4. MORTALITY Unknown. LIFESPAN 13.3 years in captivity. **Status and Threats** Widespread and tolerant of some habitat conversion. Hunted in Cambodia, China and Laos for the meat and pet trades, but apparently persists in areas of high hunting pressure if this is not in combination with significant habitat conversion. CITES Appendix III – India; Red List LC, population trend Decreasing.

# RUDDY MONGOOSE
*Herpestes (Urva) smithii*

HB 39–47cm; T 35–41cm; W 1.75–2.7kg
Large mongoose with grizzled, rusty-tinged greyish-brown fur. Long tail ends in black-tasselled tip lacking in similar sympatric mongooses, e.g. Indian Grey Mongoose (page 56). **Distribution and Habitat** C and S India, and Sri Lanka. Inhabits dry forest, thorn scrub and dry grassland–forest mosaics to 2,200m; avoids evergreen forest. Occurs in disturbed forest, but avoids heavily modified habitats near humans. **Feeding Ecology** Known to eat rodents, birds and reptiles. Foraging is mainly diurno-crepuscular and solitary. Largely terrestrial, but apparently a capable climber that hunts arboreally and carries prey into trees (unusual behaviour for mongooses, if true). Readily scavenges, including from roadkill. **Social and Spatial Behaviour** Poorly known. Largely solitary, but groups of 2–5 adult-sized individuals are fairly common; group composition unknown. **Reproduction and Demography** Unknown. **Status and Threats** Widespread but poorly known; common in some areas, e.g. C India. Habitat loss and localised hunting are main threats. CITES Appendix III – India; Red List LC, population trend Unknown.

# STRIPE-NECKED MONGOOSE
*Herpestes (Urva) vitticollis*

HB 43–53cm; T 23–33.5cm; W ♀ 1.7–2.7kg, ♂ 2.6–3.4kg
Distinctive large mongoose with an obvious black neck stripe, rufous-brown hindquarters and grizzled grey-brown forequarters; some individuals are entirely rufous except for the head. Tail has a conspicuous black-tasselled tip. **Distribution and Habitat** Sri Lanka, SW India and Similipal Hills near Kolkata. Inhabits evergreen and moist deciduous forests and dense grassland clearings. Also lives in teak plantations and rice fields. **Feeding Ecology** Eats small mammals, birds, reptiles, eggs and presumably a wide variety of invertebrates. Preys on mammals to the size of Black-naped Hare and pursues young ungulate fawns. Foraging is diurnal and solitary. Scavenges from carrion and refuse dumps. **Social and Spatial Behaviour** Poorly known; sightings are of singletons or pairs. **Reproduction and Demography** Unknown. Thought to have 2–3 young. MORTALITY Unknown. LIFESPAN Almost 13 years in captivity. **Status and Threats** Restricted distribution and uncommon. Habitat loss and hunting are the main threats, but poorly understood. CITES Appendix III – India; Red List LC, population trend Stable.

■ Collared Mongoose  ■ Crab-eating
Mongoose  ■ Brown Mongoose
■ Ruddy Mongoose
■ Stripe-necked Mongoose

Plate 23

COLLARED
MONGOOSE

CRAB-EATING
MONGOOSE

BROWN
MONGOOSE

RUDDY
MONGOOSE

STRIPE-NECKED
MONGOOSE

# CAPE GREY MONGOOSE
## *Herpestes pulverulentus*

### SMALL GREY MONGOOSE
HB 29–41.5cm; T 20.5–34cm; W 0.49–1.25kg
Small, pale to dark grizzled grey with paler underparts and dark grey lower limbs. **Distribution and Habitat** South Africa, Lesotho and SE Namibia. Occurs in most habitats with cover, to 1,900m; absent from very open and arid areas. Occurs on farmland and in urban parkland. **Feeding Ecology** Eats small vertebrates and invertebrates, especially small rodents and insects. Occasionally kills neonate grysboks and juvenile Cape Porcupine. Foraging is diurno-crepuscular, terrestrial and solitary. Scavenges from carrion (including roadkills) and dumps. **Social and Spatial Behaviour** Solitary. Adult males occasionally associate loosely in pairs. Largely non-territorial; breeding females defend exclusive small areas. Range size 0.3km² (1 ♀) and 0.55–0.92km² (♂s). **Reproduction and Demography** Seasonal. Births peak August–December. Gestation approximately 60 days. Litter size 1–3. MORTALITY Prey of various larger predators, especially raptors. LIFESPAN 8.8 years in captivity. **Status and Threats** Common habitat generalist that adapts well to human presence. No significant threats. Red List LC, population trend Stable.

# SOMALI SLENDER MONGOOSE
## *Herpestes ochraceus*

### SOMALIAN SLENDER MONGOOSE
HB 25–29cm; T 22–27.3cm; W *c.*0.3–0.75kg
Uniformly pale grizzled grey to dark grey-brown. Tail lacks a black tip, distinguishing it from Common Slender Mongoose, with which it was formerly classified. **Distribution and Habitat** Somalia, E Ethiopia and NE Kenya. Inhabits semi-arid open woodland and hilly areas to 600m. **Feeding Ecology** Unknown. Assumed to resemble other slender mongooses. **Social and Spatial Behaviour** Unknown. Assumed to be largely solitary. **Reproduction and Demography** Unknown. **Status and Threats** Probably common, with few threats, but very poorly known. Red List LC, population trend Unknown.

# KAOKOVELD SLENDER MONGOOSE
## *Herpestes flavescens*

### BLACK SLENDER MONGOOSE, ANGOLAN SLENDER MONGOOSE
Includes **BLACK MONGOOSE** *H. nigrata*
HB 31–35.5cm; T 31–37cm; W 0.55–0.9kg
Small mongoose with 2 colour morphs: uniformly very dark reddish brown to black; and pale tawny red with a black tail tip. Some authorities treat the black form as a separate species, Black Mongoose (*H. nigrata*). **Distribution and Habitat** Endemic to SW Angola and NW Namibia. Occurs in arid habitats with cover;

avoids true desert. Black form inhabits isolated granite kopjes and associated woodland. **Feeding Ecology** Small rodents, especially Dassie Rat, and insects are the main prey. Also includes birds, reptiles, arachnids, eggs and fleshy seeds. Foraging is diurnal and terrestrial (although thought to raid White-tailed Shrike nests), and solitary; adults congregate at carcasses but feed separately. Scavenges carrion (mainly for carrion-eating flies), refuse and handouts at tourist lodges. **Social and Spatial Behaviour** Solitary; males occasionally form loose pairs. Ranges overlap extensively, and adults use the same dens but not concurrently. Range estimates known only for males, 0.13–1.45km² (Erongo Mountains, Namibia). **Reproduction and Demography** Unknown. **Status and Threats** Considered relatively common, with no serious threats. Red List LC, population trend Unknown.

# COMMON SLENDER MONGOOSE
## *Herpestes sanguineus*

### SLENDER MONGOOSE, BLACK-TIPPED MONGOOSE
HB 27.5–35cm; T 19.4–33cm; W 0.37–0.79kg
Very variable colour, but typically grizzled tawny or reddish brown with a black tail tip. Melanistic individuals occur. **Distribution and Habitat** Ubiquitous in sub-Saharan Africa except the W Congo Basin, coastal Namibia, and Eastern Cape and Western Cape, South Africa. Occurs in most habitats (including anthropogenic ones) except true desert and rainforest. **Feeding Ecology** Insects, reptiles and small rodents are the main prey, as well as birds, amphibians, eggs, arachnids and wild fruits. Foraging is diurnal, terrestrial and typically solitary; males sometimes travel (and presumably forage) in temporary pairs. Scavenges from carrion (mainly for sarcophagous flies), dumps and handouts. **Social and Spatial Behaviour** Solitary, but males may form groups of 2–4 that jointly defend territory from other males. Range estimates 0.25–1km². Density estimates 3–6/km² (Serengeti NP, Tanzania). **Reproduction and Demography** Seasonal. Birth peaks coincide weakly with rainy periods: October–March (southern Africa), October–November and February–April (E Africa). Gestation 60–70 days. Litter size 1–4. MORTALITY Main predators are large raptors. LIFESPAN 8 years in the wild, 12.6 in captivity. **Status and Threats** Very widespread and common. No serious threats. Red List LC, population trend Stable.

# EGYPTIAN MONGOOSE
## *Herpestes ichneumon*

### ICHNEUMON, LARGE GREY MONGOOSE
HB 50–61cm; T 43.5–58cm; W ♀ 2.2–4kg, ♂ 2.6–4.1kg
Large mongoose, uniformly grizzled grey with a dark face, dark lower limbs and black-tipped tail. **Distribution and Habitat** Most of Africa except the Sahara, Congo Basin, arid southern Africa and NE Africa. Also Portugal and Spain (possibly introduced), and the Middle East. Inhabits woodland, grassland, wetland, semi-desert and montane areas, plus cultivated land and farmland. **Feeding Ecology** Eats vertebrates to the size of hares, invertebrates, fruits and fungi. Resistant to snake venom. Occasionally takes poultry. Foraging is nocturno-crepuscular, terrestrial and solitary. Scavenges from carrion. **Social and Spatial Behaviour** Generally solitary; forms groups of 1 male with 1–3 females and their offspring in Israel. Average range estimates (both sexes) 0.38km² (South Africa) to 3.1km² (Spain). Density estimates 0.1–2/km². **Reproduction and Demography** Seasonal. Births peak October–December (southern Africa), September–February (E Africa) and May–July (Spain). Gestation about 63–70 days. Litter size 1–4. Females (Israel) communally raise kittens. MORTALITY Predation mainly from large raptors and Iberian Lynx (page 34; Spain). LIFESPAN 13 years in captivity. **Status and Threats** Widespread and common. Locally vulnerable to persecution and poisoning of rodent prey. Red List LC, population trend Stable.

■ Cape Grey Mongoose
■ Somali Slender Mongoose
■ Egyptian Mongoose
■ Kaokoveld Slender Mongoose
■ Common Slender Mongoose

Plate 24

CAPE GREY
MONGOOSE

SOMALI SLENDER
MONGOOSE

KAOKOVELD
SLENDER
MONGOOSE

COMMON SLENDER
MONGOOSE

EGYPTIAN
MONGOOSE

# LONG-NOSED MONGOOSE

## Herpestes naso

### LONG-SNOUTED MONGOOSE

HB 44–61cm; T 32–43cm; W 1.9–4.5kg

Large, dark mongoose with a long muzzle and prominent black nose. Fur grizzled dark brown with pale underfur, but the impression in the field is very dark brown or near black. Sometimes classified in the unique genus *Xenogale* due mainly to distinctive dentition and genetic characteristics; recent molecular evidence confirms the Marsh Mongoose as its closest relative. **Distribution and Habitat** Endemic to C Africa, from SE Nigeria to SE DR Congo, west of the Rift Valley. Inhabits rainforest, usually near streams, watercourses and swampy areas with dense, tangled understorey. Avoids open forest, but sometimes forages on burnt grassland close to forest edges. **Feeding Ecology** Omnivorous, eating mainly arthropods (particularly beetles, crickets, termites, ants and millipedes), rodents and shrews. Also eats snails, frogs, reptiles, birds, fish, fruits and small bats. Rarely takes prey larger than 4–5kg; Blue Duiker, primates, pangolins and African Brush-tailed Porcupine identified in scats, but are probably scavenged. Foraging is diurnal, terrestrial and solitary. **Social and Spatial Behaviour** Solitary. Both sexes establish stable ranges that differ little in size (based on 1 study with 5 radio-collared animals). Range size, including both independent subadults and adults, 0.1–1km². **Reproduction and Demography** Very poorly known. Young animals observed March–May (W Africa), and a litter of 3 is recorded. MORTALITY Poorly known; recorded in Leopard (page 48) and Black-legged Mongoose (page 64) scats (possibly scavenged in the latter). LIFESPAN 11 years in captivity. **Status and Threats** Regarded as rare, but poorly known. Common in some areas, e.g. Dzanga-Sangha forest, SW Central African Republic. Forest loss and bushmeat hunting produce local declines, e.g. Niger Delta, Nigeria. Red List LC, population trend Decreasing.

# MARSH MONGOOSE *Atilax paludinosus*

### WATER MONGOOSE

HB 44.2–62cm; T 25–41cm; W 2.4–4.1kg

Large, dark mongoose with a distinctive blunt triangular profile to the face. Shaggy fur uniformly dark reddish brown to black, except for pale tawny patch around the mouth and chin. Toes long, slender and completely unwebbed, which is unique among mongooses; all other species possess a degree of webbing. **Distribution and Habitat** Sub-Saharan Africa; absent from arid NE Africa, and most of Namibia, Botswana and C South Africa. Inhabits dense wet habitat from sea-level to 3,950m, including streams, swamps, marshes, wet forest, mangroves, estuaries and coastal areas. Inhabits anthropogenic watercourses such as dams and canals, provided there is cover and prey. **Feeding Ecology** Unique among mongooses in taking mainly aquatic prey, especially crabs, aquatic insects, molluscs and amphibians, as well as rodents. Takes small amounts of fish, birds, eggs and fruits. Occasionally kills larger terrestrial mammals, including other carnivores, e.g. Cape Grey Mongoose (page 60) and Yellow Mongoose (page 66). Sometimes kills poultry. Foraging is nocturno-crepuscular and solitary. Excellent swimmer, able to dive for prey for up to 15 seconds, but forages mainly in the shallows and on banks. Prey is located by sight or by feeling in mud and crevices with its long, extremely dextrous digits. Scavenges from carrion. **Social and Spatial Behaviour** Solitary. Occupies stable ranges that tend to be arranged along watercourses. Range size differs little between sexes, and ranges are scent-marked extremely regularly with obvious latrines. Range size 0.54–2.04km². The only density estimate is 1.8/km² (KwaZulu-Natal, South Africa). **Reproduction and Demography** Aseasonal in much of its range; weakly seasonal in southern Africa, where breeding occurs in wetter periods, August–February. Gestation 69–80 days. Litter size 1–3. MORTALITY Poorly known; predation rarely recorded except by domestic dogs. LIFESPAN 19 years in captivity. **Status and Threats** Widespread and relatively common in much of its range. Vulnerable to destruction of watercourses by clearing, siltation and pollution, which causes local declines, and popular as bushmeat in W and C Africa. Red List LC, population trend Decreasing.

# WHITE-TAILED MONGOOSE

## Ichneumia albicauda

HB 47–71cm; T 34.5–47cm; W 1.8–5.2kg

Largest mongoose. Tall, long-legged and slender, usually pale grey to grizzled grey with blackish lower legs and a bushy silvery-white tail. A dark morph occurs, with a black tail and denser covering of black guard hairs over the body. **Distribution and Habitat** Widespread in sub-Saharan Africa except NE Africa, the Congo Basin and arid SW Africa; occurs on the S Arabian Peninsula. Inhabits moist and dry woodlands, savannah, scrub and grassland; avoids open desert and dense forest. Tolerates anthropogenic habitats including farmland, plantations and orchards. **Feeding Ecology** Chiefly insectivorous, eating medium to large nocturnal arthropods, especially termites, ants, dung beetles, crickets, grasshoppers and their larvae. Additionally eats small mammals to the size of cane rats, amphibians, birds, and small amounts of fruits and vegetable matter. Occasionally raids poultry. Foraging is nocturnal, terrestrial and mainly solitary, although pairs sometimes forage together, and up to 9 congregate at food patches such as termite flushes. Scavenges from carrion and human refuse. **Social and Spatial Behaviour** Predominantly solitary. Occasionally forms loosely associated male–female pairs, and related females (usually mothers and daughters) sometimes share a range, forming small female clans with their offspring. Adults occupy enduring ranges that may overlap within and between sexes; aggressive behaviour between neighbours appears to be rare. Female ranges are slightly smaller than those of males; range size 0.4–4.3km², exceptionally to 8km². Density in very high-quality habitat (Serengeti NP, Tanzania) reaches 4.3/km². **Reproduction and Demography** Seasonal. Births appear to coincide with wet periods, October–February (southern Africa), and March–April and October–December (E Africa). Litter size 1–4. MORTALITY Occasionally killed by larger predators, but produces a nauseating anal secretion combined with an impressive threat display that probably deters predation. LIFESPAN 14 years in captivity. **Status and Threats** Widely distributed, common and present in many protected areas. Killed on roads, during predator-control operations and by dogs in rural areas, but not threatened. Red List LC, population trend Stable.

■ Long-nosed Mongoose

■ Marsh Mongoose

■ White-tailed Mongoose

**Plate 25**

LONG-NOSED
MONGOOSE

MARSH MONGOOSE

Dark form
defensive posture

WHITE-TAILED
MONGOOSE

# BUSHY-TAILED MONGOOSE
## *Bdeogale crassicauda*

Includes SOKOKE BUSHY-TAILED MONGOOSE *B. omnivora*
HB 40–50cm; T 18–30cm; W 1.3–2.1kg
Stocky, dark mongoose with a prominent bushy tail. Colour typically dark blackish-brown with chestnut or tawny-brown underfur on the head, throat and body; tail and legs always blackish. Sokoke Bushy-tailed Mongoose, from the coastal forests of N Tanzania and E Kenya, is sometimes treated as a distinct species, *B. omnivora*; it has a paler body colour, with more obvious light tawny underfur. **Distribution and Habitat** Eastern Africa, from S Kenya to N Zimbabwe and west to S DR Congo. Occurs mostly in dense woodland savanna, dry and wet forests, wooded grassland, and hilly areas with rocky or shrubby cover. **Feeding Ecology** Eats largely insects, small reptiles, frogs and toads, land snails, and scorpions and other arachnids. Small rodents are recorded, but it appears to be relatively clumsy in handling vertebrates such as rats and large snakes. Captive animals refuse fruits. Foraging is nocturnal, terrestrial and solitary. **Social and Spatial Behaviour** Poorly known. Solitary. No range or density estimates; it is the most frequently photographed small carnivore during camera-trapping surveys in Tanzania's Eastern Arc Mountains. **Reproduction and Demography** Poorly known. Litters recorded November and December in Kenya (based on very few records). Females have 2 pairs of teats, suggesting litter size of 2–4. MORTALITY Unknown. Confirmed predators include Crowned Eagle, Gaboon Viper and Spotted Hyaena (page 54). LIFESPAN Unknown. **Status and Threats** Rarely seen and has a patchy distribution, but widely distributed and appears common in certain areas. No significant threats at species level, but illegal logging, combined with hunting, represents a threat to forest populations, e.g. Arabuko-Sokoke, Kenya, and Zanzibar, Tanzania. Red List LC, population trend Unknown (Sokoke Bushy-tailed: VU, population trend Decreasing).

# JACKSON'S MONGOOSE
## *Bdeogale jacksoni*

HB 50.8–57.1cm; T 28.3–32.4cm; W 2–3kg
Large, grizzled silver-grey mongoose with a bushy white tail and black or dark brown lower legs. Yellowish tinting on the cheeks, throat and sides of the neck. Considered by some authorities to be the same species as Black-legged Mongoose; that species is larger, with a very robust skull, and the 2 species do not overlap in range. **Distribution and Habitat** Endemic to SE Uganda, and C and S Kenya, with an isolated population in the Udzungwa Mountains, Tanzania (900km to the south). Possibly occurs elsewhere in Tanzania's Eastern Arc Mountains. Recorded only in dense lowland forest, bamboo forest and montane forest to 3,300m. **Feeding Ecology** Eats chiefly small forest rodents, e.g. vlei and marsh rats, soft-furred and brush-furred mice, and forest-floor insects, especially army ants, termites and beetles. Millipedes, snails, lizards and eggs are also recorded. Foraging is

nocturnal, terrestrial and solitary. Scavenges from carrion. **Social and Spatial Behaviour** Poorly known. Likely to be solitary; reports of pairs and groups numbering up to 4 are probably breeding pairs and mothers with grown litters. **Reproduction and Demography** Unknown. **Status and Threats** Dependent on forested habitat and limited to a series of isolated populations in a very restricted distribution. Ongoing forest clearing and degradation are the main threats. Probably also killed for bushmeat, although carnivores (apart from otters) appear not to be highly sought after in its range. Red List NT, population trend Decreasing.

# BLACK-LEGGED MONGOOSE
## *Bdeogale nigripes*

BLACK-FOOTED MONGOOSE
HB 46–65cm; T 29–40cm; W 2–4.8kg
Large, short-haired mongoose with silver-grey or yellowish-grey fur and black legs. Tail moderately bushy and varies from bright white to cream. Erythristic individuals occur, in which the silver-grey coloration is replaced by brownish red. Skull very robust, with short, rounded ears and a large nose, giving the head a blunt dog-like appearance. **Distribution and Habitat** C Africa, from the Rift Valley and E DR Congo to SE Nigeria and S Republic of the Congo. Reports from N Angola are now rejected. Found only in rainforest to 1,000m, mainly in dense ground cover associated with undisturbed forest. Rarely found in disturbed forest. **Feeding Ecology** Eats mainly terrestrial arthropods (chiefly ants, termites, beetles and grasshoppers) and small mammals, especially forest shrews and rodents; African Brush-tailed Porcupine and Long-nosed Mongoose (page 62) are also recorded as prey (possibly scavenged). Additionally eats snakes, lizards, frogs, toads and small amounts of fruits. Local people also report that it takes wild and cultivated fruits, including bananas and oil palm fruits. Foraging is nocturnal and solitary. Hunts mostly on the ground, but there is one observation of an individual hunting a young Potto with great agility in a tree 15m above the ground. **Social and Spatial Behaviour** Solitary. There are reports of pairs, probably breeding adults or mothers with large juveniles. **Reproduction and Demography** Poorly known. Records of litters cluster in November–January, suggesting that breeding occurs at the start of the dry season, but this is based on very few observations. Local people report litters numbering 1–2. MORTALITY Poorly known; most documented mortality is anthropogenic. LIFESPAN 15.5 years in captivity. **Status and Threats** Considered rare, although this is due in part to it inhabiting dense equatorial forest where it is poorly known. Widespread, with large parts of its range in relatively pristine condition, but thought to have undergone general decline due to forest loss and fragmentation. Also hunted as bushmeat, and one of the most frequently killed carnivores by people hunting with dogs, e.g. caught in 52% of hunts and represents about 25% of all carnivores caught by Bambuti hunter-gatherers in Ituri Forest, DR Congo. Red List LC, population trend Decreasing.

■ Bushy-tailed Mongoose   ■ Jackson's Mongoose

■ Black-legged Mongoose

**Plate 26**

BUSHY-TAILED
MONGOOSE

JACKSON'S MONGOOSE

BLACK-LEGGED MONGOOSE

# MEERKAT *Suricata suricatta*

### SURICATE, SLENDER-TAILED MEERKAT

HB 24.5–29cm; T 17.5–24cm; W 0.62–0.97kg

Small mongoose with coarse yellow-brown to pale greyish-tan fur and dark eye patches. Back marked with short, dark brown streaks, producing brindled (not striped) appearance. **Distribution and Habitat** Endemic to arid SW Africa: Botswana, South Africa, Namibia and extreme SW Angola. Inhabits semi-arid desert, dry open savannah, dry scrubland and grassland. **Feeding Ecology** Eats chiefly arthropods on the soil surface and subsurface, especially beetles, millipedes, centipedes, termites, scorpions, spiders, and various insect eggs, pupae and larvae. Resistant to scorpion venom and the noxious secretions of millipedes. Also eats small rodents, herptiles, birds (mainly fledglings) and eggs. Not a poultry pest. Foraging is strictly diurnal, in large social groups. Prey is captured individually; not shared except with pups. **Social and Spatial Behaviour** Intensely social. Lives in family groups of 3–20 individuals (exceptionally to 49) comprising a dominant breeding pair, offspring from successive litters and some unrelated immigrant adults. Group members cooperate to rear young, avoid predation and defend communal range. Clashes over territory are sometimes fatal. Group ranges 2–10km². Density estimates 0.32–1.69/km², fluctuating significantly depending mainly on rainfall (and therefore insect availability) and predation. **Reproduction and Demography** Seasonal. Breeding in wet summer, September–March. Dominant pair does most of the breeding. Subordinate females produce about 25% of litters; most of the pups from these are killed by the dominant female or abandoned. Gestation about 70 days. Litter size 3–7. Females have up to 3 litters a year. All adults help raise pups; babysitters remain at the den when the group forages, and all adults provision pups. Unlike in Banded Mongoose (page 70), pups do not have an escort and beg from any adult. MORTALITY 80% (pups) and 32% (adults), mainly from predation and infanticide (on pups). LIFESPAN 8 years in the wild, 12 in captivity. **Status and Threats** Widespread, common and secure. No major threats at population level. Introduced bovine tuberculosis killed 6% of S Kalahari meerkats (Kuruman River Reserve, South Africa) in 2002–15, but this did not impact the population. Red List LC, population trend Stable.

# SELOUS'S MONGOOSE

## *Paracynictis selousi*

HB 39–47cm; T 28–43.5cm; W 1.4–2.2kg

Slender, medium-sized mongoose with a grizzled, pale tawny-grey coat, darkening along the tail to the tip, which is greyish white. Lower legs blackish brown. **Distribution and Habitat** Endemic to SC Africa from S Angola to Malawi to N and E Botswana, NE South Africa and S Mozambique. Inhabits mainly dry and wet woodland savannah, scrub, grassland and cultivated areas with cover. **Feeding Ecology** Based on limited records, eats invertebrates (especially locusts, grasshoppers, termites and beetles), small rodents, herptiles and birds. Foraging is nocturnal and solitary. **Social and Spatial Behaviour** Poorly known. Most

records are solitary; pairs are reported but composition is unknown. **Reproduction and Demography** Apparently seasonal, with births occurring mainly in the wet season, August–March. Litter size 2–4. MORTALITY Unknown; 1 record of predation by a Martial Eagle. LIFESPAN Unknown. **Status and Threats** Widespread, occurring in large areas of intact habitat. Considered uncommon compared with sympatric mongoose species based on mostly ad hoc survey efforts. Red List LC, population trend Unknown.

# YELLOW MONGOOSE

## *Cynictis penicillata*

HB 27–46cm; T 25–29cm; W 0.44–0.9kg

Small mongoose with ginger-tawny to greyish-yellow fur. Southern individuals are larger, and generally more reddish with a white-tipped tail, compared with smaller greyish animals in the north, which usually lack white tail tip; however, red and grey forms occur in the same population e.g. Etosha NP, Namibia. **Distribution and Habitat** Endemic to southern Africa, from extreme S Angola through Namibia, Botswana and South Africa. Inhabits open semi-arid habitat, including semi-desert, grassland, fynbos heath, scrubland and open bushland. Occurs in rangeland. **Feeding Ecology** Mainly insectivorous, preferring termites, beetles, grasshoppers and locusts, but eats a wide variety of invertebrates and small vertebrates to the size of large rats, as well as small amounts of fruits. Occasionally raids domestic poultry and eggs. Foraging is mainly diurnal and usually solitary or in pairs. Scavenges from carrion and human refuse. **Social and Spatial Behaviour** Mostly travels and forages alone or in pairs, but lives in small family groups averaging 3–4 adults (exceptionally to 13) that reproduce cooperatively. Groups share a defined communal range, or individual group members occupy different areas of a large, loosely shared range with little overlap except at dens. Average individual range size 0.1–0.49km² (♀s) to 1.02km² (♂s). **Reproduction and Demography** Seasonal. Breeding in wet summer season, August–February, with 2 litters produced in quick succession. All group females breed. Gestation 60–62 days. Litter size 1–5, averaging 2. Females den communally, and all adults provision and guard pups. MORTALITY Large raptors are the main predators. Rabies in South Africa is often fatal, although its effects on populations are unknown. LIFESPAN 15 years in captivity. **Status and Threats** Widespread and common. Wholesale eradication campaigns to control rabies induce local declines; these programmes are now selectively applied to certain hotspot areas near humans. Red List LC, population trend Stable.

# MELLER'S MONGOOSE

## *Rhynchogale melleri*

HB 44–48.5cm; T 28–41.2cm; W 1.7–3kg

Large mongoose with a distinctive blunt, slightly bulbous muzzle, and grizzled, pale to dark brownish-grey fur. Tail colour can be black, brownish grey or pale greyish white within the same population. **Distribution and Habitat** C Tanzania, S DR Congo, Malawi, Mozambique, Zambia and NE South Africa. Inhabits mainly open woodland, savannah and grassland, but possibly has broader habitat tolerances; recently found in bamboo forest at 1,850m (Udzungwa Mountains, Tanzania). **Feeding Ecology** Poorly known, but mainly insectivorous, apparently eating chiefly termites; almost always found in association with termite mounds. Also eats small vertebrates. Foraging is thought to be nocturnal, terrestrial and solitary. **Social and Spatial Behaviour** Unknown. Believed to be solitary. **Reproduction and Demography** Believed to be seasonal based on a few records; births occur in the wet summer season, November–January. Litter sizes of up to 3 are reported. MORTALITY and LIFESPAN Unknown. **Status and Threats** Status poorly known; never properly surveyed. Widespread, occurring in many large protected areas. Red List LC, population trend Unknown.

■ Meerkat
■ Selous's Mongoose

■ Yellow Mongoose
■ Meller's Mongoose

**Plate 27**

Mobbing behaviour

MEERKAT

SELOUS'S
MONGOOSE

YELLOW
MONGOOSE

MELLER'S MONGOOSE

# POUSARGUES'S MONGOOSE
*Dologale dybowskii*

### SAVANNAH MONGOOSE
HB 25–33cm; T 16–23cm; W 0.3–0.4kg
Very small mongoose with grizzled, dark brown fur, paler underparts and dark lower limbs. Head and neck dark brownish grey, grizzled with greyish hairs and a lighter rufous-tinged throat 'ruff'. Similar to dwarf mongooses and sometimes classified with them in the genus *Helogale*; separated mainly on the basis of anatomical differences, especially in the skull and dentition. Lacks the upper lip groove of both the Somali Dwarf and Common Dwarf mongooses. **Distribution and Habitat** NW Uganda, NE DR Congo, S Central African Republic, southern South Sudan. Known from dry savannah, savannah–forest mosaics and montane-forest grassland. **Feeding Ecology** Has small, reduced dentition and long, robust front claws, suggesting its feeding ecology is similar to that of dwarf mongooses, with a specialisation mainly on surface invertebrates. One specimen had termites, millipedes and small seeds in its stomach; a foraging group (Semliki WR, Uganda) dug in loose soil, turned over stones and took surface insects. **Social and Spatial Behaviour.** Museum records and sightings indicate it is solitary, although it shares many evolutionary similarities with social species such as Banded Mongoose (page 70); a loosely associated group of 8 was observed in Semliki WR (2013). **Reproduction and Demography** Unknown. Litter of 4 reported from DR Congo. MORTALITY and LIFESPAN Unknown. **Status and Threats** Unknown. Until 2013, Pousargues's Mongoose was known from only 31 museum specimens and unconfirmed sightings. There are recent unequivocal photos from Chinko, Central African Republic; Semliki WR; and Garamba NP, DR Congo. Red List DD, population trend Unknown.

# SOMALI DWARF MONGOOSE
*Helogale hirtula*

### DESERT DWARF MONGOOSE, ETHIOPIAN DWARF MONGOOSE
HB 20–27cm; T 15–18cm; W 0.22–0.35kg
Very small mongoose with longer, paler fur than Common Dwarf Mongoose. Colour warm tawny or grizzled, pale grey-brown, with contrasting dark brown digits. In the field, appears shaggier and less reddish than Common Dwarf Mongoose. **Distribution and Habitat** Somalia, SE Ethiopia and E Kenya; possibly Djibouti and extreme NE Tanzania (Mkomazi NP). Inhabits arid to semi-arid open woodlands, scrub and grassland to 600m, and thought to be largely independent of standing water. **Feeding Ecology** Unknown. Assumed to be similar to that of Common Dwarf Mongoose. Cheek teeth are more robust, suggesting small vertebrates might be relatively more important in the diet. **Social and Spatial Behaviour** Known to live in large groups similar to Common Dwarf Mongoose, but there are no details. **Reproduction and Demography** Unknown. **Status and Threats** Unknown. Said to be common in some areas, but its status has never been properly assessed anywhere, and its range is completely overlapped by that of Common Dwarf Mongoose, which might lead to misidentification. Red List LC, population trend Unknown.

# COMMON DWARF MONGOOSE
*Helogale parvula*

### DWARF MONGOOSE
HB 16–23cm; T 14.2–18.2cm; W 0.21–0.34kg
Smallest mongoose (both Pousargues's and Somali Dwarf mongooses are comparable, but have very few verified measurements). Fur smooth, sleek and uniformly coloured. Colour variable, typically grizzled tawny brown, red-brown or dark brown with warm-coloured underparts. Melanism occurs, in which most or all of a population is black, e.g. Erongo Mountains, C Namibia. **Distribution and Habitat** From the Horn of Africa, through E Africa (E of the Rift Valley), S DR Congo, Mozambique, Zambia and Angola to N Namibia, N Botswana and NE South Africa. Inhabits a wide variety of habitats with high densities of termitaria, including dry and wet woodland savannah, brush, scrubland and open forest. Occurs in pastoral areas. **Feeding Ecology** Almost entirely insectivorous, with the diet dominated by surface and subsurface invertebrates, especially termites, beetles, grasshoppers, millipedes, centipedes and scorpions. Also eats small mammals, reptiles, frogs, birds and small amounts of fruits, including berries. Breaks open large eggs by throwing them backwards through its hind legs at the ground or against a rock. Rarely kills poultry, but known to take the eggs of domestic fowl. Foraging is strictly diurnal and terrestrial; occasionally climbs to heights of 2.5m, digging arthropods and small vertebrates from bark crevices and tree hollows (and dens overnight in hollows). Forages as a group, but spreads out individually to search for prey, most of which is caught and consumed alone. Large snakes are killed cooperatively (it is resistant to snake neurotoxins), and adults sometimes cooperate to kill large rats. **Social and Spatial Behaviour** Intensely social. Lives in complex extended groups of 2–32, averaging 9–12 adults and subadults that defend a stable group range. Each group is led by a dominant breeding pair, usually the oldest individuals of each sex, which bond for life. The group's remaining adults are made up of their grown offspring or unrelated immigrants. Group members are extremely social, engaging in constant contact and cooperative behaviours, including territorial defence, scent-marking, predator vigilance, raising young, grooming and sleeping together. Adults rescue pups from danger, and groups sometimes provision injured or invalid members. Group range size 0.27–0.96km². Density estimates 3.9–30.9/km². **Reproduction and Demography** Generally aseasonal, but births peak during wetter periods in strongly seasonal habitat, e.g. N Kenya. Group females synchronise oestrus, and all adults in a group mate; the alpha male monopolises the alpha female, and she is often the only female to reproduce successfully. Despite mating, subordinate females are suppressed behaviourally and physiologically, and produce few litters. Of subordinate litters born, most do not survive due to infanticide by the alpha female; they are more likely to be tolerated during favourable conditions. Gestation 49–53 days. Litter size 2–6, averaging 2–3. Dominant female can produce up to 4 litters a year in favourable conditions. Subadults remain in the group, disperse voluntarily to seek breeding opportunities or are forced out following a takeover; females are more likely than males to remain in their natal group. MORTALITY Annually to 59% (emerged pups to 1 year), and 26% (adult ♀s) to 32% (adult ♂s). Major predators include large raptors, monitor lizards, puff adders, large mongooses and Honey Badger (page 158). LIFESPAN 10 (♂s) and 14 (♀s) years in the wild, 18 in captivity. **Status and Threats** A widespread generalist that attains very high densities in some areas. Occurs in many protected areas and does not suffer major threats at population level. Red List LC, population trend Stable.

■ Pousargues's Mongoose
■ Somali Dwarf Mongoose

■ Common Dwarf Mongoose

Plate 28

POUSARGUES'S
MONGOOSE

SOMALI DWARF
MONGOOSE

Scent-marking
at den

COMMON DWARF
MONGOOSE

# GAMBIAN MONGOOSE
*Mungos gambianus*

HB 30–45cm; T 23–29cm; W 1–2.2kg
Medium-sized stocky mongoose with coarse, grizzled reddish-grey-brown fur. Yellowish throat and chest are demarcated by a distinctive black or dark brown streak running from the ear to the foreleg. Tail ends in a dark tip. Behaviour and ecology thought to parallel those of closely related Banded Mongoose, but have never been studied. **Distribution and Habitat** Endemic to W Africa, from Gambia and S Senegal to the Niger River, Nigeria. Occurs in dry to semi-moist woodlands, open savannah, grassland and coastal scrub. **Feeding Ecology** Poorly known, but resembles Banded Mongoose in eating mainly arthropods on the soil surface, as well as small vertebrates such as rodents, snakes and lizards. Forages in social groups and is strictly diurnal. **Social and Spatial Behaviour** Highly social. Lives in family groups typically comprising 5–15 individuals, but occasionally reaching 30–40 (reported from Côte d'Ivoire, Gambia and Senegal). **Reproduction and Demography** Poorly known. Young animals recorded January–February and September (Ghana), and June (Sierra Leone). MORTALITY Unknown; large raptors assumed to be the main predators. LIFESPAN Unknown. **Status and Threats** Status poorly known. Fairly widespread and common in some protected areas, e.g. Niokolo-Koba NP, Senegal, and Upper Niger NP, Guinea. Sought after as bushmeat but effects of hunting are unknown. Red List LC, population trend Stable.

# BANDED MONGOOSE *Mungos mungo*

**STRIPED MONGOOSE**
HB 30–45cm; T 17.8–31cm; W 0.9–1.9kg
Medium-sized mongoose with short, coarse fur. Grizzled, pale grey-brown to dark brown with 10–15 dark, narrow transverse bands across the mid-back and rump. Juveniles lack the bands until around 8–10 weeks old and are easily mistaken for dwarf mongooses. **Distribution and Habitat** Widespread in sub-Saharan Africa; absent from forested W and C Africa, and arid southern Africa. Found in all types of woodland, savannah and grassland; does not occur in desert, semi-desert or montane habitat. Tolerates farmland and cultivated areas. **Feeding Ecology** Mainly insectivorous, eating arthropods on the soil surface or subsurface, especially millipedes, dung beetles, termites, ants, grasshoppers and crickets, plus their larvae and eggs. Also takes rodents, shrews, lizards, small snakes, amphibians, birds, fledglings, eggs and some fruits. Not considered a poultry pest. Foraging is strictly diurnal and in large social groups; most prey is captured individually and hunting is not cooperative. Eagerly investigates ungulate dung (especially of elephants and rhinos) for dung beetles, and occasionally grooms Warthogs for ticks and other external parasites. Scavenges from human refuse in villages, tourist camps and rubbish dumps. **Social and Spatial Behaviour** Intensely social. Lives in large, cohesive family groups, typically of 12–20 individuals, which cooperate to raise pups, watch for predators and defend a communal range. Groups numbering up to 70–75 are occasionally recorded, usually under super-abundant food availability like that around refuse dumps in tourist lodges. Group adults are inter-related as both males and females may stay in their natal group; generally, group males are more closely related to other males, and females are more closely related to females. Groups are territorial and defend their ranges against other groups in clashes that are sometimes fatal. Group ranges 0.3–2km² (Queen Elizabeth NP, Uganda). Density estimates 2.4–3/km² (KwaZulu-Natal, South Africa, and Serengeti NP, Tanzania) to 18/km² (Queen Elizabeth NP). **Reproduction and Demography** Breeding occurs in wetter periods in regions with marked seasonality, otherwise aseasonal. Most adults in a group breed. Females synchronise oestrus and give birth within a few days of each other in a communal den; litters born out of synchrony are much less likely to survive. Gestation 60–63 days. Litter size 1–6, averaging 3. Males compete among each other for females, and dominant males sire most pups, but most males mate. All group adults contribute to pup care; 1–2 babysitters remain at the den when the group forages, and all adults groom, carry, play with and provision pups; females suckle any pup. When pups leave the den at 5 weeks, they are attached to an individual 'escort' that feeds and protects its pup until independence at around 3 months. MORTALITY 72% (birth to independence) and 14–33% (adults), mainly from predation and infanticide (on pups). LIFESPAN 17 years in captivity. **Status and Threats** Very widespread, common and secure. Disappears from intensively modified habitat, but not threatened. Red List LC, population trend Stable.

# LIBERIAN MONGOOSE
*Liberiictis kuhni*

HB 42.3–46.8cm; T 19.7–20.5cm; W (1 ♂) 2.3kg
Fairly large mongoose with a narrow head and long, mobile snout. Uniformly dark brown with tawny-orange underfur, a pale throat and chest, and a distinctive dark neck stripe. Classification is disputed, but Gambian and Banded mongooses are thought to be its closest relatives. **Distribution and Habitat** Endemic to Côte d'Ivoire and Liberia. Occurs in primary and secondary rainforest, usually associated with swampy areas and sandy streambeds where earthworms are abundant. **Feeding Ecology** Thought to be an earthworm specialist, with small amounts of other arthropods, small vertebrates and fruits also consumed. Captives eat ground beef, commercial dry dog food, chicks, fish and live insects. Foraging is diurnal and in small social groups. Uses its extremely well-developed front claws to excavate leaf litter and soil, and thrusts its long, flexible nose into turned soil to locate prey. **Social and Spatial Behaviour** Social. Forms small groups, typically of 4–6, although larger groups are sometimes observed. Adult males often travel alone and visit numerous groups for brief periods of 1–3 days, suggesting the social system might resemble that of coatis (page 144), with female groups and solitary males, but group composition is unclear. Range estimates unknown. Density estimates 1.5/km² (Tai NP, Côte d'Ivoire). **Reproduction and Demography** Poorly known. A few records suggest breeding occurs in the wet season, May–September. MORTALITY Unknown. Crowned Eagle is a known predator. LIFESPAN Unknown. **Status and Threats** Very restricted distribution and dependent on earthworm-rich wet forest. Habitat loss and bushmeat hunting are serious threats. Red List VU, population trend Decreasing.

■ Gambian Mongoose

■ Banded Mongoose
■ Liberian Mongoose

**Plate 29**

GAMBIAN
MONGOOSE

BANDED
MONGOOSE

Grooming
Warthog

LIBERIAN MONGOOSE

# ANGOLAN CUSIMANSE
*Crossarchus ansorgei*

### ANSORGE'S CUSIMANSE
HB 32–36cm; T 20.8–22cm; W 0.6–1.5kg
Medium-sized cusimanse with shaggy, dark brown fur and dense reddish-brown underfur. Lower face pale tawny and may have white flashes along the cheeks and eyebrows. Until 1984, only two specimens existed, one of which is still the only Angolan record from 1908. It is now known to be more widely distributed but remains essentially unstudied. **Distribution and Habitat** Endemic to W and C DR Congo and NW Angola in 2 disjunct populations; not clear if it occurs in between. All records are from rainforest. **Feeding Ecology** Poorly known but assumed to resemble other cusimanses, with a diet of forest-floor invertebrates and small vertebrates. Captive individuals refuse fruits, including berries, and mushrooms. Foraging is likely to be diurnal, terrestrial and social. **Social and Spatial Behaviour** Highly social, living in groups with as many as 20 members, but no details are known. **Reproduction and Demography** Unknown. **Status and Threats** Rare compared to sympatric Alexander's Cusimanse based on lower frequencies in bushmeat surveys (10% of hunted carnivores compared to 42% for the latter). Unlike Alexander's Cusimanse, it is not recorded outside intact rainforest and may be forest-dependent. Red List LC, population trend Decreasing.

# FLAT-HEADED CUSIMANSE
*Crossarchus platycephalus*

### CAMEROON CUSIMANSE
HB 30–36cm; T 15.6–21cm; W 0.5–1.5kg
Small cusimanse similar to Common Cusimanse, but with a flatter, wider skull and paler coloration. Sometimes considered conspecific with Common Cusimanse, but recent exhaustive craniometric and molecular analyses establishes the two as distinct species separated by the Dahomey Gap. **Distribution and Habitat** S Nigeria through S Cameroon, extreme SW CAR to Equatorial Guinea, N Gabon and NW Republic of the Congo; there are equivocal records from S Benin. Inhabits dense rainforest to 1,600m, as well as forest–savanna mosaics and forest farmland. **Feeding Ecology** Poorly known, but resembles other cusimanses, with a diet of forest-floor invertebrates and small vertebrates. Forages in shallow water for freshwater crabs, which appear to be important prey. Foraging is diurnal, social and mainly terrestrial; 2 adults were seen to pursue a large Forest Cobra 3m into a tree (it escaped). **Social and Spatial Behaviour** Highly social but poorly known. Family groups are relatively small for cusimanses, typically comprising 5–8 members, although up to 25 are recorded. **Reproduction and Demography** Poorly known. Believed to be aseasonal, with a litter size of 2–5. **MORTALITY** and **LIFESPAN** Unknown. **Status and Threats** Status poorly known. Relatively widespread and apparently persists in degraded habitat, e.g. Niger Delta, suggesting resilience to forest loss. Heavily hunted for bushmeat; hunters in S Nigeria set nets

around dens, often killing entire family groups as they emerge at dawn. Red List LC, population trend Unknown.

# COMMON CUSIMANSE
*Crossarchus obscurus*

### LONG-NOSED CUSIMANSE, WEST AFRICAN CUSIMANSE
HB 30–37cm; T 14.6–21cm; W 0.45–1kg
Small, stocky cusimanse with grizzled, shaggy, dark brown to blackish fur and paler underfur. Fur on the head and face is shorter and paler than fur on the body, typically tawny or reddish brown. **Distribution and Habitat** Endemic to coastal W Africa, from W Guinea and Sierra Leone to the Ghana–Togo border. Inhabits mainly dense understorey of rainforest and riparian forest to 1,500m. Occurs in logged forest and plantations with understorey. **Feeding Ecology** Eats mainly forest-floor invertebrates, especially millipedes, ants, termites, earthworms, beetles, grasshoppers, insect larvae, spiders and snails. Also takes rodents, small birds, herptiles and eggs; captives eat fruits, including berries. Cusimanses forage diurnally and socially in large groups in which individuals mostly search for prey individually. They cooperatively hunt large prey, including cobras and giant-pouched rats, e.g. Gambian Rat is hunted by 1 or more cusimanses entering holes to flush it to the surface, where it is caught by the group. Foraging is terrestrial; rarely pursues prey above the ground, but climbs vine tangles to 25m to den. **Social and Spatial Behaviour** Highly social. Lives in cohesive territorial groups with up to 20 members. Group structure unclear, but may be an aggregation of 2–3 family units (possibly inter-related), each comprising a mated adult pair and offspring from 1 or more litters. Group range size estimates 0.28–1.4km². Density in good-quality habitat 13.2–17/km². **Reproduction and Demography** Aseasonal in captivity, but most known wild births occur January–February and May–June. Gestation 53–60 days. Litter size 2–5. Breeding adults provide most of the care for pups, but non-breeding adults assist by guarding pups, carrying them between dens and provisioning them with prey. **MORTALITY** Poorly known; mortality of juveniles to 6 months estimated at 45.5% (based on few observations). Large diurnal raptors, especially Crowned Eagle, are major predators. **LIFESPAN** 13 years in captivity. **Status and Threats** Has a relatively restricted distribution that is under considerable human pressure, but not dependent on undisturbed forest and reaches high densities in suitable habitat. Exploited heavily for bushmeat. Red List LC, population trend Unknown.

# ALEXANDER'S CUSIMANSE
*Crossarchus alexandri*

HB 35–44cm; T 20.8–32cm; W 1–2kg
Largest cusimanse, with long, shaggy, dark fur, conspicuous whorls on the neck and long dorsal hairs producing an inconspicuous crest. **Distribution and Habitat** Endemic to forested DR Congo and W Uganda; a disjunct population occurs on Mt Elgon on the Uganda–Kenya border. Inhabits lowland and montane rainforests, especially in swampy areas. Occurs near villages and cultivated areas. **Feeding Ecology** Poorly known but resembles other cusimanses, with a diet comprising mainly forest-floor invertebrates, small vertebrates and some fruits. Foraging is diurnal, terrestrial and social. **Social and Spatial Behaviour** Highly social but poorly known. Family groups are relatively small for cusimanses, typically having up to 10 members. **Reproduction and Demography** Unknown. A pregnant female collected in Virunga NP, DR Congo, had 6 embryos. **MORTALITY** and **LIFESPAN** Unknown. **Status and Threats** Believed to be widespread and relatively common based on high frequency in bushmeat surveys. Appears resilient to habitat modification, but severe degradation – combined with hunting, especially in DR Congo – represents a local threat. Red List LC, population trend Decreasing.

■ Angolan Cusimanse
■ Flat-headed Cusimanse

■ Common Cusimanse
■ Alexander's Cusimanse

**Plate 30**

ANGOLAN
CUSIMANSE

FLAT-HEADED
CUSIMANSE

COMMON
CUSIMANSE

ALEXANDER'S CUSIMANSE

Foraging group

# FALANOUC *Eupleres goudotii*

HB 45–65cm; T 22–25cm; W 1.6–4.6kg
Very distinctive euplerid with an extremely slender head, a stout body and a long bulbous tail. Some authors recognise 2 species – Eastern Falanouc (*E. goudotii*) and the larger Western or Giant Falanouc (*E. major*), restricted to NW Madagascar – but recent molecular analysis confirms a single species. **Distribution and Habitat** Madagascar, in humid and deciduous forests and associated marshland from sea-level to 1,600m. Also recorded from mesic, open grassy patches in forest, and from fragmented, degraded forest habitats. **Feeding Ecology** Almost exclusively insectivorous/ vermivorous, with an exceptionally elongated snout and small conical teeth specialised for eating earthworms, slugs, snails and insect larvae. Captive animals eat frogs and small meat pieces, but otherwise refuse vertebrate prey. Long, non-protractile claws well suited for excavating prey. Accumulates up to 20% of its body weight as fat in the tail during the cold dry season, presumably to cope with reduced prey availability. Cathemeral. **Social and Spatial Behaviour** Probably solitary; all wild observations are of single animals or females with young. Both sexes mark prominent bushes and rocks with their ano-genital glands, but it is unclear if this demarcates territorial boundaries. **Reproduction and Demography** Captive animals mate July–September; births November–January; 1 record of a wild kitten in January. All captive births are singletons, but twins reportedly occur. Kittens are surprisingly precocious, able to accompany the mother after 2–3 days, and weaned by 9 weeks. MORTALITY Poorly known; domestic dogs are thought to be a serious predator. LIFESPAN Unknown. **Status and Threats** Secretive, solitary and poorly known, but thought to be naturally rare. Not restricted to undisturbed forest as previously assumed. Actively sought after by bushmeat hunters; since the 2009 *coup d'état* in Madagascar, high levels of illegal settlement in protected areas (e.g. Masoala NP) have accelerated habitat loss and greatly increased intensity of bushmeat hunting using dogs. CITES Appendix II; Red List VU, population trend Decreasing.

# FOSA *Cryptoprocta ferox*

## FOSSA

HB 70–80cm; T 61–70cm; W ♀ 5.5–6.8kg, ♂ 6.2–8.6kg
Madagascar's largest carnivore. Typically reddish to chocolate brown; reports of melanism are unconfirmed. Kittens are born with pearl-grey fur that darkens fully to adult colour by 5–6 months. **Distribution and Habitat** Madagascar. Inhabits forest and woodland to 2,600m, from dry woodland savannah with <400mm rainfall to rainforest with >6,000mm rainfall. Reaches the highest densities in western dry deciduous forest. **Feeding Ecology** Formidable predator, able to kill all indigenous species, including the largest lemurs (predation on adult Indris is equivocal). Primates frequently dominate the diet, but it opportunistically switches to other prey depending on availability. Rodents, tenrecs and other carnivores, including Narrow-striped Boky (page 76) and Fanaloka, are important prey at some sites; birds, reptiles, amphibians and invertebrates are also eaten. Records of Bushpig and cattle are almost certainly from scavenging. Kills domestic chickens. Foraging is cathemeral (nocturnal where there is high human and dog activity), and both terrestrial and in trees, where it displays exceptional agility. Usually hunts alone, but cooperative hunting has been anecdotally reported for breeding pairs and mother–young groups; an observation exists of 3 adult males driving Verreaux's Sifaka to the ground, where it was caught and shared. **Social and Spatial Behaviour** Solitary and probably territorial; vigorously marks range borders with pungent ano-genital secretions, but territories overlap by up to 30% and adults congregate at mating sites. Range size reaches 13km² (♀s) and 27km² (♂s), and is largest during the dry season, probably due to dispersed water and prey. Density estimates 0.9–0.12/km² (logged and primary forest, Ranomafana NP) to 5.5/km² (very high-density population, dry forest, Kirindy). **Reproduction and Demography** Likely seasonal. Mates September–December, usually in trees at traditional sites used by many females. Up to 8 males attend an oestrous female, fighting for access, and females mate with multiple males. Gestation ~90 days. Litter size 2–4, rarely up to 6 (captivity). Development of kittens is unexpectedly slow; weaning at around 4–5 months, and independence at around 12 months. MORTALITY Poorly known. Humans and domestic dogs are the only predators; people kill significant numbers in some areas. LIFESPAN 23 years in captivity. **Status and Threats** Restricted to peripheral forests of Madagascar, where forest loss and fragmentation are the key threats, combined with human hunting for meat (at high rates locally, especially for a top carnivore) and retributively for chicken depredation. Feral domestic dogs impact on densities, and the species is vulnerable to exotic diseases from dogs and cats, although impacts are unquantified. All threats have escalated since the 2009 Madagascar *coup d'état*. CITES Appendix II; Red List VU, population trend Decreasing.

# FANALOKA *Fossa fossana*

## SPOTTED FANALOKA, MALAGASY CIVET

HB 40–45cm; T 21–26.4cm; W 1.3–1.9kg
Genet-like, with parallel rows of dark spots and blotches on a grizzled, light brown background. Bushy tail is usually marked with brown bands, absent in some animals. **Distribution and Habitat** N and E Madagascar, primarily in humid and dry forests to 1,300m. Most common in well-watered lowland rainforest, but also occurs in dry forested canyons of *tsingy* (limestone karst) with no permanent water at Ankarana. Absent from forest fragments >2km from intact forest. **Feeding Ecology** Hunts small prey such as rodents, tenrecs, small birds, reptiles, amphibians and invertebrates. In rainforest, hunts in shallow streams for freshwater crustaceans, eels and amphibians. Stores fat in its tail for the winter dry season, up to 25% of its body weight. Foraging is mainly nocturnal and terrestrial, although it is an accomplished climber and sometimes hunts in small trees. **Social and Spatial Behaviour** Solitary. Spatial patterns are poorly known, but a brief study indicates that females and males inhabit discrete home ranges of 0.07–0.52km². Adults vigorously scent-mark ranges and males guard oestrous females, suggesting territoriality. Density estimates 1.4/km² (logged forest) to 3.2/km² (unlogged forest; Ranomafana NP). **Reproduction and Demography** Seasonal. Mates August–September; births October–December. Gestation 80–89 days. All recorded litters comprise only 1 kitten, which is well developed at birth, able to walk at day 3 and weaned by 8–10 weeks. MORTALITY Poorly known; Fosa is a confirmed predator, and human hunters remove significant numbers from some populations. LIFESPAN Unknown in the wild, 11 years in captivity. **Status and Threats** Widespread within its limited distribution and seems to reach high densities. However, does not colonise human-modified habitats and is vulnerable to human hunting. Persecuted as a supposed predator of chickens (unsubstantiated but possible) and eaten by people in rural areas. Human threats have escalated since the 2009 Madagascar *coup d'état*. CITES Appendix II; Red List VU, population trend Decreasing.

■ Falanouc    ■ Fosa ■ Fanaloka

**Plate 31**

FALANOUC

FOSA

FANALOKA

# BROWN-TAILED VONTSIRA
*Salanoia concolor*

**BROWN-TAILED MONGOOSE, SALANO**
Includes **DURRELL'S VONTSIRA** *S. durrelli*
HB 35–38cm; T 16–20cm; W *c.*0.78kg
Uniformly dark chocolate brown to light brown. Paler underparts, Durrell's Vontsira is now recognised as the same species. **Distribution and Habitat** NE Madagascar to 1,000m. Most records are from intact rainforest, occasionally from secondary forest and cultivated land. **Feeding Ecology** Mainly insectivorous; direct observations involve individuals extracting larvae from rotting wood and leaf litter. Foraging is mainly diurnal and terrestrial; climbs well and possibly forages arboreally. Blamed for raiding poultry, but this is dubious given its weak dentition. **Social and Spatial Behaviour** Poorly known. Groups with up to 5 individuals suggest adult pairs with dependent young. Groups with different-aged kittens suggest offspring from previous litters remain with the family. **Reproduction and Demography** All records of kittens are November–January, suggesting seasonal breeding. Observed litters comprise 1 kitten. MORTALITY and LIFESPAN Unknown. **Status and Threats** Very limited distribution and narrow habitat preferences, presumably vulnerable to deforestation and bushmeat hunting. Locally common at Betampona Reserve. Red List VU, population trend Decreasing.

# NARROW-STRIPED BOKY
*Mungotictis decemlineata*

**BOKIBOKY, NARROW-STRIPED MONGOOSE**
HB 26.4–29.4cm; T 19.1–21.5cm; W 0.45–0.74kg
Distinctive grizzled grey fur with yellowish underparts and narrow orange-brown stripes. **Distribution and Habitat** SW Madagascar, restricted mainly to intact dry deciduous and baobab forests to 400m. Absent from degraded forest. **Feeding Ecology** Feeds chiefly on insects, larvae and snails in the soil, leaf litter and rotting logs; also small reptiles and eggs. Occasionally preys on mouse and dwarf lemurs, small rodents and tenrecs. Lemurs are apparently hunted cooperatively. Large prey, including Malagasy Giant Rat (1–1.2kg), is probably scavenged. Foraging is largely diurnal and terrestrial. **Social and Spatial Behaviour** Gregarious, with complex sociality based on stable units of related adult and young. Males associate loosely in groups of 2–4, which disintegrate during breeding, when males join female units. Males may be aggressive to each other while breeding. Families occupy stable ranges that are marked vigorously at borders, but aggression between groups is rare. Range estimates 0.24–0.6km² (♀), and 0.5–1.3km² (♂; Kirindy Forest). Density estimates 17–25 adults and mobile young/km², averaging 15 adults/km² (Kirindy Forest). **Reproduction and Demography** Seasonal. Mates July–December (peak August; Kirindy Forest); females may breed late, to February, if a first litter is lost early. Gestation 90–105 days. Litter size is typically 1. Group females may synchronise breeding, but typically only the oldest, dominant female reproduces successfully.

**MORTALITY** Known predators include Madagascar Ground Boa, Fosa (page 74) and domestic dog. Annual mortality 6–22% (juveniles) and 7–23% (adults; Kirindy Forest). LIFESPAN 10.7 years in captivity. **Status and Threats** Very limited and fragmented range, placing it under significant pressure from habitat loss and bushmeat hunting. Red List EN, population trend Decreasing.

# RING-TAILED VONTSIRA
*Galidia elegans*

**RING-TAILED MONGOOSE**
HB 30–38cm; T 26–39.1cm; W ♀ 0.66–0.89kg, ♂ 0.9–1.09kg
Most conspicuous euplerid. Rich chestnut-red with contrasting chocolate bands on the tail. Eastern animals are darker. **Distribution and Habitat** Madagascar, in most forest types to 1,950m, as well as secondary forest and clearings close to cover. **Feeding Ecology** Feeds mainly on small rodents, tenrecs, reptiles, bird nestlings and eggs, and invertebrates, but capable of taking larger prey, e.g. Greater Dwarf Lemur (600g). Record of a 1.2kg woolly lemur was likely scavenged. Forages terrestrially to 15m in trees, excavates rodents from burrows and fishes for aquatic prey in shallow water. Largely diurnal. **Social and Spatial Behaviour** Forms male–female pairs with dependent young. Males also occur alone; unclear if pairs form only for breeding. Family groups maintain ranges of 0.2–0.25km. **Reproduction and Demography** Weakly seasonal. Mates July–November. Gestation 75 days. One kitten born October–December; families sometimes have different-aged litters, suggesting biannual breeding. MORTALITY and LIFESPAN Unknown. **Status and Threats** Most common and widespread euplerid. Persecuted for killing poultry and often killed by dogs accompanying hunters; bushmeat hunting is a serious threat in eastern rainforests. Red List LC, population trend Decreasing.

# BROAD-STRIPED VONTSIRA
*Galidictis fasciata*

**BROAD-STRIPED MALAGASY MONGOOSE**
Includes **GRANDIDIER'S VONTSIRA** *G. f. grandidieri*
HB 30–34cm; T 25–29.3cm; W 0.52–0.74kg.
*G. f. grandidieri*: HB 39.5–48cm; T 28–32.5cm; W 1.2–2.3kg
Until 2017, classified as 2 species based mainly on superficial differences. However, genetic differences are slight, and Grandidier's Vontsira is now recognised as an isolated subspecies (*G. f. grandidieri*). Grandidier's is better studied, and is poorly known elsewhere. Pale, grizzled grey-beige fur with dark brown to black longitudinal stripes, apparently narrower in Grandidier's. Grandidier's is larger, but few measurements of specimens elsewhere are recorded. **Distribution and Habitat** E Madagascar in humid lowland forest, usually to 700m. Sometimes in degraded secondary forest. Grandidier's restricted to ~450–1,500km² in SW Madagascar in dry, spiny forest. **Feeding Ecology** Known largely for Grandidier's. Eats mainly small prey, chiefly hissing cockroaches, grasshoppers, arachnids and small vertebrates weighing <10g. Largest recorded prey weighs 140–200g, e.g. Lesser Hedgehog Tenrec and Madagascar Turtle-dove, with 1 record of a 369g snake. Forages mainly on the ground, but sometimes climbs small trees in pursuit of prey. Sometimes raids research camp stores, and reputedly kills chickens. Largely nocturnal and terrestrial. **Social and Spatial Behaviour** Observations and camera-trap images suggest adult pairs; occasional sightings of male-dominated groups of up to 5 (Grandidier's) suggest more complex social patterns. Rare in surveys, suggesting low densities. **Reproduction and Demography** Unknown. Females have a single pair of teats, suggesting 1–2 young. MORTALITY and LIFESPAN Unknown. **Status and Threats** Habitat loss, hunting for bushmeat, and introduced Small Indian Civet (page 88) and domestic dog are the main threats. Red List VU, Population trend Decreasing. (Grandidier's Vontsira: EN (evaluated prior to 2017), population trend Decreasing.)

■ Brown-tailed Vontsira ■ Narrow-striped Boky ■ Ring-tailed Vontsira    ■ Broad-striped Vontsira

**Plate 32**

BROWN-TAILED
VONTSIRA

NARROW-
STRIPED
BOKY

RING-TAILED VONTSIRA

BROAD-STRIPED
VONTSIRA

Grandidier's
Vontsira

# BANDED LINSANG
*Prionodon linsang*

HB 37.9–45cm; T 33–37.5cm; W 0.59–0.8kg
The 2 species of linsang are classified in their own family, Prionodontidae. Banded Linsang is very small and slender, with a delicate, elongated neck and head. Fur is cream to yellow-buff, with large dark bands across the spine, and interconnected blotches running in parallel bands lengthways along the body. Feet genet-like, with fully protractile claws. **Distribution and Habitat** Java, Sumatra, Borneo, and Peninsular Malaysia into S Thailand and S Myanmar. Occurs mainly in primary and secondary forests to 2,700m, with a handful of records from degraded habitats such as plantations. **Feeding Ecology** Primarily carnivorous, taking small terrestrial and arboreal vertebrates, including rodents, birds, reptiles and frogs; invertebrates such as large cockroaches are also eaten. Captive animals refuse fruits. Extremely agile and hunts both in the canopy (at least to 8m) and on the ground; descends trees rapidly head first. Hunting is mainly nocturnal. **Social and Spatial Behaviour** Very poorly known. Considered solitary; reports of pairs and trios are probably mother–young groups. Range size and density have never been studied. **Reproduction and Demography** Poorly known. Litters and pregnant or lactating females recorded April–October, but it is unknown if this represents seasonal breeding. Litter size 1–3. Juveniles reach adult size at 4 months. MORTALITY Unknown. LIFESPAN 10.7 years in captivity. **Status and Threats** Difficult to monitor and status is poorly known. Forest loss is considered the main threat, although the extent to which the species can adapt to logged areas is unknown, and it occurs in better-protected higher altitudes. Appears occasionally in wildlife markets, probably reflecting its natural rarity. CITES Appendix II; Red List LC, population trend Decreasing.

# SPOTTED LINSANG
*Prionodon pardicolor*

HB 31–45cm; T 30–40cm; W 0.55–1.2kg
Similar to Banded Linsang but less richly marked, with small, discrete round spots covering the body in roughly parallel rows. Spots along the back sometimes fuse over the spine, giving a similar appearance to the dorsal bands in Banded Linsang. The 2 species apparently do not overlap, but their ranges are poorly delineated and they may co-occur in S Thailand and S Myanmar. **Distribution and Habitat** Nepal, Bhutan, NE India, S China, and Southeast Asia to S Cambodia and S Vietnam. Inhabits lowland, hill and mountain forests to 2,700m (with equivocal records to 4,000m), bamboo forest, forest–grassland mosaics and dense moist grassland scrub. Occurs in some disturbed habitats, including secondary forest and mosaics of pine plantations and cultivated areas. **Feeding Ecology** Similar diet to Banded Linsang's, comprising mainly small terrestrial and arboreal vertebrates such as rodents, birds, reptiles and frogs. Captive female in a semi-natural enclosure hunted terrestrial mice and voles by observing them from tree perches and descending quickly head first to catch and kill them on the ground. She ate 4–6 small rodents a day. Mainly nocturnal. Three observations of scavenging from the kill of a Tiger (page 44) (Chitwan NP, Nepal). **Social and Spatial Behaviour** Virtually unknown. Usually reported as solitary. Captive female liberally marked her enclosure with urine and faeces in prominent places. **Reproduction and Demography** Poorly known. Very limited records of litters cluster in February–August, numbering 1–2 young. MORTALITY Virtually unknown; 2 adults drowned in an open well in Nepal, unlikely to be a regular occurrence. LIFESPAN Unknown. **Status and Threats** Status poorly known. Rarely seen or recorded in surveys and wildlife trade, but not necessarily due to rarity; semi-arboreal lifestyle makes it difficult to see and somewhat insulated from snaring. Main threats assumed to be habitat loss and hunting, both of which occur at high intensity throughout its range. Occurs in many protected areas in its range. CITES Appendix I; Red List LC, population trend Decreasing.

# SMALL-TOOTHED PALM CIVET
*Arctogalidia trivirgata*

THREE-STRIPED PALM CIVET,
JAVAN SMALL-TOOTHED PALM CIVET
HB 43.2–53.2cm; T 46.3–66cm; W 2–2.5kg
Small civet with a long tubular tail exceeding the head–body length. Coloration very variable, including golden yellow (especially in Java), various shades of grey, and tawny brown to very dark brown. All forms typically have paler underparts, a dark tail, and 3 dark dorsal stripes or parallel rows of interconnected spots (sometimes indistinct). The inside of the ear is bright pink, contrasting conspicuously with the surrounding dark fur colour, especially while spot-lighting; ear tip is white in populations north of the Kra Isthmus. Recent genetic evidence shows the Borneo population is distinct from the rest of the range (which clusters as 1 clade), although with insufficient data to confirm species-level differences. **Distribution and Habitat** Borneo, W Java, Sumatra, continental Southeast Asia to S China, NE India and E Bangladesh. Occurs in primary moist and dry evergreen forests at 150–1,500m. Known from degraded forest in Laos, provided canopy cover is intact; tolerance for more modified habitat is unclear. **Feeding Ecology** Omnivorous. Fruits, especially figs, are a key food, at least during seasonal fruiting peaks. Also eats small vertebrates such as tree squirrels, and invertebrates. Captive animals eat bananas, apples, oranges, grapes, tomatoes and meat. Foraging is nocturnal and almost entirely arboreal in upper canopy; occasionally seen in understorey and (rarely) on the ground. Mostly forages alone, but often feeds in close proximity to other individuals in fruiting trees. **Social and Spatial Behaviour** Poorly known. Assumed to be solitary; sightings comprise around 82% single animals and 18% pairs, but pair composition is unknown. Based on limited telemetry, 2 Borneo males had ranges of 0.16–0.78km² (Danum Valley). **Reproduction and Demography** Poorly known. Mating observed in dense canopy at a height of 8m, in February (Seima Forest, Cambodia). In captivity, gestation is 45 days and litters number 1–3. Weaning occurs at around 2 months. Captive females can have 2 litters a year. MORTALITY Unknown. LIFESPAN 15.8 years in captivity. **Status and Threats** Status poorly known mainly due to highly arboreal lifestyle. Almost never appears in camera-trapping and other ground-based surveys; however, night spot-lighting shows it is locally common in some areas. Forest loss and hunting are the main threats; it is somewhat insulated from the latter except where night shooting is employed. Considered endangered in Java. CITES Appendix II; Red List LC, population trend Decreasing.

■ Banded Linsang ■ Spotted Linsang ■ Small-toothed Palm Civet

Plate 33

BANDED
LINSANG

SPOTTED
LINSANG

SMALL-TOOTHED
PALM CIVET

# MASKED PALM CIVET *Paguma larvata*

HB 50.8–87cm; T 50.8–63.6cm; W 3–5kg
Large palm civet with a highly variable body colour, typically greyish brown but ranging from pale blond to dark reddish brown. Most forms have a distinctive black-and-white facial mask, which also varies considerably; Sundaic animals often have a golden or pale grizzled face without a discrete mask pattern. **Distribution and Habitat** S and SE China, the Himalayan region from N Pakistan to NE India, the Andaman Islands, Indochina, Sumatra and Borneo. Introduced (presumably) in Japan. Occurs mainly in deciduous, evergreen and peat-swamp forests. Inhabits degraded forest, plantations and farmland with cover. **Feeding Ecology** Omnivorous, feeding mainly on fruits, small mammals and invertebrates. Diet shifts seasonally to track fruit availability, e.g. June–October in C China, while rodents and birds are mainly consumed November–May. Raids cultivated fruits, including bananas, figs, kiwifruit and mangoes, and occasionally kills domestic poultry. Foraging is mainly nocturnal, and both arboreal and terrestrial. Forages alone, but congregates amicably at dumps and feeding stations, where it scavenges food waste and handouts. Scavenges carrion. **Social and Spatial Behaviour** Solitary. Adults are not strictly territorial, but avoid overlap in small core areas. Range size 1.9–3.7km² (♀s) and 1.8–5.9km² (♂s). No published density estimates, but very common in suitable habitat. **Reproduction and Demography** Reported as both seasonal and aseasonal, breeding once or twice a year, but there are few accurate data from the wild. Gestation 51–56 days. Litter size 1–4, averaging 2–3. **MORTALITY** Poorly known; humans are the main cause of mortality in most of its range. **LIFESPAN** 15 years in captivity. **Status and Threats** Widespread and common, but also exposed to very high levels of harvest. Common in Asian wildlife markets, where it is sold mainly for meat. Farmed in China, where wild populations have declined significantly from overharvesting. Carries the SARS coronavirus, but effects on wild populations are unknown. CITES Appendix III – India; Red List LC (NT in China), population trend Decreasing.

# COMMON PALM CIVET
## *Paradoxurus hermaphroditus*

**MUSANG, TODDY CAT**
HB 42–71cm; T 33–66cm; W 2–5kg
Medium-sized to large palm civet, varying from tawny grey to very dark grey, marked with longitudinal rows of small dark spots that merge into 3 narrow dorsal stripes. Most forms have a variable dark facial mask, dark legs and a dark tail. Recent genetic analysis identified 3 major clades, proposed as separate species: *P. hermaphroditus* (S Asia, including Sri Lanka, S China and mainland Southeast Asia), *P. musanga* (mainland Southeast Asia, Sumatra, Java and other small Indonesian islands) and *P. philippinensis* (Mentawai Islands, Borneo and the Philippines). This awaits confirmation. **Distribution and Habitat** Indian subcontinent, including Sri Lanka, S China, Indochina, Sumatra, Java, Borneo and the Philippines. Inhabits forest, woodland and wooded scrub from lowlands to 2,400m. Lives close to humans

on plantations and farmland, and in villages. **Feeding Ecology** Mainly frugivorous, eating wild and cultivated fruits, nectar and sap. Often consumes coffee berries (passed beans are highly sought after for 'civet coffee', for which civets are also farmed, mainly in Indonesia). Also eats arthropods and small vertebrates, especially in non-fruiting periods. Often raids fruit plantations, and (rarely) kills poultry. Foraging is solitary, nocturno-crepuscular and mainly arboreal. Scavenges food waste from village and rice-field dumps. **Social and Spatial Behaviour** Solitary. Marks prominent sites on branches and on the ground with piles of faeces, and ranges sometimes overlap extensively. Range sizes 0.06–1.4km² (♀s) and 0.17–4.2km² (♂s). **Reproduction and Demography** Thought to be aseasonal. Gestation 61–63 days (captivity). Litter size 2–5. **MORTALITY** Predators include large cats, and possibly large raptors and pythons. **LIFESPAN** 22.4 years in captivity. **Status and Threats** Widespread, common and tolerant of disturbed habitats. Hunted for meat (especially in China), captured as pets or rodent catchers, and killed by fruit farmers for raiding orchards; in concert, these threats may produce local declines. However, the species is resilient and persists in disturbed and heavily harvested areas. CITES Appendix III – India; Red List LC (VU on Mentawai), population trend Decreasing.

# BINTURONG *Arctictis binturong*

**BEARCAT**
HB 61–97cm; T 50–84cm; W 9–20kg
Largest civet. Unmistakable, with shaggy black fur often tipped with silvery white, giving a grizzled appearance. Face usually pale, varying from slightly grizzled to completely silvery grey. Ears have a white rim and very long hair on the outer surface. Long, bushy tail is prehensile. Subspecies on Palawan Island, the Philippines, is sometimes considered a separate species, Palawan Binturong (*A. whitei*), evidence for which is limited. **Distribution and Habitat** NE India, Bhutan, E Bangladesh, extreme S China, Indochina, Sumatra, Java, Borneo and Palawan (the Philippines). Presence in E Nepal uncertain. Inhabits mainly dense primary and secondary forests, and dry forest–grassland mosaics. Occurs in reduced densities in logged forest, and avoids heavily modified habitat. **Feeding Ecology** Poorly known in the wild. Omnivorous. Fruits are assumed to be the main food, with figs apparently favoured; often seen in fig trees. Also eats small vertebrates and arthropods. Captive animals eat a wide variety of fruits, vegetables, ground beef, eggs and milk. Not known to kill poultry. Foraging is solitary and nocturno-crepuscular. Arboreal, but often comes to the ground to move between trees and feed on fallen fruits. **Social and Spatial Behaviour** Solitary. Ranges are stable and overlap considerably, suggesting lack of territoriality. Only range estimates are from Thailand, 4km² (1♀) and 4.7–20.5km² (♂s). **Reproduction and Demography** Aseasonal (captivity). Gestation 84–99 days. Litter size 1–6, averaging 2–2.5. Captive females may have 2 litters a year. **MORTALITY** Predation apparently rare, perhaps due to the combination of its mainly arboreal lifestyle, large size and ability to mount a formidable defence. **LIFESPAN** 22.7 years in captivity. **Status and Threats** Apparently adapts poorly to modified habitat, e.g. plantations, and estimated to have declined by more than 30% since 2000 as a result of forest loss in combination with heavy hunting for wildlife markets; both threats are rampant across its range, especially in Southeast Asia. CITES Appendix III – India; Red List VU (CR in China and Southeast Asia), population trend Decreasing.

■ Masked Palm Civet

■ Common Palm Civet

■ Binturong

**Plate 34**

MASKED
PALM CIVET

COMMON PALM
CIVET

BINTURONG

# GOLDEN PALM CIVET
*Paradoxurus zeylonensis*

HB 50.2–58cm; T 43.7–52.5cm; W *c*.3.6kg
Medium-sized civet with a tail as long as the head–body length. Uniformly yellow-beige to golden brown, sometimes with a rich russet tinge, and paler underparts. Some individuals have 3 faint dorsal stripes. A dark brown form occurs, usually with a yellowish or white tail tip. Some authors split this species into three, but recent genetic analysis confirms a single species. **Distribution and Habitat** Endemic to Sri Lanka, where it is patchily distributed in discontinuous fragments of suitable habitat. Occurs in dry and wet forests from lowlands to cloud forest. Apparently tolerant of some habitat modification, but much less likely than sympatric Common Palm Civet (page 80) to be near agriculture, plantations and settlements. **Feeding Ecology** Poorly known but believed to be omnivorous, feeding chiefly on fruits, as well as small vertebrates and invertebrates. Mainly nocturnal and believed to be chiefly arboreal, but it is trapped and camera-trapped on the ground. **Social and Spatial Behaviour** Very poorly known. Most records are of solitary individuals. Range size and density have never been studied. **Reproduction and Demography** Poorly known. Litter size reported as 1–3, but there are few verifiable records. MORTALITY and LIFESPAN Unknown. **Status and Threats** Relatively widespread and often locally common, especially in Sri Lanka's wet zone and highlands. Ongoing habitat loss, especially in highland areas, is the main threat. Red List LC, population trend Unknown.

# BROWN PALM CIVET
*Paradoxurus jerdoni*

JERDON'S PALM CIVET
HB 51–61.5cm; T 44–50cm; W 2–4.3kg
Medium-sized civet with a long tail, typically very dark brown with slightly lighter sides and hindquarters, and pale underparts. Some animals are dramatically lighter over the torso, ranging from light brown to pale tawny grey and (rarely) golden, with only the head, forequarters and lower hind limbs retaining the dark brown coloration. Complete leucism is recorded. Tail sometimes has a prominent yellowish or white tip, mainly in lighter individuals. **Distribution and Habitat** Endemic to Western Ghats, S India. Inhabits evergreen forest at 500–1,300m, most commonly above 1,000m. Occurs in forest mosaics with highly modified habitat, including coffee and cardamom plantations. **Feeding Ecology** Mainly frugivorous, with the diet dominated by wild and cultivated fruits, seeds and flowers. Also eats invertebrates such as insects, centipedes, snails and crabs; small mammals, birds and reptiles are occasionally taken. Animal prey is taken mainly in the dry, non-fruiting season. Primarily arboreal, but readily travels and forages on the ground. Foraging is nocturnal and solitary; individuals sometimes feed close together in fruiting trees. **Social and Spatial Behaviour** Solitary. Ranges are small and overlap; conflict in shared areas is reduced by time-sharing, in which individuals largely avoid each other. Rests during the day in Indian Giant Squirrel dreys, tree hollows or vine tangles, or on tree limbs. Male ranges are larger than female ranges. Limited range estimates (monitored for <1 year) 0.06–0.18km$^2$ (♀s) and 0.1–0.56km$^2$ (♂s). **Reproduction and Demography** Poorly known. Very limited observations of kittens report litter size as 1–2. MORTALITY Known mortality is mainly anthropogenic. LIFESPAN Unknown. **Status and Threats** Restricted distribution, but appears to be fairly common in much of its range. Also tolerates plantations, provided the natural canopy is left intact, as is often the case with coffee, and persists in small forest fragments surrounded by modified habitat. Main threat is habitat loss and conversion to intensive plantation production such as tea, eucalyptus and teak. Illegally hunted for meat. CITES Appendix III – India; Red List LC, population trend Stable.

# SULAWESI CIVET
*Macrogalidia musschenbroekii*

SULAWESI PALM CIVET, CELEBES PALM CIVET
HB 65–71.5cm; T 44.5–54cm; W 3.9–6.1kg
Large civet with a long tubular tail. Light chestnut to tawny brown, with rich yellow-brown underparts clearly demarcated from the upper fur colour. Has small, faint brown spots on the upper hindquarters, and tail is marked with alternating light and dark bands. Genetic data suggest Sulawesi Civet belongs in the subfamily Hemigalinae (page 9) rather than the palm civet subfamily Paradoxurinae, but this awaits confirmation. **Distribution and Habitat** Endemic to Sulawesi, where it is confirmed from the North, Central and South-east peninsulas. Inhabits lowland forest, montane forest to 2,600m and savannah–forest mosaics. Occurs in agricultural areas surrounded by forest. **Feeding Ecology** Omnivorous, with a diet dominated by rodents and fruits, especially of palm trees. Also takes Sulawesi Dwarf Cuscus and birds, including the large mound-building Philippine Scrubfowl and Maleo. Local people report that it takes piglets of Sulawesi Warty Pig, but this remains unconfirmed. Readily kills domestic chickens in villages, and captive animals take fruits such as bananas and papayas. Extremely agile and thought to forage both arboreally and terrestrially. Mainly nocturnal. **Social and Spatial Behaviour** Poorly known. All records are of solitary individuals. No range or density estimates; it is very rare in wildlife surveys. **Reproduction and Demography** Entirely unknown. Females have 2 pairs of teats, suggesting small litters comparable with those of other palm civet species. MORTALITY Adults do not have any predators except humans and their dogs. LIFESPAN Unknown. **Status and Threats** Status poorly known, but very restricted distribution combined with extremely high rates of forest clearing are reasons for concern. More than 50% of Sulawesi's forest was lost in 1985–97, and the species is now absent from many lowland areas that previously provided suitable habitat. It is better protected in highland areas, which are more difficult to exploit. Apparently not sought after for food, but persecuted for raiding chickens. Red List VU, population trend Decreasing.

■ Golden Palm Civet

■ Brown Palm Civet

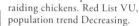
■ Sulawesi Civet

**Plate 35**

GOLDEN
PALM CIVET

BROWN
PALM CIVET

SULAWESI
CIVET

# OWSTON'S CIVET *Chrotogale owstoni*

## OWSTON'S PALM CIVET

HB 56–72cm; T 35–47cm; W 2.5–4.2kg

Slender, long-tailed civet with a very narrow head, pointed muzzle and large ears. Fur is creamy white to buff with pale peach underparts. Has 4–6 broad dark bands across the back, and small spots dotting the sides, neck and limbs. **Distribution and Habitat** Endemic to Vietnam, Laos and S China; uncertain in Cambodia. Occurs primarily in lowland and montane forests. Recorded in degraded forest near cultivation. **Feeding Ecology** Much-reduced dentition and a handful of records from the wild suggest that it eats primarily earthworms (which are relished in captivity) and other terrestrial invertebrates, including centipedes, grasshoppers, mantises and snails. Captive animals take meat, fruits, vegetables and small vertebrates (geckos, frogs and tadpoles), but largely refuse rodents. Blamed for taking poultry in villages, which is doubtful. Primarily terrestrial (but captives climb well) and nocturnal. **Social and Spatial Behaviour** Very poorly known. All camera-trap records are of solitary individuals or females with kittens. **Reproduction and Demography** Seasonal in captivity. Mates late January–mid-February; births April–May. Gestation 77–87 days. Litter size 1–3. Weaning at 12–18 weeks. Sexual maturity at 18 months. Captive males groom, sleep and forage with the kittens. MORTALITY and LIFESPAN Unknown. **Status and Threats** Very restricted distribution, which is under intense pressure from habitat clearing and hunting. Being ground-dwelling, the species is vulnerable to very high levels of snaring and trapping throughout its range. Red List EN, population trend Decreasing.

# BANDED CIVET *Hemigalus derbyanus*

## BANDED PALM CIVET

HB 41–56.5cm; T 23.5–37.5cm; W 1–3kg

Very similar to Owston's Civet, but with smaller ears, darker buff to tawny-rufous fur with 4–8 bands, and no small spots; the 2 species do not overlap in their ranges. Distinctive orange-buff coloration on the underparts does not develop until adulthood. **Distribution and Habitat** Borneo, Sumatra (and associated small islands), Peninsular Malaysia, peninsular Thailand and possibly peninsular Myanmar. Inhabits forest, mainly in lowland areas below 800m; occurs to 1,200m on Borneo. Occurs in moderately disturbed habitats, including secondary forest and *Acacia* plantations near intact forest fragments. **Feeding Ecology** Poorly known, but available records indicate it is largely insectivorous, eating mainly earthworms and insects; occasionally takes crustaceans and small vertebrates, including frogs, lizards and rodents. Fruits and plant matter are not recorded in the diet, although captive animals eat bananas. Foraging is nocturnal. Dietary records suggest it forages mainly on the ground (although it climbs well), especially along rivers and riverine habitat. **Social and Spatial Behaviour** Virtually unknown. Sightings and camera-trap records are usually of solitary animals. **Reproduction and Demography** Poorly known. Litter size 1–2 (captivity). Juveniles reach adult size at 6 months. MORTALITY Virtually unknown; 1 record of predation by a

Blood Python (Sumatra). LIFESPAN Unknown. **Status and Threats** Status poorly known, but its close association with lowland forest and largely terrestrial behaviour make it very vulnerable to habitat loss and hunting; both threats are intense in its range. CITES Appendix II; Red List NT, population trend Decreasing.

# HOSE'S CIVET *Diplogale hosei*

HB 47.2–54cm; T 30–33.5cm; W (1 ♀) 1.3kg

Similar shape and size to Banded Civet, but uniformly dark brown without markings, contrasting with bright white underparts, neck and lower face. Head is narrow and elongated, with a slightly bulbous appearance to the muzzle. One of the least known viverrids. **Distribution and Habitat** Endemic to Borneo, where it is confirmed only from the N and NE of the island. Inhabits intact rainforest and montane forest at 450–1,700m. **Feeding Ecology** Virtually unknown. Very long whiskers and partly webbed feet with fur between the pads suggest a semi-aquatic diet, but there are no records from the wild. The only animal ever kept in captivity, an adult female, ate fish, shrimp, chicken and processed meat; she refused fruits and boiled rice. All records (including behaviour in captivity) are nocturnal and terrestrial. **Social and Spatial Behaviour** Unknown. All records are of solitary animals. **Reproduction and Demography** Unknown. **Status and Threats** Status very poorly known. Probably declining due to forestry and habitat conversion to plantations and agriculture. Hunting is also a likely threat. Red List VU, population trend Decreasing.

# OTTER CIVET *Cynogale bennettii*

## SUNDA OTTER CIVET

HB 57.5–68cm; T 12–20.5cm; W 3–5kg

Very distinctive semi-aquatic civet. Grizzled, dark brown with pale creamy-brown underparts. Small ears and a bulbous muzzle with very long whiskers. Small, obvious white patches above the eyes and on the cheeks. Feet have long, dextrous digits and are partially webbed. Another species, Lowe's Otter Civet (*C. lowei*), described from a skin found in N Vietnam, is now confirmed by genetic analysis to be a young Eurasian Otter (page 194). **Distribution and Habitat** S Thailand, extreme S Myanmar (unconfirmed), Malaysia, Sumatra and Borneo. Occurs primarily in wet lowland forest and swamp forest. Recent records are from dry forest, bamboo and logged forest. **Feeding Ecology** Semi-aquatic and assumed to forage mainly along waterways for small aquatic prey, but there are no diet records from the wild. Has been observed in shallow water searching among stones with its stiff whiskers, and digging in moist leaf litter. Terrestrial and mainly nocturnal; recent camera-trap data from Sumatra show occasional diurnal activity. **Social and Spatial Behaviour** Unknown. All camera-trap records are of solitary individuals or females with kittens. **Reproduction and Demography** Virtually unknown. Litter size 1–3, based on very few records. MORTALITY and LIFESPAN Unknown. **Status and Threats** Status poorly known, but it is not common anywhere and is severely threatened by forest loss and pollution of waterways, both of which are extreme in its range. Conversion of peat-swamp forest to oil palm plantations is a particular concern. Vulnerable to snares due its terrestrial behaviour. CITES Appendix II; Red List EN, population trend Decreasing.

■ Owston's Civet ■ Banded Civet    ■ Hose's Civet

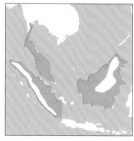

■ Otter Civet

**Plate 36**

OWSTON'S CIVET

BANDED CIVET

HOSE'S CIVET

OTTER CIVET

## MALABAR CIVET *Viverra civettina*

HB 76–85cm; T 30–40cm; W 6.6–8kg
Large terrestrial civet with buff-grey fur marked with small spots that are most distinct on the sides and flanks, becoming paler and diffuse on the forequarters. Has the distinct black-and-white throat stripes, dark lower legs and banded tail of all *Viverra* species; the only similar sympatric species is Small Indian Civet (page 88). Formerly classified with Large-spotted Civet (which does not occur in India); the possibility of it being an introduced population of this species cannot be excluded. **Distribution and Habitat** Endemic to Western Ghats, India. Known from only a handful of records in lowland forest and forest–plantation mosaics. **Feeding Ecology** Unknown. Assumed to be omnivorous, with a diet similar to that of Large Indian Civet. **Social and Spatial Behaviour** Unknown. Assumed to be solitary like other *Viverra* civets. **Reproduction and Demography** Unknown. **Status and Threats** Declared 'possibly extinct' in 1978, before being rediscovered in 1987; one fresh skin recovered since, in 1990. Otherwise, no recent records despite significant survey efforts. Its range is exposed to high levels of forest loss and hunting, and it may be extinct. CITES Appendix III – India; Red List CR, population trend Decreasing.

## LARGE-SPOTTED CIVET
### *Viverra megaspila*

HB 72–85cm; T 30–37cm; W 8–9kg
Large civet with a pale buff-grey coat marked with discrete large spots. Erectile black dorsal crest runs from the nape to the base of the tail, continuing as a black dorsal stripe to the tail tip (lacking in Large Indian Civet). Head is heavy with a slightly bulbous muzzle. **Distribution and Habitat** S China and Indochina to Peninsular Malaysia. Inhabits mainly lowland primary forest below 300m, rarely up to 780m. Occurs in logged areas, but disappears from small, fragmented forest blocks. **Feeding Ecology** Unknown. Assumed to be omnivorous, with a diet similar to that of Large Indian Civet. Camera-trap records indicate it is nocturnal and terrestrial. **Social and Spatial Behaviour** Unknown. All camera-trap records are of solitary animals. Density unknown, but occurs in much lower frequencies than sympatric *Viverra* species during camera-trap surveys (except in S Laos). **Reproduction and Demography** Unknown. **Status and Threats** Thought to have undergone more than a 50% decline in the last 15 years. Its lowland forest habitat is exposed to very high levels of degradation and hunting; especially vulnerable to snaring due to its terrestrial habits. Red List EN, population trend Decreasing.

## MALAY CIVET *Viverra tangalunga*

**ORIENTAL CIVET**
HB 54–77.3cm; T 26–39.5cm; W 3–7kg
Smallest of the *Viverra* civets, with a slender build, narrow skull, and short and slender muzzle. Tail has 10–15 narrow dark rings, compared with 4–8 broad bands in other *Viverra* species.

**Distribution and Habitat** Peninsular Malaysia, Sumatra, Borneo, Sulawesi and the Philippines. Two records from Java, which are probably human-assisted. Inhabits primary and secondary lowland and montane forests to 1,200m. Tolerates logged forest, plantations and agricultural areas near forests. **Feeding Ecology** Omnivorous. Eats small vertebrates, invertebrates (including toxic animals such as scorpions, millipedes and giant centipedes) and fruits. Civets in intact forest eat proportionally more fruits, whereas those in logged forest eat proportionally more rodents, insectivores, birds and herptiles, probably reflecting availability. Blamed for killing poultry. Foraging is solitary, nocturno-crepuscular and terrestrial. Scavenges food waste and handouts from villages, camps and dumps. **Social and Spatial Behaviour** Solitary and apparently non-territorial. Ranges are stable and often overlap, in some cases extensively. Range estimates include 0.28–1.28km² (♀s) and 0.39–2.83km² (♂s). Ranges in logged forest are slightly larger than in intact forest. Density estimates 0.9/km² (logged forest) to 2.8/km² (unlogged forest), and 2.6–3.1/km² in forest with hunting (Sulawesi). **Reproduction and Demography** Poorly known, but thought to be aseasonal. Gestation unknown. Litter size 1–2, rarely 3. MORTALITY Poorly known; roadkill is often the main cause of death in logging areas. LIFESPAN 5 years in the wild, 12 in captivity. **Status and Threats** Status poorly known but it is widespread and tolerant of modified habitat. Less common in areas of high human influence, but persists even in areas exposed to high rates of hunting. Hunted for meat and persecuted for killing poultry. Red List LC, population trend Stable.

## LARGE INDIAN CIVET *Viverra zibetha*

HB 75–85cm; T 38–49.5cm; W 8–9kg
Large civet with a typical *Viverra* appearance, but in which the spots are indistinct and interconnected, giving a mottled or marbled appearance. Dark bands on the tail are very broad, and each band may have a brownish inner ring. Sometimes regarded as a distinct species in Vietnam, *V. tainguensis*, evidence for which is dubious. **Distribution and Habitat** S and C China, Nepal, Bhutan, NE India, Indochina to Peninsular Malaysia. Occurs mainly in evergreen and deciduous primary and secondary forests to 3,080m (India). Does not tolerate heavily modified habitat but inhabits plantations, and occurs near villages provided hunting pressure is modest. **Feeding Ecology** Omnivorous, with a similar diet to that of other *Viverra* species, but with more robust dentition that suggests greater carnivory. Diet includes small mammals, birds, herptiles, fish, eggs, insects, crabs and fruits. Kills domestic poultry. Foraging is solitary, nocturno-crepuscular and terrestrial. Scavenges from villages and dumps. **Social and Spatial Behaviour** Poorly known. Solitary and apparently non-territorial. Range estimates 2.7–12km² (Thailand). **Reproduction and Demography** Poorly known but thought to be aseasonal, with 2 litters per year. Gestation unknown. Litter size 1–4. MORTALITY Unknown. LIFESPAN 20 years in captivity. **Status and Threats** Still widespread and common in much of its range, with wide habitat tolerance. However, habitat loss and high levels of hunting constitute serious threats that have extirpated it from large areas, e.g. much of SE China. Large size and terrestrial habits make it especially vulnerable to hunting. CITES Appendix III – India; Red List LC, population trend Decreasing.

■ Malabar Civet

■ Large-spotted Civet

■ Malay Civet  ■ Large Indian Civet

**Plate 37**

MALABAR
CIVET

LARGE-SPOTTED
CIVET

MALAY
CIVET

LARGE INDIAN
CIVET

# SMALL INDIAN CIVET
## *Viverricula indica*

### LESSER ORIENTAL CIVET, RASSE
HB 45.5–68cm; T 30–43cm; W 2–4kg
Small terrestrial civet, buff-grey to tawny brown, marked with small brown or black spots running in longitudinal lines along the body. Lower limbs uniformly black or dark brown. Tail marked with alternating light and dark bands, and ending in a pale tip, distinguishing it from similar terrestrial civets. The most commonly kept Asian civet (mainly in India and Thailand) for perineal gland secretion used in perfume and traditional medicinal preparation. **Distribution and Habitat** S Asia, from E Pakistan through the Indian subcontinent, Sri Lanka, S and C China, Taiwan, Indochina, Sumatra, Java and Bali. Introduced in Madagascar, Zanzibar (Tanzania), Socotra (Yemen) and Comoros. Occurs in all kinds of forest, scrubland, grassland and riverine habitats to 2,500m. Thrives in disturbed and edge habitats, and is more common in degraded areas than in undisturbed closed-canopy forest. Lives in rural, agricultural and pastoral habitats. **Feeding Ecology** Omnivorous, eating a wide variety of mainly animal prey, especially small mammals, insects and earthworms. Also eats small birds, herptiles, eggs, crustaceans, arachnids, snails, fruits (including berries) and young buds. Raids domestic poultry. Foraging is strictly nocturno-crepuscular, with most activity taking place well after sundown. Forages alone, mostly on the ground; climbs well into the lower canopy to raid birds' nests and feed on fruits. Scavenges, including from carrion, villages and dumps. **Social and Spatial Behaviour** Solitary. Leaves faeces in prominent locations, but extent of territoriality is unclear; captive animals mark their surroundings prodigiously with the perineal scent gland, 6.3–8.2 times/2 hours (non-breeding) to 11.5–19.5 times/2 hours (breeding). Male range size 2.2–3.1km²; female range size poorly known but thought to be smaller. No density estimates, but often the most common small carnivore in secondary and degraded forests. **Reproduction and Demography** Poorly known in the wild. Captive animals (within their natural distribution) have 2 mating periods, February–May and August–December. Births occur November–February and May–July. Gestation 65–72 days. Litter size 2–5. Weaning at 2–3 months. MORTALITY Poorly known; most documented mortality is anthropogenic. LIFESPAN 9 years in captivity. **Status and Threats** Widespread, adaptable and common, including in altered habitats. In Southeast Asia and China, very often killed in snares for meat and for scent. Farmed for scent in India and increasingly in Thailand, where thousands of animals are kept in captivity; farm stock is maintained largely by taking animals from the wild, but the species is resilient to harvest and remains fairly widespread in areas of collection. Frequently killed on roads and by domestic dogs, probably reflecting the species' ability to reach high densities in anthropogenic habitats. CITES Appendix III – India; Red List LC, population trend Stable.

# AFRICAN CIVET
## *Civettictis civetta*

HB 67–84cm; T 34–47cm; W 7–20kg
Africa's only true civet species, and also its largest viverrid. Unmistakably marked with bold black spots and blotches on a buff to reddish-brown background, with dark lower limbs, a black facial mask and alternating black-and-white throat stripes. Black individuals occur, mostly in equatorial forest. Dark dorsal crest runs from the neck to the tail, which is raised in alarm. Kept in Ethiopia, Niger and Senegal for perineal gland secretion ('musk'), used in perfume manufacture. Ethiopia produces around 90% of the world's supply from >3,000 captive civets. **Distribution and Habitat** Widely distributed in most of sub-Saharan Africa except arid SW Africa. Inhabits most habitats with cover, including forest, wet and arid woodland savannah, scrubland, wetland, mangroves and montane heathland to 5,000m. Absent from very arid areas except along river courses. Occurs in modified habitats with cover, including secondary forest, plantations (especially 'coffee forest' – coffee with selectively maintained shade trees) and farmlands with cover. **Feeding Ecology** Omnivorous. Catholic diet, but the most important food groups are terrestrial insects (mainly beetles, locusts, grasshoppers, termites and millipedes), fruits and small mammals, which fluctuate in relative importance depending on seasonal availability, e.g. insects peak during the wet season. Also eats birds, eggs, herptiles, arachnids, snails, crabs, molluscs and shallow-water fish, e.g. mudskippers. Occasional larger vertebrate prey includes lagomorphs, Springhare, small mongooses and 1 record of a domestic cat. Tolerant of noxious foods such as millipedes, unripe *Strychnos* fruits and highly decayed carrion. Takes domestic poultry, and cultivated fruits and grains, including coffee berries (the passed beans are highly valued by coffee farmers in Ethiopia). Occasional claims of predation on lambs are dubious. Foraging is nocturno-crepuscular and solitary. Most hunting is terrestrial; climbs to feed on fruits, but is clumsy in trees. Scavenges, including from kills of larger carnivores, human refuse and handouts in tourist camps. **Social and Spatial Behaviour** Solitary. Deposits faeces in latrines or 'civetries', which may have territorial significance. Also scent-marks assiduously with its perineal scent gland on conspicuous natural and anthropogenic objects, including tree trunks, grass stems, rocks, fence posts and signposts. Scent marks are detectable to humans for up to 4 months in the dry season. Only range estimate is 11.1km² (subadult ♂; Ethiopian farmland). Density estimates 7.5–14.2/100km² (protected high-quality habitat, South Africa). **Reproduction and Demography** Thought to be aseasonal, with possible weak wet-season birth peaks in E and southern Africa. Captive females can have 2–3 litters a year, which likely applies in the wild. Gestation 60–81 days (captivity). Litter size 1–4, averaging 2–3. Weaning at 14–16 weeks. Females (captive) first give birth at 14–24 months. MORTALITY Confirmed predators include Lion (page 46), Leopard (page 48), Spotted Hyaena (page 54), African Wild Dog (page 110) and domestic dogs. Rabies occurs but population impacts are unknown. LIFESPAN 15 years in captivity. **Status and Threats** Widespread and relatively tolerant of habitat change. Sought after for meat in W and C Africa, and valued for traditional religious and medical beliefs in much of its range, which can denude populations locally, especially in concert with habitat loss. Civet farms rely on wild-caught animals, which may have local impacts, especially in Ethiopia. Often killed unintentionally during predator-control operations on southern African farmland, e.g. 6 civets are killed for every jackal (the intended target) in South Africa. CITES Appendix III – Botswana; Red List LC, population trend Unknown.

■ Small Indian Civet    ■ African Civet

**Plate 38**

**SMALL INDIAN CIVET**

Defensive posture

**AFRICAN CIVET**

Melanistic form

# ABYSSINIAN GENET *Genetta abyssinica*

### ETHIOPIAN GENET
HB 40.8–43cm; T 38–40.3cm; W 1.3–2kg
Pale sandy-grey genet with contrasting dark spots that form 2 unbroken stripes on each upper side. Dark dorsal stripe often splits into 2 narrow parallel stripes with a pale centre. Highland animals are darker, with wider dark stripes and tail bands. **Distribution and Habitat** Eritrea, Ethiopia, E Sudan, Djibouti and extreme NW Somalia. Inhabits montane forest, heath and dense alpine grassland to 3,750m; a few records from semi-arid lowland woodland savannah. **Feeding Ecology** Mainly carnivorous. Rodents (especially grass and brush-furred mice), small birds and insects comprise the main prey, based on a small scat collection in the dry season. Also eats fruits. Foraging is generally nocturnal, but highland animals are also diurnally active, possibly because Afro-alpine rodents are mainly diurnal. **Social and Spatial Behaviour** Unknown. All records are of solitary adults. **Reproduction and Demography** Unknown. **Status and Threats** Status unknown. There are only 20 museum specimens and a handful of field sightings, but the species has a wide altitudinal and habitat range. There is intense grazing and agricultural pressure in the highland areas of its range. Red List DD, population trend Unknown.

# HAUSA GENET *Genetta thierryi*

### THIERRY'S GENET
HB 44.3–45cm; T 40–43cm; W 1.3–1.5kg
Slender, pale genet with small, widely spaced rufous-brown spots on a yellow-buff background. Dorsal stripe may be indistinct until the mid-back. Rufous colouring often infuses the dark bands on the tail, especially those closest to the body. **Distribution and Habitat** W Africa, from N Senegal to Nigeria and Cameroon. Occurs in rainforest, dry and moist savannah woodland, and dry wooded steppe. **Feeding Ecology** Unknown. Assumed to be mainly carnivorous and nocturnal like other genets. **Social and Spatial Behaviour** Unknown. Assumed to be solitary. **Reproduction and Demography** Unknown. Subadults 8–10 months old recorded in November in S Mali, suggesting breeding coincides with the cool dry season, but this observation is based on very few records. Females have 2 pairs of teats. MORTALITY and LIFESPAN Unknown. **Status and Threats** Considered rare based on a few sightings and records, but intensive surveys are lacking. Large areas of its range are exposed to severe forest conversion and hunting. Red List LC, population trend Unknown.

# SERVALINE GENET *Genetta servalina*

HB 44.5–51cm; T 36.8–48.5cm; W *c*.2.3–3kg
Dark genet, densely marked with small, tightly spaced block-like spots, and with dark lower limbs. Has orderly rows of semi-connected spots along the spine that do not form a continuous dorsal stripe, and lacks a dorsal crest. **Distribution and Habitat** Equatorial Africa, encompassing the Congo Basin eastwards to W Kenya, with discontinuous populations in the Eastern Arc Mountains and Zanzibar, Tanzania. Occurs in rainforest, dense woodland savannah, thicket, bamboo forest and montane forest to 3,500m. **Feeding Ecology** Chiefly carnivorous. Rodents, shrews and invertebrates (mainly beetles, locusts, grasshoppers and termites) are the most important prey. Also eats small reptiles, birds and small amounts of fruits. Reportedly raids poultry on Zanzibar. Foraging is thought to be nocturnal and mainly terrestrial. Has been observed scavenging from carrion. **Social and Spatial Behaviour** Unknown. Assumed to be solitary from sightings and camera-trap images. **Reproduction and Demography** Unknown. Kittens reported from Uganda in February–August (few records). MORTALITY and LIFESPAN Unknown. **Status and Threats** Wide distribution, much of which comprises intact forest. Based on camera-trapping, common in some sites, e.g. Udzungwa Mountains, Tanzania. Forest loss, combined with bushmeat hunting, can be expected to produce local declines. Red List LC, population trend Unknown.

# CRESTED GENET *Genetta cristata*

### CRESTED SERVALINE GENET
HB 49.5–62.2cm; T *c*.43cm; W *c*.2.5kg
Slender, dark genet with oatmeal-coloured fur and dense, evenly spaced black spots that become stripes on the neck and shoulders. Wide black dorsal stripe can be erected as a crest. Head is long and narrow, with large eyes that give it a slightly bug-eyed appearance. **Distribution and Habitat** Endemic to SE Nigeria and SW Cameroon, with equivocal records from Gabon and Republic of the Congo. Inhabits dense lowland and montane forests to 1,000m. Occurs in secondary forest, forest–plantation mosaics and scrub near cultivated areas, but avoids human settlements. **Feeding Ecology** Small mammals and insects are the most important prey, based on a small number of records. Two captives allowed to roam freely also caught frogs and lizards. Nocturno-crepuscular. **Social and Spatial Behaviour** Unknown. Likely to be solitary. **Reproduction and Demography** Unknown. Records of pregnancies and kittens reported from late August–December. MORTALITY and LIFESPAN Unknown. **Status and Threats** Very restricted distribution that is exposed to high levels of forest loss and bushmeat hunting; both probably constitute serious threats. Unknown if it occurs in any protected areas. Red List VU, population trend Decreasing.

# GIANT GENET *Genetta victoriae*

HB 55–60cm; T 41.3–49cm; W 2.5–3.5kg
Dark-coloured genet with small, closely spaced spots that intermingle high on the sides to give an almost speckled appearance near the spine. Dark dorsal stripe is discontinuous and can be erected as a crest. Dark tail bands are very wide, with narrow pale bands in between. **Distribution and Habitat** Endemic to E DR Congo, possibly into W Rwanda (there is an equivocal photo record from Nyungwe Forest NP, Rwanda, 2005) and extreme SW Uganda. Occurs in rainforest and lowland deciduous forest. **Feeding Ecology** Unknown. Assumed to be similar to that of other genets. **Social and Spatial Behaviour** Unknown. Assumed to be solitary. **Reproduction and Demography** Unknown. Females have only 1 pair of teats, suggesting litters of 1–2. MORTALITY and LIFESPAN Unknown. **Status and Threats** Very poorly known, but has a relatively wide range, much of which comprises intact forest. Reported as locally common in some sites. Hunted for bushmeat and presumably vulnerable to forest loss. Red List LC, population trend Unknown.

■ Abyssinian Genet ■ Hausa Genet    ■ Crested Genet
■ Sevaline Genet                ■ Giant Genet

**Plate 39**

ABYSSINIAN
GENET

HAUSA
GENET

SERVALINE
GENET

CRESTED
GENET

GIANT GENET

# SMALL-SPOTTED GENET
*Genetta genetta*

### COMMON GENET
HB 46.5–52cm; T 42–51.6cm; W ♀ 1.4–2.3kg, ♂ 1.6–2.6kg
Pale grey to buff-grey genet, marked with small black spots that become blotches on the neck and shoulders. Black erectile dorsal crest. Tail has a white tip, distinguishing it from other sympatric genets. Namibian–South African population is sometimes considered a separate species, the Feline Genet or South African Small-spotted Genet (*G. felina*). **Distribution and Habitat** Ubiquitous in Africa, except in the Sahara, Congo Basin and a narrow band across N Mozambique and Zambia; also occurs in Portugal, Spain, France (European populations are likely introduced ~eighth century CE or earlier), SW Saudi Arabia, coastal Yemen and Oman. Occupies many habitats, including forest, woodland, scrubland, wooded grassland and rocky areas. Tolerates modified habitats with cover, including plantations and agricultural areas. **Feeding Ecology** Eats mainly small rodents and insectivores, as well as birds, herptiles, arthropods, eggs and small amounts of fruits, including berries. Sometimes raids poultry. Foraging is solitary, mainly nocturnal, and both arboreal and terrestrial. Scavenges from carrion and food waste at tourist camps and villages. **Social and Spatial Behaviour** Solitary. Male ranges overlap multiple female ranges, with low intrasexual overlap. Range estimates known mainly from Europe: 0.33–11.9km². Density estimated at 0.33–0.98/km² (Spain). **Reproduction and Demography** Apparently weakly seasonal, with 2 birth peaks per year in E and N Africa and Europe (March–June and September–December), and 1 peak in southern Africa (September–February). Gestation 70–77 days. Litter size 1–5, averaging 2. MORTALITY Killed by many larger predators; predation from Iberian Lynx (page 34) possibly reduces density (Spain). LIFESPAN 21.6 years in captivity. **Status and Threats** Widely distributed, common and occupies a wide variety of habitats. Hunted in some areas for meat and fetishes, and disappears from areas of intense habitat conversion. Red List LC, population trend Stable.

# MIOMBO GENET *Genetta angolensis*

### ANGOLAN GENET
HB 44–48cm; T 38–43cm; W *c*.1.5–2.5kg
Small, slender genet. Grizzled ochre, tinged with brown or grey, and marked with brown to black spots. Black dorsal stripe and mid-dorsal crest, dark lower hind legs and a dark-tipped tail. Melanistic individuals occur. **Distribution and Habitat** Endemic to SC Africa, from C Tanzania/N Mozambique through Malawi, Zambia, S DR Congo and Angola. Restricted to open moist miombo woodland and wooded grassland. **Feeding Ecology** Poorly known. One dead specimen (Kafue NP, Zambia) had eaten insects, fruits and grass. Small vertebrates are likely to be important prey. All records nocturno-crepuscular. **Social and Spatial Behaviour** Unknown. Likely to be solitary.

**Reproduction and Demography** Unknown. **Status and Threats** Status unknown, but widespread and often common throughout Africa's miombo woodlands, which are relatively intact. Presumably killed for meat and fetishes (like all genets). Red List LC, population trend Unknown.

# JOHNSTON'S GENET *Genetta johnstoni*

HB 47–51.4cm; T 46.2–49.5cm; W 2.2–2.6kg
Small, slender genet with a narrow, elongated face and slightly bug-eyed appearance. Coat is yellowish grey with tightly spaced, dark brown or rufous-brown spots. Spots coalesce into 1–2 broken stripes along the upper sides, above which there is a black dorsal stripe. Lower limbs blackish. Tail has a dirty white tip with a faint dark band. **Distribution and Habitat** Endemic to coastal W Africa, from SE Senegal to extreme SW Ghana. Occurs in rainforest and associated dense habitat, including swamp forest, with 2 records from moist woodland savanna. **Feeding Ecology** Poorly known, but reduced dentition suggests arthropods are a chief component of the diet. Primarily nocturnal. **Social and Spatial Behaviour** Unknown. Likely to be solitary. **Reproduction and Demography** Unknown. Females have only 2 teats, suggesting small litters of 1–2. MORTALITY Crowned Eagle is a confirmed predator. LIFESPAN Unknown. **Status and Threats** Very restricted distribution and appears partially or wholly dependent on forest that is under intense pressure in W Africa from agriculture, logging and mining. Also faces severe hunting pressure across much of its range. Seen frequently in parks such as Tai NP (Côte d'Ivoire), the protection of which is increasingly necessary for its conservation. Red List NT, population trend Decreasing.

# AQUATIC GENET *Genetta piscivora*

### FISHING GENET
HB 44.5–49.5cm; T 34–41.5cm; W *c*.1.5kg
Unique genet with dense, dull red to chestnut-red fur; lacks markings, but sometimes has a dark dorsal line. Bushy tail is black and lower limbs are blackish. Face has conspicuous white brows between the eyes, white patches under the eyes, and white cheeks, chin and throat. **Distribution and Habitat** Endemic to E DR Congo, between the Congo River and Rift Valley. May occur in W Uganda and Nyungwe Forest NP, Rwanda, but there are no unequivocal records. Only around 30 known records, all from rainforest at 460–1,500m, mostly near very small streams with sandy bottoms. **Feeding Ecology** Believed to eat primarily fish. Stomachs of collected specimens contained only fish, and captive animals steadfastly refuse frogs, crustaceans and mice. Captives use a unique hunting method: they slap the surface of water and rest the tips of their long whiskers on it, thought to flush fish and detect vibrations from their movement. After several 'tests', they submerge the head to capture a fish with a swift open-mouthed lunge, taking barbell, catfish, squeaker and *Labeo* carp measuring up to 30cm. A captive kitten a few weeks old instinctively tapped the surface when first presented with a dish of water. **Social and Spatial Behaviour** Unknown. Thought to be solitary. **Reproduction and Demography** Unknown. Single record of a pregnant female, collected in December with 1 foetus. MORTALITY and LIFESPAN Unknown. **Status and Threats** Considered naturally rare, based on reports from local hunters and trappers, and the very low frequencies in which it appears in wildlife and market surveys. Opportunistically hunted in some areas for bushmeat, but the extent to which this represents a threat is unknown. Fully protected in DR Congo, but protection is nominal in much of its range. Red List NT, population trend Decreasing.

■ Small-spotted Genet

■ Miombo Genet  ■ Johnston's Genet
■ Aquatic Genet

**Plate 40**

SMALL-SPOTTED
GENET

MIOMBO
GENET

JOHNSTON'S
GENET

AQUATIC
GENET

# RUSTY-SPOTTED GENET
*Genetta maculata*

### CENTRAL AFRICAN LARGE-SPOTTED GENET
HB 41.1–52.1cm; T 39.5–54cm; W ♀ 1.3–2.5kg, ♂ 1.4–3.2kg
Sandy-grey to rufous-grey genet with large blotches, usually rufous-brown surrounded by a black border, or solid black with a rufous tinge. No dorsal crest. Tail has a black tip. **Distribution and Habitat** Sub-Saharan Africa, from S Burkina Faso and W Ghana to Eritrea, south to C Namibia and KwaZulu-Natal, South Africa. Occurs in forest, woodland and moist savannah, and absent from very arid habitat. Inhabits cultivated areas, plantations and peri-urban areas. **Feeding Ecology** Mainly carnivorous, with rodents and insects comprising the most important prey, but eats a very wide range of small vertebrates and invertebrates. Rarely kills mammals to the size of juvenile Red Duiker. Occasionally eats fruits and seeds; a population in the Shimba Hills, Kenya, atypically eats mainly fruits and seeds. Raids domestic poultry. Foraging is solitary, nocturnal, and both arboreal and terrestrial. Scavenges, including handouts and refuse at tourist camps and from kills of large carnivores. **Social and Spatial Behaviour** Solitary. Adults mark their ranges assiduously, including at large latrines used by multiple individuals, but aggressive territorial defence is rare. Average range estimates 2.8km$^2$ (♀s) to 5.9km$^2$ (♂s) in Kenya. **Reproduction and Demography** Weakly seasonal. Breeding associated with the warm wet season, peaking August–March (southern Africa), and October–May (E Africa). Gestation 70–77 days. Litter size 2–5. MORTALITY Many mammalian and avian predators, but rates are unknown. LIFESPAN Unknown. **Status and Threats** Widely distributed, common and occupies many habitats, including anthropogenic areas. Persecuted for killing poultry, and hunted for meat and fetishes; thousands are killed in South Africa for religious regalia worn by the 'Shembe' Nazareth Baptists. Red List LC, population trend Unknown.

# CAPE GENET *Genetta tigrina*

### LARGE-SPOTTED GENET
HB 43–56cm; T 39–46cm; W ♀ 1.4–1.9kg, ♂ 1.6–2.1kg
Very similar to Rusty-spotted Genet, with which it was formerly classified. Differs in having a mid-dorsal crest (apparent only when alarmed), and generally has larger, more widely spaced blotches. The 2 species overlap in S KwaZulu-Natal near the Eastern Cape provincial border. **Distribution and Habitat** Endemic to South Africa, from S KwaZulu-Natal to Western Cape, and extreme E Lesotho. Occurs in mesic habitats along the coastal strip, including forest, woodland, dense grassland and fynbos. Tolerates anthropogenic habitats with cover. **Feeding Ecology** Very similar to that of Rusty-spotted Genet; small vertebrates and invertebrates are the main prey. Raids domestic poultry. Foraging is solitary, nocturnal, and both arboreal and terrestrial. Scavenges from dumps and at tourist camps; likely to scavenge carrion. **Social and Spatial Behaviour** Solitary. Less well known than Rusty-spotted Genet, but spatial patterns are

essentially the same. Range estimates unknown. **Reproduction and Demography** Poorly known. Breeding records cluster December–February. Litter size 1–3. MORTALITY Has many predators, but death rates are unknown. LIFESPAN 9.5 years in captivity. **Status and Threats** Common and widespread in a limited distribution. Killed for taking poultry and hunted for bushmeat, but effects on populations are apparently minimal except in concert with severe habitat modification. Thousands are killed in South Africa for religious regalia worn by the 'Shembe' Nazareth Baptists. Red List LC, population trend Stable.

# PARDINE GENET *Genetta pardina*

### WEST AFRICAN LARGE-SPOTTED GENET
HB 41–55.3cm; T 39–49cm; W to 3.1kg
Similar to both Rusty-spotted and Cape genets, with which it was formerly classified. Small rectangular, dark brown or rufous-brown spots, and no dorsal crest. **Distribution and Habitat** Endemic to W Africa from the Mauritania–Senegal border to the Ghana–Togo border. Occurs in forest, woodland and moist scrubland. Inhabits plantations and cultivated areas with cover. **Feeding Ecology** Poorly known; rodents, invertebrates and fruits occur in the stomachs of dead specimens. Primarily nocturnal. **Social and Spatial Behaviour** Unknown. Likely to be solitary. **Reproduction and Demography** Unknown. Records of young suggest breeding January–February. MORTALITY and LIFESPAN Unknown. **Status and Threats** Restricted distribution, but it is a habitat generalist and considered common. Frequently appears in bushmeat markets, which may constitute a local threat. Red List LC, population trend Unknown.

# KING GENET *Genetta poensis*

HB *c.*60cm; T *c.*41.5cm; W *c.*2–2.5kg
Dark genet with elongated rectangular black or dark brown spots that often coalesce into long blotches in closely spaced rows. Formerly classified with Pardine Genet. Known from only 10 museum specimens; no wild records since 1946. **Distribution and Habitat** Endemic to coastal W and C Africa, from Liberia to Republic of the Congo; unequivocal presence limited to 3 patches in Liberia/W Côte d'Ivoire, S Ghana and coastal Republic of the Congo, but distribution may be more continuous. Recently reported from bushmeat markets in S Nigeria, but identification is equivocal. All records are from intact rainforest. **Feeding Ecology** Assumed to be similar to that of other genets. **Social and Spatial Behaviour** Unknown. Assumed to be solitary. **Reproduction and Demography** Unknown. **Status and Threats** Status unknown. Mostly known from hunters and markets, suggesting hunting is a threat, especially in W Africa. Large areas of rainforest are intact in much of its possible range, e.g. Gabon, where it would be considered secure if present. Red List DD, population trend Unknown.

# BOURLON'S GENET *Genetta bourloni*

HB *c.*49.5cm; T *c.*41cm; W *c.*1.5–2kg
Similar to Pardine Genet but much darker, with dark spots that often fuse into long blotches, especially on the neck, shoulders and rump. Tail dark with broad bands connected by a dark dorsal line. Formerly classified with Pardine Genet, but recognised as a separate species in 2003 from 29 museum specimens. **Distribution and Habitat** Endemic to Liberia, E Sierra Leone, S Guinea and W Côte d'Ivoire, where it occurs only in rainforest. **Feeding Ecology** Unknown. Assumed to be similar to that of other genet species. **Social and Spatial Behaviour** Unknown. Assumed to be solitary. **Reproduction and Demography** Unknown. **Status and Threats** Very restricted distribution, and exposed to high levels of forest loss and bushmeat hunting. Red List VU, population trend Decreasing.

■ Rusty-spotted Genet  ■ Cape Genet  ■ King Genet
■ Pardine Genet  ■ Bourlon's Genet

Plate 41

RUSTY-SPOTTED
GENET

CAPE GENET

KING GENET

PARDINE
GENET

BOURLON'S
GENET

# LEIGHTON'S OYAN *Poiana leightoni*

### WEST AFRICAN LINSANG, LEIGHTON'S LINSANG

HB 30–38cm; T 35–40cm; W 0.5–0.7kg

Very small, slender genet-like species, with soft yellow-buff fur fading to white or creamy-white underparts. Marked with irregular oval, dark brown blotches that become small spots on the limbs and neck. Tail has 10–12 chevron-shaped dark rings. Has been considered a subspecies of Central African Oyan, with which it does not overlap. **Distribution and Habitat** Endemic to W Africa, confirmed only in SW Côte d'Ivoire and W Liberia. Presence in SW Guinea needs confirmation. All records are from rainforest. **Feeding Ecology** Unknown. Size and dentition suggest it eats small vertebrates such as rodents, birds and herptiles, as well as invertebrates. Arboreal with protractile claws, and thought to forage mainly in the canopy. **Social and Spatial Behaviour** Unknown. Assumed to be solitary. Local people (Liberia) report that it builds nests from leaves in the tree canopy similar to squirrels' dreys, which may be occupied by a number of individuals. **Reproduction and Demography** Unknown. **Status and Threats** One of the least known carnivores, confirmed from only 12 museum records. The most recent records are 2 skins collected in E Liberia in 1988–89. Restricted to a very localised range that is exposed to high levels of forest loss and bushmeat hunting. Both are considered serious threats, but the species' current status is entirely unknown. Red List VU, population trend Decreasing.

# CENTRAL AFRICAN OYAN
*Poiana richardsonii*

### AFRICAN LINSANG, RICHARDSON'S LINSANG

HB 32–40cm; T 34–40.2cm; W ♀ 0.45–0.5kg, ♂ 0.51–0.75kg

Very similar to Leighton's Oyan. Distinguished by slightly darker background coloration, yellow-brown with a grey or reddish cast, which is more densely marked with spots and blotches. Markings sometimes coalesce into elongated blotches or stripes along the back and dorsal area. Tail has 10–12 wide bands interspersed with narrow 'shadow' rings that are more distinct than in Leighton's Oyan. **Distribution and Habitat** Endemic to the Congo Basin, in S Cameroon, extreme S Central African Republic, Equatorial Guinea (including Bioko Island, where it is the only native carnivore), Gabon, Republic of the Congo and DR Congo to the Rift Valley. Occurs in lowland and montane rainforests. **Feeding Ecology** Unknown. Assumed to have a diet similar to that predicted for Leighton's Oyan. All records are nocturno-crepuscular. Arboreal, but has been observed on the ground, where it probably also forages. **Social and Spatial Behaviour** Unknown. All sightings and records are of solitary animals. **Reproduction and Demography** Unknown. One record of a female lactating in October (Cameroon), and local people report it has 2 offspring, but there are no verified records. MORTALITY and LIFESPAN Unknown. **Status and Threats** Status unknown. Assuming it occurs throughout the Congo Basin, there are large

areas of intact forest where it is probably secure. Occasionally appears in the bushmeat trade, e.g. Bioko Island, although it is probably not especially sought after due to its very small size and arboreal, nocturnal habits. Forest loss, combined with hunting, is likely to produce local declines. Red List LC, population trend Unknown.

# AFRICAN PALM-CIVET
*Nandinia binotata*

### NANDINIA, TWO-SPOTTED PALM-CIVET

HB 37–62.5cm; T 34–76.2cm; W 1.2–3kg

Classified as the only species in the family Nandiniidae and not closely related to Asian palm civets (Paradoxurinae; page 82). Medium-sized genet-like species with a long tail that equals or exceeds the head–body length. Dense woolly fur, greyish brown to rusty brown on upperparts and paler buff-yellow on underparts. Lightly marked with small, dark brown spots and a unique pale spot on each shoulder; limbs are unmarked. Tail has faint dark rings that can be difficult to distinguish in some individuals. Claws are partially protractile. **Distribution and Habitat** Sub-Saharan Africa, from Senegal along coastal W Africa, through the Congo Basin to Uganda, Kenya, Tanzania (including Unguja, Zanzibar), Malawi, W Mozambique and extreme E Zimbabwe. Primarily a forest species, living in lowland and montane forests to 2,500m, forest–savannah mosaics and moist woodland savannah. Occurs in logged and disturbed forests, and in forest patches near cultivated areas. **Feeding Ecology** Primarily frugivorous. Around 80% of the diet is made up of a wide variety of wild and cultivated fruits, especially figs, African Corkwood, Sugar Plum and the pulp of African Oil Palm nuts. Commonly eaten cultivated fruits include banana, passionfruit and pawpaw. Balance of the diet consists of small mammals, birds, fledglings, eggs and arthropods. Efficient nest raider, including of weavers' nests at the ends of very thin branches, which are negotiated easily. Kills mammals to the size of Pottos and juvenile monkeys, although these rarely appear in the diet. Raids domestic poultry. Extremely agile in trees; able to hang from branches by its hind feet and descend trees rapidly head first. Foraging is nocturnal and solitary. Forages both arboreally and terrestrially; insects, fallen fruits and rodents are taken on the ground. Scavenges from carrion and village dumps, and known to drink fermenting sap from tapping vessels on palm trees. **Social and Spatial Behaviour** Solitary and territorial. Male ranges overlap multiple smaller female ranges. Fights between resident males are sometimes fatal. Unclear if territories are maintained only while breeding; there is evidence of seasonal nomadism during fruiting peaks, e.g. 12–15 individuals moving into 1km of forested valley to exploit localised fruiting of African Corkwoods. Range estimates 0.29–0.7km² (♀s) and 0.34–1.53km² (♂s). Density estimated at 2.2–3.3/km² (Bwindi Impenetrable NP, Uganda) and 5–8/km² (Gabon). **Reproduction and Demography** Thought to be weakly seasonal, with births peaking in wet periods, e.g. September–January (Gabon), and May and October (Uganda). Gestation ~64 days. Litter size 1–4, typically 2. Sexual maturity 1 year. MORTALITY Unknown. LIFESPAN 16.4 years in captivity. **Status and Threats** Widely distributed and reaches high densities in suitable habitat. Often considered the most abundant small carnivore in C African rainforest; this is supported by its common appearance in wildlife markets, e.g. Equatorial Guinea and Nigeria, but status in most of its range has never been assessed. Likely undergoing localised declines from a combination of forest loss and heavy hunting pressure. Red List LC, population trend Unknown.

■ Leighton's Oyan

■ African Palm-civet

■ Central African Oyan

**Plate 42**

LEIGHTON'S OYAN

CENTRAL
AFRICAN OYAN

AFRICAN
PALM-CIVET

Descending head first

# DINGO *Canis lupus familiaris/ Canis familiaris*

Includes **NEW GUINEA SINGING DOG OR NEW GUINEA HIGHLAND WILD DOG** *C. dingo hallstromi/C. hallstromi*
HB ♀ 70.3–101cm; ♂ 75–111cm; T 20–37cm;
W ♀ 8–17kg, ♂ 7–22kg

The Dingo has been classified as a distinct species, *Canis dingo*, or a subspecies of the Grey Wolf (page 100), *C. lupus dingo*, i.e. derived from a regional population of Grey Wolves in Asia independently of the lineage leading to the domestic dog (*C. l. familiaris/C. familiaris*). The New Guinea Singing Dog (named for its distinctive melodic howl; also known as New Guinea Highland Wild Dog) has been classified as both a subspecies of the Dingo, *C. dingo hallstromi*, and as a full species, *C. hallstromi*. A recent and comprehensive review, including genetic analyses, concluded that the 2 forms are very closely related and together comprise an ancient breed (or breeds) of domestic dog that likely arose in Southeast Asia perhaps ~10,000 years after the effective genetic separation of domestic dogs from the ancestral Grey Wolf population. Accordingly, from an evolutionary perspective, the Dingo is most correctly regarded as an archaic domestic dog that later became established in the wild. Based on fossil evidence, the Dingo colonised Australia at least 3,500–4,000 years ago, probably in association with humans; there is limited, unresolved genetic evidence that this occurred without human assistance as early as 8,300 BCE, when a land bridge connected New Guinea and Australia. Regardless, Australia is now the only place where the Dingo unequivocally lives wild. In New Guinea and Southeast Asia, it is primarily associated with humans, although often in a semi-feral state. Australian Dingoes are approximately the size of a Border Collie; New Guinea Singing Dogs have a shorter body length and shorter legs, giving them a smaller, stockier appearance. Usually tawny ginger; pale sandy, white (not albino) and black-and-tan variants occur. Tail tip and paws are usually white or cream. Sable (Alsatian-like), brindled and piebald coloration typically indicates hybridisation with modern (of European descent) domestic dogs.

## Distribution and Habitat
Commensal with humans in S Myanmar, Thailand, Laos, Cambodia, Vietnam, Malaysia, Indonesia, Borneo, Philippines, Sulawesi and New Guinea; wild in Australia, where it inhabits desert, grassland, woodland savannah, wetland, alpine moorland and forest. Occurs in rural habitats, including extensive livestock production areas, and in peri-urban areas provided there is sufficient habitat and prey. Wild populations mostly avoid intensive agriculture, although extensive sugar-cane monocultures with associated bushland are important habitats for peri-urban Dingoes (Queensland).

## Feeding Ecology
Very broad diet; 177 prey species recorded from Australia, with mammals comprising around 75% of the diet on average. At least 1 macropod – especially Red Kangaroo, Euro, and Swamp, Agile and Red-necked wallabies – features prominently in the diet across its range. Other important prey includes wombats, brushtail possums, bandicoots, introduced European Rabbit and Magpie Goose. Small rodents, mainly Spinifex Hopping-mouse, Sandy Inland Mouse, Long-haired Rat and introduced House Mouse, dominate the diet of Simpson Desert Dingoes during rodent population irruptions. A very wide variety of other items are opportunistically eaten, usually forming a small proportion of the diet, including birds, reptiles, crocodile and turtle eggs, invertebrates, fruits and seeds. Dingoes on Fraser Island (Queensland) eat mainly small to medium-sized mammals, especially Northern Brown Bandicoot, with relatively high proportions of seeds, fruits and large skinks, as well as marine species hunted and scavenged along the shore. After bandicoot, fish – almost all scavenged from people's fishing waste – are the second-most common dietary item for Fraser Island Dingoes. They also consume crustaceans and molluscs, and scavenge stranded marine turtles, whales, dolphins, Dugongs and New Zealand Fur Seal. Occasionally cannibalistic. Kills sheep, goats and cattle calves. Foraging is mainly nocturno-crepuscular, but diurnal where the Dingo is free from persecution. Forages alone or socially; large prey such as kangaroos are usually hunted cooperatively in packs, which increases hunting success, e.g. from 5.5% (alone) to 19% (packs) when hunting Red Kangaroos. Scavenges, including from livestock carcasses, human-killed feral animals (especially pigs and deer), human refuse and recreational fishing waste. Peri-urban Dingoes in Queensland eat pet food, but only rarely; diet is mainly natural rather than from human sources.

## Social and Spatial Behaviour
Free from persecution, lives in stable packs of 2–12 adults and their pups in enduring home ranges. Territorial, but often shares important resources such as waterholes with neighbouring packs. Breeding is often restricted to the alpha pair, and other pack members help raise pups by provisioning and guarding. Under persecution (around half of its Australian range), social structure may be fractured, so that packs are smaller and less stable. Individuals associate in loose 'tribes', sharing a range that is not actively defended, and foraging is mostly solitary. Size of pack territories: 4–55km² (moist, cool forest) and 32–126km² (Simpson Desert), to more than 300km² in Australian desert areas generally.

## Reproduction and Demography
Breeding is generally seasonal, most strongly in arid C Australia. Dingoes (including New Guinea Singing Dogs) differ from modern domestic dog breeds in having only a single breeding season per year. Mating period peaks April–June; births peak June–August. Gestation 61–69 days. Litter size 1–10, averaging 5. Most females first breed at around 24 months; males sexually mature at 12 months, but breeding is limited by social dynamics. Females can breed until 11 years (wild). MORTALITY Highly variable depending on the level of human persecution; on average, approximately two-thirds of Dingoes die before 2 years from natural causes (primarily starvation and intraspecific killing, including infanticide). Persecution by people is the next most significant cause of mortality, especially for adults. Occasionally killed by Water Buffalo, Red Kangaroo and Wedge-tailed Eagle (pups). LIFESPAN 13.3 years in the wild, 20 in captivity.

## Status and Threats
Widespread in Australia, where it is protected in national parks, World Heritage sites and Aboriginal reserves. Elsewhere, legally regarded as a pest and persecuted, mainly in livestock-producing landscapes, including by state-sanctioned trapping and poisoning. Persecution is intense in some areas, but Dingo populations are very resilient and capable of rapid recovery. Hybridisation from modern (European) domestic dogs threatens the integrity of the ancient Dingo genotypes, worthy of conserving in their own right (even if only for what they might reveal about the early stages of dog domestication). Pure Dingoes are most common in C and N Australia, rare/possibly extinct in S and NE Australia, and probably extinct in SE and SW areas. Without intensive conservation effort, pure Dingo genotypes are unlikely to persist except perhaps on islands (e.g. Fraser Island) or in very remote areas (e.g. Tanami Desert). Red List VU, population trend Increasing overall (including hybrids), purebreds Decreasing.

■ Dingo

**Plate 43**

New Guinea
Singing Dog

Howling

**DINGO**

Black form

Typical form

Pale form

# GREY WOLF *Canis lupus*

### TIMBER WOLF, ARCTIC WOLF, TUNDRA WOLF

HB ♀ 87–117cm, ♂ 100–130cm; T 35–50cm;
SH 66–81cm; W ♀ 18–55kg, ♂ 20–79.4kg

The world's largest canid, with significant variation in size and coloration. Largest individuals (Alaska and Canada) are 3–6 times as heavy as Middle Eastern and S Asian wolves. Typically pale to dark grey, but highly variable, e.g. ginger in E to C Asia ('Himalayan Wolf' or 'Tibetan Wolf'), brown in W to N Eurasia, and white, especially in N Canada ('Arctic Wolf'). Black coloration is rare outside forested North America, and traces to interbreeding with early domesticated dogs 10,000–15,000 years ago. Grey Wolves hybridise with Coyotes (page 102), particularly in areas where Grey Wolves, and hence conspecific mates, are rare. Grey Wolf is the progenitor of the domestic dog, and they can interbreed. Dingo (page 98), treated here as a domestic dog variant, is sometimes classified as a Grey Wolf subspecies. Twelve Grey Wolf subspecies are described, most on the basis of morphology, which is unreliable. Genetically, the most distinct lineages are the Mexican Wolf (*C. l. baileyi*); wolves of coastal SE Alaska, usually recognised as *C. l. ligoni*; and Himalayan Wolves (*C. l. himalayensis*; Himalayas to Tibetan Plateau), which some scientists treat as a separate species, *C. himalayensis*.

### Distribution and Habitat

North America and Eurasia, formerly one of the most widespread mammals. Widespread in Canada and Alaska, extirpated in the lower USA except in the N Rockies and N Midwest, and relict in SW USA–Mexico, where reintroduction has established 100–110 Mexican Wolves. Widespread in Russia and C Asia, fragmented and reduced in SW Asia, the Middle East, and W and N Europe. Occupies many habitat types, including desert (to 50°C), open plains, steppe, mountainous areas, swamps, forest and Arctic tundra (to –56°C). Although tolerant of habitat modification, rarely inhabits agricultural and pastoral areas due to intense anthropogenic persecution.

### Feeding Ecology

Highly opportunistic and proficient pack hunter. Diet varies extensively by region and season, but medium to large ungulates are usually the mainstay, e.g. Musk-ox, bison, Moose, Elk, Red Deer, Reindeer/Caribou, White-tailed Deer, roe deer, wild sheep, ibex and Wild Boar. Juvenile and debilitated individuals are more often killed, but even a single Grey Wolf is capable of killing healthy adults, especially during winter. When ungulates are less vulnerable (spring–summer), the diet is more diverse, with increased consumption of beavers, hares, rodents, waterfowl, fish and fruits. Kills smaller carnivores, especially Coyotes, and occasionally Pumas (page 38) and young Black Bears (page 136), Brown Bears (page 138) and (exceptionally) Polar Bears (page 140). Livestock is readily killed, especially during spring–summer, when wild prey disperses and stock occupies productive grazing areas; livestock (including semi-domestic Reindeer) is the most important prey for many Eurasian populations. Unprovoked attacks on humans are very rare and usually attributed to rabies,

e.g. 2 fatalities by healthy wolves in North America since 1900. Hunting is cathemeral, with greater diurnalism where it is protected. Hunting is highly social; pack members exchange the lead in chases and cooperatively bring down large prey. Can reach 64km/h and has extraordinary endurance, maintaining pursuit to 8km (with an exceptional record of 21km). Hunting success rates 10–49% for packs (North America). Scavenges, including from refuse dumps and appropriated carcasses from other carnivores.

### Social and Spatial Behaviour

Highly social and territorial, living in packs numbering up to 42 but typically 2–15. Nucleus of the pack is a mated adult pair, accompanied by adult offspring. Pack size fluctuates depending on dispersal of offspring, which is affected by food availability. Dispersal is low in productive years, producing large packs with up to 4 generations of grown offspring. Most offspring ultimately disperse and seek non-related adults to form new packs. Recruitment of unrelated individuals (especially to replace a lost breeder) or small groups of dispersers occurs occasionally in established packs. Packs occupy enduring ranges that are usually defended aggressively from other packs. Range size 33–4,335km², averaging 69–2,600km². Ranges increase locally during winter and with increasing latitude; largest ranges recorded are from Alaska and the Canadian Arctic. Wolves following migratory herds have massive ranges of 63,000–100,000km² annually that are not defended. Density estimates 5/1,000km² (NW Alaska) to 92/1,000km² (Isle Royale, Canada), but rarely exceeding 40/1,000km².

### Reproduction and Demography

Seasonal. Mating January–April depending on latitude, with pups born March–June. Gestation 60–75 days, typically 62–65. Litter size 1–13, averaging 4–7. Pack's dominant female is normally the only breeder, although multiple females (probably close relatives) occasionally breed under high prey availability. All pack members help raise pups by provisioning the mother and pups at the den, and by defending pups from predators. Weaning at around 8–10 weeks. Pups leave the den permanently and travel continually with the pack from 4–6 months by September–October. Dispersal is usually at 11–24 months, but is recorded at 5–60 months. Inter-litter interval typically 12 months; 2 litters a year produced on rare occasions. Sexual maturity at around 10 months for both sexes, although breeding opportunities rarely arise before 3 years. MORTALITY Annual pup mortality averages 34%, ranging from 9% (Denali NP, Alaska) to 61% (N Wisconsin). Adult mortality from 14%, to 44% where heavily persecuted. Human hunting and trapping are often the main cause; in unexploited populations, starvation (mostly of pups) and aggression from other wolves are the main factors. Disease is an important cause of death, although population effects are poorly known. Wolves occasionally die in hunting accidents and are killed by bears, Puma (page 38) and Amur Tiger (page 44). LIFESPAN 13 years in the wild, 17 in captivity.

### Status and Threats

Widespread and stable in most of its northern range, especially in Alaska, Canada, Kazakhstan and Russia (total combined estimate 113,000–127,000 wolves). None the less, it has lost an estimated third of its historic range, mainly in the USA/Mexico, W Europe and S Asia, where it is mostly threatened or endangered. Chief threat is persecution by humans, often as part of state-sanctioned control programmes. Diseases, especially canine parvovirus, mange and rabies produce local declines. Reintroduction of 31 individuals to Yellowstone NP in 1995–96 has been highly successful, growing to approximately 1,900 animals in 6 states in 2016; reintroduction to the SW USA (Mexican Wolf subspecies) has been less successful. Legally hunted and trapped in at least 15 countries, with the largest numbers killed in Canada (4,000 annually), Russia (10,000–20,000 annually) and Mongolia. CITES Appendix I – Bhutan, India, Nepal and Pakistan, Appendix II – elsewhere; Red List LC, population trend Stable.

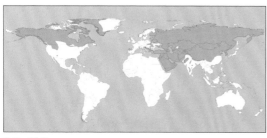
■ Grey Wolf

**Plate 44**

**GREY WOLF**

Pack howling

Arabian form

Mexican form

Tibetan form

Eurasian form

# COYOTE *Canis latrans*

### BRUSH WOLF, PRAIRIE WOLF

HB 74–95cm; T 26–46cm; W ♀ 7.7–14.8kg (exceptionally to 25kg), ♂ 7.7–18.1kg (exceptionally to 34kg)

Generally uniformly coloured, from frosted grey to rufous-brown, with pale underparts and often a greyish or 'salt-and-pepper' saddle. Tail is typically infused with dark brown to black hairs, and usually dark-tipped (rarely white-tipped). Varies very widely geographically and seasonally; northern and winter individuals are generally larger and paler/greyer. Rufous sides, outer legs and backs of ears are common in eastern and southern (including Central American) individuals. Melanistic, leucistic, brindled, sable (Alsatian-like) and blond individuals occur, particularly in eastern North America, where admixture with domestic dogs is most prevalent ('Eastern Coyote', page 104).

### Distribution and Habitat

N Alaska and Canada (except NE Canada), throughout the USA and Meso-America to Panama. Recorded east of the Panama Canal for the first time in 2013; not confirmed from Colombia (as of 2017). At the time of European settlement, Coyotes were restricted to non-forested W and C North America. Habitat conversion, with a concomitant increase in White-tailed Deer and extirpation of Grey Wolves (page 100), fostered their expansion across virtually the entire North American continent and Meso-America in 200 years. Now inhabits virtually all habitat types, from Arctic tundra to deserts, tropical and montane forest, and heavily modified anthropogenic habitats, including all kinds of agricultural land and suburban–urban areas, even in large cities, e.g. Chicago and New York.

### Feeding Ecology

Extremely opportunistic generalist that consumes virtually any edible food source. Vertebrate prey is most important, mainly rodents (chiefly squirrels, mice and voles), lagomorphs, juvenile ungulates and carrion. A wide variety of other small to medium-sized mammals are also taken incidentally, including armadillos, Virginia Opossums and mesocarnivores, e.g. Northern Raccoons (page 142), Striped Skunks (page 150), foxes and Bobcats (page 36; probably juveniles). Capable of killing adult large ungulates, including 4 recent records of 2–5 Coyotes killing Moose older than 20 months (Ontario, Canada), but large mammals are rarely killed, and debilitated individuals, such as those weakened in deep snow, are usually targeted. Scavenging of winter- and wolf-killed large ungulates is particularly important to northern populations, e.g. scavenged Moose is the main dietary item in Cape Breton Highlands NP, Canada. Mammalian prey is always supplemented by a wide variety of other food sources, especially fruits, seeds, vegetables, grains (including crops), eggs and invertebrates. Diet varies very widely regionally and seasonally. Coyotes adjust intake of different food types depending on local availability, for example, different fruits including blackberries, wild plum, wild grape, black cherry and persimmon peak at different times in the diet of Coyotes in Longleaf Pine habitat (Joseph W. Jones Ecological Research Center, Georgia) as the fruiting season progresses. Birds are typically ancillary prey; waders, shorebirds and waterfowl form a large part of the diet on protected islands off the coast of South Carolina. Coyotes take small livestock (goats, sheep and young calves) and poultry. Domestic pets, especially cats and less so small dogs, are eaten rarely; cats occur in 0–2% of scats collected in urban and suburban studies.

■ Coyote

Attacks on people are very rare and not as prey; attacks occur most often during the breeding and pup-rearing season, when adults are very defensive. There are 2 recorded human fatalities, a 3-year-old child (California, 1981) and an adult woman killed by a pair (Cape Breton Highlands NP, 2009). Foraging is mainly diurno-crepuscular, but generally nocturnal near humans, particularly where hunted. Usually forages alone, less often in pairs. Where large ungulates are available, Coyotes may hunt socially, usually as pairs or small family groups; typically the alpha pair is responsible for the attack, and younger animals play little part. Sometimes associates with foraging American Badgers (page 158), snatching rodents flushed from cover or burrows as the badger digs. Large groups, including non-relatives, congregate relatively amicably at large carcasses. Scavenges, including from carnivore (especially Grey Wolf) kills, human refuse, pet food and bird feeders.

### Social and Spatial Behaviour

Sociality is extremely flexible, changing regionally and temporally depending on food availability. Basic social unit is a territorial monogamous pair that may breed for life. 'Associate' individuals, usually grown offspring of previous litters, remain with the pair under high food availability, forming packs numbering up to 10. Associates help raise pups and defend territories, although not to the extent of the breeding pair. Large packs occur where ungulates are the main prey, while pairs and trios are typical where prey is small. Some Coyotes never join packs and live as solitary nomads. Average resident territory size (excluding small breeding ranges) 2–3km² (SW USA) to 42–61km² (Minnesota). Territories in urban habitats range from 5–36km² (resident) to 27–115km² (transient). Density varies very widely, depending on habitat, season, protection and Grey Wolf density, e.g. 1–9/100km² (Alberta) to 150–230/100km² (Texas); urban populations reach extremely high densities, e.g. up to 600/100km² in Chicago.

### Reproduction and Demography

Seasonal. Mating January–March, with pups born April–June. Gestation 58–65 days. Maximum litter size 11, averaging 4–7. Pups weaned at 5–7 weeks; dispersal from 6 months. MORTALITY Humans are the main cause of death, mainly from shooting or trapping; collisions with vehicles comprise 35–62% of mortalities in urban areas. Grey Wolf is the chief natural predator. Annual mortality (adults and subadults) is lower in protected and urban populations (20–47%), compared to trapped and hunted populations (50–70%). LIFESPAN 15.5 years in the wild (rarely beyond 8), 18 in captivity.

### Status and Threats

Extremely widespread, common and resilient. Coyotes are heavily hunted, trapped and persecuted across much of their North American range, but populations are very resistant to persecution. Official control actions, largely in response to complaints of livestock depredation, killed more than 77,000 Coyotes in the USA in 2016. Very tolerant of habitat modification; deforestation to open habitat actually favours Coyotes. Combined with extirpation of Grey Wolves (the main natural predator and competitor), such habitat conversion has enabled colonisation outside its historic range, e.g. E Canada, E USA and E Central America, which continues today. Red List LC, population trend Increasing.

**Plate 45**

Hunting with American
Badger in prairie dog town

COYOTE

Raiding
bird
feeder

Central American
form

# GREY WOLF–COYOTE HYBRIDS

The canids depicted opposite have all been (and sometimes still are) classified as discrete species in eastern North America. Recent (2016) compelling genetic evidence indicates that all are hybrid populations of Coyote (page 102) and Grey Wolf (page 100). The analysis suggests that Coyotes and Grey Wolves diverged from a common ancestor very recently, within the last 117,000 years, making them sufficiently closely related to interbreed occasionally and produce fertile offspring. The amount of admixture correlates with Grey Wolf declines in eastern North America following European colonisation; this opened up the large canid niche to Coyotes and allowed them to expand eastward into the void. Faced with reduced opportunities for reproduction, remaining Grey Wolf individuals mated with Coyotes, and their fertile hybrid pups formed part of an expanding Coyote population that rapidly colonised former Grey Wolf distribution. Accordingly, continuous, large populations of Alaskan Grey Wolves almost never hybridise, and average 8–8.5% Coyote ancestry. Wolves from Algonquin Provincial Park, Ontario, thought to be pure Eastern Wolf (see below), actually have 32.5–35.5% Coyote ancestry, while Red Wolves in CE USA (see below), where human pressures on Grey Wolves were early, intense and sustained, have 70–80% Coyote ancestry – they are now more Coyote than Grey Wolf.

Coyotes and Grey Wolves continue to exchange genetic material today, although hybridisation is most prevalent where and when wolf persecution is intense and Coyote populations expand; there is little evidence of ongoing hybridisation in some populations with mixed ancestry where persecution has relaxed. Wolves of the western Great Lakes region are recovering from historic low numbers around a century ago, when their Coyote ancestry (21.7–23.9%) is assumed to have largely arisen. Great Lakes Grey Wolves today are not limited in mating opportunities with other Grey Wolves (strictly speaking, *mostly* Grey Wolf, from a genetic perspective), and are more likely to kill Coyotes rather than breed with them.

Grey Wolf–Coyote hybrid populations not only reveal the intriguing challenges in defining species (see the box 'How many species of carnivores?', page 7); they also present a quandary for conservationists. Does having mixed ancestry mean they do not warrant conservation efforts? They are fascinating in their own right and have similar aesthetic and ecological value to 'true' species. They fulfil an important regulatory role as the major predators of super-abundant White-tailed Deer, a species that causes hundreds of human deaths and tens of thousands of injuries through road accidents, as well as an estimated US$3.5 billion in damage to crops, nursery plants and tree seedlings each year across eastern North America. Medium-sized wolf-like canids such as the Red Wolf and Eastern Coyote defy traditional categorisation as species, yet they are better suited to modern anthropogenic eastern North America than the original Grey Wolf occupants, which need vast wilderness areas with very large ungulate prey.

## EASTERN COYOTE
### Canis latrans var. (Canis 'oriens')

*See Coyote (page 102) for species account*
Advocates have proposed that the Coyote in NE North America warrants recognition as a unique species, *Canis 'oriens'* (often referred to as 'Coywolf'), with little validity. Eastern Coyotes tend to be larger than western Coyotes, but there is continuous variation in size from west to east; they are not significantly genetically differentiated nor reproductively isolated from western or southeastern Coyotes. The Eastern Coyote is essentially a Coyote with some Grey Wolf genes that, in the absence of competing Grey Wolves, has undergone natural selection for a slightly larger ecotype to exploit White-tailed Deer more effectively. As well as having Grey Wolf ancestry, Eastern Coyotes have hybridised with domestic dogs. All sampled individuals are mainly Coyote, with some that have almost no Grey Wolf genes, but none is exclusively Coyote, and none completely lacks dog genes. The mix of genes gives rise to wide morphological variation, including coat colour variants such as brindled, sable (Alsatian-like) and blond (depicted opposite), rarely seen in other populations.

## RED WOLF *Canis 'rufus'*

HB ♀ 99–120cm, ♂ 104–125cm; T 30–46cm; SH 66–76cm; W ♀ 16–30kg, ♂ 21–41kg

The Red Wolf's status is controversial. There is ongoing debate over whether hybridisation was pre-historic (~10,000 BCE) or since European colonisation; and some taxonomists suggest it is not a hybrid but instead evolved very recently from a common ancestor with the Coyote. Regardless, its biological profile – updated from the first edition of this book – is included here to provide ecological data broadly representative of the canid hybrid populations now inhabiting eastern North America.

Reddish fur, becoming pale ginger to cream on the lower limbs, and distinctive white throat and chest patches. **Distribution and Habitat** Extinct in the wild except for a reintroduced population occupying 6,000km² in E North Carolina, USA, which inhabits pine forest–wetland mosaics, marshland and agricultural land with cover. **Feeding Ecology** Eats mainly White-tailed Deer, raccoons, Marsh Rabbit and small rodents. Livestock is eaten, although recent records are all of carrion. Hunting is nocturno-crepuscular, and usually in small packs or singly. **Social and Spatial Behaviour** Forms small family packs of 2–12 animals, comprising a dominant breeding pair and its offspring. Packs are territorial and occasionally kill unrelated intruders. Females disperse at higher rates than males, and some individuals never disperse, remaining in the pack as non-breeding helpers. Resident pack range size averages 68.4km² (range, 25–190km²); ranges for transients are much larger, average 319km² (range, 122–681km²). **Reproduction and Demography** Seasonal. Mating February–March; births April–May. Gestation 61–63 days. Litter size averages 3–5, exceptionally to 10. MORTALITY Rates low for canids: 32% (pups), 21% (yearlings) and 19% (adults) annually. Shooting and roadkills are the main causes; natural deaths account for a quarter of the total, mainly from intraspecific killing, sarcoptic mange and starvation (of pups). LIFESPAN 20 years in captivity. **Status and Threats** Treated as an endangered species by the US government and declared Extinct in the Wild by 1980. Reintroduced from captivity in 1987 and formerly numbered up to 130; there are currently fewer than 50 in the wild, including pups (2018). Humans are the main threat. Given recent genetic data, its conservation status is uncertain; it is still (2018) treated as a distinct species by the US Fish and Wildlife Service. Red List CR, population trend Decreasing.

## EASTERN WOLF
### Canis lupus var. (Canis 'lycaon')

*See Grey Wolf (page 100) for species account*
The Eastern Wolf has been variously classified as a distinct species, *Canis 'lycaon'*, the same species as Red Wolf, a hybrid between Red Wolf and Grey Wolf, or (as in this book) a Coyote-admixed population of the Grey Wolf. Historically, its range was defined as S Quebec and Ontario, centred on Algonquin Provincial Park, although this is contiguous with Grey Wolf distribution across E Canada. Algonquin Provincial Park wolves have historically been heavily hunted by people (including official culling programmes as recently as the 1960s; they have been protected since), and wolves are legally hunted and trapped throughout the area considered Eastern Wolf range. Resulting hybridisation with Coyotes is typical of heavily hunted wolf populations; this declines along a cline north and west into more continuous and less hunted Grey Wolf range in Canada.

**Plate 46**

EASTERN
COYOTE

RED
WOLF

EASTERN
WOLF

# EURASIAN GOLDEN JACKAL
## Canis aureus

GOLDEN JACKAL, ASIATIC JACKAL, INDIAN JACKAL, COMMON JACKAL
HB ♀ 69–85cm, ♂ 70–90cm; T 20–38cm; SH 35–48cm; W ♀ 4.9–13.6kg, ♂ 6.7–14.5kg
The only jackal in Eurasia. Until 2011, it included the species now classified as the African Wolf. It is now uncertain whether the Eurasian Golden Jackal occurs anywhere in Africa; there is a possible hybrid zone from Egypt to Israel. Uniformly tawny grey to greyish brown, without discrete markings except a greyish mantle in some populations; bushy tail usually has a dark tip (never white). Melanism occurs very rarely and may be the result of hybridisation with domestic dogs. **Distribution and Habitat** Arabian Peninsula to SE Europe, and C Asia to Indochina; may occur in Egypt. Inhabits semi-desert, grassland, dry woodland, forest, and agricultural and semi-urban areas. **Feeding Ecology** Omnivorous, eating mainly rodents, hares, lizards, snakes, invertebrates, fruit, seeds, mast and vegetable matter, including crops. Small fawns e.g. of Chital and rarely to Sambar size, are taken. Birds are usually ancillary prey but dominate diet locally or seasonally, e.g. mostly migratory egrets, Garganey and coucals are the main winter prey in Patna Bird Sanctuary, India. Jackals inhabiting a mangrove island in the Gulf of Kachchh, India, eat almost exclusively crabs and fish. Takes small stock and poultry, these dominating the diet (kills and carrion combined) in some sites, e.g. Greece and Israel. Foraging is mainly nocturnal, and crepuscular/diurnal where protected. Hunts singly, in adult pairs or in small family groups. Caches surplus food in shallow holes, and scavenges: congregations of up to 18 adults are recorded at large carcasses and in dumps. **Social and Spatial Behaviour** Breeding pair is the main social unit, often accompanied by grown helpers from previous litters. Pairs are usually formed during the breeding season, but persist year-round under high food availability. Pairs defend a core territory centred on dens, and may defend larger territories under high food availability. Territories 3–30km² (India). A collared female in Thailand occupied 151km² in mostly agricultural habitat. Densities 0.1–1.5/km² (Greece, Hungary, Romania) to 15/km² (very high prey availability, with no large carnivores, Keoladeo NP, India). **Reproduction and Demography** Seasonal; births often coincide with peak food supply, such as birth flushes of ungulates or rodents, e.g. December–May (Israel) and April–June (India, C Asia). Gestation 63 days. Maximum litter size 8, typically 3–6. MORTALITY Poorly known; sometimes killed by large cats, Grey Wolf (page 100) and domestic dogs. LIFESPAN 16 years in captivity. **Status and Threats** Generally common and widespread. Slowly declining outside protected areas in some countries, but expanding range in Europe (possibly due to historic Grey Wolf declines), most recently into Austria, Czech Republic, Denmark, Estonia, Germany, Italy, Latvia, Lithuania, Poland and Switzerland. Very tolerant of human activities and converted landscapes, but disappears under agricultural intensification (often with associated use of poisons) and urbanisation. Vulnerable to transmission of disease, especially rabies and distemper by feral dogs in anthropogenic landscapes. CITES Appendix II – India; Red List LC, population trend Increasing.

■ Eurasian Golden Jackal
■ African Wolf

# AFRICAN WOLF
## Canis lupaster

AFRICAN GOLDEN WOLF, GOLDEN WOLF
HB ♀ 74–100cm, ♂ 76–105cm; T 20–26cm; SH 38–50cm; W ♀ 6.5–14.5kg, ♂ 7.6–15.5kg
Prior to 2011, misclassified as a Golden Jackal subspecies. Morphological and genetic analyses has shown that the canid previously assigned to Golden Jackal in Africa is a distinct species, Canis lupaster (sometimes called C. anthus), which is more closely related to Grey Wolf (page 100). Western and northern African Wolves are larger, more variable in appearance, and tend to be more 'wolf-like' than E African individuals, which closely resemble Eurasian Golden Jackal. Yellow-grey to greyish brown, with pale underparts, breast shield and throat, often with a greyish mantle, and russet or ginger undertones on upperparts. Tail is usually interspersed with blackish hairs, especially dorsally, and has a black tip (never white). **Distribution and Habitat** Former distribution of Golden Jackal in Africa is now assumed to be African Wolf range: N Tanzania to Senegal, throughout C, W and N Africa. Very wide habitat tolerance; inhabits semi-desert, grassland, woodland, forest, and agricultural and semi-urban habitats. Penetrates deeply into very arid habitat in the Sahara, where it is associated with massifs, vegetation or the presence of livestock. Recorded from sea-level to 3,800m (Bale Mountains, Ethiopia). **Feeding Ecology** Omnivorous and highly opportunistic, with a broad diet. Capable of killing ungulates to the size of adult Thomson's Gazelle, but most kills are of small vertebrates to the size of hares. Common prey includes mice, rats, mole rats, gerbils, cane rats, ground squirrels, hares, reptiles, birds and eggs. In Algeria, Wild Boar comprises 20% (Djurdjura NP) to 41% (Tlemcen HR) of diet by biomass, presumably mainly scavenged although piglets may be hunted. Barbary Macaque, Dama Gazelle, Red Fox (page 114) and domestic cat are also recorded from scats in Algeria. Invertebrates, especially dung beetles, grasshoppers, locusts, termites and larvae, are readily consumed. Eats fruit, seeds and vegetable matter, including cultivated crops. Takes small stock; Ethiopian pastoralists in the Guassa highlands consider it to be the main livestock predator, mainly of sheep, although dietary analysis found sheep to be only rarely consumed. Foraging is mainly nocturnal, especially where persecuted, but frequently crepuscular/diurnal where protected. Forages singly or in small family groups; larger prey is more often taken by groups. Caches surplus food in shallow diggings, and scavenges from carcasses and human refuse; individuals in Ethiopian montane farmlands take rodents caught in human hunters' traps. Congregates at large carcasses and in dumps. **Social and Spatial Behaviour** Known mainly from E Africa (especially Serengeti NP, Tanzania), when studied as Golden Jackal. Breeding pair is the main social unit, often accompanied by grown helpers from previous litters. Pairs typically form during the breeding season, but persist year-round in good conditions. They defend a core territory around dens, and may cooperate to establish larger territories, depending on food availability. Territory size 1.1–20km², with densities of up to 4/km² (Serengeti NP). Densities in Guassa highlands are 0.03/km² (natural bushland) to 0.31/km² (human dump site). **Reproduction and Demography** Seasonal, with births coinciding with peak food supply, e.g. December–April (E Africa). Gestation 63 days. Maximum litter size 8, typically 3–6. MORTALITY Poorly known; sometimes killed by Lions (page 46), Leopards (page 48) and domestic dogs. Humans are likely the main cause of mortality for many populations; Ethiopian pastoralists (Guassa highlands) kill them by plugging den entrances with stones. LIFESPAN 16 years in captivity. **Status and Threats** Generally common, although declining outside protected areas, where persecution is intense. Very tolerant of human activities and prospers in livestock and farming areas despite often high levels of persecution. They have been extirpated where poisoning (usually illegal) occurs. Red List NE, population trend Unknown.

Plate 47

EURASIAN GOLDEN
JACKAL

Eurasian
Golden
Jackal

Threat postures

African
Wolf

AFRICAN
WOLF

# DHOLE *Cuon alpinus*

### ASIATIC WILD DOG

HB 80–113cm; T 32–50cm; SH 42–55cm;
W ♀ 10–17kg, ♂ 15–21kg

Superficially resembles a large jackal. Pale tawny brown to rich russet-brown with a dark-tipped tail. Northern temperate individuals are usually more reddish, with contrasting bright white underparts. **Distribution and Habitat** W and S China, Nepal, Bhutan, India, Southeast Asia, Sumatra and Java; patchily distributed in N China; uncertain in SE Russia and C Asia, where there are no confirmed records for >30 years. Inhabits forest, forest–grassland mosaics and montane scrubland. Avoids open habitat, and agricultural and pastoral areas. **Feeding Ecology** Pack hunter that mostly kills ungulates, with Chital, Red Muntjac and Sambar preferred across much of its range; also Blackbuck, Nilgai, Swamp Deer, Gaur, Asiatic Buffalo, Banteng, Blue Sheep, Markhor, Himalayan Tahr, gorals and Wild Pig. Juveniles are often selected, but packs are capable of killing adults of all but the largest species. Large Indian Civet (page 86) was a preferred prey species during a short-term study in Salakpra WS, Thailand. Livestock is sometimes killed, especially when unguarded and where natural prey is depleted. People in SE Thailand blame Dholes for most losses of free-roaming poultry, possibly due to confusion with Eurasian Golden Jackals (page 106). Foraging is usually diurno-crepuscular and cooperative. Scavenges, including kleptoparasitism from other carnivores, e.g. Leopard (page 48). **Social and Spatial Behaviour** Lives in packs of 2–15 adults and their pups, exceptionally totalling 30 individuals. Packs have a dominant breeding pair and are biased towards males because females disperse more often. Packs occupy defined home ranges, though the extent of territorial defence is unknown. Pack range estimates (telemetry) 12–49.5km² (mixed evergreen forest, Phu Khieo WS, Thailand) and 26.1–202.8km² (dry forest, Pench NP, India). A pack of 6 in lowland forest used 100km², as estimated by camera-traps (Khao Ang Rue Nai, Thailand). **Reproduction and Demography** Seasonal. Breeding October–April (India) and January–May (Java). Gestation 60–63 days. Litter size 4–12. Breeding usually restricted to the dominant pair, although multiple females occasionally breed and subordinate males sometimes mate with the alpha female. Pack members assist reproduction by guarding, provisioning at the den and regurgitating food to pups. A monitored pack in Baluran NP, Java, denned in burrows on steep slopes with dense vegetation and moved pups to new dens every 2 weeks on average. **MORTALITY** Poorly known; Tiger (page 44) and Leopard are known predators. **LIFESPAN** 16 years in captivity. **Status and Threats** Endangered and declining, chiefly from persecution, habitat loss and prey declines due to human hunting. Extirpated from at least 75% of former range. Likely extinct in its former E and C Asian range, and in Southeast Asia restricted to large protected areas. S and C India is the species' stronghold, where it reaches high densities in small protected areas; reasonably tolerated in non-protected areas, where it is generally not significantly involved in conflict with humans or hunted for illegal trade of body parts. CITES Appendix II; Red List EN, population trend Decreasing.

# ETHIOPIAN WOLF *Canis simensis*

### SIMIEN JACKAL, ABYSSINIAN WOLF, SIMIEN FOX

HB ♀ 84.1–96cm, ♂ 93–101.2cm; T 27–39.6cm; SH 53–62cm;
W ♀ 11.2–14.2kg, ♂ 14.2–19.3kg

Rich tawny rufous with white underparts and bright white markings on the lower face, throat, chest and lower legs. Tail has a white base, darkening to a chocolate-brown tip. Hybrids with domestic dogs have a stockier build and lighter, duller coat. Despite its confusing array of common names, the species is most closely related to Coyote (page 102) and Grey Wolf (page 100). **Distribution and Habitat** Restricted to 7 isolated populations at 3,000–4,500m in Ethiopia. Inhabits open highland habitats, especially montane grassland, heath and shrubland. Avoids agricultural areas, which reach 3,500–3,800m in parts of its range. **Feeding Ecology** Feeds almost exclusively on small diurnal mammals, especially mole rats, rats and Starck's Hare. Infrequent prey includes Rock Hyrax, juvenile Grey Duiker, reedbucks and Mountain Nyala, as well as birds such as Blue-winged Goose juveniles and francolins, and their eggs. Foraging is largely diurnal and solitary, with most kills made by individual wolves stalking rodents or digging them from burrows. Small packs of 2–4 sometimes cooperatively pursue prey, especially hares and young antelopes. Rarely kills sheep lambs; does not kill cattle calves, and often forages among herds and Gelada Baboon troops, which may assist hunting by providing cover and flushing rodents. Appropriates kills from raptors and scavenges, including from livestock carcasses. Caches surplus food in shallow holes. **Social and Spatial Behaviour** Forms packs of 2–13 adults that defend small, stable territories from other packs. Pairs or small packs occur where prey availability is low. Males rarely disperse, so packs contain up to 8 related adult males, as well as 1–3 adult females that may or may not be related; some females remain in their natal pack, while others disperse for breeding opportunities. Average territory size ranges from 6km² in productive habitat to 13.4km² in poor habitat. Estimated densities include 0.1–0.25/km² in poor habitat or unprotected areas, to 1–1.2/km² in optimum protected habitat. **Reproduction and Demography** Seasonal. Mating August–November; births October–January. Gestation 60–62 days. Litter size 2–6. Reproduction is largely by the pack's alpha pair, but the dominant female also mates with visiting males from neighbouring packs. All pack members provision pups at the den, and subordinate females sometimes assist in suckling (it is unclear if extra nursing females are pseudo-pregnant or absorb/abandon their own litters). Pups weaned from 10 weeks, and accompany the pack from 6 months. Sexual maturity at 18–24 months. **MORTALITY** Most mortality is anthropogenic and natural factors are poorly known; predation has not been observed, but may occur on pups by Spotted Hyaena (page 54), African Wolf (page 106) and large eagles. **LIFESPAN** 12 years in the wild. **Status and Threats** Endangered, with approximately 360–440 adults (>1 year old), of which <250 are breeding adults in 7 disjunct populations. Extreme pressure on habitat for agriculture and livestock is the chief threat, combined with exotic disease, especially rabies and distemper, from domestic dogs. More than half of the remaining Ethiopian Wolves live in the Bale Mountains, where numbers have declined by ~30% since 2008 (to approximately 210 adults >1 year old) due to successive disease epidemics. Roadkills, persecution and hybridisation with domestic dogs (mainly in the Bale Mountains) are lesser threats. Red List EN, population trend Decreasing.

■ Dhole

■ Ethiopian Wolf

**Plate 48**

Northern form

**DHOLE**

Southern form

Defending their kill
from a wild pig

Pack at den

**ETHIOPIAN
WOLF**

# AFRICAN WILD DOG *Lycaon pictus*

### PAINTED DOG, CAPE HUNTING DOG

HB 76–112cm; T 30–42cm; SH 61–78cm;
W ♀ 17–26.5kg, ♂ 21–36kg

Africa's largest canid, with coarse fur coloured a mottled patchwork of tawny, black and white. Tail has a conspicuous white tip, extending variably along the length; some individuals have an entirely white tail. Very rarely, the tail is tipped black. Coloration varies very widely within and between populations; southern African individuals tend to be tawnier, while E and NE African animals tend to be darker, but colour is not reliable for identifying origin. Coloration is unique to each individual, allowing identification for life. Little sexual dimorphism; males are slightly heavier than females and recognisable by a prominent penile sheath. There is little regional variation in size.

### Distribution and Habitat

Sub-Saharan Africa, mainly in E and southern Africa, with scattered populations across Sahelian W and C Africa. Reaches highest densities in woodland savannah, but occurs widely in open grassland, semi-desert and scrubland. Absent from C African forest, but inhabits forest patches in E Africa. Penetrates deeply into true desert, but cannot permanently colonise very arid areas. Tolerant of habitat modification, but rarely inhabits pastoral landscapes due to intense persecution.

### Feeding Ecology

Highly efficient pack hunter capable of taking prey as large as adult zebras and female African Buffaloes, but mostly kills medium-sized antelope species; each population focuses on 1–2 of the most common locally available species. Typical prey includes Impala, Nyala, Red Lechwe, Thomson's Gazelle and Blue Wildebeest (usually to subadult size). Largest preferred prey is Greater Kudu, in which adult females (135kg) are commonly killed (Namibia). Able to switch to smaller prey, especially where large species are absent or in low numbers, e.g. outside protected areas in N Kenya, Kirk's Dik-dik (3–7kg) comprises 70% of prey. Bushbuck, duikers, Steenbok and Warthog are also important prey in some areas. Opportunistically kills smaller prey, including hares, small carnivores (e.g. Bat-eared Fox; page 120) and reptiles, but these form an insignificant proportion of the diet. Kills small livestock, but depredation is rare where wild prey is available, even when it is heavily outnumbered by stock. No records of predation on humans. Hunting is almost always diurnal and highly social, often preceded by a frenzy of greeting between pack members. Reaches speeds of 66km/h and has terrific endurance, with chases extending for 2km. Hunts are highly coordinated and cooperative; pack members fan out and run in relays to maximise opportunities for capture, sometimes yielding more than 1 kill per hunt. Prey is killed cooperatively, usually by many pack members after capture by 1 dog; large and dangerous prey, e.g. Warthog and wildebeest, is often restrained by the head while other dogs disembowel and dismember it. Although this appears cruel (contributing to pastoralists' hatred for the species), the prey usually dies within 2–4 minutes. Hunts have high success rates, 42–70%, which increase with the number of adults present. Occasionally scavenges, including appropriating carcasses from other packs, Leopard (page 48), Spotted Hyaena (page 54) and (very rarely) Lion (page 46).

### Social and Spatial Behaviour

Intensely social, with pack members in almost constant association. Packs form around the dominant breeding pair, with up to 28 adults, but normally average 5–10 adults accompanied by yearlings and pups; the pack size occasionally exceeds 50, including pups old enough to travel. Same-sex adults in the pack are usually related to one another but not to opposite-sex adults. Packs usually form through interchange of same-sex subgroups, typically dispersing littermates that join opposite-sex subgroups. Both sexes may disperse, with females dispersing sooner but settling nearer to their natal range than males. Occupies enduring defined ranges that are often very large and overlap those of other packs. Active territorial defence is infrequent, but occurs in overlapping areas and around den sites, where inter-pack encounters are aggressive and sometimes fatal. Range size 150–2,460km², averaging 423–1,318km² and dropping to 50–260km² when young pups are in the den. Due to its wide-ranging behaviour, the species naturally occurs at low densities that fluctuate significantly depending on pup survival, e.g. 5/1,000km² (semi-arid savannah, N Botswana), 2.8–22.5/1,000km² (dry savannah, N Kruger NP), 16–24/1,000km² (Selous GR, Tanzania) and 19–39/1,000km² (mesic woodland, S Kruger NP).

### Reproduction and Demography

Weakly seasonal. Pups born year-round, but most litters coincide with peak prey availability, e.g. March–June (Serengeti NP, Tanzania) and April–September (Kruger NP). Gestation 69–73 days. Litter size typically 10–11, exceptionally to 21. Pack's dominant female is usually the only breeder. All pack members cooperate to help raise pups by provisioning the mother at the den, regurgitating food to the pups and guarding the den. Helpers are essential for raising litters, and small packs (<4 adults) rarely reproduce successfully. Subordinate females occasionally breed, but their pups survive only when prey availability is high (they are sometimes 'stolen' and raised by the dominant female); otherwise, they are frequently killed by the dominant female or die from starvation brought about by harassment of subordinate mother(s). Weaning is at around 8 weeks, and pups emerge from the den at around 12–16 weeks, after which they travel with the pack. Dispersal occurs most often at around 21–22 months for females (range 13–31), and 28 months for males (range 17–43). Inter-litter interval averages 12–14 months. Sexual maturity is at around 2 years for both sexes, but breeding usually occurs with social dominance at around 4–5 years. MORTALITY 25% (Selous GR) to 65% (Kruger NP) of pups die in their first year. Adult mortality 23–28% for prime adults, rising to around 50% for older adults. Main natural causes are Lions, other African Wild Dogs and infectious diseases such as rabies and canine distemper. LIFESPAN 11 years in the wild, 16 in captivity.

### Status and Threats

The species has undergone a drastic loss of range and is now extinct in at least 25 of 39 original range countries. Total numbers are estimated at 6,600 adults in 39 subpopulations, of which only 1,400 are mature individuals. African Wild Dogs were actively destroyed by wildlife managers until the 1970s; they are now protected throughout their range, although anthropogenic factors overshadow natural deaths, even in protected populations. Persecution, incidental killing in snares, roadkills and exotic disease transmitted by domestic dogs are the main causes of death. The species now persists predominantly in areas with large parks. The main strongholds are the Okavango–Kaudom–Hwange ecosystem, Kafue NP and Luangwa Valley, Zambia; Selous GR–Mikumi NP and Ruaha–Rungwa ecosystems, Tanzania; and Kruger NP, South Africa. Red List CR in W Africa and N Africa (Algeria only, if not already extinct there), EN elsewhere, population trend Decreasing.

■ African Wild Dog

Plate 49

**AFRICAN
WILD DOG**

Pack members
greeting

# BLACK-BACKED JACKAL
*Canis (Lupulella) mesomelas*

### SILVER-BACKED JACKAL
HB ♀ 66–85cm, ♂ 69–90cm; T 27–38cm; SH 38–48cm;
W ♀ 5.9–10kg, ♂ 6.4–11.1kg

Recent molecular analyses show that the 2 African jackal species are not closely related to Eurasian Golden Jackal (page 106), as formerly thought. Indeed, they diverged early (estimated ~3.5 million years ago) from the lineage that gave rise to the *Canis* clade of large, wolf-like species (see page 9) and may warrant being grouped separately within a distinct genus, *Lupulella* (adopted by some authorities). African jackals are most closely related to the African Wild Dog (page 110), and are not closely related to other *Canis* species. Black-backed Jackal is recognisable by its dark-edged silver-grey saddle on a buff to rufous-brown body, and grizzled, dark bushy tail. Pups show adult coloration, including saddle and dark tail, from a very young age (compare with Side-striped Jackal pups). Melanism is not recorded. Usually the most conspicuous jackal where it occurs, due to preference for open areas and aggressive dominance over other similar-sized canids. **Distribution and Habitat** Two disjunct populations, in southern and E Africa. Occurs in true desert, grassland, montane meadows, arid to mesic woodland savannah, and agricultural habitats. Recorded from sea-level to 3,660m (Mt Kenya, Kenya). **Feeding Ecology** Generalist omnivore. Recorded killing adult Springbok, Thomson's Gazelle and Impala, but typical prey includes rodents, Springhare, hares, and young or small ungulates, especially 'hider' species such as Bushbuck and Grey Duiker. Juvenile Cape Fur Seals are readily killed by coastal-living jackals near seal colonies. Birds, reptiles, eggs, invertebrates and carrion are also important food items. Readily takes poultry and small livestock. Foraging is mainly nocturnal, especially where it is persecuted, but often crepuscular/diurnal where it is protected. Usually forages alone or in pairs, but up to 12 adults cooperate to kill large prey, and large congregations gather relatively amicably at carcasses and in food-rich patches like seal colonies. Readily scavenges, including from large carnivore kills and human refuse; caches food for later. **Social and Spatial Behaviour** Monogamous and territorial, forming breeding pairs that may endure for life and defend territories from other pairs. Up to 3 helpers accompany a pair and help to raise pups, including regurgitating food for them and the mother. Coastal Namibian jackals commute up to 20km from their territories to feed at a fur seal colony (Cape Cross Seal Reserve) along shared 'highways'. Commuters avoid and are tolerated by territorial residents as they travel, and residents mostly abandon territorial defence at the colony itself except during the denning period. Territories range from an average of 1.0km$^2$ (Hwange NP, Zimbabwe) to 24.9km$^2$ (coastal Namibia). Densities peak during the breeding season, e.g. 0.5–0.8/km$^2$ (non-breeding) to 0.7–1/km$^2$ (breeding; Hwange NP). Density estimates 40/100km$^2$ (Giant's Castle GR, South Africa), 62/100km$^2$ (Kalahari, possibly applying only to riverine areas) and as high as 220/100km$^2$ (Cape Cross Seal Reserve, representing density only in the area of the seal colony). **Reproduction and Demography** Seasonal. Mating May–August; births June–November. Gestation ~60 days. Maximum litter size 6, typically 3–4. Pups weaned at 8–9 weeks. Sexually mature at 11 months. MORTALITY Predators include Leopards (page 48), Lions (page 46), Spotted Hyaenas (page 54) and, occasionally, Cheetahs (page 40) and African Wild Dogs. Very susceptible to domestic dog diseases (especially rabies) near settlements, although populations recover quickly. LIFESPAN 14 years in captivity. **Status and Threats** Widespread and common in protected and pastoral areas. Persecuted intensely on farmland (especially in southern Africa), but is very resilient, and anthropogenic population declines appear to be only temporary. Red List LC, population trend Stable.

# SIDE-STRIPED JACKAL
*Canis (Lupulella) adusta*

HB ♀ 65–76cm, ♂ 66–81cm; T 30–41cm; SH 41–48cm;
W ♀ 6.2–10kg, ♂ 5.9–12kg

Grizzled buff-grey, with a characteristic pale stripe (often outlined with a dark border) along the flanks and a distinctive white-tipped dark tail. Pups are typically uniformly buff-grey without obvious body markings, except for obvious white-tipped tail, until >5–6 months old. Melanism is not recorded. **Distribution and Habitat** Southern, W and C Africa; replaced by Black-backed Jackal in arid southern Africa, and African Wolf (page 106) in arid N Africa. Inhabits wooded grassland, woodland savannah, marshland, montane areas and forest edges. Uses more open natural habitats, e.g. open grasslands, in the absence of Black-backed Jackals and African Wolves. Avoids very open habitat but can utilise agricultural areas with cover, and occurs in peri-urban and urban areas near major cities. **Feeding Ecology** The most omnivorous and least predatory jackal species, rarely killing prey larger than gazelle fawns. Diet varies widely locally and seasonally; mainly includes a wide range of fruits, seeds and crops, as well as small rodents, hares, Springhare, small birds, insects and carrion. Free-range poultry is sometimes killed. More strictly nocturnal than other jackals, perhaps to reduce competition with Black-backed Jackal, but becomes crepuscular when unmolested. Forages alone, but family groups gather at rich patches such as termite nests, and up to 12 from various families congregate to scavenge from carrion or dumps. **Social and Spatial Behaviour** Monogamous, forming mated pairs that may be lifelong. Resident pairs maintain exclusive use of a core territory, with edges shared by neighbouring pairs. Yearling offspring often remain in the territory, sometimes forming groups of up to 7 with the resident pair, although it is unclear if they act as helpers. Range size 0.15–0.56km$^2$ outside breeding, expanding to 0.55–1.6km$^2$ during breeding. Density estimates 7/100km$^2$ (depleted savanna, Niokolo-Koba NP, Senegal) and 54–79/100km$^2$ (W Zimbabwe) in non-breeding season, to 97/100km$^2$ (W Zimbabwe) in breeding season. **Reproduction and Demography** Seasonal. Mating June–July; births August–November. Gestation 57–60 days. Litter size 4–6. Pups weaned at 8–10 weeks. Sexually mature at 11 months. MORTALITY Preyed on by larger carnivores, including domestic dogs near human habitation. Vulnerable to diseases such as rabies and canine distemper. LIFESPAN 10 years in captivity. **Status and Threats** Widespread and common. Tolerant of habitat conversion, and persists in suburban and agricultural habitats. Persecuted in human-dominated areas as a livestock predator, and many are killed by snares and vehicles, but human-caused deaths probably produce only local declines unless they are associated with poisoning or disease outbreaks. Thought to be expanding in some areas, e.g. NE South Africa, where Black-backed Jackals are heavily persecuted. Red List LC, population trend Stable.

 Black-backed Jackal    ■ Side-striped Jackal

**Plate 50**

BLACK-BACKED
JACKAL

Gathering at
carcass

Black-backed
Jackal pup

Side-striped
Jackal pup

SIDE-STRIPED
JACKAL

# ARCTIC FOX *Vulpes lagopus*

### POLAR FOX, WHITE FOX, BLUE FOX

HB ♀ 50–65cm, ♂ 53–75cm; T 25–42.5cm;
W ♀ 3.1–3.7kg, ♂ 3.6–6.7kg

The northernmost canid and the only canid species to change colour seasonally. Two distinct colour morphs: white winter morph moults to grey-brown with cream underparts in summer; blue morph is pale bluish brown in winter and dark grey-brown in summer. White morph is more common, but blue dominates on islands and in coastal areas. **Distribution and Habitat** Circumpolar in the Arctic. Restricted to Arctic and tundra habitats, mostly north of the treeline in Canada, the USA (Alaska), Greenland, Russia, Finland, Norway, Sweden and Iceland. Inhabits most Arctic islands and winter sea ice to within 60km of the North Pole. **Feeding Ecology** Small rodents, chiefly lemmings and voles, are critical, especially to inland populations, which fluctuate with rodent 'boom-bust' cycles. Other food includes fruits, eggs, birds to the size of geese, ground squirrels, Arctic Hare and infrequent kills of Reindeer/Caribou neonates. Coastal foxes also eat molluscs, crabs, fish, seabirds, and the carcasses of seals and whales; sometimes kills Ringed Seal pups. Blamed for killing domestic sheep lambs, although these are probably scavenged. Foraging is largely nocturno-crepuscular (light during the Arctic summer) and solitary, but congregates at large carcasses. Caches surplus food; 1 larder contained more than 500 eggs. Scavenges from bear and Grey Wolf (page 100) kills, winter-killed Reindeer and human refuse. **Social and Spatial Behaviour** Usually solitary and monogamous, forming tight-knit breeding pairs that are territorial near the den. Pairs usually separate after raising pups, but remain in the territory year-round, pairing up again each spring to breed. Helpers from previous litters sometimes linger, forming extended family groups that persist if food is plentiful. Coastal home ranges are generally smallest (5–21km²), with high densities (4–8/100km²) due to more reliable food availability; inland ranges 15–60km² and densities 0.09–3/100km². Individuals may wander spectacular distances, possibly driven by rodent crashes, e.g. 2,300km over 3 years by an Alaskan male. **Reproduction and Demography** Seasonal. Mating February–May; births April–July. Gestation 52–54 days. Litter size typically 3–11, exceptionally reaching 19 in rodent booms. Pups weaned at 7–8 weeks, reaching independence at 12–14 weeks. Most disperse in autumn, but they may overwinter on their parents' range; some (mainly females) become helpers. Both sexes mature at 10 months, but most individuals do not breed until their third year. MORTALITY Survival is tied to rodent abundance; up to 50% of adults and 80% of pups die in poor years, and populations collapse by up to 80%. Predators include Red Fox (especially of pups), large raptors, Wolverine (page 164), Grey Wolf and bears. Domestic dogs kill Arctic Foxes near human settlements and may also transmit disease. LIFESPAN Maximum 10–11 years in the wild, typically under 5; 15 in captivity. **Status and Threats** More than 100,000 Arctic Foxes are trapped annually for their dense fur, but populations appear to tolerate hunting if pressure is relaxed during poor food years. In Iceland, legally killed as pests by sheep farmers and eider-down collectors. Northwards expansion of Red Fox due to climate warming and human subsidies is causing Arctic Fox declines and range contraction in lowland Fenno-Scandinavia, possibly more widely. Protected in Finland, mainland Norway and Sweden, where historic population crashes have not recovered; unprotected elsewhere. Red List LC, population trend Stable.

# RED FOX *Vulpes vulpes*

### CROSS FOX, SILVER FOX, COMMON FOX
### Includes NORTH AMERICAN RED FOX *V. fulva*

HB ♀ 45–68cm, ♂ 59–90cm; T 28–49cm;
W ♀ 3.4–7.5kg, ♂ 4–14kg

The world's most widespread and abundant wild carnivore. Typically various shades of rich red-brown, but highly variable, including platinum-tipped black ('silver fox'), an intermediate morph called 'cross' and pale silvery blond. All morphs (except albinos) have black-backed ears, and white-tipped tails are typical but not ubiquitous. Sometimes classified as 2 species based on genetic analyses showing divergence ~209,000 years ago: Eurasian Red Fox (*V. vulpes*) and North American Red Fox (*V. fulva*). **Distribution and Habitat** North America, Eurasia and N Africa. Occurs in virtually all habitats to 4,500m, including farmland, suburbs and cities north of the Tropic of Cancer, except the northernmost Arctic and deserts of the SW USA. Introduced to Australia in the mid-1800s, where it has serious impacts on native wildlife. **Feeding Ecology** Highly opportunistic, eating mainly reptiles, birds and small mammals to the size of hares; also eggs, amphibians, fish, invertebrates, fruits, acorns, fir cones, sedges, fungi and tubers. Kills juvenile small stock and poultry, and consumes crops such as wheat and corn. Hunting is terrestrial (although it is recorded occasionally climbing to 8m) and mostly nocturno-crepuscular, often more diurnal in winter and where it is undisturbed. Usually forages alone, but aggregates in food-rich patches, e.g. shorebird nest colonies and dumps. Caches surplus food for later use, and has an excellent memory for larder sites. Readily scavenges: ungulate carcasses (including of domestic livestock) can be especially important in winter, and scavenges from human refuse, bird feeders and compost heaps. **Social and Spatial Behaviour** Usually solitary and monogamous. Mated pair is the main social unit, but sociality during breeding is very flexible. With sufficient food, may form groups comprising 1 male and up to 5 vixens (probably related). Group-breeding females may den alone or together; younger females are mostly non-breeding helpers from previous litters. Range size is resource-dependent, from 0.2km² (Oxford, UK) to 50km² (Oman). Density estimates 0.1/km² (Arctic tundra), 1–3/km² (temperate forest, Canada and W Europe) and exceptionally reaching 30/km² with abundant food, e.g. urban areas where foxes are subsidised. **Reproduction and Demography** Seasonal. Mating is in winter, usually December–February, earlier in southerly latitudes (Australia: June–October). Births usually March–May. Oestrus 1–6 days; gestation 49–55 days. Litter size reaches 12 depending on food availability, typically 3–8. Pups weaned at 6–8 weeks, and most disperse from age 6 months before the next breeding season. Some young females remain as helpers. Sexually mature at 9–10 months. MORTALITY First-year mortality reaches 80% and averages 50% for adults, mainly due to humans. Large raptors, other carnivores and domestic dogs kill Red Foxes, although humans are overwhelmingly their main predator. Major vector for rabies, with outbreaks causing intermittent population crashes. LIFESPAN Maximum 9 years in the wild, typically <5; 15 in captivity. **Status and Threats** Remarkable adaptability and resilience enables it to tolerate intense persecution, with some 1–2 million wild individuals killed annually for the fur trade, and perhaps the same amount again by sport hunters and pest control. Unprotected in most of its range; exports of furs from India are restricted. CITES Appendix III – India; Red List LC, population trend Stable.

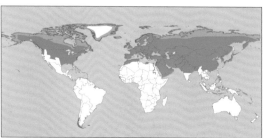

■ Arctic Fox ■ Red Fox

**Plate 51**

White form,
winter

White form,
summer

**ARCTIC FOX**

Blue form,
winter

Blue form,
summer

Pale form

**RED FOX**

'Silver'
form

Typical form

# KIT FOX *Vulpes macrotis*

HB 45.5–54cm; T 25–34cm; W ♀ 1.6–2.2kg, ♂ 1.7–2.7kg
Smallest fox on mainland North America. Tawny grey with ochre sides, neck and legs. Closely related to Swift Fox; hybrids occasionally occur in a narrow band of overlap in Texas and New Mexico. **Distribution and Habitat** W USA and N Mexico. Inhabits semi-arid to arid desert scrub and grassland. Can occupy urban and agricultural areas. **Feeding Ecology** Eats mainly mice, rats, kangaroo rats, ground squirrels, prairie dogs, lagomorphs and insects; also small birds, reptiles, carrion, wild cactus fruits and crops, e.g. tomatoes and almonds. Foraging is mainly nocturnal and solitary. Scavenges from livestock carcasses and human refuse. **Social and Spatial Behaviour** Monogamous, normally mating for life. Helpers, usually grown daughters, often remain with the pair. Ranges are stable, with exclusive core denning areas. Range size (both sexes) averages 2.5–11.6km². Densities fluctuate widely depending on prey oscillations: 10–170/100km², averaging 44/100km². **Reproduction and Demography** Seasonal. Mating December–January; births February–March. Gestation 49–55 days (estimated). Litter size 1–7. Weaning at around 3 months and independence at 5–6 months. MORTALITY Average annual mortality 65% (juveniles) and 45% (adults), mainly from Coyote (page 102) predation and starvation during prey shortages. LIFESPAN 7 years in the wild, 20 in captivity. **Status and Threats** Secure but has undergone significant local declines, e.g. California and Mexico, from habitat conversion and eradication of prey colonies, e.g. prairie dog and kangaroo rat towns. Threatened in California and Oregon, endangered in Colorado, vulnerable in Mexico. Red List LC, population trend Decreasing.

# SWIFT FOX *Vulpes velox*

HB 47.5–54cm; T 25–34cm; W ♀ 1.6–2.3kg, ♂ 2–2.95kg
Very similar to Kit Fox, with more rounded ears and a shorter tail. **Distribution and Habitat** Mid-western North America, from Alberta to New Mexico. Restricted to short- to medium-grass prairies and grassland. Tolerates dry land agricultural areas. **Feeding Ecology** Diet dominated by prairie dogs, ground squirrels, mice and lagomorphs, plus wild fruits, seeds, insects, small birds, reptiles, eggs and carrion. Foraging is solitary and mainly nocturno-crepuscular. **Social and Spatial Behaviour** Mated pairs are typical, but sociality is flexible; trios and extra-pair breeding occur. Pairs/groups maintain exclusive core areas with overlapping edges; neighbours are often related. Range size (both sexes) 7.6km² (Colorado) to 25.1km² (W Kansas). **Reproduction and Demography** Seasonal. Mating December (Oklahoma) to March (Canada); births March–May. Gestation 50–55 days. Litter size 3–6, exceptionally to 8. MORTALITY Rates average 67–95% (juveniles) and 36–57% (adults), mainly from Coyote (page 102) predation. LIFESPAN 8 years in the wild, 14 in captivity. **Status and Threats** Extirpated from about 60% of its historic range, from massive prairie conversion and intense persecution of prey. Extirpated from Canada by 1938; now present as a small reintroduced population. Red List LC, population trend Stable.

# INDIAN FOX *Vulpes bengalensis*

## BENGAL FOX

HB ♀ 46–48cm, ♂ 39–57.5cm; T 24.5–32cm;
W ♀ 2–2.9kg, ♂ 2.3–3.6kg
Slender, fine-featured fox with a narrow face, yellow-grey to silvery-grey fur and a black-tipped tail. **Distribution and Habitat** Endemic to the Indian subcontinent. Inhabits hot, semi-arid grassland, plains, scrub and open, dry forest. Occurs on agricultural land. **Feeding Ecology** Omnivorous, eating mainly small mammals and insects, supplemented by birds, reptiles, eggs, fruits, seeds and fresh shoots. Foraging is solitary and nocturno-crepuscular; often diurnal on cool or overcast days. Scavenges from carrion, but rarely since feral dogs dominate carcasses. **Social and Spatial Behaviour** Monogamous in mated pairs. Other adults sometimes associate with pairs, but do not help raise pups; their role and relatedness is uncertain. Range estimates average 1.6km² (♀s) and 3.1km² (♂s). Densities fluctuate due to rodent cycles and disease outbreaks, usually 1–15/100km², reaching 150/100km² in ideal conditions. **Reproduction and Demography** Seasonal. Mating November–January; births January–May. Gestation 50–53 days. Litter size 2–4. Both parents provision and guard pups. MORTALITY Disease is implicated in population crashes. LIFESPAN 8 years in captivity. **Status and Threats** Relatively widespread, but occurs at low densities in habitats that are under strong development pressure. Naturally vulnerable to population crashes, exacerbated by hunting pressure from people for food. CITES Appendix III – India; Red List LC, population trend Decreasing.

# CORSAC FOX *Vulpes corsac*

## CORSAC, STEPPE FOX

HB ♀ 45–50cm, ♂ 45–59.5cm; T 19–34cm;
W ♀ 1.6–2.4kg, ♂ 1.7–3.2kg
Medium-sized fox with pale, tawny-grey fur (silky and frosted in winter) and a black-tipped tail. **Distribution and Habitat** C Asia, from W Russia to NE China. Inhabits steppes, grassland, shrubland, semi-desert and desert. **Feeding Ecology** Omnivorous and opportunistic, exploiting seasonal fluctuations in food, especially of rodents, e.g. lemmings, voles, ground squirrels, gerbils and jerboas. Also consumes birds, reptiles, insects and carrion. Foraging is solitary and usually nocturnal; diurnalism increases when feeding young pups and during food shortages. Scavenges, including from human refuse, Grey Wolf (page 100) kills and winter-killed livestock. **Social and Spatial Behaviour** Forms monogamous breeding pairs, although it is unknown if they are permanent or territorial, and 2 females sometimes den together with their pups. Juveniles may become helpers. Range size (pairs) 3.5–11.4km² (C Mongolia), occasionally to 35–40km² in poor habitat. **Reproduction and Demography** Seasonal. Mating January–March; births mid-March–May. Litter size 2–10, averaging 5–6. Gestation 52–60 days. Both parents provision and guard pups; helpers sometimes assist. MORTALITY Average adult mortality 34% (protected reserve, C Mongolia), mainly from human hunting and Red Fox (page 114) predation. LIFESPAN 9 years in captivity. **Status and Threats** Widespread and locally common, but heavy hunting pressure for furs and rodent-poisoning campaigns (especially in China) are pervasive. Extirpated in many areas, especially in Russia and its former republics. Red List LC, population trend Decreasing.

■ Kit Fox ■ Swift Fox

■ Indian Fox

□ Corsac Fox

**Plate 52**

KIT FOX

SWIFT FOX

INDIAN FOX

CORSAC FOX

# BLANFORD'S FOX *Vulpes cana*

### KING FOX, ROYAL FOX, AFGHAN FOX
HB ♀ 34–45cm, ♂ 38.3–47cm; T 26–36cm; W 0.8–1.6kg
Very small fox with distinctive dark 'tear' lines along the muzzle. Brown-grey fur is interspersed with long black guard hairs, and very bushy tail usually has a black (rarely white) tip. **Distribution and Habitat** E Egypt, Arabian Peninsula and C Asia. Inhabits semi-arid to arid rocky desert and mountainous habitats. Independent of water. **Feeding Ecology** Largely insectivorous and frugivorous, eating mainly beetles, crickets, grasshoppers, ants, termites, scorpions, wild capers, olives, grapes and melons. Small rodents, birds and (rarely) reptiles are also hunted; newborn ibex records are probably carrion. Foraging is usually solitary and nocturnal, with increased crepuscularity in winter. **Social and Spatial Behaviour** Forms territorial monogamous pairs that cooperate to raise pups, but are fairly solitary outside the breeding period. Non-breeding yearling females (possibly from previous litters) are often tolerated by resident pairs. Range size (both sexes) 0.5–2km², averaging 1.6km². Density estimates 0.5–2/km² (Israel) to 8/km² (high-quality habitat with abundant carrion, Jordan). **Reproduction and Demography** Seasonal. Mating January–February (Israel); births late February–May. Gestation 50–60 days. Litter size 1–3. Males groom, guard and accompany pups (2–4 months) on foraging excursions. MORTALITY Rabies and old age appear to be the main mortality factors. Red Fox (page 114) is a confirmed predator. LIFESPAN <5 years in the wild, 6 in captivity. **Status and Threats** Fairly widespread and common. Locally threatened by habitat development, especially in coastal areas, and incidentally killed by poison set for other species. CITES Appendix II; Red List LC, population trend Stable.

# PALE FOX *Vulpes pallida*

### PALLID FOX, AFRICAN SAND FOX
HB 38–55cm; T 23–28.5cm; W 1.2–3.6kg
Very small fox, uniformly pale sandy cream except for dark-tipped tail (distinguishing it from Rüppell's Fox). Ears medium-sized, in proportion to the head and lacking the oversized appearance in Rüppell's Fox and Fennec (page 120). **Distribution and Habitat** Sub-Saharan Africa, in a narrow band from W Senegal–Mauritania to Eritrea and Ethiopia. Inhabits very arid, sandy and stony deserts, and dry savannah. Occurs near human settlements. **Feeding Ecology** Primarily insectivorous, eating mainly weevils, scarabs, grasshoppers and scorpions; small mammals, especially gerbils and jerboas, are also taken. Robust molars suggest fruits, seeds and plant matter are consumed, but these appeared very rarely in scats collected in SE Niger. Largely nocturnal. **Social and Spatial Behaviour** Mostly seen in pairs and small groups, probably mated pairs with offspring, suggesting patterns similar to those of other small foxes. Range estimates average 5.6km² with minimal overlap, suggesting territoriality (Termit and Tin Toumma National Nature and Cultural Reserve, Niger) **Reproduction and Demography** Probably seasonal. Gestation (captivity) 51–53 days. Litter size 3–6. MORTALITY Poorly known; occasionally killed by domestic dogs. LIFESPAN Unknown. **Status and Threats** One of the least known canids; status unknown.

■ Blanford's Fox  ■ Pale Fox     ■ Rüppell's Fox  ■ Tibetan Fox

Occasionally killed near settlements, and used locally for traditional medicines, e.g. Sudan, for asthma. Red List LC, population trend Unknown.

# RÜPPELL'S FOX *Vulpes rueppellii*

### SAND FOX
HB 35–56cm; T 25–39cm; W ♀ 1.1–1.8kg, ♂ 1.1–2.3kg
Small, fine-featured fox with large ears and a slender face. Body colour near white to greyish brown, often with a silvery sheen due to dark guard hairs. Long, bushy tail has a white tip. **Distribution and Habitat** N Africa (Sahara), the Arabian Peninsula and C Asia. Independent of water and inhabits semi-arid to very arid habitats, including sandy and stony deserts, rocky steppes, massifs, scrub and vegetated watercourses. Occurs near human habitation. **Feeding Ecology** Omnivorous. Eats small mammals, birds, lizards, insects and plant matter, including wild fruits (especially dates), desert succulents and grass (probably an emetic). Foraging is solitary and nocturno-crepuscular. Most hunting is terrestrial; climbs palm trees for dates. Scavenges from carrion and human refuse. **Social and Spatial Behaviour** Monogamous, forming mated territorial pairs, but larger aggregations of up to 15 suggest more complex sociality. Territories are largely exclusive, although large ranges overlap significantly. Female range sizes 13.2km² (Saudi Arabia) to 53.8km² (Oman); male ranges 20.9–84.4km². Density estimates 0.7–1.05/km² (fenced reserve, Saudi Arabia). **Reproduction and Demography** Seasonal. Mating November–February (Saudi Arabia); births March–May. Gestation 52–56 days. Litter size 2–6. Pups independent at 4 months and disperse at 6–10 months. MORTALITY Rabies, distemper and predation are the main factors; Steppe Eagle and Pharaoh Eagle-owl are confirmed predators. LIFESPAN 7 years in the wild, 12 in captivity. **Status and Threats** Widespread and quite common. Killed indiscriminately during poisoning campaigns, and absent in heavily grazed areas. Expanding Red Fox (page 114) range (in association with human settlements) displaces Rüppell's Fox; it is almost extinct in Israel as a result. Red List LC, population trend Stable.

# TIBETAN FOX *Vulpes ferrilata*

### TIBETAN SAND FOX, SAND FOX
HB 49–70cm; T 22–29cm; W ♀ 3–4.1kg, ♂ 3.2–5.7kg
Very distinctive stocky fox with a long, narrow muzzle, small ears and small, wide-set eyes on a broad face. Body grizzled grey with white underparts, and a rufous cape, head and lower legs. **Distribution and Habitat** Restricted to the Tibetan Plateau in Ladakh (India), N Nepal, and through S and C China; presence in N Bhutan is unconfirmed. Inhabits remote, cold, semi-arid to arid steppes, meadows, grassland and slopes at 2,500–5,200m. Tolerates ambient temperatures of –40°C to 30°C. **Feeding Ecology** Eats mainly small mammals, especially pikas (with which it is closely associated), mice and zokors. Also eats hares, marmots, birds, lizards, insects and berries. Eats carrion, including scavenging Grey Wolf (page 100) kills, and follows foraging Brown Bears (page 138) to mop up flushed rodents. Hunts alone and appears diurnal, possibly reflecting the activity patterns of pikas. **Social and Spatial Behaviour** Poorly known. Monogamous breeding pairs are typical, but adult trios with pups are recorded. Pairs are found in close proximity, especially in food patches like pika colonies, suggesting the species is not strongly territorial. Densities are naturally low, reaching 2–4/km² with abundant prey and low hunting pressure. **Reproduction and Demography** Seasonal. Mating December–March; births February–May. Litter size 2–5. Gestation 50–55 days. MORTALITY and LIFESPAN Unknown. **Status and Threats** Widespread and inhabits remote areas, somewhat insulating it from human threats. Given its strong association with pika colonies, the gravest threat is the state-sanctioned rodent poisoning affecting most of the Tibetan Plateau. Red List LC, population trend Unknown.

**Plate 53**

BLANFORD'S
FOX

PALE FOX

RÜPPELL'S
FOX

TIBETAN FOX

# FENNEC *Vulpes zerda*

### FENNEC FOX

HB 33.5–39.5cm; T 12.5–23cm; W 0.8–1.9kg

Smallest canid, with proportionally the largest ears in the family. Pale cream to sandy red, with lighter underparts, a dark-tipped tail and a dark caudal spot. Soles of the feet are fully furred for traversing hot, loose sand. **Distribution and Habitat** Restricted to N Africa; reports from the Arabian Peninsula are unverified. Extremely well adapted to deserts; water-independent. Prefers stable sand dunes for burrows, but occupies all semi-arid/arid habitats. **Feeding Ecology** Eats very small prey, chiefly small rodents, lizards, geckos, birds to the size of sandgrouse, invertebrates and their larvae, eggs, fruits (especially dates) and tubers. Reportedly raids poultry coops, although evidence is anecdotal. Forages alone, largely at night, becoming more crepuscular/diurnal in winter. Prodigious digger, catching most prey by speedy excavation after locating it with its extremely sensitive hearing. Caches surplus food in little excavations, and sometimes enters human settlements to scavenge. **Social and Spatial Behaviour** Poorly known. Thought to form territorial breeding pairs in enduring ranges; observed groups with up to 10 individuals suggest extended families with helpers. Density is unknown but they are often the most common mammal (aside from rodents) recorded in surveys. **Reproduction and Demography** Thought to be seasonal (but breeds year-round in captivity). Mating January–February; births March–April. Gestation 50–52 days. Litter size 1–4. Pups weaned at 61–70 days. MORTALITY Putative predators include large owls, African Wolf (page 106) and domestic dogs. LIFESPAN 13–14 years in captivity. **Status and Threats** Status uncertain, but probably secure by virtue of inhabiting very remote regions. Main threat is trapping for the tourist pet and domestic fur trades, which drives local extinctions around settlements. CITES Appendix II; Red List LC, population trend Stable.

# CAPE FOX *Vulpes chama*

HB 45–61cm; T 25–40.6cm; W 2–3.3kg

The only small, light-coloured fox in southern Africa. Body fur grizzled silver-grey, blending into pale tawny-reddish limbs, neck and head. Long, bushy tail has a characteristic dark tip. **Distribution and Habitat** SW Angola, Namibia, Botswana and South Africa; possibly Swaziland and Lesotho. Favours semi-arid/arid habitats extending into moderately mesic scrub habitat in South Africa and Botswana. Occurs on farmland. **Feeding Ecology** Eats chiefly mice and gerbils; also invertebrates, small birds, reptiles and fruits. Largest kills are hares and Springhare. Very rarely kills newborn sheep and goats; most livestock consumed is scavenged. Forages alone, usually at night, with activity peaks after dusk and before dawn. Most prey is captured after prolonged listening at burrows or holes, ending with frenzied digging. Surplus food is cached. Eats carrion, although rarely visits large carnivore kills. **Social and Spatial Behaviour** Usually solitary and monogamous. Breeding pairs are typical, with both parents raising pups. Helpers occur rarely, and adult females (possibly related) occasionally den together. Solitary outside breeding, but pairs share the same range year-round. Range size of pairs 1–32.1km². Density estimates 0.05–0.3/km². **Reproduction and Demography** Broadly seasonal, weakly so in some regions. Seasonal populations mate from June; most births August–December. Gestation 51–52 days. Litter size 1–6, typically 2–4. Pups begin hunting at around 15–16 weeks, reaching independence at 5 months. MORTALITY Adult mortality 26–52% (South Africa), depending on densities of Black-backed Jackal (page 112), the most important predator. Other predators include large raptors, owls and large carnivores, including domestic dogs. Contracts rabies, but is apparently less susceptible than other canids. LIFESPAN <7 years in the wild. **Status and Threats** Many thousands of Cape Foxes are killed, mainly in South Africa and Namibia, for perceived livestock losses, deliberately and as 'by-catch' in trapping and poisoning campaigns targeting jackals and Caracal (page 26). Despite this, the species often prospers on farmland that lacks larger predators (especially jackals) and has expanded its range in some areas. Red List LC, population trend Stable.

# BAT-EARED FOX *Otocyon megalotis*

HB 46.2–60.7cm; T 23–34cm; W 3.4–5.4kg

Grizzled, smoky grey, with black legs and a bushy black-edged tail. Unique dentition, with a range of 46–50 total teeth, the most for any placental land mammal. **Distribution and Habitat** Two disjunct populations in southern and E Africa. Favours arid or semi-arid grassland and open woodland savannah. Inhabits farmland and degraded habitat provided insecticide use is limited. **Feeding Ecology** Almost entirely insectivorous, eating particularly 2 termite genera with which its distribution overlaps almost completely. Also eats other invertebrates, small reptiles, rodents and some fruits, especially in the dry season. Does not kill livestock or poultry, but eats insect larvae in livestock carcasses, sometimes incurring blame for depredations. Forages mainly by sound, typically in family groups. Feeding aggregations of up to 15 individuals from different families occur when termites are abundant. Foraging is chiefly nocturnal, but shifts diurnally in winter, reflecting changes in termite activity. Does not cache food and rarely scavenges. **Social and Spatial Behaviour** Monogamous pair is typical, but sometimes forms extended groups with 1 male and 2–3 related females that breed communally and allo-suckle pups. Insectivorous diet precludes female provisioning at the den, so the male is essential for guarding pups and allowing mothers to forage. Ranges overlap and territorial defence is limited to the den area. Range size 1–8km². Densities fluctuate depending on food and season, e.g. 2.3/km² (non-breeding) to 9.2/km² (breeding; Mashatu GR, Botswana), and 0.7–14/km² (Kalahari, South Africa). **Reproduction and Demography** Seasonal. Pairs mate for life. Mating July–September; births October–December. Gestation 60–75 days. Litter size 1–6, averaging 3. Pups weaned at 10–15 weeks, but remain with the parents until the following June–July; many disperse, although some stay as helpers. MORTALITY Adult mortality 25–30% (South Africa), mainly from predation by Black-backed Jackal (page 112) and disease episodes (rabies and canine distemper). Other predators include large raptors, owls and larger carnivores, but groups vigorously mob predators, often deterring predation. LIFESPAN 9 years in the wild, 13 in captivity. **Status and Threats** Reasonably widespread and tolerant of habitat conversion, but mistakenly persecuted as a livestock predator and cannot persist where insecticide kills off prey. Disease outbreaks associated with domestic dogs sometimes trigger severe local die-offs. Red List LC, population trend Stable.

■ Fennec ■ Cape Fox          ■ Bat-eared Fox

**Plate 54**

FENNEC

CAPE FOX

BAT-EARED
FOX

Listening for
termites

# ISLAND FOX *Urocyon littoralis*

### ISLAND GREY FOX, CHANNEL ISLANDS FOX
HB 45.6–63.4cm; T 11.5–32.2cm; W 1.07–2.7kg
Smallest North American canid, very similar to Grey Fox but much smaller. An insular dwarf form of Grey Fox, separated for 10,400–16,000 years, and genetically distinct. **Distribution and Habitat** Restricted to 6 Channel Islands off the California coast, USA. Occupies all island habitats, including grassland, chaparral scrub, woodland, coastal scrub and dunes. Avoids degraded areas such as overgrazed pasture. **Feeding Ecology** Omnivorous, focusing on the most abundant food source, which differs by habitat and island. The most important food types are small mammals (especially deer mice), insects and fruits (especially prickly pears, and also berries). Also eats seeds, acorns, birds, nestlings, eggs and crustaceans. Cathemeral, with nocturnal activity peaks. Forages on the ground, climbs shrubs for fruits and birds' nests, and scales cliffs for seabird eggs and chicks. **Social and Spatial Behaviour** Monogamous and territorial, living as mated pairs with offspring, which usually remain until their second year; adult offspring are often tolerated even after they are living independently. Resident males chase and fight with other males, mainly during the breeding season. Ranges are among the smallest for any canid: 0.15–0.87km². **Reproduction and Demography** Seasonal. Mating January–March; births February–May (peaking April). Gestation 50–53 days. Maximum litter size 5, typically 1–3. Pups weaned at 6–8 weeks and forage with adults from 2 months. MORTALITY Recent Golden Eagle colonisation on northern Channel Islands led to hyperpredation, prompting population crashes. Exotic disease (especially canine distemper) reduced the Santa Catalina Island population by 95% in 1998–2000. LIFESPAN 10 years in the wild, 15 in captivity. **Status and Threats** Restricted to small, isolated populations that are greatly vulnerable to random events. Golden Eagle predation and exotic disease (and less so roadkill) produced calamitous declines on 4 of the 6 islands, reducing the total population from 6,000, to 1,500 in 2002. Aggressive conservation interventions (especially captive breeding and reintroduction, vaccination against canine diseases and relocation of Golden Eagles) have since reversed declines; by 2011, total population had increased to 5,500 (including >4,000 mature adults) and annual survival rates to >85%. Red List NT, population trend Increasing.

# GREY FOX *Urocyon cinereoargenteus*

### NORTHERN GREY FOX, TREE FOX
HB ♀ 52.5–58cm, ♂ 56–66cm; T 28–44.3;
W ♀ 2–3.9kg, ♂ 3.4–7kg
Grizzled grey body colour, bordered by a sharp edge of rufous on the neck, sides and legs, changing to white underparts, chest and cheeks. Long, bushy tail has a black dorsal stripe and tip. **Distribution and Habitat** Extreme SE Canada, most of the USA, Meso-America, extreme N Colombia and N Venezuela. Inhabits temperate and tropical forests, woodland, brush, semi-arid scrubland, agricultural habitats and peri-urban areas. Avoids very open areas such as grassland and prairie. **Feeding**

**Ecology** The most omnivorous North American fox. Hunts mainly rodents and rabbits in winter, but greatly expands its diet in other seasons as different foods become available. Can be almost exclusively insectivorous in summer, while fruits, seeds and nuts comprise up to 70% of its diet in autumn. Also eats small herptiles, birds, eggs and carrion. Foraging is mainly nocturnal and solitary. The most arboreal of canids, and forages both terrestrially and in trees up to 18m. **Social and Spatial Behaviour** Monogamous and territorial, living as mated pairs with offspring. It is unclear if pair bonds are permanent or if offspring remain as helpers. Territory size differs little between sexes, ranging from 0.13km² (Wisconsin) to 27.6km² (Alabama), averaging 1–6.7km². Density estimates 0.4/km² (California) to 1.5/km² (Florida). **Reproduction and Demography** Seasonal. Mating January–April; births March–early June. Gestation 60–63 days. Maximum litter size 10, typically 3–5. Pups weaned at 6–8 weeks and accompany foraging adults from 3 months. MORTALITY Most important predator is Coyote (p. 102), which suppresses populations in some areas. Distemper and rabies produce local crashes. LIFESPAN 4–5 years in the wild, 14 in captivity. **Status and Threats** Widespread and common. Legal trapping is the main source of mortality; trapping is not regarded as a threat, although it probably contributes to localised population impacts in combination with disease epidemics. Red List LC, population trend Stable.

# RACCOON DOG *Nyctereutes procyonoides*

### TANUKI
HB 49–70.5cm; T 15–23cm; W 2.9–12.5kg
Grizzled dark grey to buff-grey, with a black facial mask, chest, legs and feet. White (leucistic) individuals occur. An ancient canid lineage with no close relatives, and classified in its own genus. Some authors consider the Japanese population a distinct species, *N. viverrinus*, based on limited genetic and morphological evidence. **Distribution and Habitat** Japan, SE Russia, W Mongolia, E China, Korean Peninsula and extreme N Vietnam. Introductions and escapes from fur farms have established populations throughout N, E and W Europe. Inhabits a variety of forest types, shrubland, farmland and urban areas. **Feeding Ecology** Omnivorous. Rodents are the mainstay, supplemented by small herptiles, birds, eggs, fish, crustaceans and carrion. Fruits, including berries, and seeds are important in late summer–autumn before hibernation. New leaves and flowers are consumed mainly in spring, and insects peak in the diet in summer. Eats crops, including oats, corn, maize, watermelon and fruits, and urban populations exploit garden fruits such as gingko and persimmon, e.g. Japan; rarely raids poultry. Foraging is mostly terrestrial and nocturnal. Adult pairs forage together, but often some distance apart. It is the only canid that hibernates, in November–March in areas with severe winters. **Social and Spatial Behaviour** Strictly monogamous, forming permanently mated pairs that share a territory, usually moving and denning together. Territory cores are exclusive, especially while breeding, but range edges overlap. Territory sizes 0.07km² (urban, Japan), 6.1km² (subalpine habitat, Japan) and to 20km² (SE Russia, introduced). **Reproduction and Demography** Seasonal. Mating February–March; births April–June. Gestation 59–70 days. Litter size averages 4–9, exceptionally reaching 19. Pups weaned at 5 weeks, and forage with adults shortly thereafter. MORTALITY Sarcoptic mange, distemper and rabies cause population declines, but impacts appear temporary. LIFESPAN 5 years in the wild, 13 in captivity. **Status and Threats** Abundant in much of its original range, and widely considered a pest where it has been introduced. Very tolerant of suburban and agricultural habitats. Up to an estimated 370,000 are killed annually on roads in Japan, apparently without producing population declines. Fur farms in China maintain a staggering 10 million Raccoon Dogs (2009), presumably mostly captive-bred. Red List LC, population trend Stable.

■ Island Fox ■ Grey Fox    ■ Raccoon Dog

**Plate 55**

ISLAND FOX

GREY FOX

Tree climbing

RACCOON
DOG

# CHILLA *Lycalopex griseus*

### ARGENTINE GREY FOX, SOUTHERN GREY FOX
HB 50.1–66cm; T 11.5–34.7cm; W 2.5–5kg
Small, pale, grizzled grey fox, with rufous-buff lower legs and a rufescent head tinged with grey. Lower thighs have a distinctive dark patch, and the lower jaw is conspicuously dark. **Distribution and Habitat** S Peru to Tierra del Fuego on both sides of the Andes; Peruvian population may be disjunct, as the species is thought to be absent from the Atacama Desert. Inhabits grassland, shrubland, steppes and *Nothofagus* thickets in lowlands and Andean foothills (rarely to 4,000m). Tolerates ranching, agriculture and plantations. **Feeding Ecology** Eats mainly small rodents, European Hare and carrion. Where small mammal availability declines, the diet includes more fruits, arthropods, reptiles and birds. Kills domestic poultry and (very rarely) lambs. Foraging is largely nocturno-crepuscular, and solitary or as loosely associated pairs with offspring during breeding. Buries excess food. **Social and Spatial Behaviour** Forms monogamous breeding pairs, occasionally with female helpers, which help raise pups. Pairs associate loosely outside breeding season. Range size 1.4–2.8km². **Reproduction and Demography** Seasonal. Mating August–September; births October. Gestation 53–58 days. Litter size 4–6. Males help raise pups and provision mother at den. Two mothers (possibly related) may cooperate to raise litters. MORTALITY Killed by domestic dogs and canine diseases, but impacts are unknown. LIFESPAN Unknown. **Status and Threats** Widespread and locally common, especially in its southern range. Once heavily hunted for fur, which has declined, leading to population recovery in some areas. Killed for depredation and in the false belief that it transmits disease to livestock. CITES Appendix II; Red List LC, population trend Stable.

# DARWIN'S FOX *Lycalopex fulvipes*

HB 48–59.1cm; T 17.5–25.5cm; W ♀ 1.8–3.7kg, ♂ 1.9–4kg
Small, stocky fox, dark grey-brown with contrasting white underparts, rufous extremities and a dark bushy tail. **Distribution and Habitat** Endemic to Chile, on Chiloé Island and on the mainland coastal range. Mainland population formerly thought to be restricted to Nahuelbuta NP, but recently confirmed from a much larger area. Relies on dense southern temperate (Valdivian) forest, but tolerates forest mosaics with dunes, beaches and pasture patches. **Feeding Ecology** Eats mainly small vertebrates, insects, crustaceans, fruits and seeds. Largest recorded prey, Southern Pudú (10kg) and Magellanic Penguin, is probably scavenged. Foraging is solitary, but congregates at food patches. Cathemeral; foraging mainly nocturnal in Nahuelbuta, perhaps to avoid larger Chilla (absent from Chiloé). Scavenges, including from fishing waste, pet food and carrion. **Social and Spatial Behaviour** Solitary. Forms monogamous pairs, which associate mainly for breeding on Chiloé but persist year-round in Nahuelbuta. Range size (both sexes) averages 1.5–3km². Density estimates 0.95–1.14/km². **Reproduction and Demography** Poorly known. Seasonal. Observed litters occur October–January. Gestation unknown. Litter size estimated at 2–3. Both parents help raise pups. MORTALITY

Rates in Nahuelbuta are 7–16% annually (juveniles and adults combined). Puma (page 38) is a confirmed predator (mainland only); no natural predators on Chiloé. Killed by domestic dogs at both sites. LIFESPAN Unknown. **Status and Threats** Formerly thought to number <250 adults in 2 populations, but recent range extensions significantly increase the estimated population to ~640–900. None the less, Darwin's Foxes are still strongly threatened by habitat loss to logging, and widespread occurrence of feral domestic dogs and associated disease. CITES Appendix II; Red List EN, population trend Decreasing.

# SECHURAN FOX *Lycalopex sechurae*

### SECHURA DESERT FOX, SECHURA FOX
HB 50–78cm; T 27–34cm; W 2.6–4.2kg
Slender head with a narrow, long muzzle, large rufous-backed ears and a rufous ring around the eyes. **Distribution and Habitat** Coastal NW Peru and extreme SW Ecuador. Inhabits desert, associated beaches and sea cliffs, dry forest and Andean foothills to 1,000m. Occurs in agricultural areas. **Feeding Ecology** Omnivorous and opportunistic. Fruits and seeds comprise much of the diet; also small rodents, birds, reptiles, insects, scorpions and carrion. Coastal individuals eat crabs, and seabirds (probably scavenged) and their eggs. Occasionally takes poultry and domestic guinea pigs; blamed for killing goats (unlikely). Foraging is primarily nocturnal and solitary; congregates in small groups at large carcasses. **Social and Spatial Behaviour** Poorly known. Sightings are largely of single adults or females with pups. **Reproduction and Demography** Poorly known. Births probably peak October–January. MORTALITY Roadkills common in N Peru; impacts unknown. LIFESPAN Unknown. **Status and Threats** Very limited distribution; status poorly known. Appears to tolerate rural and agricultural areas. Vulnerable to persecution, and religious ceremonial uses as amulets and handicrafts. Red List NT, population trend Unknown.

# CULPEO *Lycalopex culpaeus*

### ANDEAN FOX
HB 44.5–92.5cm; T 31–49.5cm; W ♀ 3.9–10kg, ♂ 3.4–13.8kg
Largest South American fox, powerfully built and with a robust head. Light to dark grey, with tawny extremities and pale underparts. **Distribution and Habitat** Extreme S Colombia to southern tip of South America. Inhabits all Andean habitats, from dry desert to temperate rainforest, and from coasts to 4,800m (higher than other South American canids). Occurs on ranchland. **Feeding Ecology** More carnivorous and predatory than other South American foxes. Eats mainly rodents, introduced and native lagomorphs, and ungulates (wild and domestic), mostly as carrion but recorded killing young Alpacas, Vicuñas, Llamas and Guanacos (up to 33kg); Northern Pudú (5–10kg) and Little Red Brocket (8–14kg) dominate the diet in Podocarpus NP, Ecuador. Also consumes fruits, birds, invertebrates and herptiles. Kills small livestock, generally young lambs but occasionally adults, e.g. a 3.6kg juvenile fox killed a 24kg goat by suffocation. Generally forages alone and is cathemeral; strictly nocturnal where hunted. Scavenges. **Social and Spatial Behaviour** Solitary and territorial. Forms pairs for breeding; male assists in caring for pups. Range estimates (both sexes) typically 4.5–8.9km², but as large as 800km². **Reproduction and Demography** Seasonal. Mating August–October; births October–late December. Gestation 55–60 days. Litter size 3–8, averaging 5. MORTALITY Rates for juveniles 20% (not hunted) to 92% (hunted), and for adults 31% (not hunted) to 49% (hunted). Chief predators are domestic dogs and Puma (page 38). LIFESPAN 11 years in the wild. **Status and Threats** Widespread, common and resilient. Benefits from pastoral/agricultural conversion with introduction of exotic lagomorphs. Intensely persecuted as a livestock pest and extirpated from extensive sheep-ranching areas. CITES Appendix II; Red List LC, population trend Stable.

■ Chilla ■ Darwin's Fox          ■ Culpeo ■ Sechuran Fox

**Plate 56**

CHILLA

DARWIN'S FOX

SECHURAN
FOX

CULPEO

# HOARY FOX *Lycalopex vetulus*

### HOARY ZORRO, SMALL-TOOTHED DOG
HB 49–71cm; T 25–38cm; W 2.5–4kg
Small, slender fox, grizzled grey with buff lower legs and underparts, and with a less crisply contrasting chest and throat patches than in similar foxes. Smallest canid in its range. **Distribution and Habitat** Endemic to Brazil. Inhabits mainly open *cerrado* savannah, and occasionally associated woodland, forest and floodplains. Occurs in pastoral, agricultural and plantation habitats. **Feeding Ecology** Largely insectivorous, with a diet dominated by harvester termites, dung beetles and grasshoppers. Also eats small rodents, birds, reptiles, wild fruits and grasses. Evidence for poultry depredation is equivocal. Foraging is largely nocturnal, singly or as pairs with offspring. Most prey is taken on the soil surface; flips cattle dung for termites and dung beetles. **Social and Spatial Behaviour** Forms monogamous breeding pairs that inhabit a defined range and cooperate to raise pups. Unclear whether pairs are permanent, and there is no evidence of extended family groups with helpers. Range size 3.8–4.6km². **Reproduction and Demography** Seasonal. Mating late May–June; births July–August. Gestation 50 days (estimated). Litter size 2–5. Weaning at around 3 months. Males help groom, guard and chaperone pups on foraging excursions. MORTALITY Maned Wolves (page 128) are putative predators. In C Brazil in 2007–13, 30 of 70 foxes monitored in non-protected habitat were killed by people (including road mortalities) and their dogs. LIFESPAN 8 years in captivity. **Status and Threats** Widespread, common and tolerant of some habitat conversion to pasture and agriculture. Persecuted (probably mistakenly) for poultry depredation, and roadkills are frequent. Rabies and sarcoptic mange are confirmed, although population impacts are unknown. Red List LC, population trend Unknown.

# PAMPAS FOX *Lycalopex gymnocercus*

### AZARA'S FOX
HB ♀ 50.5–72cm, ♂ 60–74cm; T 25–41cm;
W ♀ 3–5.7kg, ♂ 4–8kg
Medium-sized fox, grizzled grey with reddish ears, neck and lower limbs. Throat, chest and lower hind limbs creamy white. Smaller than sympatric Culpeo (page 124). **Distribution and Habitat** Extreme SE Brazil, E Bolivia, NE Argentina, Paraguay and Uruguay. Optimal habitat is pampas grassland, but also inhabits scrub, open woodland, pasture and agricultural land. **Feeding Ecology** Adaptable omnivore with a diet that shifts depending on availability. Most important food items are small rodents, European Hare, grassland birds, insects and fruits. Eats carrion, especially livestock carcasses. Rarely kills newborn lambs. Foraging is solitary, but congregates at large carcasses. Cathemeral, becoming largely nocturnal where persecuted. Scavenges. **Social and Spatial Behaviour** Solitary. Forms monogamous pairs, but appears to associate only during the breeding season. Range estimates 0.4–1.8km². Reported densities typically 1–3/km², peaking at 5.85/km² in optimal pampas habitat free of persecution. **Reproduction and Demography** Seasonal. Mating July–August;

■ Hoary Fox ■ Pampas Fox    ■ Crab-eating Fox ■ Short-eared Dog

births September–December. Gestation 55–60 days. Maximum litter size 8, typically 3–4. Pups weaned at 2 months. Both parents guard pups, and males provision females and pups at the den. MORTALITY Predators include Puma (page 38) and domestic dogs. LIFESPAN 14 years in captivity. **Status and Threats** Widespread, common and tolerant of agricultural/pastoral conversion, but legal control and bounties for perceived livestock depredation kill many tens of thousands, resulting in local population declines. CITES Appendix II; Red List LC, population trend Stable.

# CRAB-EATING FOX *Cerdocyon thous*

### CRAB-EATING ZORRO
HB 57–77.5cm; T 22–41cm; W 4.5–8.5kg
Medium-sized fox, with coarse, grizzled dark grey fur, giving it a dark bristly appearance. Muzzle and lower limbs usually conspicuously dark. **Distribution and Habitat** E Panama (a recent range expansion since 1999–2000 into agriculture-dominated landscapes), N Colombia, Venezuela, E and S Brazil, E Bolivia, Paraguay, N Argentina and Uruguay. Occupies all kinds of forest, woodland, grassland and marshland to 3,690m (Colombia), as well as pastoral and agricultural habitats. **Feeding Ecology** Omnivorous, with a catholic diet, especially fruits, insects and small mammals. Also eats birds, reptiles, eggs, amphibians, land crabs, insects and carrion. A pair was filmed killing a 2.5m Boa Constrictor (Mato Grosso do Sul, Brazil). Raids poultry and kills small lambs (rarely). Foraging is mainly nocturno-crepuscular and as pairs with pups, or alone. Congregates in larger groups on turtle-nesting beaches and at carcasses. **Social and Spatial Behaviour** Monogamous, forming mated pairs occupying exclusive territories. Yearling offspring often remain with the resident pair, forming family groups of up to 7. Dispersers may settle near their parents and interact amicably as adults. Range size for adults 0.5–10.4km², averaging 2.2–5.3km². Density estimates 0.55/km² (Brazilian scrub savannah) to 4/km² (Venezuelan Llanos). **Reproduction and Demography** Possibly seasonal, with dry-season breeding peaks, although births occur year-round in some areas. Gestation 52–59 days. Litter size 3–6. Pups weaned at 12 weeks. MORTALITY Killed by larger carnivores like domestic dogs; common as roadkill. LIFESPAN 9.2 years in the wild, 11.5 in captivity. **Status and Threats** Widespread, common and adaptable; deforestation to agricultural mosaics actually favours the species and it has expanded its range in some areas. CITES Appendix II; Red List LC, population trend Stable.

# SHORT-EARED DOG *Atelocynus microtis*

### SMALL-EARED DOG
HB 72–100cm; T 25–35cm; SH *c*.35cm; W 9–10kg
Medium-sized canid with short, sleek, uniformly coloured fur ranging from very dark brown to rufous-grey. Face long and slender, and ears conspicuously small. Classified in its own genus; most closely related to Bush Dog (page 128). **Distribution and Habitat** Restricted to W lowland Amazonia, in Colombia, Ecuador, Brazil, Peru and Bolivia. Inhabits undisturbed primary forest and is usually associated with rivers. Avoids human presence and disturbed habitats. **Feeding Ecology** Poorly known; fish dominate the diet in Cocha Cashu, Peru. Other food includes agoutis, small marsupials, rodents, birds, crabs, frogs and fruits. Has been observed hunting in waterholes and swimming after prey; its elongated shape, sleek fur and partially webbed toes may be adaptations for semi-aquatic hunting. **Social and Spatial Behaviour** Poorly known. Most sightings are of individuals, suggesting it is solitary, but adult pairs have been observed foraging together. **Reproduction and Demography** Poorly known. Observed litters cluster in the dry season (May–December). MORTALITY Unknown. LIFESPAN 11 years in captivity. **Status and Threats** Naturally rare and relies on intact forest. Amazon deforestation is a serious threat, and domestic dog diseases were implicated in an apparent population decline in Peru. Red List NT, population trend Decreasing.

**Plate 57**

HOARY FOX

PAMPAS FOX

CRAB-EATING
FOX

SHORT-EARED
DOG

# BUSH DOG
## *Speothos venaticus*

HB 57.5–75cm; T 11–15cm; SH *c.*30cm; W 5–8kg
Small, stocky dog unlike any other canid, with a long body, short legs and short, bushy tail. Broad head is bear-like with small eyes and short, rounded ears. Body colour varies from blond to dark brown; usually tawny blond on the neck and head, and dark brown on the legs and tail. **Distribution and Habitat** N Argentina and N Paraguay, through much of Brazil into N South America, N Ecuador to Panama–Costa Rica border; first confirmed in Costa Rica (Las Tablas Protected Zone, Talamanca Mountains) in 2016. Closely tied to intact forest and forest savannah, including well-vegetated *cerrado* and pampas grassland. Occurs on ranchland and in agricultural areas, but is dependent on forest fragments in disturbed habitats. **Feeding Ecology** Eats mainly small mammals up to its own weight, especially pacas, agoutis, Nine-banded Armadillo, Brazilian Rabbit, opossums and rats. Large terrestrial reptiles, e.g. tegu lizards, and birds, e.g. tinamous, are also taken. Packs supposedly kill large prey, including Capybara, brocket deer and rhea, by biting the legs until the quarry tires: a report exists of a pack of 6 harassing and badly wounding an adult Brazilian Tapir. Sometimes eats *Cecropia* fruits. Local people report that it occasionally takes chickens. Foraging is mostly diurnal, and it sleeps in burrows overnight; there are a handful of observations of nocturnal hunting. Hunts socially, mainly by prolonged pursuit through thick vegetation, assisted by its long, squat body shape. Readily takes to water during pursuits, and enters and excavates burrows in pursuit of prey. **Social and Spatial Behaviour** Most social of small canids, living in small packs of 2–12 (generally 2–6) that are in constant close contact, including sleeping in groups. Pack composition is thought to comprise a monogamous breeding pair with its grown offspring. Pack members help raise pups by provisioning mothers at the den during nursing. Spatial behaviour is poorly known; the few recorded range sizes are very large for such a small canid: a pack inhabiting mainly native *cerrado* savannah forest covered 141km², compared to 709km² for a pack occupying mainly ranchland and agriculture with *cerrado* fragments (both packs in Mato Grosso, Brazil). **Reproduction and Demography** Aseasonal, although birth peaks possibly occur in the wet season. Gestation averages 67 days (65–83 days in captivity). Litter size 3–6, exceptionally to 10. Pups weaned from 4 weeks. Sexual maturity at 10 (♀s) to 12 (♂s) months. MORTALITY Poorly known; predation by large cats is reported by local people. LIFESPAN 10.4 years in captivity. **Status and Threats** Widespread but nowhere abundant, and appears to be naturally rare. Conversion of forested habitat for livestock and agriculture is the main threat. Occasionally killed on roads and as a perceived predator of poultry. Captive individuals are vulnerable to canid diseases such as distemper and parvovirus. CITES Appendix I; Red List NT, population trend Decreasing.

# MANED WOLF
## *Chrysocyon brachyurus*

HB 95–115cm; T 28–50cm; SH 70–74cm; W 20.5–30kg
Tall, very long-legged canid with tawny-rufous fur, dark on the neck and shoulders, with black socks and a white-tipped bushy tail. Face fox-like, with very large ears, a white throat and a black muzzle. Melanism is very rare, with a single record from Veredas do Acari Sustainable Reserve, SE Brazil. Despite its common name, it is not closely related to wolves and belongs in its own genus; its closest relative (but distant none the less) is thought to be Bush Dog. **Distribution and Habitat** C and S Brazil, E Bolivia, E Paraguay and NE Argentina; occasional records in extreme SE Peru and N Uruguay. Inhabits primarily *cerrado* and pampas savannah, woodland–savannah mosaics, shrub forest and seasonally flooded wetland such as the Pantanal. Occurs on ranchland and in agricultural areas with cover. **Feeding Ecology** Omnivorous, with a very broad diet of both plant and animal matter; at least 102 fruits and 157 animal species are recorded in Brazil alone, although small vertebrate prey is most important by weight. Common prey includes mice, spiny rats, cavies and small armadillos, as well as small birds, arthropods and (less so) reptiles, including venomous snakes. Occasionally kills tamandua and brocket deer; one record of predation on an adult Pampas Deer, which was killed by a throat bite. Wolf Apple is consumed year-round and is the most important fruit in the diet. Diet expands in the wet season to include more fruits, such as bell peppers, coffee and papaya, as well as new grass. Readily kills chickens, and possibly takes juvenile small stock, although reports are equivocal. Foraging is cathemeral and solitary. Scavenges, including from roadkill carcasses and human refuse. **Social and Spatial Behaviour** Basic social unit is a monogamous pair that shares and defends a common territory from other pairs. Most behaviour, including hunting, is solitary; pairs occasionally rest and travel together, but longer associations occur only when breeding. Territories are stable, marked constantly with urine and faeces, and used equally by both pair members. No difference in range size between males and females, except that female ranges decrease during breeding. Resident pair territory size averages 75km² (*cerrado*, Noel Kempff Mercado NP, Bolivia) and 80.2km² (*cerrado*, Emas NP, Brazil). Extensive non-territorial ranges in Emas NP average 188km². Densities are naturally low, 1.6–8/100km² in Brazilian and Bolivian protected *cerrado* and Pantanal. **Reproduction and Demography** Seasonal. Mating April–June; most births occur in the dry season, June–September. Gestation 56–67 days. Litter size 1–7, averaging 3. Weaning at around 15 weeks, but pups may accompany the mother from 7 weeks. Role of the male in raising pups is unclear; captive males regurgitate food and groom pups, and wild males often accompany mothers and young pups. Sexual maturity at 12 months, but first breeding is probably during the second year. MORTALITY Annual adult and subadult mortality 35% and 36%, respectively (Emas NP). Most mortality is anthropogenic; Puma (page 38) and domestic dogs are confirmed predators. LIFESPAN 15 years in captivity. **Status and Threats** Lives at naturally low densities, and its habitat is under intense pressure from agricultural development. In Brazil, roadkills are one of the leading causes of death, and domestic dogs on ranches often kill Maned Wolves; dogs may also be a source of exotic disease, although effects on populations are unknown. Frequently killed for folkloric medicine, especially in Bolivia, and in retribution for depredation on poultry. CITES Appendix II; Red List NT, population trend Unknown.

■ Bush Dog

■ Maned Wolf

**Plate 58**

BUSH DOG

Family group

Hunting
rodents

MANED
WOLF

# GIANT PANDA
## *Ailuropoda melanoleuca*

HB 120–180cm; T 8–16cm; SH 71–86cm;
W ♀ 70–100kg, ♂ 85–125kg

Unmistakable and probably the most recognisable mammal on Earth. The distinctive white-and-black coloration is not aposematic as in skunks and other black-and-white carnivores. It has been suggested that it helps pandas locate one another in dense habitat during the breeding season, although they clearly utilise scent-marking and calls to find mates, as do most carnivores. The ear and eye markings are thought to be important for intraspecific communication. Cubs are tiny at birth, weighing only around 100g, relatively much smaller compared with the mother's size than in all other bears. Cubs have sparse white fur: black markings appear gradually by 3–4 weeks. The forefoot has a 'false thumb', actually a greatly modified sesamoid bone (normally tiny in bears) with its own pad, which helps in grasping and manipulating bamboo, the species' main food source.

### Distribution and Habitat
Restricted to 6 mountain ranges in the C China provinces of Sichuan (which has about 75% of the population), Gansu and Shaanxi. Formerly widespread across C and SW China, into N Myanmar and N Vietnam. Dependent on temperate montane forest with abundant bamboo at altitudes of 1,200–4,100m. Suitable habitat now occurs only on steep rugged slopes that are inaccessible for agriculture.

### Feeding Ecology
The most specialised and herbivorous of bears, and indeed of carnivores, with more than 99% of the diet made up of bamboo. Eats more than 60 bamboo species, moving seasonally between altitudes to exploit the availability of different types as they germinate and grow. Most parts of the plant are consumed, but it prefers leaves and shoots, which are high in protein and easier to digest than stems and branches. Although it is a capable climber, it eats on the ground, usually in dense stands of bamboo, in a sitting or reclining position. It occasionally eats other items, particularly in years of bamboo die-off, when it is forced to seek other food, including leaves, shoots, roots and the bark of other plants, crops (including wheat, kidney beans and pumpkin) and fruits. Recorded occasionally scavenging from carrion and human refuse. Foraging occurs day and night, with about 50–55% of the time spent eating or gathering bamboo; adults eat 12–15kg a day. Unlike in other bears, foraging patterns do not change during the year to maximise periods of high food abundance. As food is available year-round, Giant Pandas do not hibernate. Females fast for a limited period of 2–3 weeks when they give birth.

### Social and Spatial Behaviour
Solitary and non-territorial, with considerable overlap in home ranges. Individuals may remain in small core areas ≤3km² for extended periods; these overlap little between same-sex adults, although it is unknown if they are actively defended as territories. Range size 1–60km², averaging 5–15km², and changes seasonally as different bamboo species flower and Giant Pandas migrate vertically to track food. Usually stays in high altitudes during summer and spring, and descends to lowlands in winter to forage and avoid deep snow. Unusually among bears, it appears that young females disperse and young males settle close to their natal range. Density estimates are poorly known and controversial; 48/100km² estimated for Mabian NR, Sichuan.

### Reproduction and Demography
Giant Pandas have a reputation for poor reproduction, but this arises from the difficulties of breeding them in captivity. Wild Giant Pandas have a similar reproductive output to other bears. Seasonal. Mating March–May. Oestrus 12–25 days; gestation 97–163 days (averaging 145–146 days in the wild), with delayed implantation. Cubs born August–September. Litter size 1–2 (very rarely 3); with twins, the mother often ignores the second cub, which dies. It is the only bear that regularly gives birth to more cubs than it raises, the reasons for which are unknown. Weaning at 8–9 months. Independence at around 1.5 years. Inter-litter interval 2–3 years, averaging 2.2. Sexual maturity at 4.5 years for both sexes: earliest breeding 5–7 years for females and probably similar for males. Females can reproduce until their early 20s, males until age 17. MORTALITY Post-emergence (i.e. excluding abandoned twins), most cubs survive, with mortality estimated at 10–30%. Adult mortality normally ≤10% for both sexes, except in occasional years of mass bamboo die-offs, when starvation is a serious threat, e.g. at least 138 adults starved in a die-off event in the mid-1970s. No definite records of predation: Giant Panda remains have been found in Leopard (page 48) scats, although it is not clear if the bears were killed or scavenged. Brown Bear (page 138), Asiatic Black Bear (page 134) and Dhole (page 108) co-occur and could plausibly kill subadults and perhaps adults. Cubs are helpless for a prolonged period and could be killed also by Snow Leopard (page 42), Mainland Clouded Leopard (page 42), Asiatic Golden Cat (page 24) and Yellow-throated Marten (page 170). LIFESPAN Maximum 26 years in the wild, 37 in captivity.

### Status and Threats
Numbers in the wild (excluding dependent young <1.5 years of age) estimated to have increased to ~1,860 in 2014 from ~1,200 in 1988, although the species' shyness and the rugged habitat make accurate population estimates challenging. They are strictly protected in China and now rarely killed by humans; occasionally killed unintentionally in snares set for ungulates. Reforestation has led to a ~12% increase in occupied range since 2004, although continued destruction of habitat for forestry and agriculture is a grave threat elsewhere in the range. Now restricted to 33 subpopulations in 6 mountain ranges, each of which is an isolated island surrounded by deforested areas and cultivated land. Within each, habitat is further fragmented by cultivation and forestry, so that most populations number fewer than 50 adults; 18 contain fewer than 10 individuals. An estimated 67% of the population is protected in 67 reserves, but both protected and non-protected areas remain vulnerable to human activities. As well as ongoing habitat conversion, pressures include bamboo-shoot collection by local people, expanding livestock populations and associated grazing pressure, and infrastructure development, especially the building of highways and dams that further fragments habitat. CITES Appendix I; Red List VU, population trend Increasing.

■ Giant Panda

**Plate 59**

Reclining
feeding posture

**GIANT PANDA**

Female with
newborn

Handstand
urination

# SUN BEAR *Helarctos malayanus*

### HONEY BEAR, MALAYAN SUN BEAR

HB 100–140cm; T 3–7cm; SH 70cm; W ♀ 25–50kg, ♂ 34–80kg
Smallest bear, with short jet-black (occasionally chocolate-brown) velvety fur, very small ears and a pale muzzle and chin. Named for its distinctive orange, yellow or cream chest patch, which is highly variable in shape and sometimes absent altogether. **Distribution and Habitat** Occurs patchily, from E Bangladesh throughout Indochina to Malaysia, Sumatra and Borneo. Recorded barely in Yunnan, S China, but very rarely, and possibly only as transients from Myanmar. A published 2017 photo record from extreme S Tibet was actually an Asiatic Black Bear (page 134). Extinct in Singapore. Optimum habitat is dense lowland dry and wet forests, as well as montane evergreen forest and swamp forest, from sea-level to 3,000m. Extends into marginal habitats such as mangroves and plantations, provided dense forest is nearby. **Feeding Ecology** Omnivorous, with a narrow diet dominated by insects, honey and fruits. Eats more than 100 species of insects, especially social species such as ants, termites and bees. Breaks into nests with its powerful claws, and uses its extremely long tongue to consume adult insects, larvae, eggs, honey, honeycomb, beeswax and nesting resin. Fruits are also extremely important, with more than 40 species eaten, especially figs. Occasionally eats other invertebrates such as earthworms and scorpions, reptiles (including small turtles), rodents and birds' eggs. Eats little vegetation, but apparently relishes coconut-palm growth shoots ('hearts'); their extraction kills the trees and creates conflict in plantations. Also may raid fruit orchards and crops such as sugar cane, potatoes and manioc. Livestock depredation is almost unknown, except for exceptional attempts at raiding poultry coops. Scavenges from human dumpsites, especially when natural food is scarce. Foraging is mainly diurnal when undisturbed, but almost exclusively nocturnal when close to humans. Highly arboreal, adeptly climbing trees to forage for fruits and insect nests, and building large nest platforms from branches for resting. Does not hibernate. **Social and Spatial Behaviour** Solitary; reported to gather occasionally around fruiting trees. Spatial patterns poorly known; unlikely to be strongly territorial, but 4 collared males in Borneo occupied small exclusive core areas of less than 1km² with larger overlapping ranges of 6.2–20.6km². Two females in poor habitat had small ranges of around 4km². Density estimates 4.3–5.9/100km² (Khao Yai NP, Thailand). **Reproduction and Demography** The only bear species that is not seasonal at all (although reproduction is very poorly known in the wild). Gestation short, 95–97 days (captivity), suggesting no delayed implantation. One cub (exceptionally 2) born in a tree cavity or hollow log. First reproduction 3 years for females, probably later for males. MORTALITY Poorly known. Humans cause most deaths in many populations. Vulnerable to starvation in poor fruiting years, when conflicts with humans (and related retributive killings) also rise. Confirmed predators include Tiger (page 44) and Reticulated Python (1 known case, of an old, starvation-weakened adult). LIFESPAN Unknown in the wild, 24–25 years in captivity. **Status and Threats** Numbers have declined an estimated 35% since the mid-1980s, chiefly due to

pervasive commercial hunting, and deforestation from logging and conversion to plantations. Hunted mainly for gall bladders for traditional Chinese medicinal use, and for bear-paw soup. Hunting reduced one Thai Sun Bear population by an estimated 50% in 20 years. CITES Appendix I; Red List VU, population trend Decreasing.

# SLOTH BEAR *Melursus ursinus*

HB 140–190cm; T 8–17cm; SH 60–92cm; W ♀ 50–100kg (exceptionally to 120kg), ♂ 70–150kg (exceptionally to 190kg) Solid black coloration, rarely chocolate brown or reddish brown, with a crescent-shaped whitish-cream patch on the chest, and a pale muzzle and face. Fur is long and shaggy. **Distribution and Habitat** Restricted to Sri Lanka, India (90% of the range) and Nepal; extends very marginally into S Bhutan, these are likely vagrant bears from India. Formerly Bangladesh, where it is now presumably extinct. Lives primarily in dry or moist forest, scrubland, savannah and grassland, mostly in lowlands below 1500m, but occasionally to 2,000m, e.g. Western Ghats, India. **Feeding Ecology** The only bear species adapted for myrmecophagy, with flexible, protrusible lips and nostrils that it can seal when sucking termites and ants. Switches mainly to fruits, especially figs, during the fruiting season; mostly eats fallen fruits rather than foraging in trees, although it is a capable climber, e.g. to access honey. Eats tubers, roots and some flowers, but otherwise consumes little vegetation. Rarely eats meat, aside from exceptional meals of small vertebrates and carrion. Feeds on crops, including sugar cane, maize, rice, potatoes and sweet potatoes. Livestock depredation is virtually unknown. Has a reputation for unpredictability and aggression, and may attack people, e.g. 350 injuries and 16 fatalities in Madhya Pradesh, India, in 2001–15. Attacks occur mostly in fields and adjacent forest when people are collecting non-timber forest products, e.g. bamboo, seeds and flowers, or grazing livestock; humans are rarely hunted as prey. Foraging is mainly nocturnal. Pregnant females den for up to 2 months, although it is unclear if they actually hibernate; other cohorts are active year-round. **Social and Spatial Behaviour** Solitary and non-territorial. Home ranges often overlap extensively, and individuals may feed in close proximity without interacting, although females appear to maintain small exclusive core areas. Home range size averages 2km² (♀s) to 4km² (♂s) in Sri Lanka, to 25–100km² in Panna NP, India. Density estimates 6–8/100km² (dry forest habitat, Panna NP) to 27/100km² (productive Terai grassland and forest, Royal Chitwan NP, Nepal). **Reproduction and Demography** Seasonal. Mating May–July. Gestation 4–7 months (captivity), with delayed implantation. Litter size 1–3 (usually 2), with cubs born November–January. Cubs emerge from the den at around 6–10 months, and ride on the mother's back for up to 6 months, probably as a defence against predation. Weaning at 12–14 months, and cubs accompany the mother for 1.5 or 2.5 years, depending on food availability. First breeding at 4 years for females, probably later for males. MORTALITY Poorly known. Humans are the main predator; natural predation of adults is rare, but is known by Tiger (page 44) and Leopard (page 48). LIFESPAN 40 years in captivity. **Status and Threats** Reasonably secure inside protected areas, but outside suffers heavily from habitat fragmentation and anthropogenic killing. Killed retributively and preventively in conflict situations, as well as for commercial trade in its parts, particularly gall bladders. In some parts of India and Nepal, females are killed and cubs captured to be trained mainly by Kalandar gypsies as 'dancing bears', illegal (since 1972) and enforced (since 2009), but still practised in the India–Nepal border region. CITES Appendix I; Red List VU, population trend Decreasing.

■ Sun Bear

■ Sloth Bear

**Plate 60**

SUN BEAR

SLOTH BEAR

Female
carrying cub

# ANDEAN BEAR *Tremarctos ornatus*

### Spectacled Bear

HB 130–190cm; T <10cm; SH 70–90cm;
W ♀ 60–80kg, ♂ 100–175kg (exceptionally to 200kg)

The only bear in South America. Typically black, occasionally reddish brown, with variable, pale facial 'spectacles' that usually extend onto the throat and chest, and are unique to individuals. **Distribution and Habitat** Endemic to the tropical Andes in Venezuela, Colombia, Ecuador, Peru and Bolivia; recently confirmed in NW Argentina (but probably transient dispersers) and possibly occurs in Darién region, Panama. Optimum habitat is high-elevation humid forest and *páramo*, but it inhabits a variety of forests, woodland and grassland at 250–4,750m. An isolated population lives in coastal desert scrub forest around Cerro Chaparrí, NW Peru. **Feeding Ecology** Perhaps the most herbivorous of bears after Giant Panda (page 130), eating mainly bromeliads and fruits (especially of the fig and avocado families). Opportunistically eats cacti, moss, orchids, bamboo, tree wood, palms, honey, invertebrates, birds and small mammals. Mountain Tapirs are sometimes observed with wounds suggestive of bear attacks, and a camera-trap photo from Colombia shows an Andean Bear unequivocally attacking an adult tapir. Kills cattle, including adults, and occasionally sheep, donkeys and horses. Eats crops, particularly corn, and is considered a major crop pest in some places. Foraging is primarily diurnal (0600–2100), although probably more nocturnal where it is persecuted. Given that its preferred food is above ground, it is highly arboreal. Builds a large nest-like 'feeding platform' by pulling fruiting branches into a bunch to support its weight while feeding; this possibly doubles as a rest bed. Readily scavenges, especially from livestock carcasses. With food available year-round, does not hibernate. **Social and Spatial Behaviour** Solitary, but reported to feed in groups (of up to 9) in cornfields and cactus groves. Spatial patterns are poorly known, but like other bears it is unlikely to be strongly territorial. Home ranges of radio-collared bears in Ecuador overlap considerably and average 34km² (♀s) to 150km² (♂s). Density estimates 7.5/100km² (N Ecuador). **Reproduction and Demography** Seasonal. Mating in the only well-studied wild population (NW Peru) occurs December–January with births late-June to mid-October. Gestation 160–255 days (captivity) with delayed implantation. 1–4 cubs (usually 2) are born. They emerge at around 3 months, coinciding with the following fruiting season, and accompany the mother for up to 14 months (possibly longer). First reproduction at 4 years for both sexes (captivity). MORTALITY Poorly known. Humans are the main cause of death in many populations, estimated to be at least 180 bears annually (a minimum estimate) across the range. LIFESPAN Unknown in the wild, 36 years in captivity. **Status and Threats** Reduced to an estimated 42% of its historical range, now present in only 260,000km² in many isolated populations scattered along the Andes. The largest, least fragmented intact sites are in Peru and Bolivia. Habitat destruction from forestry and agriculture is the chief threat, although human hunting is equally grave for many populations. Killed mainly for crop raiding and cattle killing, as well as for fur, meat and some traditional medicinal use. Dairy cow production is increasing rapidly in parts of the range, e.g. N Ecuador, driving an escalation of conflict-related killing. CITES Appendix I; Red List VU, population trend Decreasing.

# ASIATIC BLACK BEAR *Ursus thibetanus*

### Himalayan Black Bear, Moon Bear,
### Tibetan Black Bear

HB ♀ 110–150cm, ♂ 120–189cm; T <12cm; SH 70–100cm;
W ♀ 40–140kg, ♂ 60–200kg

Solid black coloration, often paler on the muzzle and face, and usually with a characteristic crescent-shaped cream patch on the chest. A rare chocolate-brown morph exists, and a highly variable blond morph is known from Cambodia, Laos and Thailand. **Distribution and Habitat** Southern Asia in a narrow band mostly associated with mountains, from SE Iran across C Asia into Southeast Asia (except Malaysia) and S China, including Taiwan, NE China, the Russian Far East, the Korean Peninsula and Japan. Lives primarily in temperate and tropical forested habitats in hilly and mountainous terrains to 4,300m. Avoids open country, but enters plantations, agricultural fields and open alpine meadows in forested habitat. Westernmost population, in S Pakistan/Iran, lives in arid thorn forest. **Feeding Ecology** Chiefly herbivorous, with 80–90% of the diet comprising plant matter. Diet varies seasonally as it moves between habitats and elevations, tracking food availability. In spring, eats mainly succulent young vegetation, including grass, leaves, forbs and bamboo shoots, switching to fruits (including berries) in summer, and hard mast such as oak acorns, beechnuts, walnuts, chestnuts and hazelnuts in autumn. Invertebrates are consumed when available, typically peaking in summer. Vertebrates to the size of small (10–20kg) ungulates such as muntjacs and serows are also eaten. Active hunting occurs, although most meat is probably scavenged. Both sexes hibernate in winter in the northern part of its range (October–May; Russia), while only pregnant females hibernate in the tropics; southern bears that do not hibernate eat mainly hard mast and fruits. Feeds in fruit orchards, plantations (where it ring-barks trees to access the tender cambium) and crops, especially corn and oats. Humans are rarely attacked, and probably never as prey. Foraging is mainly diurnal, although nocturnal activity increases in autumn, when hard mast is abundant, e.g. Taiwan. Readily scavenges, especially from mammals caught in hunters' traps. **Social and Spatial Behaviour** Solitary and appears non-territorial. Home range size averages 26km² (♀s) to 66km² (♂s) in Japan, and 117km² (1 ♀) and 27–202km² (♂s) in Taiwan. Ranges overlap extensively, but females and young males avoid productive areas where adult male ranges concentrate during autumn (Taiwan). Density estimates 8–29/100km² (Khao Yai NP, Thailand). **Reproduction and Demography** Likely seasonal, especially in temperate areas; poorly known from the tropics. Mating May–July. Gestation 6–7 months (captivity), with delayed implantation. 1–3 cubs (most often 2) born December–March (Russia). Cubs accompany the mother for 2–3 years. Sexual maturity 3–4 years for both sexes (captivity). MORTALITY Humans are the main cause of death in many populations. Known natural predators of adults include Brown Bear (page 138), Tiger (page 44) and (rarely) other Asiatic Black Bears. LIFESPAN Unknown in the wild, 36 years in captivity. **Status and Threats** Chief threats are habitat loss, combined with intense human hunting that feeds a massive commercial market for bear products, mainly bile used in the Asian medicinal trade and paws for luxury restaurants. Bear farms are common in China, Vietnam and, increasingly, Laos for bile production. Some are ostensibly self-supporting, but many do not breed bears, and wild bear products are more valuable, fuelling ongoing hunting and capture of wild bears. Relict in Iran (<200) and South Korea (~40, a reintroduced population in Jirisan NP). Sport hunting is legal only in Russia (75–100/year) and Japan (around 500/year); illegal and/or nuisance killing results in an additional 500 and 1,000–2000 deaths, respectively. CITES Appendix I; Red List VU, population trend Decreasing.

■ Andean Bear

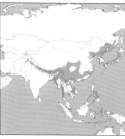
■ Asiatic Black Bear

**Plate 61**

ANDEAN
BEAR

ASIATIC
BLACK BEAR

Blond
form

# AMERICAN BLACK BEAR
## *Ursus americanus*

HB ♀ 120–168cm; ♂ 129–188cm; T <12cm; SH ♀ 63–85cm, ♂ 72–103.5cm; W ♀ 40–150kg (exceptionally to 190kg), ♂ 60–300kg (exceptionally to 400kg)

Smallest of North America's bears and endemic to that continent. Colour is highly variable, most often black but also many shades of brown ('Cinnamon Bear', common in the W USA); a grey-blue morph, 'Glacier Bear', in Alaska and NW Canada; and a cream morph, 'Kermode Bear', which occurs only in coastal British Columbia (10–25% of the population). There is some evidence that Kermode adults are more successful than black individuals at catching salmon in daylight (but not in darkness), possibly because their light coloration is less conspicuous to salmon against daylit sky. Except in the Kermode morph, the muzzle is usually a contrasting shade of buff-brown, useful for distinguishing the species from Brown Bear (page 138). Cubs of any colour may be born into the same litter, and brown cubs often darken after their second year, occasionally becoming black by adulthood. Up to 80% of cubs have a white chest patch that usually disappears but is retained in some adults.

## Distribution and Habitat
Widespread and abundant in most of Canada, and the E and W USA (including Alaska), becoming patchy and fragmented in the S USA and N Mexico. Adaptable, and occupies a wide range of forested habitats from sea-level to 3,500m. Generally avoids areas without cover, although a unique population has colonised open coastal tundra in NE Canada since the recent local extinction of Brown Bears. Readily occupies human landscapes, e.g. farmland and peri-urban areas, provided there is cover.

## Feeding Ecology
Omnivorous, feeding mainly on vegetation, with a relatively small proportion of the diet consisting of animal matter. As in other bears, the diet shifts seasonally, reflecting available food sources. Eats mainly new grasses, buds, shoots and forbs in spring; fruits and soft mast in summer; and hard mast such as hazelnuts, oak acorns and Whitebark Pine nuts, and berries, including huckleberries and buffalo berries, in autumn. Kills are made opportunistically in any season, but especially of winter-debilitated and newborn ungulates in spring. A capable hunter that is recorded killing animals to the size of Moose cows, but most kills are the size of White-tailed Deer fawns or smaller, e.g. rodents, birds, reptiles, fish and invertebrates. Carrion eater, especially of winter-killed ungulates after emerging from hibernation in spring. Readily exploits foods from human sources, especially during autumn hyperphagia. Occasionally kills livestock and eats crops such as apples, oats and corn, and can become a pest by raiding domestic beehives, suburban bird feeders, refuse bins, dumpsters, campgrounds and refuse dumps. Humans are sometimes killed: although rare, kills are thought to be mainly predatory rather than in defence of food or cubs. There are very few records of female Black Bears attacking humans while defending cubs. Foraging is mostly solitary and diurnal, with early-morning and late-afternoon peaks; becomes more nocturnal in human-dominated areas. Forms tolerant congregations at food-rich sites like refuse dumps. Hibernates throughout its range for 3–7 months; in its southern range, where food is available year-round, only pregnant females and mothers with yearling cubs hibernate.

■ American Black Bear

## Social and Spatial Behaviour
Mostly solitary, except mothers with emerged cubs that stay in family groups for 16–18 months. Non-territorial, with enduring home ranges that overlap considerably with those of other adults. Females sometimes establish exclusive areas in their home range that they defend from other females, probably related to raising cubs. Excursions up to 200km outside their own range are fairly common in periods of food scarcity, especially during autumn hyperphagia; individuals typically return to their own range to hibernate. Depending on food availability, range size is 2–1,100km², exceptionally reaching 7,000km² in the NE Canadian tundra, where food is especially scarce. Ranges expand in seasons, years and regions of low food availability. Male ranges are typically 2–10 times the size of female ranges. Average range sizes include 6.9km² (♀s) and 51.2km² (♂s) in Tennessee, 17.1km² (♀s) and 22.4km² (♂s) in California, 28km² (♀s) and 318km² (♂s) in Massachusetts, 48.8km² (♀s) and 112.1km² (♂s) in Idaho, and 295km² (♀s) and 495km² (♂s) in Manitoba. Females mostly settle near their natal range; males disperse more widely. Dispersal distance is typically 10–220km. Density estimates 20/100km² (SC Alaska), 40–50/100km² (N Montana) and 120–150/100km² (SW Washington).

## Reproduction and Demography
Seasonal. Mating mid-May–July, occasionally as late as September in southern areas. Oestrus is 'seasonally constant', lasting until conception or the end of the breeding period. Gestation 200–253 days, with delayed implantation. Cubs born January–February (rarely December). Litter size 1–5, average 2–2.5. Weaning at 5.5–7 months. Independence at 16–17 months. Inter-litter interval usually 2 years, longer when food availability is low. Sexually mature at 2.5–3 (♀s) and 3.5 (♂s) years; earliest breeding at 3–8 (♀s; average 4.5–5.6 years) and 3.5–8 (♂s) years. Reproduction by females is possible until at least age 20. MORTALITY On average, 35% (eastern populations) to 46% (western populations) of cubs die in their first year, but cub mortality ranges from 0% (wilderness, Nevada) to 83% (urban area, Nevada). Mortality averages 23–28% (often much higher for individual populations, especially close to people) following independence, mainly from starvation and human causes, declining to on average 12% (western) to 18% (eastern) for adults. Even in populations not hunted, humans are often the main cause of death, especially from roadkills and problem animal control. Adults have few predators except Brown Bears (page 138) and Grey Wolf (page 100) packs, typically of hibernating individuals killed in their dens. Cubs are additionally vulnerable to predation by adult male American Black Bears, and occasionally by Bobcats (page 36) and Coyotes (page 102); there is at least 1 record of Golden Eagle predation. LIFESPAN Maximum 24 (♀s) and 20 (♂s) years in the wild, 32 in captivity.

## Status and Threats
Widespread and globally secure, with a total population estimated at 850,000–950,000. Has disappeared from large areas of its southern and mid-western US historic range, where remaining populations are patchy, and some are threatened (Florida and Louisiana) or endangered (Mexico). Vulnerable to severe habitat loss and fragmentation, but thought to be recolonising or increasing in much of its range. As many as 40,000–50,000 are legally killed annually by sport hunters and trappers in the USA and Canada. Sport hunting is illegal in Mexico. Poaching, illegal killing and roadkills are serious local threats for some populations. CITES Appendix II; Red List LC, population trend Increasing.

**Plate 62**

Typical
form

**AMERICAN
BLACK BEAR**

Kermode
form

Cinnamon
form

Glacier
form

# BROWN BEAR *Ursus arctos*

## GRIZZLY BEAR

HB ♀ 140–228cm; ♂ 160–280cm; T 6.5–21cm; SH 90–152cm; W ♀ 55–277kg, ♂ 135–725kg

Second-largest terrestrial carnivore after the closely related Polar Bear (page 140). Massively built, with a distinctive shoulder hump, distinguishing it from similarly coloured morphs of American Black Bear (page 136). Colour is variable, ranging from light blond through various shades of brown to near black. Some individuals have blond tips to the hairs, giving a grizzled appearance, hence the name Grizzly Bear (used only in North America). Cubs often have a white or blond collar that usually fades after their first year, but sometimes persists in adults, especially in Eurasian populations. Size varies significantly, seasonally within populations and regionally between populations: smallest bears are W Eurasian, e.g. Syrian Bear (*U. a. syriacus*, the subspecies inhabiting Iran to Turkey), while bears with access to abundant salmon, e.g. in coastal habitats of Alaska, British Columbia and eastern Russia, are largest.

## Distribution and Habitat

The most widespread bear, ranging across NW North America, the Russian Far East and through northern Asia, including Japan, to Fenno-Scandinavia, and south in progressively fragmented populations through the Tibetan Plateau to the Himalayas, SW Iran, Turkey and W Europe. Inhabits a wider variety of habitat types than any other ursid, including all types of temperate forest, coastal habitats, meadows, grassland, steppes, tundra and semi-desert, from sea-level to 5,000m.

## Feeding Ecology

Highly omnivorous and opportunistic, with the broadest diet of any bear species, comprising all types of fungi, plant matter, invertebrates, fish, reptiles, birds, eggs and mammals. In most populations, the diet changes seasonally as bears move between habitats and elevations, reflecting food availability. In spring and early summer, they eat mainly grasses, shoots, sedges and forbs, and actively hunt newborn ungulates such as Elk, Moose and Caribou/Reindeer calves. Fruits, including berries, become increasingly important during summer and early autumn; roots and bulbs are also eaten, and may become critical in autumn for some inland populations if fruit crops are poor. Super-abundant salmon is a key food source for many coastal populations, especially in autumn during the spawning run. Invertebrates and hard mast are also important in summer and autumn, given their high fat content, e.g. Rocky Mountain bears in high talus slopes eat up to 40,000 Army Cutworm moths daily, and harvest Whitebark Pine nuts from American Red Squirrel middens almost exclusively. Meat dominates the diet at the end of winter as the bears emerge from hibernation to scavenge carcasses of winter-killed ungulates, and hunt weakened Moose, Elk, bison, Caribou/Reindeer, Wild Boar and various deer species; adult Musk-ox occasionally recorded. Occasionally kills livestock, raids crops and ransacks domestic beehives, typically peaking during autumn hyperphagia and especially when natural food sources are poor. Humans are sometimes killed, usually in defence of carrion or cubs, but occasionally as food. Loses 5–43% of its body mass during winter hibernation. Foraging is mostly solitary, but large seasonal congregations gather at food-rich sites like spring meadows, salmon runs, alpine-moth aggregations and refuse dumps. May cache food, especially large carcasses, by covering it with dirt and vegetation, and often lies close to the pile. Readily scavenges, including from human refuse.

## Social and Spatial Behaviour

Solitary, but emerged cubs (≥3 months old) accompany their mothers for up to 3 years, and adults congregate amicably at seasonal feeding sites. Not classically territorial. Adults maintain enduring home ranges that often overlap extensively; subordinate bears give way to dominant individuals in well-defined dominance hierarchies that segregate individuals and prioritise access to food and mates. Range size is smallest in populations with concentrated dependable food sources such as salmon, e.g. 24–89km² (♀s) and 115–318km² (♂s) in coastal Alaska and British Columbia. Ranges generally increase inland where food sources are more dispersed, e.g. 281km² (♀s) to 874km² (♂s) in Yellowstone NP, USA; up to 2,434km² (♀s) and 8,171km² (♂s) in the C Canadian Arctic. Subadult bears occupy areas of up to 20,000km², e.g. C Canadian Arctic, before settling into their adult range. Females tend to settle near their natal range, while males disperse more widely. Density estimates 1–3/1,000km² (Norway), 3–4/1,000km² (Arctic National WR, Alaska), 14–18/1,000km² (Yellowstone NP), 47–80/1,000km² (Glacier NP, USA), 135–190/1,000km² (Abruzzo NP, Italy), to 191–551/1,000km² (coastal Alaska).

## Reproduction and Demography

Seasonal. Mating April (Eurasia) to mid-May (North America) until July. Oestrus 10–30 days; gestation 210–255 days, with delayed implantation. Cubs born January–March. Litter size typically 1–3, rarely to 6. Adoption and exchange of emerged cubs sometimes occurs. Weaning at around 18 months, independence at 2–3 years, occasionally as long as 4.5 years. Inter-litter interval averages 3.5 years, range 2–6, depending on food availability. Sexual maturity at 3.5 (♀s) and 5–5.5 (♂s) years; earliest breeding at 4–8.1 (♀s) and 5–8 (♂s) years. Reproduction by females possible until age 28. MORTALITY 13–44% of cubs die in their first 1.5 years. Adult mortality ≤10% (♀s) and 6–38% (♂s), higher rates occurring in hunted populations. Even in populations that are not hunted, humans are often the main cause of death. Adults have few predators except other Brown Bears and (rarely) Tigers (page 44; Russia). Both sexes (but usually males) occasionally kill cubs, and males sometimes kill other adults. Cubs are occasionally killed by Grey Wolf (page 100) and Golden Eagle (1 confirmed record). LIFESPAN Maximum 25–30 years in the wild, reportedly 47 in captivity.

## Status and Threats

Still widespread and relatively common in much of its northern range, with large numbers in W Canada (~25,000), Alaska (~33,000) and Russia (100,000–125,000). The next largest subpopulations are in W Europe, excluding Russia, and are fragmented (~15,400); W China (~5,000–6,000); and Hokkaido, Japan (~2,200). Southern range has undergone significant contraction and severe fragmentation into numerous very small and isolated populations. Extirpated from Mexico, most of the lower 48 United States, and most of its former range in Europe and the Middle East. Formerly occurred in N Africa, perhaps until the mid-1800s in Morocco and Algeria, and the only modern bear species to inhabit Africa. Globally secure, but small isolated populations are vulnerable to contact with humans. Legal sport hunting occurs in at least 18 range countries, with the largest numbers killed in Canada, Finland, Romania, Russia, Slovakia and the USA (Alaska only). Some 300–800 bears, a very high percentage of the population, are killed annually on Hokkaido to limit the population and manage conflict. CITES Appendix I – Bhutan, China, Mongolia, Mexico and Himalayan populations, Appendix II – elsewhere; Red List LC, population trend Stable.

■ Brown Bear

**Plate 63**

Kodiak Island
form, male

**BROWN
BEAR**

Grizzly form,
female

Syrian form

Cubs

# POLAR BEAR *Ursus maritimus*

HB ♀ 180–247cm, ♂ 200–285cm; T 6–21cm; SH 120–170cm;
W ♀ 150–450kg, ♂ 300–655kg (exceptionally to 800kg)
The world's largest terrestrial carnivore. The bear's white fur is actually unpigmented and transparent, its shifting hue depending on reflected light, e.g. golden at sunset/sunrise and bluish when it is cloudy or misty. Impurities such as oils from kills also stain the fur, contributing to a dirty cream or yellowish colour. Skin is pink in young cubs, but completely black (as on nose) in adults; it was once thought to enhance the absorption of ultraviolet (UV) light, but the transparent hairs actually absorb UV before it reaches the skin. Hairs are also hollow, increasing insulation (and the reason why captive animals sometimes appear greenish due to algal growth inside the hair). Closely related to Brown Bear (page 138); ranges of the 2 species overlap minimally, chiefly in the W Canadian Arctic, where wild hybrids are rarely recorded – 2 were shot by hunters in Canada's Northwest Territories, in 2006 (Banks Island) and 2010 (Victoria Island).

## Distribution and Habitat
Circumpolar in the Arctic: Canada, the USA (Alaska), Russia, Norway (Svalbard) and Greenland. Transient in N Iceland, where it is usually shot, e.g. 2 in June 2008. Reliant on sea-ice habitats mostly within 300km of the coast, where marine productivity is the highest. Follows retreating ice northwards in summer where possible, e.g. N Greenland, where summer ice remains near the coast; otherwise forced inland, e.g. Hudson Bay, Canada. After the first few months of life, many individuals spend their entire lives on sea-ice.

## Feeding Ecology
The most carnivorous bear species and profoundly dependent on seals and sea-ice for hunting; cannot hunt in open water. The most important prey species is Ringed Seal, followed by Bearded Seal, Harp Seal and Hooded Seal. Seals are caught by 'still-hunting', which involves patiently waiting at breathing holes, sometimes for hours; by carefully stalking basking seals either on ice or from water; or by 'pole-driving' into seal birth dens to catch newborn pups. Walruses are occasionally hunted, sometimes by stampeding colonies at haul-out sites, e.g. Wrangel Island, Russia, resulting in dozens of crushed animals, which are scavenged. Recorded killing Narwhals and Beluga Whales, usually when the whales are trapped in ice. During lean periods, e.g. summer, when some populations are restricted to ice-free land, opportunistically eats berries, kelp, grasses, fish, seabirds, eggs, small mammals, hares and Reindeer/Caribou, but it cannot survive indefinitely on this diet. Humans are killed extremely rarely, typically by starving male bears; 20 fatalities globally 1870–2014. Polar Bears have a prodigious ability to fast when food is scarce, dependent on extensive fat reserves accumulated from seals. Fasting bears enter a similar physiological state to hibernation, but remain active and alert. This can occur during food shortages in any season (in contrast to other bears, which fast only during winter hibernation). Pregnant females can fast for 8 months from the time they leave the ice to den until the next ocean freeze-up after birth. Healthy males and non-pregnant females easily fast for 4–6 months, but apart from sheltering temporarily in severe weather, they do not overwinter in dens. Foraging is mostly solitary, but congregations form around large carcasses, Walrus colonies and dumps. Readily scavenges, e.g. from beached whales and refuse.

■ Polar Bear

## Social and Spatial Behaviour
Solitary, but emerged cubs (≥3 months old) always accompany their mothers, and bears congregate amicably at food-rich areas and while waiting for the freeze-up, when unrelated adults often engage in highly social behaviour such as play-fights. Extremely mobile and has the largest home ranges of any carnivore; utilises different areas in its range depending on ice dynamics, but does not wander randomly as once thought. Annual ranges are smaller in near-shore areas with stable ice, averaging 50,000km², compared with ranges on drift ice, which average 250,000km². Hudson Bay females have annual ranges of 8,470–311,646km² (average 106,613km²), while Beaufort Sea (Canada/Alaska) female ranges are 13,000–597,000km² (average 149,000km²). Straight-line movements (i.e. minimum estimates) can exceed 50km per day and 6,200km per year. Easily swims 25–40km and capable of extraordinary endurance in water: a monitored Beaufort Sea female swam continuously for 232 hours, covering 687km, in 2–6°C water. Ranges and movements are thought to be similar for both sexes, but males are rarely radio-collared as their neck circumference exceeds their head size.

## Reproduction and Demography
Seasonal. Mating March–June. Oestrus duration poorly understood, but mating associations last 2–4 weeks; gestation 195–265 days, with delayed implantation. Cubs born mid-November–mid-January in traditional denning areas near the coast or in drift ice, where snowfall and topography allow excavation of snow dens. Litter size 1–3 (4 exceptionally recorded from captivity), most often 2. Weaning and independence occur together, coinciding with the mother's next breeding season, normally at 30 months, sometimes at 18 or 42 months, depending on food availability. Inter-litter interval averages 3.1–3.6 years. Both sexes are sexually mature at 3–3.5 years, but earliest breeding is at 4–6 (♀s) and 6–8 (♂s). Reproduction is possible until age 27 (♀s) and over 20 (♂s). MORTALITY Depending on resources, 25–65% of cubs die in their first year, most from starvation. Survival rates increase each year of life until prime adult natural mortality is 1–4%. Adults have no predators except other Polar Bears and humans; male bears are sometimes infanticidal, and Grey Wolves (page 100) are (rarely) recorded killing young cubs. There are occasional records of Walruses killing bears when attacked. LIFESPAN 32 (♀s) and 29 (♂s) years in the wild, 42 in captivity.

## Status and Threats
Total numbers estimated at 20,000–25,000 in 19 relatively discrete subpopulations. Protected by a 5-nation treaty that restricts hunting to indigenous communities (Canada, Alaska and Greenland), or prohibits hunting (Norway/Svalbard and Russia, largely unenforced in the latter, where illegal hunting in E Russia is estimated to kill 100–200 bears a year). Annually, 700–800 bears are legally hunted, most (~500) in Canada, which is also the only range state that permits sport hunting, under the quota to native people. Excessive harvest causes population declines and is a short-term threat in some areas, e.g. in the Chukchi Sea subpopulation (hunted legally in the US and illegally in Russia). Given the species' strict dependence on sea-ice, global warming is now recognised as the greatest long-term threat; southern-most populations are already impacted by earlier than usual sea-ice thaws, e.g. S Beaufort Sea and W Hudson Bay, and display lowered condition and survival, and escalated conflict with people in their search for food; the former is 1 of 3 (and possibly 5) subpopulations known to be declining. CITES Appendix II; Red List VU, population trend Unknown.

**Plate 64**

Pole-driving
for seal pups

Play-fighting

**POLAR BEAR**

Cubs

Waiting for
ocean freeze-up

# PYGMY RACCOON *Procyon pygmaeus*

### COZUMEL RACCOON
HB 35–43cm; T 22–35cm; W ♀ 2.9–3.5kg, ♂ 3–4.1kg

The smallest raccoon, with orange-tinged fur on the tail and along the spine, especially in males. Has been classified as a Northern Raccoon subspecies, but recent genetic analysis shows it is a distinct species. Three other insular Caribbean populations, formerly called Bahamas Raccoon (*P. maynardi*), Barbados Raccoon (*P. gloveralleni*; extinct) and Guadeloupe Raccoon (*P. minor*), are actually introduced Northern Raccoons. **Distribution and Habitat** Endemic to Cozumel Island, Mexico. Relies heavily on mangroves, coastal wetland and (less so) adjacent tropical rainforest. **Feeding Ecology** Omnivorous, with more than 50% of the diet made up of crabs; insects, fruits, and marine turtle eggs and nestlings make up most of the balance. Foraging is solitary and mainly nocturnal. Individuals near settlements are heavier, suggesting they scavenge from food refuse. **Social and Spatial Behaviour** Poorly known. Thought to be essentially solitary, analogous to low-density unsubsidised Northern Raccoon populations. Limited telemetry data suggest a provisional range size of 0.7km². **Reproduction and Demography** Poorly known. Births believed to occur mainly November–January. MORTALITY No natural predators, but killed by feral dogs and possibly introduced Boa Constrictors. Frequent hurricane devastation of habitat causes significant mortality and drastic population declines. LIFESPAN Unknown. **Status and Threats** Occurs only on Cozumel Island, where it numbers fewer than 250 mature individuals. Depends strongly on coastal habitats, which are under intense development pressure for tourism infrastructure and associated roads; habitat loss and roadkills, in concert with frequent hurricanes, drive rapid and severe population decline. Red List CR, population trend Decreasing.

# NORTHERN RACCOON *Procyon lotor*

### COMMON RACCOON
HB 44–62cm; T 19.2–40.5cm; W ♀ 1.7–7.1kg (exceptionally to 10kg), ♂ 2.4–11kg (exceptionally to 28kg)

Largest and most familiar raccoon. Colour usually grizzled grey-brown, but varies from cinnamon to near black. All forms have the characteristic dark mask with pale eyebrows, banded tail and pale feet. Albinism occurs. Northern individuals, e.g. Idaho, can be twice as large and heavy as southern ones, e.g. S Florida. Tres Marias Raccoon (Tres Marias Islands, Mexico) was considered a separate species, but is now classified as a Northern Raccoon subspecies (*P. l. insularis*). **Distribution and Habitat** S and C Canada, USA, Mexico and Central America to the Panama Canal. Introduced in W Eurasia, Japan and on some Caribbean islands. There is almost no habitat it cannot occupy, but it prefers edge habitats and areas associated with water. Lives in close association with humans, including in urban areas and large cities. **Feeding Ecology** Extremely omnivorous and opportunistic, eating virtually all available edible items. Wilderness populations eat mostly fruits, hard mast, aquatic crustaceans, molluscs, amphibians, eggs, nestlings and small mammals. Many populations live largely or entirely on anthropogenic foods, including grains, crops, pet food, bird food and refuse. Sometimes kills domestic poultry. Foraging is mainly nocturno-crepuscular and solitary; congregates at food patches such as dumps. Most food is found by its keen sense of smell, and captured or handled with its very dextrous front feet; often 'washes' food in water, although as clean food is also submerged, the actual purpose is unclear. Does not hibernate, but northern populations may overwinter in dens for weeks or months, during which time they live off accumulated fat. **Social and Spatial Behaviour** Sociality and spatial behaviour are very flexible, depending on food availability. In natural settings, it is essentially solitary and defends ranges against same-sex individuals. Under high food availability, neighbouring females (usually related) have small, closely spaced ranges with high overlap, and males form coalitions of 3–4 that cooperate to defend a territory from other males. Average range size 0.05–0.8km² (urban), 0.5–3km² (rural) and to 25.6km² (wilderness). Density estimates 0.5–6/km² (wilderness), 1–27/km² (rural) and to 111/km² (urban). **Reproduction and Demography** Seasonal. Most populations mate February–March, with births April–June; southern populations are more variable. Gestation 54–70 days. Litter size 1–8, averaging 2–5. Kittens largely independent by 17–18 weeks, but often rejoin the mother for winter denning; the family finally breaks up the following spring. MORTALITY Highly variable, depending on latitude and harvest; 10–83% (juveniles), and 16–55% (yearlings and adults). Most mortality is from disease (canine distemper and rabies) and human harvest. LIFESPAN 12.5 years in the wild (typically <5), 17 in captivity. **Status and Threats** Widespread and extremely adaptable. Widely killed for fur in Canada and the USA, peaking at more than 5 million/year in 1979–80. Populations are very resilient to harvest, which is not considered a threat. Red List LC, population trend Increasing.

# CRAB-EATING RACCOON
## *Procyon cancrivorus*

HB 54–76cm; T 25–38cm; W 3.1–7.7kg

Slender raccoon with a short, dense coat. Fur is greyish brown with a buff, tawny or rufous shade, especially where the body colour transitions to the paler underparts. Legs and feet are dark grey-brown, in contrast to Northern Raccoon, which always has pale feet. The 2 species overlap in S Costa Rica and W Panama. **Distribution and Habitat** S Costa Rica to N Argentina and Uruguay, and Trinidad. Inhabits a wide variety of habitats usually associated with water in forest, brush, wooded grassland, swamps and wetland, and on coastlines. Occurs in dry Chaco scrubland, where water sources are mostly man-made. Tolerates rangeland and plantations; rarely occurs in urban areas. **Feeding Ecology** Omnivorous, eating mainly crabs, crayfish, snails, insects and fruits, especially of palms. Small lizards, snakes, birds, rodents and fish are also eaten. Apparently forages in coastal caves, either for dying bats or insects attracted to bat droppings on the cave floor. Sometimes kills poultry and causes damage in fruit plantations. Foraging is mostly nocturnal, solitary and terrestrial. **Social and Spatial Behaviour** Poorly known. Solitary. Density estimates 6.7/km² (dry wooded rangeland, Paraguayan Chaco). **Reproduction and Demography** Poorly known. Births apparently peak February–June (Suriname). Litter size 2–3. MORTALITY and LIFESPAN Unknown. **Status and Threats** Widespread and probably fairly common. Habitat loss is the main threat. Fairly widely persecuted as a pest and hunted for sport, but effects on populations are unknown. Frequently killed on roads in Brazil. Red List LC, population trend Decreasing.

■ Pygmy Raccoon
■ Northern Raccoon

■ Crab-eating Raccoon

**Plate 65**

PYGMY RACCOON

NORTHERN
RACCOON

CRAB-EATING
RACCOON

# MOUNTAIN COATI *Nasuella olivacea*

Includes **EASTERN MOUNTAIN COATI** *N. meridensis*
HB 40–54cm; T 19.2–30cm; W 1–1.5kg
Smallest coati. Dark olive-brown, with paler, rufous-tinged brown on the throat and chest. Face narrow and elongated, tapering to a sharp point at the nose, which is naked. Recent molecular and morphological analyses suggest sufficient differences to recognise 2 species, Western Mountain Coati (*N. olivacea*; Colombia and Ecuador) and Eastern Mountain Coati (*N. meridensis*; Venezuela), but this remains tentative. **Distribution and Habitat** Endemic to the Andes of Colombia, Ecuador and Venezuela. Inhabits cloud forest and *páramo* shrubland at 1,300–4,250m. Does well in reforested plantations of Andean Alder. Occurs in peri-urban areas with forest near major cities, e.g. Cali and Bogotá. **Feeding Ecology** Eats mainly adults and larvae of soil invertebrates, especially beetles, grasshoppers, locusts, millipedes, centipedes and ants. Frogs are the most common small vertebrate prey (based on limited data). Also eats fruits, leaves, grass roots and moss. Blamed for killing poultry and raiding potato crops, although neither is definite. Thought to forage diurnally in social groups. Leaves behind large areas of turned soil, with many distinctive diggings made by the claws and probing nose; one moss bank of 35m² had more than 5,000 such holes. **Social and Spatial Behaviour** Poorly known. Observed in small groups and individually, suggesting sociality resembles that of other coati species. Group size typically 6–8, although bands of 50–80 have been reported. The only range estimate is 0.11km² (single ♂ monitored for 3 months, Colombia). **Reproduction and Demography** Unknown. A litter of 4 is reported. MORTALITY and LIFESPAN Unknown. **Status and Threats** Limited distribution, with narrow habitat tolerances. Range is under significant pressure from agriculture, logging and pine plantations. Persecuted as a pest, and hunted in some regions for meat and fur. Red List NT (EN for presumed isolated Venezuelan population, assessed separately as *N. meridensis*), population trend Decreasing.

# SOUTH AMERICAN COATI *Nasua nasua*

**BROWN-NOSED COATI, RING-TAILED COATI**
HB 43–59cm; T 42–55cm; W 2–7.2kg
Large coati, typically pale to dark olive-brown, but colour varies from bright ginger to almost black. Most forms have a white lower jaw and buff or orange-buff throat. Muzzle is dark compared with that of White-nosed Coati; the 2 species do not overlap. **Distribution and Habitat** East of the Andes in Colombia and Venezuela to N Argentina and N Uruguay. Introduced to Isla Róbinson Crusoe, Chile. Occurs to 2,500m in rainforest, cloud forest, riverine forest, dry Chaco scrub, and wooded habitat in *cerrado* and Pantanal savannah. Tolerates disturbed habitats with cover, e.g. pasture–woodland mosaics. **Feeding Ecology** Omnivorous, eating mainly ground-litter invertebrates, especially beetles, ants, millipedes and arachnids, as well as fruits. Occasionally takes small vertebrates, and is an important predator of caiman nests. Foraging is social, diurnal and mainly terrestrial, but also above ground among vine tangles and bromeliads. Most food is found by smell. Scavenges from carrion, human refuse and handouts. **Social and Spatial Behaviour** Social. Forms matrilineal bands of related females and their offspring, numbering 5–30 (exceptionally to 65). Adult males are usually solitary and temporarily join bands for breeding, although they sometimes accompany bands year-round, e.g. Iguazú NP, Argentina. Range size estimates include 7.6–54.4km² for bands and 2.2–9.6km² for solitary males. Density estimates 6.2–13/km² (intact forest). **Reproduction and Demography** Seasonal. Mating August–October; births October–November (Iguazú NP). Gestation 65–77 days. Litter size 1–7 (captivity). Group females synchronise births; they leave the band to give birth alone. MORTALITY Under low predation (Iguazú NP), annual mortality 19.7–43.4% (juveniles), and 29.2% (band females). Known predators include Ocelot (page 28), Puma (page 38) and Jaguar (page 50). LIFESPAN 17.7 years in captivity. **Status and Threats** Wide distribution and wide habitat tolerances, including the ability to occupy modified areas. Important meat species for some subsistence hunting communities. CITES Appendix III – Uruguay; Red List LC, population trend Decreasing.

# WHITE-NOSED COATI *Nasua narica*

**COATIMUNDI**
HB 43–68cm; T 42–68cm; W 3.5–5.6kg
Similar to South American Coati, but usually dark or reddish brown with pale 'frosting' on the forequarters, a white muzzle and less distinct bands on the tail (sometimes entirely absent). Coatis on Cozumel, Mexico, are very small and sometimes treated as a separate species, Dwarf Coati (*N. nelsoni*). **Distribution and Habitat** SW USA, Mexico, Central America and Colombia west of the Andes. Inhabits wet and dry forests, woodland and scrub, and lives along vegetated watercourses in arid areas. Occurs close to humans in modified habitats with cover. **Feeding Ecology** Omnivorous. Eats mostly ground-litter invertebrates and fruits, which constitute 88–100% of the diet. Small vertebrates generally comprise <5% of the diet; an important predator of marine turtle nests. Sometimes raids cultivated fruits and gardens, and (rarely) kills poultry. Foraging is social, diurnal and mainly terrestrial, but it is a capable climber that also forages in the subcanopy. Scavenges from carrion, human refuse and handouts. **Social and Spatial Behaviour** Social. Similar to South American Coati, with matrilineal bands of 5–22 (exceptionally to 30). Adult males are more solitary than in South American Coati, and rarely accompany bands except during breeding. Range size estimates include 0.19–0.41km² (tropical forest, Panama) to 7.9–22.4km² (semi-arid forest, Arizona) for bands, and 0.15–0.54km² (Panama) to 3.5–10.7km² (Arizona) for solitary males. Density estimates 1.7/km² (Arizona) to 50–70/km² (Costa Rica, Panama). **Reproduction and Demography** Seasonal. Timing depends on location, with births April–May (Central America) and June (Arizona). Gestation 70–77 days. Litter size 1–6. Females synchronise births; they give birth alone and integrate the kittens with the group at 5–6 weeks. Males disperse to become solitary at 20–24 months. MORTALITY Most natural mortality is from predation, e.g. 76% of known deaths in SE Arizona are by Puma (page 38); Jaguar (page 50), Ocelot (page 28), large raptors and Boa Constrictor are also predators. Capuchin Monkeys are significant predators of nest young, killing 100% of juveniles in some bands, e.g. Santa Rosa NP, Costa Rica. Canine distemper and rabies have produced die-offs in Arizona. LIFESPAN 9 years in the wild, 17 in captivity. **Status and Threats** Widespread, adaptable and secure in most of its range. Important for subsistence hunters, which can lead to local declines, e.g. N Mexico. Indiscriminate predator control, including by poisoning in the USA, has led to large declines. The unusual Cozumel population numbers less than 150 and is endangered. CITES Appendix III – Honduras; Red List LC, population trend Decreasing.

■ Mountain Coati

■ South American Coati
■ White-nosed Coati

**Plate 66**

MOUNTAIN
COATI

SOUTH
AMERICAN
COATI

Group
foraging

WHITE-NOSED
COATI

# RINGTAIL *Bassariscus astutus*

HB 30.5–42cm; T 31–44.1cm; W 0.8–1.1kg
Smallest procyonid in North America, with an unmistakable long, bushy tail marked with black-and-white rings. Can be confused only with the closely related Cacomistle where the 2 species overlap in S Mexico. **Distribution and Habitat** USA, from S Oregon through the SW, and Mexico to Oaxaca. Inhabits rocky desert areas, desert grassland, canyons, chaparral scrub and various forest types. Tolerates agricultural areas with cover, and human settlements including suburban areas. **Feeding Ecology** Eats arthropods, fruits and small vertebrates to the size of hares; mice and squirrels are typical mammal prey. Raids birds' nests for eggs and fledglings, and feeds on agave nectar. Rarely raids poultry. Foraging is both terrestrial and arboreal, and exclusively nocturnal. Scavenges from carrion, human refuse and hummingbird feeders. **Social and Spatial Behaviour** Solitary. Ranges overlap extensively, with little evidence of territorial defence; male–female pairs sometimes associate loosely, but do not share dens (although captive animals are tolerant and den together). Range size 0.05–2.3km². Density estimates 1–4/km², exceptionally reaching 10.5–20/km² (Central Valley, California). **Reproduction and Demography** Seasonal. Mating February–May; most births May–June. Gestation 51–54 days (the shortest among procyonids). Litter size 1–4, exceptionally 5 (captivity). MORTALITY Adult mortality (Trans-Pecos, Texas) 81%, mainly from predation by Great Horned Owl and, less so, Coyote (page 102), Northern Raccoon (page 142) and Bobcat (page 36). LIFESPAN 16.5 years in captivity, much lower in the wild. **Status and Threats** Widespread and relatively common. Legally trapped in SW USA, although fur is poor quality; effects of trapping are unknown. Red List LC, population trend Unknown.

# CACOMISTLE *Bassariscus sumichrasti*

CENTRAL AMERICAN CACOMISTLE
HB 38–47cm; T 39–53cm; W 0.7–1.2kg
Very similar to Ringtail, but larger and with muted facial markings, a darker body colour and dark lower legs. Tail is less strikingly banded, with up to a third of the tip coloured dark brown or blackish. **Distribution and Habitat** S Mexico to W Panama. Occurs primarily in rainforest, evergreen forest, dry forest and dense scrub, mostly associated with mountainous areas. Tolerates secondary forest, plantations and overgrown pasture. **Feeding Ecology** Diet similar to Ringtail's, but insects and fruits appear to be more important than vertebrates. Associated with bromeliads, which are rich sources of small prey as well as water. Foraging is nocturno-crepuscular and mainly arboreal. **Social and Spatial Behaviour** Poorly known. Thought to be solitary. Extensive range overlap (wild) and mutual tolerance of adults (captivity) suggests some social tendencies. Male ranges are slightly larger than those of females; ranges average 0.17–0.23km². **Reproduction and Demography** Poorly known. Gestation 63–65 days. Litter size 1–2. MORTALITY and LIFESPAN Unknown. **Status and Threats** Status poorly known. Locally common and able to occupy small forest fragments, but has disappeared from much of its former range due to deforestation. Hunted locally for meat by indigenous people. Endangered in Costa Rica. CITES Appendix III – Costa Rica; Red List LC, population trend Unknown.

# OLINGOS *Bassaricyon* spp.

Northern Olingo: HB 35–49cm; T 40–53cm; W 1–1.6kg. Western Lowland or Panamanian Olingo: HB 29–37cm; T 37–42cm; W 1–1.2kg. Eastern Lowland Olingo: HB 30–49cm; T 35–53cm; W 0.9–1.6kg. Olinguito: HB 32–40cm; T 33–43cm; W 0.75–1.1kg
A recent revision of the genus clearly delineated 4 species, one of which (Olinguito) is new to science: Northern Olingo (*B. gabbii*), Western Lowland or Panamanian Olingo (*B. medius*), Eastern Lowland Olingo (*B. alleni*) and Olinguito (*B. neblina*). Olingos look similar to one another, typically yellowish brown to tan-brown with creamy or golden underparts; the head is often dark, either greyish or dark brown. Olinguito is the most distinctive and smallest, with shaggy fur that varies from black-tipped tan to rich russet-brown, and distinctly small, round, low-set ears. Olingos are easily confused with the Kinkajou (page 148), especially as they sometimes feed in the same fruiting tree. Olingos are smaller and have long tubular tails that lack Kinkajou's tapering prehensile tip. **Distribution and Habitat** Northern Olingo: Honduras–Nicaragua border to C Panama. Western Lowland Olingo: E Panama to W South America, west of the Andes. Eastern Lowland Olingo: South America, E of the Andes from Venezuela to Bolivia. Olinguito: endemic to the Colombian and Ecuadorean Andes. All olingos inhabit moist tropical forest; Olinguito is restricted to highland cloud forest. Olingos' ability to tolerate human-modified habitats is unclear; Northern Olingos apparently occur in secondary forest and plantations. **Feeding Ecology** Olingos eat mainly fruits, as well as nectar and flowers. Animal prey is rare, but Northern Olingos have been observed killing deer mice, and in one case a Variegated Squirrel; they may sometimes snatch hummingbirds from hummingbird feeders (which they also plunder for sugar-water). Foraging is mostly nocturnal, exclusively arboreal and usually solitary, but olingos congregate in fruiting trees; observations of Eastern Lowland Olingo groups suggest communal foraging by small social groups, possibly family members. **Social and Spatial Behaviour** Olingos are usually observed alone and thought to be mainly solitary, but groups of 2–6 Eastern Lowland Olingos occur in Amazonia, Brazil. Only 1 range estimate exists, for a male Western Lowland Olingo: 0.24km². Olingos are thought to occur in naturally low densities, although 20.4 Eastern Lowland Olingos/km² was estimated in N Brazilian Amazonia; Western Lowland Olingo is much less common than Kinkajou in Panamanian surveys. **Reproduction and Demography** Poorly known. Gestation in captive Northern Olingos 72–75 days, and 1 young is born. Wild births appear to peak in the dry season (Costa Rica), but births are recorded year-round in captive Northern Olingos. Mating by Eastern Lowland Olingos was recently observed in June (Los Amigos Biological Station, Peru). MORTALITY Unknown. LIFESPAN 25.3 years (a captive Northern Olingo), doubtless much less in the wild. **Status and Threats** Status of all species is poorly known. However, they are dependent on forest, occur in low densities and appear less tolerant of human disturbance than most procyonids. All have probably declined due to deforestation and habitat fragmentation. Indigenous people hunt olingos for meat, and they are sometimes captured for the pet trade. Northern, Western Lowland and Eastern Lowland olingos: Red List LC, population trend Decreasing. Olinguito: Red List NT, population trend Decreasing.

■ Ringtail
■ Cacomistle

■ Northern Olingo
■ Western Lowland Olingo

■ Eastern Lowland Olingo
■ Olinguito

**Plate 67**

RINGTAIL

CACOMISTLE

WESTERN
LOWLAND
OLINGO

OLINGUITO

EASTERN
LOWLAND
OLINGO

NORTHERN
OLINGO

# KINKAJOU *Potos flavus*

HB 40.5–76cm; T 37–57cm; W 1.4–4.6kg
Dense, uniformly coloured velvety fur, ranging from honey brown to dark wood brown with lighter golden underparts. Rounded head has large eyes, small forward-facing ears and a short muzzle. Together with Binturong (page 80), the only carnivore with a prehensile tail. Related to, and resembles, olingos (page 146), but is 2–3 times larger and has a slender, tapering tail compared to olingos' bushy, non-tapering tail. **Distribution and Habitat** C Mexico to C Bolivia and SE Brazil. Inhabits a variety of closed-canopy tropical forests, including cloud forest, rainforest and dry forest, from sea-level to 2,500m. Occurs close to humans, including in forested urban parks and plantations with natural canopy. **Feeding Ecology** One of the most frugivorous mammal species, with ripe fruits comprising 90–99% of the diet. Balance is made up of nectar, flowers, and young leaves and buds. Eats fruits from more than 100 tree species, most importantly figs, which produce fruits year-round. Seeds are consumed, but most are passed intact. Substantial amounts of ants and insects are sometimes eaten, probably incidentally while eating fruits and nectar. Captives consume cereals, bread, meat, eggs and milk, although these are not recorded in wild individuals. Sometimes raids orchards; does not kill poultry. Foraging is almost exclusively nocturnal and entirely arboreal; rarely comes to the ground except when compelled. Forages alone, but members of the same social group congregate in fruiting trees. Can hang from its prehensile tail to use both forepaws for handling fruits, and has an extremely long tongue thought to aid it in consuming nectar from deep flowers, e.g. of Balsa Tree. Does not scavenge except to visit hummingbird feeders and feeding stations at tourist lodges. **Social and Spatial Behaviour** Sociality is unusual. The only intensively studied population (Soberanía NP, Panama) lives in small social groups comprising an adult female, her juvenile offspring, a single subadult offspring and 2 adult males. Group members share a collective range, which is defended against other groups, but individuals mostly travel and forage alone. They congregate in diurnal dens where group members groom, sleep and play together. Some adult females live solitarily in small ranges, and are visited by group males for breeding. Groups occur elsewhere in the species' range, although it is unclear if sociality follows the same pattern. Individual range size 0.11–0.5km². Density varies widely depending on fruit abundance, estimated at 12.5–30/km². **Reproduction and Demography** Aseasonal. Gestation 98–120 days. Litter size 1, rarely 2. Males do not assist in raising juveniles. Females apparently disperse (as subadults), while males remain in the group, possibly explaining the species' patrilineal group structure. MORTALITY Few predators given its nocturnal arboreal behaviour, but occasionally killed by Harpy Eagle, Black-and-chestnut Eagle, Ocelot (page 28) and Jaguar (page 50). LIFESPAN 28.7 years in captivity (and one exceptional case of 40.5 years). **Status and Threats** Widespread and common in suitable habitats. Vulnerable to forest loss due to strict arboreality, and disappears wherever habitat is converted to pasture and agriculture. Hunted in some areas for meat and captured as pets, although harvest is unlikely to constitute a significant threat. CITES Appendix III – Honduras; Red List LC, population trend Decreasing.

# RED PANDA *Ailurus fulgens*

LESSER PANDA
HB 51–73cm; T 28–53.3cm; W 3–6kg
Small, robust species with a pale to dark chestnut-brown coat, and black legs and underparts. Thick, bushy tail has alternating chestnut and buff rings. Individuals east of the Nujiang River, China, tend to be darker, with richer red coloration; western populations are paler, especially on the face and head, although there is high variability within all populations. Has formerly been classified with Giant Panda (page 130), procyonids and mustelids, but is currently treated as the only species in a unique family – the Ailuridae – related to all of these. **Distribution and Habitat** S China (most of the range), extreme N Myanmar, Bhutan, N Nepal and extreme NE India. There is unequivocal evidence for a disjunct low-altitude population on the Meghalaya Plateau, India, close to the Bangladesh border, but no definite records since the 1960s. Records from N Laos are dubious. Lives mainly in dense temperate forests with a bamboo-thicket understorey at 1,550–4,800m. Meghalaya records are from tropical forest at 700–1,400m. **Feeding Ecology** Eats almost exclusively bamboo, primarily leaves as well as new bamboo shoots in spring, which collectively comprise up to 95% of the diet. Fruits, including berries, and fungi are eaten in late summer–autumn. Captives are recorded eating small mammals, birds, insects, flowers and bark (also reported for wild animals, although authenticated observations are equivocal). Bamboo is handled with a 'false thumb', actually a highly modified sesamoid bone with its own pad (a feature shared with Giant Panda). Foraging is cathemeral, with long feeding bouts interspersed with regular rest periods. Forages alone and mostly above ground, using fallen timber, low shrubs and tree stumps to reach bamboo. **Social and Spatial Behaviour** Solitary. Groups numbering up to 5 are reported, but there is no evidence of complicated sociality; groups probably comprise females with large cubs. Adults occupy relatively small and stable ranges that often overlap extensively. They demarcate ranges with regular scent-marking and latrines. Range size 0.94–9.6km². **Reproduction and Demography** Seasonal. Mating January–mid-March; births June–July. Gestation 114–145 days (captivity). Litter size 1–4 (exceptionally 5 in captivity), averaging 2. MORTALITY In one study, 67% of cubs died before 6 months and 30% of adults died annually. Most deaths are human related; Leopard (page 48) is a known predator. LIFESPAN 14 years in captivity. **Status and Threats** Restricted to suitable bamboo habitat, which is under severe pressure from forestry, cultivation and grazing. Thought to be declining in much of its range, especially in China; a population decline of >50% is estimated across the range since 1997. Poached for meat and fur in some parts of its range. CITES Appendix I; Red List EN, population trend Decreasing.

■ Kinkajou          ■ Red Panda

**Plate 68**

**KINKAJOU**

**RED PANDA**

Western
form

Eastern form

# STRIPED SKUNK *Mephitis mephitis*

HB 17–40cm; T 15–47cm; W ♀ 0.6–3.6kg, ♂ 0.7–5.5kg
Domestic cat-sized skunk with highly variable white markings, usually variations of a V-shaped cape or double stripe along the back. Some individuals are almost entirely black; brown, reddish and albino forms also occur. The most common skunk in North America, and the species typically encountered in urban areas. **Distribution and Habitat** Southern half of Canada, throughout the USA and N Mexico. Occurs in almost every habitat in its range, to 4,200m, provided there is shelter and food. Thrives in disturbed habitats, and has probably benefited from forest conversion to pasture and fields. Common in urban areas. **Feeding Ecology** Omnivorous and highly opportunistic, feeding on all kinds of invertebrates, small mammals, birds, reptiles, amphibians, eggs, fruits, vegetables, grains and nuts. Eats carrion and readily scavenges from dumps, pet bowls and bird feeders. Sometimes raids domestic beehives and (rarely) poultry coops. Not a true hibernator as it feeds throughout the winter, but it overwinters in dens in its northern range; in severe winters, subsists entirely on fat stores for as long as 3 months. Mainly nocturno-crepuscular. **Social and Spatial Behaviour** Solitary, but adults (especially females) sometimes den together. Ranges fluctuate geographically and seasonally, depending on food availability; estimates 0.5–12km². Urban skunks typically have very small ranges, while the largest ranges are from the Canadian prairies. Density estimates vary widely, depending on food availability and associated disease outbreaks, typically 1.8–4.5/km², but varying from 0.7/km² to 38/km², with the highest numbers recorded from urban parkland. **Reproduction and Demography** Seasonal. Mating February–early March; births April–June. Gestation 59–77 days; longer gestations probably involve a short period of delayed implantation in females that mate early. Litters average 5–9, exceptionally to 18. Independence and dispersal by late August–September. MORTALITY Populations naturally have high turnover rates, with frequent crashes (and rapid recovery) from disease cycles associated with starvation in harsh winters. Natural predators include large raptors (1 Great Horned Owl nest contained the remains of 57 skunks), as well as cats and canids. LIFESPAN Averages 2–3.5 years in the wild, to 12 in captivity. **Status and Threats** Widespread, adaptable and common, and considered very secure in most of its range. Susceptible to rabies, although populations recover quickly. Red List LC, population trend Stable.

# HOODED SKUNK *Mephitis macroura*

HB 27.8–36cm; T 27.5–43.5cm; W ♀ 0.7–1.2kg, ♂ 0.8–2.7kg
Small to medium-sized skunk with variable white markings, typically 1 or 2 narrow stripes along the flanks, sometimes with a white cape. Cape and especially the tail often appear greyish or silvery due to intermixing of black hairs. Smaller than Striped Skunk, with a more slender face and snout, and a proportionally longer, luxuriant tail. Individuals increase in size from south to north. **Distribution and Habitat** SW USA (possibly excluding Texas) through Meso-America to NW Costa Rica. Occupies a wide variety of habitats to 3,110m, including grassland, shrubland, arid lowland, dry and deciduous forests, rocky areas and riverine

habitats. Occurs in agricultural areas and close to human settlements. **Feeding Ecology** Feeds mainly on invertebrates grubbed from the soil and leaf litter, as well as rodents, shrews, fruits (e.g. prickly pear) and eggs. Chiefly nocturnal. **Social and Spatial Behaviour** Solitary, but ranges overlap extensively, and adults congregate amicably at food patches, e.g. artificial feeding stations. Ranges in Mexico are 2.8–5km². Density estimates typically 1.3–4/km², although densities to 25/km² are reported in Mexico. **Reproduction and Demography** Thought to be seasonal; assumed to mate February–March, and to give birth mid-April–June. Gestation approximately 60 days. Litter size 3–8 (typically 3–5). MORTALITY Annual adult mortality in Arizona 44–76%, mostly due to predation by Coyote (page 102), Bobcat (page 36) and raptors. LIFESPAN 8 years in captivity. **Status and Threats** Secretive and inconspicuous, but probably more common than widely assumed. Can survive in human-modified habitats, and abundant in parts of its range, e.g. much of Mexico. Thought to have declined in Texas, with no recent records, but otherwise considered secure. Red List LC, population trend Increasing.

# AMERICAN HOG-NOSED SKUNK
*Conepatus leuconotus*

**COMMON HOG-NOSED SKUNK**
Includes **WESTERN HOG-NOSED SKUNK** *C. mesoleucus*
HB 34–51cm; T 12–41cm; W 2–4.5kg
Largest of the hog-nosed skunks, with a white cape rather than 2 white dorsal stripes as in other species. Tail usually completely white, occasionally with a black underside at the base. Formerly classified as 2 species, Eastern (*C. leuconotus*) and Western (*C. mesoleucus*) hog-nosed skunks, but recent molecular data indicate a single species. **Distribution and Habitat** SW USA, Mexico, and throughout Central America to N Nicaragua; records into N Costa Rica are equivocal. Occurs in desert scrub, rocky areas, grassland, cacti/thorn brush, marshland, woodland and various forest types to 3,000m. Apparently absent from evergreen forest and true desert. Inhabits pastures and ranchland, but is less tolerant of open agriculture and urban landscapes. **Feeding Ecology** Invertebrates, especially soil-living insects, grubs and larvae, comprise 50–90% of the diet. Also eats small mammals, reptiles, amphibians, carrion and a wide variety of fruits and vegetables. Drinks when water is available, but appears independent of water in arid habitats. Largely nocturnal. **Social and Spatial Behaviour** Solitary. Terrestrial (but capable and rapid climbers to >6m when pursued). Males have larger ranges than females, with extensive intra- and inter-sexual overlap (i.e. no evidence of territoriality). Adults often den together, including same-sex, and intersexual pairs outside the breeding period. Range estimates 0.3–1.04km² (♀s) and 1.1–2.5km² (♂s; ranchland, WC Texas). Density estimates 0.2–2.6/km². **Reproduction and Demography** Seasonal in the USA (probably true generally). Mating February–early March; births April–May. Gestation 60–70 days. Litter size 1–5. Independence and dispersal by late August at 12–16 weeks. MORTALITY Poorly known: observed mortality is largely anthropogenic, especially roadkill. LIFESPAN 16 years in captivity. **Status and Threats** Despite being considered a low conservation priority, it has declined sharply in the USA, thought to be from habitat loss to agriculture, pesticide use, roadkill, indiscriminate predator control and competition with feral pigs. Status poorly known in its Meso-American range, although subject to similar threats, especially in Mexico. Red List LC, population trend Decreasing.

■ Striped Skunk

■ Hooded Skunk

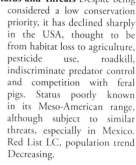
■ American Hog-nosed Skunk

**Plate 69**

STRIPED
SKUNK

HOODED SKUNK

AMERICAN
HOG-NOSED
SKUNK

# MOLINA'S HOG-NOSED SKUNK
## *Conepatus chinga*

ANDEAN HOG-NOSED SKUNK
Includes HUMBOLDT'S HOG-NOSED SKUNK OR
PATAGONIAN SKUNK *C. humboldtii*
HB 20–49cm; T 13–29cm; W 0.5–3kg
A recent comprehensive analysis, including of genetic samples, found no significant differences between Molina's Hog-nosed Skunk and Humboldt's Hog-nosed Skunk (*C. humboldtii*), and grouped them as the same species. Subsequent analysis, still unpublished at the time of writing, shows those populations formerly classified as Humboldt's (i.e. in Patagonia) are distinct, but it is still unclear whether the differences warrant species-level delineation. It is black or brownish-black furred with 2 parallel white stripes that meet on the crown and may extend to the base of the tail; some specimens lack stripes entirely. Bushy, mostly white tail is infused variably with black and brown hairs. Albinism and leucism are recorded. Fur is long and shaggy, especially in winter in temperate parts of the range, e.g. Patagonia. Humboldt's specimens were formerly distinguished by having dark brown, rufous-brown or creamy-brown fur on the back and base of the tail, extending variably down the flanks; however, these variants occur widely throughout the range. Molina's Hog-nosed Skunk is very similar in appearance to Striped Hog-nosed Skunk and there is also some dispute over whether these comprise separate species; however, the genetic differences between them are marked, and evidence to combine them is weak. **Distribution and Habitat** C Peru to SE Brazil, and south to Straits of Magellan; Patagonia is the range of the former Humboldt's Hog-nosed Skunk. Inhabits a wide variety of pampas grassland, steppe, rocky desert, bush, scrub and forested habitat, from sea-level to the Bolivian altiplano (>4,000m). Apparently avoids moist dense rainforest, and tolerates secondary forest, agricultural areas and degraded livestock pastures with cover. **Feeding Ecology** Omnivorous, feeding mainly on invertebrates (especially ground beetles and their larvae), rodents, and small reptiles and their eggs. Insects peak in the diet during summer, while rodents and carrion are more important in autumn–winter (especially in Patagonia). Eats fruits and vegetables, sometimes raiding vegetable gardens and refuse dumps. Scavenges from carrion, including the carcasses of hares, Guanacos and livestock. Primarily nocturno-crepuscular, but becomes more diurnal, especially in winter in the southern part of the range. **Social and Spatial Behaviour** Poorly known. Solitary. Male ranges are larger than female ranges. Range size averages 1km² (♀s) to 2.6km² (♂s; S Brazil). Density estimates 1.4/km² (Atlantic forest grasslands) to 3.8/km² (pampas grasslands, S Brazil). **Reproduction and Demography** Poorly known, but thought to resemble other hog-nosed skunks in breeding seasonally; juveniles are mostly recorded in spring in Patagonia. Gestation estimated at 42–60 days. Litter size 2–5. MORTALITY Poorly known. Sometimes killed by domestic dogs on ranches; known natural predators include Puma (page 38), Great Horned Owl, Crowned Eagle and Black-chested Buzzard-eagle. LIFESPAN 6.6 years in captivity. **Status and Threats** Status poorly

known, but thought to be reasonably secure. Heavy fur harvests (mainly for blankets) until the early 1980s led to inclusion on CITES in 1983, banning exports from Chile and Argentina. No longer harvested commercially, but localised hunting and capture for the pet trade occurs. Has disappeared from habitat that has been severely degraded by overgrazing and soil erosion caused by livestock and feral exotic ungulates, but is able to occupy well-managed ranchland. Due to its predilection for scavenging, it is often killed in poisoning campaigns targeting Culpeo (page 124) in livestock areas. Red List LC, population trend Decreasing.

# STRIPED HOG-NOSED SKUNK
## *Conepatus semistriatus*

HB 33–50cm; T 13.5–31cm; W 1.4–3.5kg
The larger of the South American hog-nosed skunks. Two parallel white stripes of very variable length and width run alongside the spine from the crown towards the base of the tail. Distal end of the tail is white, sometimes extending the length of the tail except for black fur at the tail's base. There is preliminary genetic evidence distinguishing the disjunct Brazilian population, possibly as a separate species, *C. amazonicus*; this awaits further study. **Distribution and Habitat** S Mexico to Venezuela, Ecuador, Colombia and N Peru, absent from the Amazon Basin, with a disjunct population in E and C Brazil. There is uncertainty over the range limits in Brazil of both *Conepatus* species, with a possible area of sympatry where their respective ranges meet in SE Brazil; Striped Hog-nosed Skunk inhabits deciduous forest, woodland savanna, shrubland and grassland with shrubby cover; it is the *Conepatus* species of Brazil's *cerrado* savannahs, including in key protected areas (e.g. Emas NP), replaced by Molina's Hog-nosed Skunk in pampas. Appears absent from rainforest. Tolerates disturbed habitats, including secondary forest, plantations, and pastures and clearings at forest edges. Recorded from suitable habitat in peri-urban areas near large cities, e.g. forest patches near Bogotá. **Feeding Ecology** Omnivorous and thought to eat mainly invertebrates grubbed from the soil surface, supplemented with small mammals, birds, reptiles, amphibians and fruits, including introduced avocado and mulberry (Emas NP). Scavenges, including from refuse dumps near settlements or tourist camps in protected areas; skunks are apparently drawn to night lighting and attendant insects at the administrative headquarters of Emas NP. **Social and Spatial Behaviour** Poorly known. Solitary. Very few range estimates are available; a radio-collared female in Venezuela covered 0.18km² in the wet season, expanding to 0.53km² in the dry season. Ranges of 3 collared males in Brazil 0.6–2.3km² (Emas NP). Thought to reach high densities, calculated at 6–12/km², although figures have not been validated by modern survey techniques. **Reproduction and Demography** Thought to be seasonal, although few data exist. Gestation approximately 60 days. Litter size 2–5. MORTALITY Poorly known. Known natural predators include Jaguar (page 50) and Puma (page 38), and there is one record of a Crane Hawk killing a juvenile. One of the most hunted bushmeat species by local people in NE Brazil. LIFESPAN 6.5 years in captivity. **Status and Threats** Status poorly known, but widespread, tolerant of some habitat conversion and thought to be reasonably secure. Localised declines are likely to occur from overhunting by people and by the presence of feral dogs; skunks are >50% less abundant in areas with dogs compared to areas without in Cayambe Coca NP, Ecuador. Red List LC, population trend Unknown.

■ Molina's Hog-nosed Skunk

■ Striped Hog-nosed Skunk

**Plate 70**

MOLINA'S
HOG-NOSED SKUNK

STRIPED
HOG-NOSED
SKUNK

# SOUTHERN SPOTTED SKUNK
## *Spilogale angustifrons*

### CENTRAL AMERICAN SPOTTED SKUNK

HB 20–25cm; T 10–14.5cm; W 0.24–0.54kg
Formerly classified with Eastern Spotted Skunk, but recent molecular data indicate that they are separate species, although this is still disputed by some authorities and they are virtually indistinguishable by appearance. Southern species is most easily differentiated by range as it is the only spotted skunk in Central America. Overlaps the very similar Western Spotted Skunk in N Mexico, and much smaller Pygmy Spotted Skunk (page 156) on Mexico's Pacific coast. **Distribution and Habitat** N Mexico to C Costa Rica. Inhabits bushland, grassland, scrub, thickets and various forest types to 2,800m. Occurs in agricultural and settled areas with cover. **Feeding Ecology** Diet dominated by invertebrates, with around 50% of prey made up of insects and larvae from leaf litter and the soil surface. Balance of the diet is made up of small rodents, lizards, amphibians, birds' eggs and plant matter, including fruits and grains. Foraging is almost entirely nocturnal. **Social and Spatial Behaviour** Poorly known, but assumed to be similar to that of other spotted skunks. Sightings are largely of single animals. Recorded denning in groups, the composition of which is unclear but most likely comprises mothers with large young. **Reproduction and Demography** Poorly known. Litter size 2–9. **MORTALITY** and **LIFESPAN** Unknown. **Status and Threats** Widespread and relatively common in much of its range. Tolerant of some human activity and able to occupy farmland and settlements. Some populations test positively for exotic carnivore diseases, probably transmitted by domestic dogs and cats, although there is no evidence of population-level effects. Red List LC, population trend Stable.

# EASTERN SPOTTED SKUNK
## *Spilogale putorius*

HB 23–33cm; T 7–28cm; W ♀ 0.2–0.48kg, ♂ 0.28–0.9kg
The spotted skunks are very similar in appearance, with some controversy over their classification. The Eastern species generally has less white than the Western species, with discontinuous white stripes broken into discrete blotches, and less white to the tail tip. The 2 species are separated by range except along the E Rocky Mountains through C Texas. When threatened, both employ a distinctive handstand display before spraying. **Distribution and Habitat** E USA to the Canadian border with Minnesota, and extreme NE Mexico. Inhabits forest, woodland, rocky habitat, brushland, vegetated dunes, and scrubby strips along canals and fences. Avoids very open habitats and wetland. Readily adapts to farmland, using outbuildings, haystacks and woodpiles for shelter. **Feeding Ecology** Feeds mainly on insects and rodents, the importance of which shifts seasonally; rodents become very important in winter when insect availability is low. Also eats birds, eggs, fruits, vegetables and carrion. Occasionally raids domestic poultry and grain stores. Does not hibernate, but winter activity diminishes in colder parts of its range. Almost entirely nocturnal. **Social and Spatial Behaviour** Solitary, but sometimes dens in small groups during winter. Occupies loosely defined home ranges that are not defended as territories. Male home ranges are 2.5–6.4 times larger than female ranges, and expand

■ Southern Spotted Skunk
■ Eastern Spotted Skunk
■ Western Spotted Skunk

significantly during the spring breeding season. Range estimates include 0.3–1.9km² (♀s, all seasons), 0.2–4km² (♂s, non-breeding seasons) and 2.2–18.2km² (♂s, spring, breeding). Density estimates 9/km² (farmland, Iowa) to 40/km² (protected coastal habitat, Florida). **Reproduction and Demography** Seasonal. Mating March–April; births May–early June. In productive years, sometimes breeds again July–September, producing a second litter. Gestation 50–65 days, with 2 weeks of delayed implantation. Litter size 2–9, averaging 5–6. Mothers provision kits in the den with food, including 1 recent (2017) record of live prey (Northern Slimy Salamander). Females first breed at 10 months. **MORTALITY** Humans and domestic carnivores are the main causes of death in studied populations. Natural predators include Coyote (page 102), Red Fox (page 114), Bobcat (page 36) and large owls. **LIFESPAN** 9.8 years in captivity. **Status and Threats** Despite reaching high abundances locally, the species has declined significantly in much of its range, particularly in the US Midwest, where it is very rare or possibly absent entirely. Causes are unclear, but may be due to a combination of historical fur overharvest (which has declined significantly since the 1970s) and intensification of farming, including widespread use of agro-pesticides. Red List VU, population trend Decreasing.

# WESTERN SPOTTED SKUNK
## *Spilogale gracilis*

HB ♀ 24–37cm; T 8.5–20.3cm; W ♀ 0.27–0.57kg, ♂ 0.26–1kg
Very similar to Eastern species in appearance, behaviour and ecology. Generally has broader, more continuous white stripes, with a larger white spot between the eyes and more white to the tail tip. **Distribution and Habitat** W USA, N Mexico and extreme SW Canada. Inhabits a variety of broken or vegetated habitats, including forest, woodland, thickets, vegetated watercourses, rocky outcrops, dry valleys, cliffs and lava fields. Occurs on farmland and in other modified habitats in association with natural or anthropogenic cover, including buildings. **Feeding Ecology** Diet similar to that of Eastern Spotted Skunk. Insects and small mammals are the main prey items, supplemented with birds, small lizards, amphibians, eggs, fruits, vegetables and carrion. Does not hibernate, but is sometimes inactive and den-bound for weeks in areas with cold winters, e.g. British Columbia. Largely nocturnal. **Social and Spatial Behaviour** Solitary. Less studied than Eastern species; most information comes from island populations off the California coast, where it does not defend territories and ranges are small; seasonal ranges of males (average 0.47km²) are larger than those of females (0.31km²). Density reaches 9–19/km² on Californian islands. **Reproduction and Demography** Seasonal. Mating September–October; births April–May. Gestation 210–230 days, with a prolonged period of delayed implantation, in contrast to Eastern species; this difference reproductively divides Western from Eastern. Litter size 2–6, averaging 3–4. **MORTALITY** Known predators include domestic carnivores, Coyote (page 102), Red Fox (page 114), Bobcat (page 36) and large raptors, but they can deter predation effectively; a skunk repeatedly usurped an adult female Puma (page 38) from her Mule Deer kill and fed on it in California. **LIFESPAN** >10 years in captivity. **Status and Threats** Widely distributed but occurs patchily across its range, and its status is poorly known. Often killed during predator-control programmes, by fur trappers and on roads. Island Spotted Skunk subspecies (*S. g. amphiala*) is considered to be 'of special concern' in California, but it has recently undergone significant increases, possibly due to former declines in Island Foxes (page 122; now reversed), combined with habitat recovery after the removal of feral livestock. Red List LC, population trend Decreasing.

**Plate 71**

SOUTHERN
SPOTTED
SKUNK

EASTERN
SPOTTED
SKUNK

WESTERN
SPOTTED SKUNK

# PYGMY SPOTTED SKUNK
## *Spilogale pygmaea*

**PYGMY SKUNK**
HB 19–21cm; T 5–8.7cm; W ♀ 0.13–0.17kg, ♂ 0.15–0.23kg
Smallest skunk. Resembles other spotted skunks, but is considerably smaller, with creamy rather than crisp white stripes. Distinct from other spotted skunks, a continuous cream-white stripe runs across the forehead and down the sides of the body, and stripes extend down the legs to the feet. **Distribution and Habitat** Endemic to Mexico's Pacific coast, from Sinaloa to Oaxaca. Inhabits various coastal habitats, including dry forest, desert scrub and vegetated dunes, usually below 350m but occasionally to 1,630m. Occurs in agricultural areas with cover. **Feeding Ecology** Feeds mainly on invertebrates, especially insect larvae and adult beetles, ants, termites, millipedes, centipedes, spiders and scorpions. Eats vertebrates less often than other spotted skunks, but rodents (especially Spiny Pocket Mice) become important in the dry season, when insect abundance declines. Occasional food includes small lizards, birds, crustaceans, snails and vegetation, including fruits and seeds. Mainly nocturnal. **Social and Spatial Behaviour** Solitary. Occupies defined territories, with male ranges overlapping 1 or more smaller female ranges. Exclusive core areas are maintained and males aggressively exclude other males, especially during the breeding season. Range size (averaged for both sexes) 0.2km². **Reproduction and Demography** Seasonal. Mating April–early August; births July–September. Gestation 43–51 days, possibly with a short period of delayed implantation. Litter size 1–6. MORTALITY Poorly known; Barn Owl and snakes are known predators. LIFESPAN Unknown. **Status and Threats** Locally abundant in some areas, but has a very restricted distribution that is under intense pressure from tourist resorts, towns and roads. Associated with such development, it is sometimes killed and stuffed as tourist souvenirs, and killed by domestic cats and dogs. Red List VU, population trend Decreasing.

# PALAWAN STINK-BADGER
## *Mydaus marchei*

**PANTOT, PHILIPPINE STINK-BADGER**
HB 32–49cm; T 1.5–4.5cm; W 0.85–2.5kg
Smaller stink-badger species, with dark chocolate-brown fur and a very short, almost absent tail. White dorsal stripe rarely extends beyond the crown and shoulders, and is sometimes very faint or absent altogether. Has well-developed anal scent glands, but secretion is apparently less noxious than that of Sunda Stink-badger, described as pungent but inoffensive, smelling faintly of almonds and ants. Never the less, the secretion is defensive, and stink-badgers are left alone by domestic dogs and cats. **Distribution and Habitat** Endemic to 3 Philippine islands: Palawan, Busuanga and Calauit. Occurs in a wide range of lowland habitats, including primary and secondary forests, swamp forest, mangroves and shrub grassland. Tolerant

■ Pygmy Spotted Skunk

■ Palawan Stink-badger
■ Sunda Stink-badger

of agricultural and settled areas, including rice paddies and cropland, provided cover is available. **Feeding Ecology** Grubs on the surface with its mobile snout, and uses its robust claws to excavate invertebrates such as worms, insects like mole crickets and beetles, and larvae. Apparently often forages near watercourses, where crabs and freshwater arthropods are eaten. Eats fallen ripened fruits, including mangoes and cheesewood fruits, possibly in part for the insects found feeding on them. Foraging is mainly nocturnal. **Social and Spatial Behaviour** Poorly known, but most observations are of singletons, suggesting solitary behaviour. Adults deposit regular scent marks on the soil surface while foraging, indicating that the anal glands are important for socio-spatial behaviour as well as for defence. **Reproduction and Demography** Poorly known. Litters thought to number 2–3, born in underground burrows. The only direct observations of wild young occur in November–March, although it is unclear whether breeding is seasonal. MORTALITY and LIFESPAN Unknown. **Status and Threats** Extremely restricted distribution, but within it the species is widespread and appears to be common. Tolerant of agricultural areas, although probably requires some undisturbed habitat; disappears from areas of extensive rice cultivation that lack cover. Ethnic Pala'wan hunt it in low numbers and it is vulnerable to being killed on roads; neither is considered to have population impacts. Red List LC, population trend Stable.

# SUNDA STINK-BADGER
## *Mydaus javanensis*

**MALAYAN STINK-BADGER, TELEDU,
INDONESIAN STINK-BADGER**
HB 37.5–51cm; T 3.4–7.5cm; W 1.4–3.6kg
Larger of 2 stink-badger species, with a longer snout and longer tail than Palawan Stink-badger. Fur is dirty black, with a dorsal white stripe that usually extends from a conspicuous crown patch to a white-tipped tail, but is reduced in some individuals. Possesses well-developed anal scent glands for defence, and can spray a pale green secretion up to 15m. Locals believe it can blind or asphyxiate dogs, and there are unconfirmed reports of people having been rendered unconscious by the secretion. **Distribution and Habitat** Java, Sumatra, Borneo and the Natuna Islands (Indonesia). Inhabits mainly forested habitat from sea-level to 2,100m. Also recorded in secondary forest, as well as fields and pastures adjacent to forested areas, suggesting some flexibility in habitat use. A prodigious digger, which dens in underground burrows it excavates or that are dug by other species such as Sunda Porcupine, with which it sometimes shares a burrow. **Feeding Ecology** Diet thought to be mainly worms and other invertebrates excavated from the soil surface, for which the large claws and elongated, probing snout are well adapted. Also recorded eating birds' eggs, some plant matter and carrion. Captive animals eat meat and eggs. Not recorded depredating poultry, but sometimes persecuted for digging up crops and plantation seedlings while foraging. Highly nocturnal; 2,268 camera-trap images from Lower Kinabatangan WS, Sabah, are all between 18:39–06:27 (2010–15). **Social and Spatial Behaviour** Unknown. Reported to occur in adult pairs or trios, although this remains to be confirmed. **Reproduction and Demography** Unknown. Litters thought to number 2–3, and are likely reared in underground burrows. **Status and Threats** Status poorly known. Likely to occur in many protected areas, and found sufficiently often in human-modified habitat to suggest it is not dependent on undisturbed forest. Does not appear to be widely hunted, although some ethnic groups consume the flesh and believe its parts have medicinal value; its patchy distribution on Borneo may be due to overhunting. Red List LC, population trend Stable.

**Plate 72**

PYGMY
SPOTTED SKUNK

PALAWAN
STINK-BADGER

SUNDA
STINK-BADGER

# AMERICAN BADGER *Taxidea taxus*

HB 42–72cm; T 10–15.5cm; W 4–12kg

Squat, low-slung badger with a broad, wedge-shaped head. Coat is grizzled yellow-grey, with buff underparts and dark limbs. Face has a black mask, black cheek stripes and a distinctive white blaze from the nose to the nape, sometimes extending along the spine. **Distribution and Habitat** SW Canada and USA (mostly west of the Mississippi river, south of Tennessee, and west of Ohio River) to C Mexico. Inhabits mainly open habitats from sea-level to 3,600m, including prairie, grassland, open woodland, scrubland and desert. Occurs on farmland but cannot tolerate intensive agriculture. **Feeding Ecology** Omnivorous, but strongly reliant on small burrowing mammals such as ground squirrels, marmots, prairie dogs, pocket gophers, voles, mice and lagomorphs. Other prey includes arthropods, birds, eggs and carrion, and occasionally reptiles, amphibians, fish and molluscs. Consumes grains, seeds and grass, but most vegetation is probably taken incidentally while eating prey. Does not kill livestock except for very rare kills of newborn lambs and poultry. Foraging is solitary and usually nocturnal. Very well adapted to excavate prey from burrows; uses its keen sense of smell to locate burrows and plug their entrances with soil and sod, or sometimes snow, rocks or other objects, to block escape routes. Coyotes (page 102) often form hunting 'partnerships' with American Badgers, which is supposedly advantageous to both species, but there is little evidence that badgers benefit. Caches surplus food in burrows and by burying carcasses, usually to jackrabbit size, but 2 records from Utah involved solitary badgers burying cattle calves weighing 18–27kg, and feeding from them for 41–52 days. Scavenges carrion and occasionally from human refuse. **Social and Spatial Behaviour** Solitary. Adults occupy stable ranges; male ranges are usually, but not always, 2–4 times larger than female ranges. Territorial behaviour is limited; there is high range overlap, adults actively avoid each other and individuals often use the same dens at different times. Average range estimates include 2.4km$^2$ (♀s) to 5.8km$^2$ (♂s) in Utah, to 13km$^2$ (♀s) to 44km$^2$ (♂s) in Illinois, with very large ranges at the distribution's extreme (SW Canada) of 9–87.3km$^2$ (♀s) and 51–450km$^2$ (♂s). Density estimates 40–500/100km$^2$, but as low as 0.4/100km$^2$ in SW Canada. **Reproduction and Demography** Seasonal. Mating late July–August; births late March–early April. Gestation 210–240 days, with delayed implantation. Litter size 1–5, averaging 2. Weaning at 6 weeks, dispersal at 3–4 months. Some females breed at 4–5 months, but most breeding follows the first winter. MORTALITY Natural mortality is mostly from starvation during prey crashes and predation; adult American Badgers are occasionally killed by bears, Puma (page 38), Grey Wolf (page 100) and Coyote. LIFESPAN 14 years in the wild, 26 in captivity. **Status and Threats** Generally common and widespread, with an estimated global population of several hundred thousand. Ongoing declines are driven by agricultural intensification on grassland, associated declines of ground squirrels and prairie dogs, and retributive killing for badgers' excavations, which can damage crops and equipment, and (rarely) cause injury to livestock. Endangered in British Columbia (<100 remaining) and Ontario (<200 remaining). Red List LC, population trend Decreasing.

# HONEY BADGER *Mellivora capensis*

RATEL

HB 74–96cm; T 14.3–26cm; W ♀ 6.2–13.6kg, ♂ 7.7–14.5kg

Powerfully built and conspicuously bicoloured, with black sides and underparts contrasting with a silver-grey to dark grey cape. Melanistic individuals occur, mostly in African rainforest. Skin is very thick and loose, providing protection against snakebites, bee stings and predators. A formidable and tenacious animal that sometimes deters Lions (page 46) and Leopards (page 48), but there are few carnivores surrounded by as many falsehoods, and they are killed by larger carnivores. **Distribution and Habitat** Sub-Saharan Africa, the Arabian Peninsula and C and S Asia, from SE Kazakhstan to Nepal and most of the Indian subcontinent. Occupies all kinds of wet and dry forests, woodland, grassland, alpine heath (to 4,050m), steppes, scrub, wetland, semi-desert and true desert. Occurs in agricultural areas with cover. **Feeding Ecology** Omnivorous and highly opportunistic. The most important prey is small mammals to the size of Springhare (2kg), and reptiles including monitors, African Rock Python and highly venomous snakes, e.g. Cape Cobra, Puff Adder (Honey Badgers are very resistant to snake neurotoxins). Occasionally kills larger vertebrates, e.g. Aardwolf (page 52), but reports of it killing large ungulates by castration are specious. Also consumes invertebrates, birds, nestlings, eggs, carrion, fruits (including berries) and seeds. Bees, and their honeycomb and honey, are readily eaten, but there is no evidence that Greater Honeyguide birds direct Honey Badgers to hives. Raids domestic beehives and poultry coops. Foraging is mainly nocturno-crepuscular, with increased diurnalism during cold winters. Forages alone, but congregates at food-rich patches. Foraging is largely by its excellent sense of smell, and most prey is excavated after following scent trails. Climbs strongly and raids nests for eggs and nestlings; raptor chicks are important seasonal prey in the Kalahari. Scavenges, including from other carnivores' kills, and at campgrounds and dumps. **Social and Spatial Behaviour** Solitary. Male ranges are massive, marked by high overlap and avoidance rather than active territorial defence; each male range overlaps as many as 13 female ranges (Kalahari). Female ranges are more exclusive, but also with little evidence of territorial defence. Moves constantly while foraging, covering up to 40km/day, averaging 14km (♂s) and 8km (♀s) between rest periods. Kalahari range size 85–194km$^2$, averaging 126km$^2$ (♀s), and 229–776km$^2$, averaging 541km$^2$ (♂s). Occurs naturally at low densities, 3/100km$^2$ (S Kalahari). **Reproduction and Demography** Aseasonal. Gestation 50–70 days. Litter size 1, rarely 2. Weaning at 2–3 months, but cubs are entirely dependent on their mothers to 10–12 months, gradually diminishing to independence at 16–22 months. MORTALITY Annual mortality under protection estimated at 46% (cubs, to independence) and 34% (adults, Kalahari), mainly by starvation, predation by large cats and hyaenas, and infanticide. LIFESPAN 7 years in the wild, 28 in captivity. **Status and Threats** Widespread, adaptable and has a broad habitat tolerance. However, it has an unusually low reproductive rate, is naturally rare and is vulnerable where directly persecuted, especially by apiarists and livestock owners; the use of poisons to target Honey Badgers is particularly grave, and has extirpated populations locally. Also killed for traditional medicinal uses and superstitious beliefs, such as claims that it excavates gravesites, and appears to be increasingly sought for bushmeat in some areas (e.g. W Africa), perhaps as other, preferred species decline. CITES Appendix III – Botswana; Red List LC, population trend Decreasing.

■ American Badger

■ Honey Badger

**Plate 73**

AMERICAN
BADGER

Burying
large calf

Raiding
bees' nest

HONEY BADGER

# SUMATRAN HOG BADGER
## Arctonyx hoevenii

HB 51–71cm; T 8–18cm; W c.4–8kg

Hog Badgers were considered to be a single species, *A. collaris*, until 2008, when a long-overdue review of the genus recognised 3 species. Sumatran Hog Badger is the smallest and darkest species, with sparse dirty-black body fur and a creamy-white tail, throat, chin and blaze. **Distribution and Habitat** Endemic to Sumatra. Restricted to 700–3,780m in the forested foothills and slopes of the Barisan Mountains. Occurs in montane and mossy forests as well as subalpine meadows; camera-trap surveys indicate it is more common in higher montane forest than in lower foothill forest. **Feeding Ecology** Thought to have a diet consisting almost entirely of soil-living invertebrates, primarily earthworms, beetle larvae and ants. Captive animals refuse raw meat, although 1 animal was trapped using a squirrel carcass as bait. Foraging thought to be mainly by a well-developed sense of smell. Grubs in soft soil with its muzzle to locate prey, which is excavated and lapped up with its long cylindrical tongue, leaving characteristic funnel-shaped depressions. Limited observations indicate it is cathemeral. **Social and Spatial Behaviour** Unknown. Early accounts suggest adults form pair bonds, but most sightings and camera-trap images are of single animals. **Reproduction and Demography** Unknown. Females have 3 pairs of mammae, suggesting litters numbering up to 6, but there are no records. MORTALITY Unknown. Reported as aggressive when threatened, and like all hog badgers uses pungent secretions from well-developed anal scent glands to deter predation. LIFESPAN Unknown. **Status and Threats** Status poorly known. Camera-trap photographs and frequency of diggings suggest it is common in intact forest at 800–2,600m. Considered a local delicacy in some areas, and snared intentionally and accidentally, but impacts are unknown. Small numbers appear in markets, e.g. in Jakarta, for the novelty pet trade. Red List LC, population trend Stable.

# NORTHERN HOG BADGER
## Arctonyx albogularis

### CHINESE HOG BADGER
HB 54.6–70cm; T 11.4–22cm; W c.5–10kg

Medium-sized hog badger with a shaggy coat that is long and soft in winter. Colour is blackish with interspersed white hairs on the hindquarters, mid-back and sides, becoming near white in some individuals. More white on the face and throat than in Sumatran Hog Badger. **Distribution and Habitat** E to S China, extreme E Mongolia, NE India and probably sub-Himalayan Bhutan, Nepal and N Bangladesh. Considered the most generalist of the hog badgers, with a wide habitat tolerance. Occurs from sea-level to 4,300m in temperate forest, scrubland and montane meadows. Lives in agricultural habitats and close to villages. **Feeding Ecology** Omnivorous and opportunistic, with a high proportion of small rodents and snails in the diet, as well as herptiles, birds,

earthworms, beetles, larvae, roots, acorns and leaves. Earthworms are especially important from late spring to autumn. Foraging is solitary and primarily nocturnal. Unlike other hog badgers, hibernates over winter (November–March) in its northern range (C China); it is not clear if it hibernates in milder areas of its range. **Social and Spatial Behaviour** Unknown. Most records are of single adults; adult pairs live amicably in captivity. **Reproduction and Demography** Poorly known, but thought to be seasonal (C China). Mating apparently April–May; births February–March, indicating a long period of delayed implantation (estimated at 5–9.5 months for a captive female). Litter size 1–6. Captive juveniles first eat solid food at 85 days; weaning and independence co-occur at 4 months. MORTALITY Unknown; allegedly preyed on by Dhole (page 108), Leopard (page 48), Grey Wolf (page 100) and Asiatic Black Bear (page 134) in C China. LIFESPAN 13.9 years in captivity. **Status and Threats** Status poorly known. It is the most widespread hog badger species and is common in some areas, but heavily hunted for human consumption and killed as 'by-catch' in snares. Severely threatened in SE China. Red List LC, population trend Decreasing.

# GREATER HOG BADGER
## Arctonyx collaris

HB 65–104cm; T 19–29cm; W 7–15kg

Largest hog badger. Robust, with a massively built skull, and described as resembling a small bear in the field. It is the lightest coloured species, pale grizzled grey to yellowish grey, with more white on the face, head and neck than in Northern Hog Badger (with which it overlaps in E Bangladesh and NE India, and possibly S China and N Myanmar); some individuals have almost entirely white or creamy-white heads. Lower limbs are black, extending variably over the shoulders and neck. **Distribution and Habitat** Southeast Asia, from E Bangladesh and NE India through Myanmar, Thailand, Laos, Cambodia and Vietnam. It probably occurs in Yunnan, China; records from Malaysia are equivocal. Occurs at 500–1,500m, primarily in undisturbed lowland and hill forests as well as bamboo stands. Reported close to villages, but rarely in modified habitat; occurs in rubber plantations close to forests. **Feeding Ecology** Poorly known; thought to be omnivorous and possibly specialises partially in earthworms (which captive animals relish) like Sumatran Hog Badger, but not to the same extent. Captive animals consume meat, reptiles, fish, bread, milk and fruits, especially plantains. Cathemeral. **Social and Spatial Behaviour** Unknown. Assumed to be solitary. **Reproduction and Demography** Very poorly known. Litter size thought to be 2–3. MORTALITY Important prey of Leopard (page 48) in Thailand and also killed by Tiger (page 44). LIFESPAN 7 years (minimum estimate) in captivity. **Status and Threats** Relatively widespread, but its large size and apparent lack of wariness of humans and dogs make it a common target of hunters. Intensively hunted in much of its range and overhunted to extinction in much of Indochina. Severely threatened in Laos, Vietnam and perhaps Myanmar, where it now occurs only patchily. Hunting intensity is lower in Thailand, where the species is considered relatively secure. Red List VU, population trend Decreasing.

■ Sumatran Hog Badger

■ Northern Hog Badger

■ Greater Hog Badger

**Plate 74**

SUMATRAN
HOG BADGER

NORTHERN
HOG BADGER

GREATER
HOG BADGER

# EUROPEAN BADGER *Meles meles*, ASIAN BADGER *Meles leucurus*, JAPANESE BADGER *Meles anakuma*

NORTHWEST ASIAN BADGER (*M. leucurus*)
ANAGUMA (*M. anakuma*)
European Badger: HB 56–87cm; T 11.5–20.5cm; W 4.8–17.1kg (exceptionally >30kg during autumn hypophagia).
Asian Badger: HB 48.5–70cm; T 11–20cm; W 3.2–10.5kg.
Japanese Badger: HB 50.5–80cm; T 14–20cm; W 4.2–9kg
Until recently, considered 1 species, Eurasian Badger (*Meles meles*), with 3 regional subspecies distributed throughout Eurasia from the UK to Japan; each subspecies is now recognised as a full species based on molecular, morphological and distributional differences. European Badger population from Turkey south of the Caucasus Mountains and Caspian Sea, to S Tajikistan, is genetically and morphologically somewhat distinct, and may be a fourth species, Southwest Asian Badger (*M. canescens*); this awaits wider consensus. European Badger is the largest badger species; Asian and Japanese badgers are smaller on average. European Badger is typically brindled silvery grey, with black legs and alternating black-and-white facial stripes. Albino, melanistic and erythristic European individuals occur. Coloration in Asian and Japanese badgers is variable. Some individuals resemble a slightly paler version of the European Badger with reduced facial stripes, but body fur colour varies from yellowish grey to greyish black or pure black; and varies similarly widely for facial markings, from narrow stripes to dark spectacles, or markings absent entirely. The degree of facial striping is least in Japanese Badger and the Far Eastern form of the Asian Badger ('Amur Badger').

## Distribution and Habitat
European Badger: UK, W Europe from Iberian Peninsula to Fenno-Scandinavia, to the west bank of Volga River, and south through Turkey to Sinai Peninsula, through N Iraq and N Iran to Afghanistan–Tajikistan border. Asian Badger: from Volga River east across S Russia, C Asia, Mongolia, E China and Korean Peninsula, including Jeju Island. Japanese Badger: endemic to Japan (Honshu, Kyushu, Shikoku, Shodoshima). Asian and European badgers are sympatric in Volga River region and Uzbekistan–Tajikistan borderlands. European Badger and Japanese Badger inhabit mainly forest and associated scrub or grassland habitats, as well as farmland, fields and urban habitats. Asian Badger inhabits forest, scrubland, grassland, steppes and semi-desert with scrub cover.

## Feeding Ecology
Omnivorous, feeding mainly on soil-living invertebrates and insects; wild and cultivated fruits (including berries), hard mast, grains, tubers and mushrooms; and small mammals such as mice, voles and shrews. Earthworms are a major component of the diet in many populations, especially of European and Japanese badgers. Asian Badgers generally occupy more arid habitats with harsh winters, where earthworms are less common in the diet.

■ European Badger ■ Asian Badger
■ Japanese Badger

Hedgehogs, rabbits, small birds, herptiles and eggs are opportunistically consumed; European Rabbit is the main component of European Badger diet in Doñana NP, Spain. Exceptionally kills very young lambs and poultry (recorded for European and Asian badgers). Foraging is mainly solitary. European Badgers congregate, sometimes in large groups of >20, at food-rich patches, including artificial feeding sites. Nocturno-crepuscular, with increased diurnalism where undisturbed. In parts of the range experiencing severe winters, all species undergo partial hibernation with opportunistic foraging, but can remain underground for months in protracted winters, living entirely off fat reserves. Scavenges from carrion, bird feeders, pet bowls and human refuse.

## Social and Spatial Behaviour
Sociality is flexible and complex, and linked to availability of clumped, rich food sources, especially earthworms. It is most gregarious and reaches highest densities where food patches are dense and frequent, e.g. lowland UK, living in large communal clans numbering up to 29, averaging 5–8 adults. Clan adults are mostly inter-related, with a minority of unrelated immigrants. Clans share territory, with extensive burrow systems called setts, where members gather to interact before setting off to forage alone. Clans actively repel strangers; neighbouring ranges may overlap, but core areas with main setts are defended, sometimes violently. Clans tend to be smaller for European Badger in southern and eastern parts of the range (linked to lower food availability), where mated pairs with shared ranges are typical. Japanese Badgers are mainly solitary in Japan, with females maintaining small, relatively exclusive ranges, which they share with offspring, often for extended periods (up to 14 months for female and 26 months for male offspring); adult males have larger ranges, which are flexible, approximately doubling in size during the breeding season, when they attempt to visit as many females ranges as possible. Asian Badgers are poorly known but assumed to follow broadly similar social patterns linked to food patch availability. Territory size 0.1–0.4km² (Japan) and 0.3–1.5km² (UK), to 4–24.4km² (Poland). Density estimates: 0.2–0.25/km² (Finland), 0.9/km² (Ireland), 1.6–2.6/km² (Poland), 4/km² (Japan, suburbs) and 4.7–25.3/km² (UK).

## Reproduction and Demography
In clans, multiple adults of both sexes breed, and females often mate with males from neighbouring clans. Breeding occurs year-round, but mating peaks February–May (European Badger, UK) and April–August (Japanese Badger), with most births December–April. Gestation includes a very variable period of delayed implantation with a range of 90–300 days. Litter size 1–5, averaging 2–3. Weaning begins at 12 weeks, but extends to 6 months under low food availability. MORTALITY Annual mortality rates estimated at approximately 50% of cubs and 30% of adults. Natural mortality occurs mainly from starvation (especially cubs) and predation; Asian Badger is preyed upon by Amur Tiger (page 44; Russia). LIFESPAN European Badger: 14 years in the wild, 16 in captivity; poorly known for other species.

## Status and Threats
Widespread, common and found in many protected areas. Main threat in Europe is roadkill, which claims 50,000 individuals in Britain and 10–15% of Danish and Dutch populations annually. Persecuted as a pest and used for illegal 'baiting' with terriers. Controversially culled as a carrier of bovine tuberculosis (bTB) in the UK, despite strong evidence that culls do not reduce incidence of the disease. Asian Badgers are widely hunted for bushmeat and traditional medicinal purposes; badger farms, e.g. in South Korea, are mostly stocked with wild-caught animals, the sustainability of which is dubious. About 200 Japanese Badgers are legally culled each year in Kyushu, apparently to reduce crop damage; this number rose to more than 6,000 in 2016 as a result of an ill-advised government bounty programme, which also killed many Masked Palm Civets (page 80) and Raccoon Dogs (page 122). All 3 species are persecuted for damage to crops, heavily in China and Japan. European Badger: Red List LC, population trend Stable. Asian Badger: Red List LC, population trend Unknown. Japanese Badger: Red List LC, population trend Decreasing.

**Plate 75**

ASIAN
BADGER

Amur
form

JAPANESE
BADGER

At sett
entrance

EUROPEAN
BADGER

Foraging in cattle pasture

# TAYRA *Eira barbara*

### GREY-HEADED TAYRA, EIRA
HB 55.9–71.2cm; T 36.5–47cm; W 2.7–7kg

Largest mustelid in Latin America, excluding otters. Typically dark smoky brown to black, often with a creamy-yellow or white throat patch and a pale head. Completely pale individuals occur, including a uniformly golden form (probably leucistic) recorded from N South America to S Brazil. The Tayra belongs in a unique genus, and its closest relatives are thought to be the Fisher (page 166) and Wolverine. **Distribution and Habitat** C Mexico, through Central America to N Argentina, Paraguay and C Uruguay. Occurs in various dry and wet forests and forest woodland, and in meadows, grassland and savannah in forested mosaics. Recorded up to 3,100m (E Andean slopes, Ecuador), generally rare above 2,000m; absent from high Andes and Brazilian *caatinga*. Tolerates agriculture, plantations and pasture in association with forest. **Feeding Ecology** Omnivorous, eating mammals to the size of agoutis, Southern Opossum, small primates (Common Marmosets, squirrel monkeys and tamarins) and neonate sloths, as well as reptiles to the size of Green Iguanas, birds, eggs, invertebrates (adults, eggs and pupae), fruits, honey and carrion. Pursues large prey, including brocket deer and large adult primates, but successful hunts are unknown; an observed attack on an adult Pale-throated Three-toed Sloth was unsuccessful. Tayras raid the nests of land-nesting reptiles for eggs, including those of various caiman species. They are recorded caching unripe fruit (plantains and sapote) in bromeliads and tree cavities for later consumption. Usually forages alone, although adult pairs and family groups are observed. Cathemeral, and equally at home on the ground or in trees. **Social and Spatial Behaviour** Poorly known. Assumed to be mainly solitary. Small social groups occur, usually assumed to comprise a female with large offspring, but this has not been confirmed. Limited data indicate that adult ranges overlap extensively. Range estimates 5.3–16km² (♀s) and 24.4km² (1 ♂) in Belize. **Reproduction and Demography** Thought to breed year-round. Gestation 63–70 days. Litter size 1–3. Weaning at around 2–3.5 months. Males are occasionally recorded with family groups, but apparently do not help raise juveniles. MORTALITY Unknown. LIFESPAN 18 years in captivity. **Status and Threats** Widespread and often common. Main threat is loss of forested habitat and agricultural intensification, leading to local endangerment, e.g. in Mexico. It is hunted in parts of its range for fur or meat, and killed as a predator of poultry, which may contribute to local declines. CITES Appendix III – Honduras; Red List LC, population trend Decreasing.

# WOLVERINE *Gulo gulo*

### GLUTTON, SKUNK-BEAR
HB 65–105cm; T 17–26cm; SH 36.5–43.2cm; W ♀ 6.6–14.8kg, ♂ 11.3–18.2kg

Largest terrestrial mustelid. Heavily built, with a bear-like head, short, powerful limbs and a bushy tail. Dark brown with a blond to rusty-brown fringe running from the shoulders along the sides; this extends in some individuals to cover the entire upper body in a pale cape. Forehead is often grizzled grey to blond. Cream to white markings on the chest are common; they extend to the front legs and feet in some individuals. **Distribution and Habitat** Circumpolar, mostly north of 50°N from Fenno-Scandinavia through Russia, N Mongolia, N China, Canada, Alaska and W USA in the Rockies. Inhabits coniferous and deciduous forests, open rocky terrain and Arctic tundra. Strongly associated with deep snow and dead timber for denning. Actively avoids areas of human disturbance, including agricultural land, roads, skiing fields and recent logging. **Feeding Ecology** Relies heavily on ungulates, particularly winter-killed or predator-killed carrion, but actively hunts ungulates (mainly juveniles; capable of killing adult Moose and Reindeer in deep snow), e.g. 28% of food items in Norway consist of Reindeer killed by Wolverines. Also actively hunts small to mid-sized vertebrates such as marmots, porcupines, beavers, ground squirrels, lagomorphs, meso-carnivores (e.g. Red Foxes; page 114), small rodents and birds, especially ground-feeders such as ptarmigans and grouse. Consumes eggs, invertebrates, fruits and fungi. Known to raid trap-lines for captured fur-bearers, scavenges hunter refuse (gut-piles etc.) and sometimes kills livestock (mainly sheep lambs). Semi-domestic, free-ranging Reindeer, both killed and scavenged, make up 40–95% of prey items in N Norway and Sweden. Scavenges whale and seal carcasses in coastal Alaska. Foraging is cathemeral, solitary and mostly terrestrial, although it is a strong climber and swimmer known to forage in trees and water. Hoards surplus food under rock piles, ice or snow, sometimes creating large caches, e.g. 20 Red Foxes and 100 ptarmigans in one cache (Russia). **Social and Spatial Behaviour** Solitary, with very large, stable ranges. Male ranges are larger and overlap multiple female ranges. Adults exclude same-sex conspecifics, but range overlap can be considerable. Covers large daily distances to 35km, driven in part by the search for carrion; summer movements tend to be larger than winter ones. Territory size estimates include 31–560km² (♀s) and 133–1,131km² (♂s) in N Sweden, 53–232km² (♀s) and 488–917km² (♂s) in NW Alaska, and 175–692km² (♀s) and 845–2,127km² (♂s) in Idaho. Subadults have ranges 2–3 times as large as adults in the same population, e.g. on average 400km² (adult ♀s) and 1,175km² (subadult ♀s), and 1,160km² (adult ♂s) and 3,292km² (subadult ♂s; Greater Yellowstone Ecosystem). Density poorly known, but it is naturally rare with low densities, estimated at 3.5/1,000km² (Greater Yellowstone) to 15.3/1,000km² (N Montana). **Reproduction and Demography** Seasonal. Mating May–August; births January–April. Wolverines require snow cover for denning, and reproduction is limited to areas with snow persisting to mid-May, the end of the denning period. Gestation 215–272 days (captivity), with delayed implantation. Litter size 1–5, averaging 2–3. Weaning at 7–8 weeks. Independence at around 8–10 months, dispersal at 12–13 months. Wolverines are excellent dispersers, regularly covering >200km and occasionally 400–500km. Females breed on average at 3.4 years. MORTALITY Annual adult and subadult mortality, respectively, is 26% and 43% (trapped), and 12% and 7% (not trapped). Most natural mortality is due to starvation and predation by large carnivores, including Grey Wolf (page 100), Puma (page 38; North America) and other Wolverines. LIFESPAN 13 years in the wild, 18 in captivity. **Status and Threats** Wide distribution, with numerous large and continuous populations, but the species occurs in very low densities, and it is sensitive to persecution and disturbance. It has declined in large areas of W USA and S Europe. Threatened by overtrapping, predator-control programmes, illegal killing for livestock depredation and habitat conversion. Given the species' strong reliance on snow cover for reproduction, climatic warming is predicted to reduce suitable habitat and fragment populations. Red List LC (VU in Europe), population trend Decreasing.

■ Tayra

■ Wolverine

**Plate 76**

TAYRA

WOLVERINE

Scanning

# FISHER *Pekania pennanti*

HB 45–65cm; T 25.3–50cm; W ♀ 1.3–3.2kg, ♂ 3.5–5.5kg (exceptionally to 9kg)

Classified in its own genus, reflecting very early divergence (with Tayra; page 164) from true martens (*Martes*). Grey-brown to silver-tipped black with paler head and shoulders, sometimes with white or cream throat, chest and groin. **Distribution and Habitat** S Canada, extreme SW Alaska, W, Mid-west and NE USA. Strongly prefers intact forest generally <1,250m with dense canopy. Uses logged forest but avoids large open areas, clear-cuts and human disturbance. **Feeding Ecology** Often specialises in North American Porcupine and Snowshoe Hare, but also eats other lagomorphs, squirrels, small rodents, birds, eggs, herptiles, invertebrates, fungi and carrion. Foxes, raccoons and skunks are recorded prey, and cannibalism is documented. Rarely kills domestic poultry. Foraging is solitary, nocturno-crepuscular and mainly terrestrial, but Fishers are extremely capable climbers; they chase porcupines to the ground, where they are killed. Fishers cache small kills, and scavenge from refuse and pet bowls. **Social and Spatial Behaviour** Solitary and territorial. Average range size generally 2.1–29.9km² (♀s) and 9.2–38.7km² (♂s); largest ranges in N British Columbia, averaging 33km² (summer, ♀s), and 122km² (summer, ♂s). Rapidly covers large distances, up to 90km in 3 days. Density 8.6–11.2/1,000km² (low-quality spruce forest, N British Columbia) to 14–52/100km² (high-quality habitat, California). **Reproduction and Demography** Seasonal. Mating March–May; births late February–early May (following year). Gestation 236–275 days, with delayed implantation (total embryonic development ~50–55 days). Litter size 1–6, averaging 2–3. Weaning at 2–3 months, and dispersal from 7–9 months. **MORTALITY** In California, where trapping is illegal, mortality is mainly from predation (60–77% of known deaths ) by Pumas (page 38), Bobcats (page 36), Coyotes (page 102) and domestic dogs, natural disease (13–23%) and human causes. **LIFESPAN** 7.5 years in the wild, 10 in captivity. **Status and Threats** Extirpated from most of historic distribution by overtrapping for furs; now recovered or reintroduced in much of eastern and Great Lakes range; recovery is poor in the Pacific Northwest. Legally trapped in most of its range, impacting populations in low-quality habitat. Red List LC, population trend Unknown.

# SABLE *Martes zibellina*

## JAPANESE SABLE

HB 35–56cm; T 11.5–19cm; W ♀ 0.7–1.6kg, ♂ 0.8–1.8kg

Honey brown to very dark brown, paler head and a small white or cream throat patch (often absent). Japanese Sables are often rich yellow or tawny brown with a light grey head, similar to some winter forms of Japanese Marten (page 168). **Distribution and Habitat** Russia (~95% of range), extreme NE Kazakhstan to North Korea and Hokkaido, Japan. Closely tied to temperate debris-rich, dense-canopy forest to 2,200m. Avoids open areas and disturbed habitat. **Feeding Ecology** Eats mainly small rodents, pikas and Mountain Hare, and also seeds, berries, nuts, invertebrates, birds, fish and freshwater crustaceans. Capable of killing adult Siberian Musk Deer in deep snow. Occasionally kills domestic poultry. Foraging is solitary, cathemeral and mostly terrestrial, although Sables are very agile climbers. Scavenges, mainly from winter-killed ungulates, and caches surplus food. **Social and Spatial Behaviour** Solitary. Average range size 7.2km² (♀s) and 13.1km² (♂s) with little intrasexual overlap (open larch taiga, NE China), and only 1.12km² (both sexes) with high intrasexual overlap (high-quality forest, Japan). **Reproduction and Demography** Seasonal. Mating June–August; births April–May (following year). Gestation 236–315 days, with delayed implantation (embryonic development 25–40 days). Litter size 1–5, averaging 2–3. Weaning at around 7–8 weeks. **MORTALITY** Trapping accounts for most mortality (especially in Russia); Red Fox (page 114) is a confirmed predator. **LIFESPAN** 5.5 years in the wild, 15 in captivity. **Status and Threats** Sable fur is highly sought after; historical overharvest caused widespread declines. Hunting bans and reintroductions have led to recovery; Russian population is now estimated at >2 million. Commercially hunted, mainly in Russia (>700,000 in 2011–12 trapping season), and farmed for fur. Red List LC, population trend Increasing.

# AMERICAN MARTEN *Martes americana*
# PACIFIC MARTEN *Martes caurina*

HB ♀ 32–40cm, ♂ 36–45cm; T 13.5–23cm; W ♀ 0.3–0.85kg, ♂ 0.47–1.3kg

Formerly classified as 1 species; genetic analyses now separate Pacific Northwest–Rocky Mountains populations as the Pacific Marten. The 2 species are extremely similar in appearance and ecology. Very variable, from tawny beige with dark limbs to uniformly dark chocolate brown. Head is usually paler, buff-brown or greyish. All forms have a cream to yellow throat and chest. **Distribution and Habitat** American Marten: Canada, Alaska, marginally into Mid-west and NE USA. Pacific Marten: Pacific Northwest coast from S British Columbia to California, and US Rocky Mountains to New Mexico. They are sympatric and hybridise in N Montana and SE Alaska. Both prefer mature temperate forest and woodland with a closed canopy and dense understorey. They avoid open or disturbed habitat, including clear-cuts and recently logged areas. **Feeding Ecology** Both species eat small rodents, and Snowshoe Hare (mainly during cyclical irruptions). Also eat invertebrates, birds, fish, herptiles, fruits and seeds. They rarely take domestic poultry. Foraging is solitary and mainly nocturno-crepuscular. They hunt terrestrially, arboreally, and under snow. They scavenge from carrion and cache excess food. **Social and Spatial Behaviour** Solitary and territorial. Average range size 2.3–27.6km² (♀s) and 4.3–45km² (♂s). Density estimates 0.4–1.5/km². **Reproduction and Demography** Seasonal. Mating July–August; births late March–April (following year). Gestation 220–275 days, with delayed implantation (embryonic development ~40 days). Litter size 1–5, averaging 2–3. Weaning at 6–7 weeks; kits kill small prey at 2.5 months. **MORTALITY** Adult mortality before trapping 7% (both sexes) increasing to 51% (♀s) to 74% (♂s) during trapping (American Marten, Maine). Mortality in unharvested populations 13–44%, mainly from predation by Bobcat (page 36), raptors and other martens. Infanticide by males occurs rarely. **LIFESPAN** 14.5 years in the wild (typically <5), 15 in captivity. **Status and Threats** Fur overharvests and forest loss have reduced populations, mainly in New England (American Marten) and coastal W USA (Pacific Marten), where they remain fragmented and rare. Both have benefited from reintroduction projects, especially American Marten. Both: Red List LC, population trend Decreasing.

■ Fisher

■ Sable

■ American Marten  ■ Pacific Marten

**Plate** 77

FISHER

SABLE

AMERICAN /
PACIFIC
MARTEN

# STONE MARTEN *Martes foina*

### BEECH MARTEN
HB 40–54cm; T 22–30cm; W 1.1–2.3kg
Typically rich, dark brown with a slightly paler, greyish head, and light tawny underfur, especially on the sides and underparts. Throat has a distinctive white or cream patch that often extends down the front legs. **Distribution and Habitat** Continental W and C Europe through C Asia, Bhutan, N India, Nepal and N Myanmar to Mongolia and China. Introduced to Wisconsin, USA. Inhabits forest, shrubland, forest edges, hedgerows and rocky hillsides to 4,200m. Occurs near humans, including in densely populated urban areas (W and C Europe). **Feeding Ecology** Diet varies seasonally and regionally with fluctuating proportions of 2 main food groups: small mammals, especially voles, mice and rabbits; and fruits, including berries. Also eats insects, birds, herptiles, eggs, seeds and other plant items. Urban populations frequently eat commensal birds like pigeons. Sometimes kills domestic poultry. Foraging is solitary and nocturno-crepuscular. Urban Stone Martens readily scavenge from refuse, bird feeders, pet bowls and handouts. **Social and Spatial Behaviour** Solitary and territorial, with male ranges overlapping multiple female ranges. Ranges tend to be smallest in urban areas, intermediate in rural areas and largest in forested habitat. Range size 0.095–8.8km², averaging 0.37–0.49km² (♀s) and 1.11–1.13km² (♂s) in rural/village areas. **Reproduction and Demography** Seasonal. Mating July–August; births March–mid-April (following year). Gestation 236–275 days, with delayed implantation (embryonic development ~30 days). Litter size 1–8, averaging 3–4. Weaning at around 6–8 weeks in late May–early June, and dispersal from 6 months. MORTALITY Most known mortality is anthropogenic. LIFESPAN 18.1 years in captivity, much lower in the wild. **Status and Threats** Widespread and adaptable, reaching high densities in urban habitats. Considered a nuisance in C Europe due to its habit of sheltering in car-engine spaces and chewing leads and hoses, e.g. 160,000 damaged cars in Germany in 2000, for which it is sometimes legally and illegally killed. Hunted for fur in India and Russia. CITES Appendix III – India; Red List LC, population trend Stable.

# PINE MARTEN *Martes martes*

### EUROPEAN PINE MARTEN, EURASIAN PINE MARTEN
HB 45–58cm; T 16–28cm; W 0.8–1.8kg
Similar to Stone Marten, with which it overlaps in most of W and C Europe, and distinguished by a yellowish throat patch. **Distribution and Habitat** UK, continental W and C Europe to Fenno-Scandinavia, W Siberia (Russia), Turkey, N Iraq and N Iran. Occurs mainly in mature intact forest, woodland and scrubland with dense understorey. Inhabits coastal shrubland, pasture and grassland with cover, but avoids open areas. Occurs near settlements, but does not readily colonise urban areas as do Stone Martens. **Feeding Ecology** Preys predominantly on small mammals, especially Field Vole, red-backed voles, field mice, Wood Lemming, squirrels and lagomorphs; a camera-trap set in Poland recorded a marten killing 2 young Red Fox (page 114)

cubs in their den. Other important prey includes invertebrates, birds, herptiles, fruits (including berries), eggs and carrion (mainly wild and domestic ungulate carcasses). Sometimes kills domestic poultry. Foraging is primarily nocturnal and solitary. Scavenges, mainly from carrion and rarely from urban sources. Caches excess food. **Social and Spatial Behaviour** Solitary and territorial, with male ranges overlapping multiple female ranges. Range size correlates with forest cover and rodent density. Smallest ranges are in mature forest with high rodent abundance, e.g. Poland and Germany; largest known ranges are in open habitat in Finland and Scotland. Average range size 1.4–9.8km² (♀s) to 2.3–28.6km² (♂s). **Reproduction and Demography** Seasonal. Mating July–August; births March–April (following year). Gestation 230–274 days, with delayed implantation (embryonic development ~30 days). Litter size 2–8, averaging 3–5. Weaning at around 6–8 weeks; dispersal from 6 months throughout winter. MORTALITY Annual mortality in protected forest (Poland) is 38.4% (adults and subadults, sexes combined), from canine distemper, winter starvation, poaching, and predation by Eurasian Lynx (page 34), Red Fox (page 114) and raptors. LIFESPAN 5 years in the wild, 17 in captivity. **Status and Threats** Formerly very heavily hunted for fur, resulting in declines and local extinctions, especially in Russia and Fenno-Scandinavia. Stricter controls have led to recovery, and it is now fairly widespread, but still harvested at questionable levels in some areas. Also illegally persecuted as a pest, the main reason it disappeared from much of the UK, where it is now recovering (especially in Scotland). Red List LC, population trend Stable.

# JAPANESE MARTEN *Martes melampus*

### YELLOW MARTEN, TSUSHIMA ISLAND MARTEN
HB 47–54.5cm; T 17–22.3cm; W 0.7–1.7kg
Small, slender marten. Rich, dark brown in colour, with a large, rich yellow throat patch; populations on Kyushu and northern Honshu moult in winter to a vivid orange-yellow with a white to pale grey head. Tail sometimes has a white tip. **Distribution and Habitat** Endemic to Japan (introduced to Hokkaido and Sado for fur, native to other islands). Records from the Korean Peninsula are equivocal. Occurs mainly in broadleaved forest, woodland and subalpine shrubland. Inhabits rural and urban areas with natural forest patches. **Feeding Ecology** Feeds mainly on small mammals, insects, centipedes, earthworms, spiders, snails, fruits (including berries) and seeds. Considered an important seed disperser in subalpine areas due to the amount of fruit it consumes. Also eats birds, frogs and various plant items. Occasionally takes domestic poultry and is easily trapped with chicks. Foraging is nocturnal and solitary. **Social and Spatial Behaviour** Adults are solitary and probably territorial; they deposit scats at range borders, with ranges overlapping little within the same sex. Range size 0.5–1km², similar for females (average 0.63km²) and males (average 0.7km², Tsushima Island). **Reproduction and Demography** Seasonal. Mating late July–mid-August; births mid-April–early May (following year). Gestation 230–250 days, with delayed implantation (embryonic development 28–30 days). All known litters number 2 (based on few observations). MORTALITY Rates unknown; main factors on Tsushima Island are roadkills (72%) and feral dogs (9%). LIFESPAN Unknown. **Status and Threats** Relatively widespread and common within its limited distribution. Main threats are habitat conversion (including to forestry monocultures), roadkills and predation by feral dogs. Legally trapped for fur (not on Tsushima Island) in December–January. Red List LC, population trend Stable.

■ Stone Marten

■ Pine Marten

■ Japanese Marten

**Plate 78**

STONE
MARTEN

PINE
MARTEN

Winter form,
Kyushu and
northern Honshu

JAPANESE MARTEN

# NILGIRI MARTEN *Martes gwatkinsii*

HB 50–70cm; T 35–50cm; W 1–3kg
Very similar to Yellow-throated Marten and considered by some authors to be the same species; separated as a distinct species in part due to its isolated, discontinuous distribution. Recent genetic analyses, which would help resolve the controversy, are lacking. Appearance of both is similar, but Nilgiri Marten is typically dark brown over the entire upper body and lacks the Yellow-throated Marten's yellow cape, with golden yellow restricted to throat and chest; the shoulders and torso sometimes tend towards pale rufous-brown. **Distribution and Habitat** Endemic to the Western Ghats, India, where most records are from 6 mostly disjunct populations, although it may occur in between. Strongly associated with evergreen forest patches and forest–grassland mosaics in undeveloped montane and hilly areas, mostly at medium to high elevations of 800–2,600m, occasionally as low as 120m. Sometimes found in adjoining (within 3km of forest) plantations of tea, coffee, cardamom, acacia and wattle. **Feeding Ecology** Poorly known. Assumed to be similar to that of Yellow-throated Marten. Has been observed pursuing Indian Giant Squirrel (with which it is sometimes confused due to strikingly similar pelage), Indian Spotted Chevrotain and Bengal Monitor, and eating the nectar of cultivated kapok trees. Raids domestic beehives, thought to be mainly for bee larvae, although honey and honeycomb are doubtless also consumed. **Social and Spatial Behaviour** Poorly known. Has been sighted singly and in pairs, consistent with the little that is known of Yellow-throated Marten sociality. It is observed and recorded in surveys at markedly lower rates than the Yellow-throated Marten, suggesting it naturally occurs at low densities. **Reproduction and Demography** Unknown. **Status and Threats** Distribution is very restricted, calculated to be about 24,500km², and very fragmented. Thought to be naturally rare based on the frequency of encounters, with an estimated total population of around 1,500 (1,000 of which are mature adults). The Western Ghats are under intense anthropogenic pressure, and further habitat loss and fragmentation are the main threats. Also killed by beekeepers as a perceived pest, and illegally hunted by some communities for meat, although both are considered to have declined in recent years, and the species is thought to be increasing in some areas where persecution was formerly pervasive. CITES Appendix III India; Red List VU, population trend Stable.

# YELLOW-THROATED MARTEN
## *Martes flavigula*

### Himalayan Yellow-throated Marten, Kharza

HB 45–65cm; T 37–45cm; W 1.3–3kg
Large marten with a long tail up to 70% the length of its body. Head, nape, hindquarters and tail are normally dark brown with a highly variable tawny-brown cape covering the rest of the upper body, although this is entirely absent in some animals, especially in Peninsular Malaysia, Borneo and Sumatra. Throat and chest are always golden lemon yellow, sometimes extending down the forelimbs. Chin and cheeks are white. **Distribution and Habitat** From the Russian Far East through the Korean Peninsula and E and S China, including Taiwan, Indochina, Sumatra, Java and Borneo, and extending through the N Indian subcontinent to N Pakistan and N Afghanistan. Inhabits temperate and tropical forests from sea-level to 4,150m. Occurs in secondary forest and plantations, but avoids open anthropogenic habitats. **Feeding Ecology** Omnivorous, with a wide, opportunistic diet, although detailed studies of feeding ecology are mostly lacking. Eats small mammals, birds (including large ones such as pheasants), reptiles, amphibians, invertebrates, eggs, fruits (including berries), flowers and nectar. Its diet shifts to take advantage of seasonal foods, e.g. focuses on fruits and flowers during spring and summer. Has been observed pursuing large mammals, including Himalayan Tahr, Himalayan Musk Deer and gorals, although the outcome was not observed. A pair was filmed attacking an injured adult Nepal Grey Langur (Jim Corbett NP, India) on the ground, which was unable to flee; the martens eventually lost interest while the langur was still alive. Seven martens were observed feeding on a Chinese Goral, and tahr has been found in scats, but they are extremely unlikely to kill such large prey and are known to take carrion, e.g. one was photographed scavenging the carcass of a Red Muntjac suspected of dying from a snakebite, Huai Kha Khaeg WS, Thailand. A marten was photographed in Chitwan NP, Nepal, carrying a dead adult Small Indian Civet (page 88), although it was unclear whether it was killed or scavenged. The nests of social insects, especially wasps and bees, are readily plundered. Beeswax appears in scats throughout the year in Jirisan NP, South Korea, although the remains of honeybees are not, suggesting honey rather than bees is the main food item. Reportedly raids poultry from coops (West Bengal, India). Primarily diurnal, with greater nocturnalism near people, and forages both terrestrially and arboreally; very agile and adept at pursuing prey in trees. Scavenges boiled rice at guardposts in Khao Yai NP, Thailand, and frequents refuse dumps. **Social and Spatial Behaviour** Poorly known. More often seen in pairs and trios than alone. Pair/group composition is unclear and may comprise females with large kittens, but almost all records involve adult-sized animals, and their frequency of occurrence suggests greater sociality than occurs in other marten species. Also found in larger groups, e.g. at carcasses, which are probably temporary aggregations. Only range estimates (Phu Khieo WS, Thailand) are 8.8km² (1 ♀) and 1.7–11.8km² (♂s). **Reproduction and Demography** Poorly known. Thought to be seasonal. Mating occurs June–August; births March–June (following year). Gestation 220–290 days, with delayed implantation. Litter size 2–5. MORTALITY Unknown. LIFESPAN 14 years in captivity. **Status and Threats** Widespread and considered secure. Presumably undergoes declines with forest loss and fragmentation. Remains relatively common even in areas with high hunting pressure, e.g. Indochina, perhaps because it has unpleasant-tasting flesh and few communities eat it. The fur is generally not considered valuable; it is hunted for fur in Afghanistan, Pakistan, Russia (Siberia) and North Korea. CITES Appendix III – India; Red List LC, population trend Decreasing.

 Nilgiri Marten     ■ Yellow-throated Marten

Plate 79

Hunting Indian
Giant Squirrel

NILGIRI
MARTEN

YELLOW-THROATED
MARTEN

# SMALL-TOOTHED FERRET BADGER
## Melogale moschata

### CHINESE FERRET BADGER
HB 31.5–42cm; T 13–21.1cm; W 0.8–1.6kg

Ferret badgers show slight external differences between the 4 well-described species, and their taxonomy is in need of review. In 2011, a fifth species, Vietnam or Cuc Phuong Ferret Badger (*M. cucphuongensis*) was described based on 2 specimens from Cuc Phuong NP, Vietnam. It differs markedly from the other species, having a very distinct elongated skull with a very narrow, slender snout, and largely unmarked brown pelage with creamy-brown underparts. Genetic analysis suggests it is likely a distinct species, although further analysis with more samples is necessary. Its tiny known distribution is also home to Small-toothed Ferret Badger and Large-toothed Ferret Badger. The latter two are sympatric in much of their ranges; they are virtually indistinguishable; the Small-toothed is slightly smaller, generally has a shorter white dorsal stripe and has markedly smaller premolars. **Distribution and Habitat** S and C China, Taiwan, N Myanmar, Laos, Vietnam and NE India; possibly Bhutan, Cambodia and Thailand. Inhabits forest, woodland, scrub and dense grassland. Tolerates cultivated areas with cover and occurs near human settlements. **Feeding Ecology** Feeds chiefly on soil-living invertebrates, especially earthworms and insects, as well as fruits and seeds. Less important food includes small mammals, herptiles, carrion and eggs. Not known to prey on poultry. Foraging is solitary and almost exclusively nocturnal. **Social and Spatial Behaviour** Ranges overlap extensively and mixed-sex groups of up to 4 adults share ranges and setts, suggesting some sociality, including possible maintenance of group ranges as in European Badger (page 162). Range size is similar for sexes and averages 1.3km² (range 0.51–4.7km²). **Reproduction and Demography** Poorly known. Thought to be seasonal. Mating assumed to be in March (China), but births occur through May–December (Taiwan). Gestation 53–80 days (captivity). Litter size 1–4. MORTALITY Unknown; rabies, canine distemper and SARS coronavirus (rarely) confirmed, but there is no evidence of population impacts. LIFESPAN 10.5 years in captivity. **Status and Threats** Status poorly known, but the species is widespread and considered common in much of its range. It is used for meat and traditional medicinal practices in Indochina, and heavily hunted in S China; despite this, it apparently remains relatively widespread. Red List LC, population trend Stable.

# LARGE-TOOTHED FERRET BADGER
## Melogale personata

### BURMESE FERRET BADGER
HB 33–43cm; T 14.5–23cm; W 1.5–3kg

Largest ferret badger, although differences between all species are slight. Dentition is relatively massive. Generally has more white coloration than other species. White dorsal stripe extends to at least the mid-point of the spine, the distal half of the tail is white and body fur has extensive white 'frosting'. Sometimes considered the same species as Bornean and Javan ferret badgers. **Distribution and Habitat** SE Nepal, NE India, Myanmar, Thailand, Indochina and S Yunnan, China; presumably Bhutan, although no certain records. Occurs in similar habitats (including anthropogenic habitats) to Small-toothed Ferret Badger. **Feeding Ecology** Diet less well known than that of Small-toothed Ferret Badger, but assumed to be similar. Considerably more massive dentition suggests it is more predatory on small vertebrates, but this remains unconfirmed. Foraging is almost exclusively nocturnal. **Social and Spatial Behaviour** Unknown. Most records are of single adults or females with young; it is unknown if it is social or semi-social, as for Small-toothed Ferret Badger. **Reproduction and Demography** Poorly known. Reputed to be seasonal, with captives giving birth mainly May–June. Litters in captivity 1–3. MORTALITY and LIFESPAN Unknown. **Status and Threats** Status poorly known, but hunting pressure is very high in most of its range and it rarely appears in camera-trap surveys, e.g. it was not photographed in 8,499 camera-trap days in 2003–06 in Nam Et–Phou Louey PA, Laos. Occurs in a number of protected areas in Thailand. Red List LC, population trend Unknown.

# BORNEAN FERRET BADGER
## Melogale everetti

### KINABALU FERRET BADGER, EVERETT'S FERRET BADGER
HB 33–45cm; T 14.5–17cm; W 1–2kg

Usually described as mainly brown (rather than greyish), with typical ferret badger markings that are less extensive than in the continental species. The only ferret badger in its range. **Distribution and Habitat** Endemic to Sabah, Borneo. All certain records are from the Kinabalu massif and Crocker Range region, N Sabah, in montane broadleaved forest habitat at 900–3,700m; a record from lowland forest in E Sabah is erroneous and it is unclear whether it occurs more widely in Borneo. **Feeding Ecology** Poorly known. Reportedly eats soil-living invertebrates (especially earthworms), lizards, small birds, rodents and fruits. Nocturnal. One record exists of scavenging in roadside refuse dumps. **Social and Spatial Behaviour** Unknown. Most records are of single adults or females with young. **Reproduction and Demography** Unknown. **Status and Threats** Status very poorly known. Extremely small known distribution, estimated at <5,000km², which includes protected areas, but much of the range is threatened by ongoing conversion to agriculture and hunting. This is possibly Borneo's most threatened carnivore. Red List EN, population trend Decreasing.

# JAVAN FERRET BADGER
## Melogale orientalis

HB 35–40cm; T 14.5–17cm; W 1–2kg

Physically indistinguishable from Bornean Ferret Badger and sometimes considered the same species (and both are sometimes treated as a subspecies of Large-toothed Ferret Badger). The only ferret badger in its range. **Distribution and Habitat** Endemic to Java and Bali. Formerly thought to be restricted to isolated montane areas, it is now suspected to be more widely distributed across Java and Bali. Preferred habitat is likely mid- to high-altitude primary and secondary forests at 800–2,230m, but it is also recorded in lowlands, including from highly modified habitats such as croplands and rubber plantations near human settlements. **Feeding Ecology** Diet is assumed to be similar to that of other ferret badgers. Anecdotally reported in association with tourist refuse in Gunung Gede Pangrango NP, W Java, but it is unclear if it scavenges from dumps. Nocturnal. **Social and Spatial Behaviour** Unknown. **Reproduction and Demography** Unknown. **Status and Threats** Status very poorly known. Known distribution is restricted and exposed to a high rate of forest loss and hunting. It has recently started appearing in small numbers in the local novelty pet trade. Red List LC, population trend Unknown.

■ Small-toothed Ferret Badger
■ Bornean Ferret Badger
■ Large-toothed Ferret Badger
■ Javan Ferret Badger

Plate 80

SMALL-TOOTHED
FERRET BADGER

LARGE-TOOTHED
FERRET BADGER

CUC PHUONG
FERRET BADGER

BORNEAN
FERRET BADGER

JAVAN
FERRET BADGER

# PATAGONIAN WEASEL
## *Lyncodon patagonicus*

**Huroncito** HB 30–35cm; T 6–9cm; W 0.2–0.25kg
Very small, pale, grizzled grey with chocolate-brown to black underparts. Wide wedge-shaped white crown covers the head, distinguishing it from the considerably larger Lesser Grison, which has a narrow white brow. **Distribution and Habitat** Endemic to Argentina and a narrow band of C to E Chile. Inhabits cold arid and semi-arid shrubland, steppes and open scrubby woodland from sea-level to 2,000m. **Feeding Ecology** Poorly known. Thought to hunt mainly small burrowing rodents such as tuco-tucos and mountain cavies; 1 record of predation on Elegant Crested Tinamou. An adult living under the ranger station at Cabo Dos Bahías WR, Argentina, scavenged handouts. The species has a novel series of forepaw muscles never previously described for mammals, possibly enhancing dexterity in handling small prey, although this is speculative. **Social and Spatial Behaviour** Unknown; assumed to be solitary. **Reproduction and Demography** Unknown. **mortality** Black-chested Buzzard-eagle is a known predator. **lifespan** Unknown. **Status and Threats** Status essentially unknown. Rarely observed or encountered during wildlife surveys, suggesting it is naturally rare. Red List LC, population trend Unknown.

# LESSER GRISON *Galictis cuja*

HB 27.3–52cm; T 12–19cm; W 1–2.5kg
Grizzled yellow-grey to brownish-grey upperparts. Black face and underparts bounded by a narrow white or creamy band across the brow to the shoulders. Moves with rapid, low-slung weasel-like movements compared to the Greater Grison's heavy, bouncing gait (reminiscent of badgers). **Distribution and Habitat** SE Peru, S Bolivia, and S and E Brazil through Paraguay, Uruguay, Argentina, and C Chile. Occurs in desert, steppes, grassland savannah, shrubland, marshland, woodland and forest from sea-level to 4,200m. Tolerates agricultural and pastoral habitats. **Feeding Ecology** Diet dominated by small mammals, especially mice, rats and cavies, and introduced European Hare and European Rabbit; often focuses almost entirely on lagomorphs under high availability. Also eats birds, small reptiles, frogs, eggs and invertebrates. Fruits are consumed rarely. Blamed for killing poultry, but depredation is poorly quantified. Cathemeral. **Social and Spatial Behaviour** Poorly known. Adults are usually observed alone but small groups, including adult pairs and their juveniles, suggest monogamous pair bonds. Up to a dozen animals recorded playing together. **Reproduction and Demography** Gestation 39 days. Litter size 2–5. Juveniles recorded March–October, suggesting weak seasonality. Mated pairs apparently cooperate to raise kittens. **mortality** Ocelot (page 28) and Black-chested Buzzard-eagle are known predators. **lifespan** Unknown. **Status and Threats** Widespread. Broad habitat tolerance and considered secure, although status is poorly quantified. Persecuted for killing poultry, often killed on roads (e.g. E Brazil) and by urban feral dogs (e.g. University of São Paulo, Piracicaba, SE Brazil). Red List LC, population trend Unknown.

# GREATER GRISON *Galictis vittata*

HB 45–60cm; T 13.5–19.5cm; W 1.4–4kg
Larger than Lesser Grison, with a proportionally shorter tail and paler, grizzled, salt-and-pepper grey fur. The 2 species overlap in E Brazil. **Distribution and Habitat** E Brazil through N South America to SE Mexico. Occurs in low and mid-elevation forest woodlands, palm savannah, grassland and wetland to 1,500m. Tolerates disturbed forest, plantations, open fields and agricultural land with cover. **Feeding Ecology** Carnivorous, eating rodents to the size of agoutis, marsupials (including Southern Opossum), reptiles, amphibians, fish, invertebrates and eggs. Captives eat fruits and some plant matter. Sometimes raids domestic poultry. Foraging is cathemeral. Hunting is terrestrial, but readily pursues prey into trees and deep water. Hunts alone, in adult pairs or in small family groups. **Social and Spatial Behaviour** Assumed to be largely solitary; adult pairs and family groups occur, but sociality is poorly understood. Only range estimate is for 1 female (Venezuela) over 2 months, 4.15km². **Reproduction and Demography** Gestation 39–40 days. Litter size 1–4. Juveniles recorded March–October, suggesting weak seasonality. Males often recorded with mothers and kittens, but it is unknown if they assist in raising juveniles. **mortality** Unknown. **lifespan** 10.5 years in captivity. **Status and Threats** Secure over much of its range, but threatened at the extremes, e.g. Mexico and Costa Rica. Tolerant of some disturbance, but hunting pressure and habitat conversion to open agriculture drives local declines. CITES Appendix III – Costa Rica; Red List LC, population trend Stable.

# MARBLED POLECAT *Vormela peregusna*

HB 28.8–47.7cm; T 14.5–20.1cm; W 0.3–0.72kg
The sole Eurasian representative of the subfamily Ictonychinae; all members possess aposematic pelage and enlarged anal scent glands used in defensive threat displays. Very dark chocolate brown, with a striking buff-yellow cape dappled with red-brown blotches. Bushy tail grizzled yellow-white, usually with a dark tip. A conspicuous white stripe encircles the face, the tops of the ears are white, and the muzzle and chin are creamy white. Assumes a distinctive arching posture when threatened, followed by ejecting a noxious anal-gland secretion if unheeded. **Distribution and Habitat** N China, Mongolia, C Asia, the Middle East and SE Europe. Inhabits temperate and arid steppes, grassland, scrubland, rocky upland, salt marshes, semi-desert and open desert habitats. Occurs in cultivated areas, orchards and vegetable gardens near settlements, and in urban parkland. **Feeding Ecology** Diet dominated by small mammals, especially ground squirrels, jirds, hamsters, voles, rats, mice and rabbits. Also consumes insects (especially during spring–summer flushes), birds, herptiles, snails and fruits. Sometimes kills domestic poultry and rabbits. Foraging is mainly nocturno-crepuscular, solitary and by scent; reputedly has poor eyesight. Eats carrion and scavenges, including raiding larders for smoked meat and cheese. Caches surplus food in burrows. **Social and Spatial Behaviour** Solitary. Limited data indicate small stable ranges with moderate overlap. Outside the breeding season, adults sometimes fight furiously. Only known range estimates (Israel) 0.5–0.6km², with little difference between sexes. **Reproduction and Demography** Seasonal. Mating March–June; births February–May (following year). Gestation 243–327 days, with delayed implantation. Litter size 1–8, averaging 4–5. Mothers reportedly use a unique (for carnivores) distraction display of feigning death and injury, belly-crawling away from hidden pups to divert predators. Weaning at 50–54 days and dispersal at 61–68 days. Females become sexually mature at 3 months; males typically breed after their first year. **mortality** Poorly known. Most documented mortality is anthropogenic. **lifespan** Almost 9 years in captivity. **Status and Threats** Nowhere common, and threatened by conversion of steppe habitats to cultivation, combined with large-scale poisoning of rodents, e.g. China and Mongolia. Killed in small numbers for fur and persecuted for killing poultry. Red List VU, population trend Decreasing.

■ Patagonian Weasel ■ Lesser Grison ■ Marbled Polecat
■ Greater Grison

**Plate 81**

PATAGONIAN
WEASEL

LESSER
GRISON

GREATER
GRISON

MARBLED
POLECAT

# STRIPED WEASEL *Poecilogale albinucha*

### AFRICAN STRIPED WEASEL, WHITE-NAPED WEASEL
HB ♀ 24–35cm, ♂ 27–33cm; T 13.8–21.5cm;
W ♀ 0.21–0.29kg, ♂ 0.28–0.38kg

Small weasel with a long sinuous body, very short limbs and a long tail. Fur is black with a yellowish-white dorsal stripe starting at the crown; stripe splits into paired stripes that run along each side. Tail is white. **Distribution and Habitat** Sub-equatorial Africa, from S Kenya and S Uganda to coastal DR Congo, and south to South Africa. Inhabits woodland savannah, grassland, scrubland, forest (its range stops at the limits of the forested Congo Basin) and vegetated semi-arid desert, e.g. the Kalahari. Occurs in plantation, agricultural and pastoral habitats. **Feeding Ecology** Rodent specialist, hunting mainly small mice, rats and mole rats to its own size; an adult may kill 3–4 rodents a night. Also eats small reptiles, insects and eggs. Foraging is mainly nocturnal, terrestrial and solitary. Forages chiefly by scent, and is well suited to entering small rodent burrows; a powerful burrower, but has not been observed excavating prey. Rodents are killed with a nape bite and vigorous kicking by the hind legs, which may dislocate the neck; large prey is sometimes killed by a throat bite. Caches surplus kills in burrows. **Social and Spatial Behaviour** Poorly known. Assumed to be solitary; most sightings are of adult individuals or females with pups. **Reproduction and Demography** Possibly seasonal. Breeding September–April (southern Africa); births from November. Gestation 30–33 days. Litter size 1–3. Weaning at 11 weeks (captivity). Sexual maturity at 8 months. MORTALITY Poorly known. Occasionally killed by Black-backed Jackal (page 112), domestic dogs and large owls. Rabies is recorded. LIFESPAN 6 years in captivity. **Status and Threats** Considered uncommon to rare, but it is inconspicuous and elusive, and there is little accurate information on its status. Killed on roads in rural areas, and highly prized for traditional medicinal use in South Africa. Red List LC, population trend Unknown.

# LIBYAN WEASEL *Ictonyx libycus*

### SAHARAN STRIPED POLECAT,
### NORTH AFRICAN STRIPED WEASEL
HB 20.7–26cm; T 11.4–18cm; W 0.2–0.6kg

Small, compact weasel with a black face, limbs and underparts. White stripes interleaved with variable black interstripes cover the body. Tail is long and white, with interspersed black hairs, and sometimes with a black tip. Fur is longish with a silky appearance. Unbroken white band encircles the face, running from the forehead behind the eyes to the base of the throat; this helps distinguish it from the similar Zorilla. It has well-developed anal glands and secretes a pungent fluid when threatened. **Distribution and Habitat** N Africa, on the edges of the Sahara in the coastal band of Mediterranean N Africa from Egypt to Mauritania, and through the Sahel from W Mali to the Sudan–Eritrea coast. Scattered records exist across the Sahara itself, but it is unclear if it occurs throughout. Occupies mainly sub-desert habitats such as stony desert, massifs, steppes, oases and sparsely vegetated dunes. Found close to settlements in cultivated areas. **Feeding Ecology** Poorly known. Thought to feed mainly on small desert rodents, birds, reptiles, eggs and invertebrates. Nocturnal. **Social and Spatial Behaviour** Unknown. Most records are of single adults; assumed to be solitary. **Reproduction and Demography** Poorly known. Thought to be seasonal; all records of young occur January–March. Litter size 1–3. MORTALITY Unknown. LIFESPAN 5.5 years in captivity. **Status and Threats** Status poorly known. Widely distributed and locally abundant in some coastal dune areas. Hunted in Libya and Tunisia in the belief that its body parts increase human male fertility. Red List LC, population trend Unknown.

# ZORILLA *Ictonyx striatus*

### STRIPED POLECAT
HB 28–38cm; T 16.5–28cm; W ♀ 0.4–1.4kg, ♂ 0.7–1.5kg

Larger than the similar Striped and Libyan weasels. Jet black with 4 white stripes that unite on the crown and run the length of the body to the tail, which is white interspersed with black hairs. Face is distinctively marked with a cluster of 3 white blotches on the forehead and on each temple. Overlaps Libyan Weasel in the Sahel. Ejects a noxious anal secretion when threatened. **Distribution and Habitat** Throughout sub-Saharan Africa, except the Sahara and Congo Basin. Occurs in a wide variety of habitats from sea-level to 4,000m, including wet and dry woodland savannahs, grassland, forest, dunes, wetland, montane heath, semi-desert and desert. Absent from equatorial forest and desert interiors. Readily inhabits agricultural and cultivated habitats. **Feeding Ecology** Eats mainly small rodents and insects. Also eats herptiles, birds, chicks, eggs, arachnids and other invertebrates. Largest prey includes Springhare, ground squirrels and large snakes, including venomous species such as cobras. Occasionally kills domestic poultry. Nocturnal and terrestrial. Hunting is solitary, but juveniles sometimes help the mother in subduing large prey such as snakes. Prey is hunted by sight and smell, with rodents and insects often killed in burrows or excavated. **Social and Spatial Behaviour** Poorly known. Adults are largely solitary. Captive males are intolerant of each other, but females with juveniles tolerate other mother–kitten families in captivity. **Reproduction and Demography** Poorly known. Reported to give birth mainly November–February in southern Africa, but lactating females are recorded February–October in E Africa. Gestation 36 days. Litter size 1–3, exceptionally to 5 (in captivity, the maximum reared being 3). Weaning at around 8 weeks. Females first breed at 10 months (captivity). MORTALITY Poorly known. Large raptors, especially Martial Eagle and owls, are confirmed predators, and it is frequently killed by domestic dogs in rural areas. LIFESPAN 13.3 years in captivity. **Status and Threats** Widespread habitat generalist and common to abundant in suitable protected habitat. Roadkills, domestic dogs and persecution for poultry depredation kill significant numbers in rural areas, but probably constitute only a localised threat. Valued in traditional medicinal beliefs in some areas. Red List LC, population trend Stable.

■ Striped Weasel

■ Libyan Weasel

■ Zorilla

**Plate 82**

STRIPED
WEASEL

LIBYAN
WEASEL

ZORILLA

# AMERICAN MINK *Neovison vison*

HB ♀ 30–40cm, ♂ 33–43cm; T 12.8–23cm;
W ♀ 0.45–1.1kg, ♂ 0.6–2.3kg

Uniformly glossy chestnut-brown to sooty black with slightly paler underparts. The chin is often but not always white; white fur on the chin rarely extends to the upper lip or throat (in contrast to European Mink; page 182). American Mink is closely related to American weasels (closest relative is thought to be Long-tailed Weasel; page 186) and only distantly related to European Mink. It is classified in its own genus with the now-extinct Sea Mink (*N. macrodon*), which was formerly distributed on the Atlantic coast of Canada and the US. **Distribution and Habitat** Most of Canada and the USA, including Alaska; absent from S USA. Introduced for fur in Argentina, Chile and Eurasia, including Japan, where it is invasive and destructive to native wildlife, including the European Mink in Europe. Inhabits densely vegetated waterways, marshes, wetlands, swamp forest and coastal beaches. **Feeding Ecology** A bold and aggressive predator capable of killing prey much larger than itself, including records of adult swans, geese, gannets and at least one case of a juvenile Harbour Seal, but typical diet comprises small mammals, birds, slow-swimming fish, herptiles, eggs and aquatic invertebrates such as crayfish and crabs. In North America, preys heavily on Muskrat, and population fluctuations of the 2 species are closely linked. An important nest predator of waterfowl and colonially nesting birds such as gulls and terns. Readily preys on domestic poultry. Foraging is solitary, nocturno-crepuscular, and both terrestrial and aquatic. Dives to depths of 6m and swims underwater for up to 35m. Caches surplus food. **Social and Spatial Behaviour** Solitary. Male ranges overlap 1 or more smaller female ranges. There can be high intrasexual overlap of ranges. Linear range size 1–4.2km (♀s) and 1.5–11.1km (♂s). Density estimates from North American wetlands vary between 1.6–5.4/km² (Wisconsin) and 25–42/km² (Louisiana cypress–tupelo swamp). **Reproduction and Demography** Seasonal. Mating February–April (to early May in Alaska); births April–June. Gestation 39–79 days, with a brief period of delayed implantation (embryonic development 30–32 days). Litter size 2–8, averaging 4–5. Weaning at 7–9 weeks. MORTALITY In North America, deaths are mainly from trapping. LIFESPAN Rarely >3 years in the wild, 8 in captivity. **Status and Threats** Widespread and common. The most important American fur-bearer and widely trapped, with 400,000–700,000 wild mink harvested each year. Threatened in S Florida by wetland modification and degradation. Red List LC, population trend Stable.

# BLACK-FOOTED FERRET
## *Mustela nigripes*

HB 38–50cm; T 11.4–15cm; W ♀ 0.76–0.85kg, ♂ 0.96–1.1kg

The only ferret native to North America, closely related to Steppe Polecat (page 180) and Western Polecat (page 182), and more distantly to other American *Mustela*. Yellowish buff on the body, darkening to dark brown on the back. Head is creamy white with a brownish-black mask, white muzzle and chocolate-brown crown. Limbs are chocolate brown to black, and the tail has a black tip. **Distribution and Habitat** Great Plains of the USA; formerly from S Alberta and Saskatchewan, Canada, to N Mexico. Extinct in the Wild by 1987 and all present populations result from reintroductions. Restricted to short to mid-grass plains and prairies in obligate association with prairie dog colonies. **Feeding Ecology** Entirely dependent on prairie dogs, which comprise around 90% of the diet. An estimated 0.4–0.6km² of prairie dog colony is needed to support one Black-footed Ferret, and breeding females need prairie dog densities of at least 1,200 individuals/km² in core areas to successfully raise pups. The most important prey species is Black-tailed Prairie Dog, followed by White-tailed Prairie Dog and Gunnison's Prairie Dog (Arizona only). Occasional prey includes small rodents such as deer mice, voles and ground squirrels, as well as cottontail rabbits and White-tailed Jackrabbit. Hunting is mainly nocturno-crepuscular and underground; pursues prairie dogs into their burrows, where most kills occur. Above-ground hunts are less successful; adult prairie dogs often mount an effective defence on the surface. Does not hibernate and hunts hibernating prairie dogs throughout winter. Sometimes caches surplus kills in burrows. **Social and Spatial Behaviour** Solitary. Adults establish enduring ranges, closely tied to active prairie dog colonies. Same-sex adults avoid each other, but ranges overlap by as much as 42% in areas of high prairie dog density. Male ranges are about twice the size of female ranges. Range sizes 0.23–1.88km², averaging 0.56–0.65km² (♀s) and 1.28–1.32km² (♂s). **Reproduction and Demography** Seasonal. Mating March–April; births May–June. Gestation 42–45 days. Litter size 1–6, averaging 3–4. Weaning at 6 weeks, and kits venture above ground at 60 days. Dispersal in late autumn at around 5–6 months. MORTALITY Rates of disappearance (including some emigration) are 53–86% annually. Main factors are disease and predation, especially by Coyote (page 102) and large raptors. LIFESPAN 12 years in captivity, but much lower in the wild. **Status and Threats** The species was decimated by exotic disease (canine distemper and plague) and the massive anthropogenic-driven decline of prairie dogs. A comprehensive captive breeding and reintroduction effort initiated in 1985 has released ferrets in the 3 native range countries at 29 sites, only 4 of which have established self-sustaining populations, in Arizona, South Dakota and Wyoming. Another 10 populations, all in the US, show limited success or are too recently established to assess. Reintroduction in Canada and Mexico has failed, and the species is again considered extinct in those countries. There are now approximately only 300 adults in the wild, which has declined from a peak of 500 in 2008. Ongoing conversion of prairie grasslands for agriculture limits available habitat to ferrets, but current population declines and reintroduction failures are driven primarily by epidemics of exotic plague. Plague is transmitted by fleas in prairie dog colonies and is now considered endemic across Black-tailed Prairie Dog range. Both Black-footed Ferrets and prairie dogs are vulnerable to infection, so ferrets experience direct mortality and strong indirect effects due to resultant, very dramatic declines (typically >90%) in their prey base. Several hundred ferrets are maintained in captivity in the US. CITES Appendix I; Red List EN, population trend Decreasing.

■ American Mink                ■ Black-footed Ferret

**Plate 83**

**AMERICAN
MINK**

Attacking
Mute Swan

**BLACK-FOOTED
FERRET**

Hunting Prairie Dog

# SIBERIAN WEASEL *Mustela sibirica*

### SIBERIAN POLECAT, KOLINSKY, HIMALAYAN WEASEL

HB ♀ 25–30.6cm, ♂ 28–40cm; T 13.5–23.5cm;
W ♀ 0.36–0.45kg, ♂ 0.43–1.15kg

Formerly classified with the closely related Japanese Weasel; it closely resembles that species but is larger and generally more brightly coloured. Uniformly rich orange-brown with slightly paler underparts. Summer coat tends to be darker brown than winter coat. Face has a dark brown to black mask with a white muzzle and chin. **Distribution and Habitat** Temperate Asia; C to Far East Russia, N Mongolia, E and S China, Korean Peninsula, and marginally into Nepal, Bhutan and N Indochina. Introduced to, and invasive in, Japan (native on Tsushima Island). Inhabits forest, forest steppe, dense grassland, vegetated scrubland and wetland. Occurs in cultivated areas, plantations and urban areas, but avoids open anthropogenic habitat. **Feeding Ecology** Small rodents and shrews are the most important prey. Also eats insects, earthworms, crustaceans, herptiles, birds, fledglings, eggs and fruits, including berries. Locally a significant nest predator of colonially nesting birds, e.g. Little Tern (Nakdong Estuary, South Korea), and occasionally raids domestic poultry. In urban habitats, scavenges from refuse, handouts (cakes, bread, etc.) and fish remains from dock areas. Foraging is mainly nocturno-crepuscular and terrestrial, although it swims well. **Social and Spatial Behaviour** Solitary. Adults live in stable ranges that overlap with those of other adults, but avoid each other, except male–female pairs when breeding. Range size estimates known only from Japan: 0.013–0.017km² (♀s) and 0.014–0.044km² (♂s). **Reproduction and Demography** Seasonal. Mating late February–March; births early April–June. Litter size 2–12, averaging 5–6. Nests in burrows and tree and rock cavities, and under buildings and haystacks in urban and rural areas. **MORTALITY** Unknown. **LIFESPAN** 8.8 years in captivity. **Status and Threats** Widespread and common in many areas. Hunted for fur (legally in Russia) and meat, but hunting is likely a threat only at the range limits, especially in Laos and S China. CITES Appendix III – India; Red List LC, population trend, Stable.

## JAPANESE WEASEL *Mustela itatsi*

HB ♀ 22.2–26.5cm, ♂ 26.8-40cm; T 8.3–16.2cm;
W ♀ 0.1–0.26kg, ♂ 0.2–0.92kg

Very similar in appearance to the Siberian Weasel and considered the same species until recently. Genetic and morphological evidence indicates they are distinct species that diverged >2 million years ago. Siberian Weasel is introduced in Japan (except Tsushima Island, where it is native), and the 2 species are sympatric and very difficult to tell apart on Kyushu, Shikoku and W Honshu (everywhere west of Nagoya). Japanese Weasel is uniformly orange-brown to tawny brown with a greyish-buff head and throat. Summer coat is typically uniformly darker brown with a greyish-brown to chocolate-brown head and neck. Face has a dark brown mask with a white muzzle and chin. **Distribution and Habitat** Endemic to Japan, occurring naturally on all large islands, except Hokkaido; introduced to Hokkaido (1880s) and a further 50 small islands in Japan. Introduced to Sakhalin Island, Russia (1932), but thought to be extinct there now. Inhabits most habitats across Japan, especially forest, dense grassland and wetlands from sea-level to 336m. Occurs in agricultural landscapes and peri-urban areas, but apparently intolerant of urbanisation and in large cities is restricted to well-vegetated riparian strips. **Feeding Ecology** Eats small rodents, insects, earthworms, crustaceans, herptiles, birds, fledglings, eggs and fruits. An urban population living in riverine habitat in outer Tokyo eats mainly fish, insects and fruits. Urban weasels apparently do not utilise anthropogenic foods (in contrast to Siberian Weasel). Foraging is mainly nocturno-crepuscular, terrestrial and semi-aquatic. **Social and Spatial Behaviour** Solitary, and thought to follow similar patterns to Siberian Weasels. Range size is poorly known, 0.01–0.31km² (♀s). **Reproduction and Demography** Seasonal. Mating late winter (February–March); births in spring, April–June. Litter size unknown, assumed to be similar to Siberian Weasel. **MORTALITY** Unknown. Killed occasionally by domestic dogs. **LIFESPAN** Unknown. **Status and Threats** Widespread and common in many areas but it is disappearing from lowlands in western Japan, now occupied by introduced Siberian Weasel (which possibly outcompetes Japanese Weasels or perhaps invades after their urbanisation-driven disappearance). Red List NT, population trend Decreasing.

## STEPPE POLECAT *Mustela eversmanii*

### STEPPE WEASEL

HB 29–56.2cm; T 7–18.3cm; W ♀ 0.4–0.8kg, ♂ 0.75–1.2kg

Formerly classified with the closely related Western Polecat (page 182); it strongly resembles that species, but tends to be lighter, with a paler face and fewer dark guard hairs over the body. The 2 species overlap in E Europe and W Russia. The domestic ferret is thought to descend from both Steppe and Western polecats. **Distribution and Habitat** E Europe through S Russia, NC Asia, Mongolia, and N and C China. Mainly inhabits steppe, grassland and vegetated semi-desert to 2,600m. Generally avoids densely vegetated areas, including most forest types. Occurs in pastures and on farmland, including areas with crops such as corn and cereals. **Feeding Ecology** Small rodents and lagomorphs are the mainstay, particularly voles, mice, gerbils, hamsters, sousliks, marmots, zokors and pikas. Also eats grassland birds (especially in spring and autumn), including grouse, ptarmigans and pheasants, plus reptiles, fish, eggs and invertebrates. Hunting is mainly nocturno-crepuscular and terrestrial, with most prey captured and killed in burrows. Occasionally scavenges, including from carrion, and caches surplus kills, e.g. up to 50 sousliks in Russian reports. **Social and Spatial Behaviour** Poorly known. Adults are solitary, with large male ranges overlapping numerous female ranges. Range estimates average 1.27km² (♀s) and 3.54km² (♂s; NW Hungary). **Reproduction and Demography** Seasonal. Mating February–April; births April–June. Gestation 36–41 days. Litter size 4–14, averaging 8–9. Weaning at around 6 weeks; dispersal at 3–4 months. Females first breed at 9–10 months. **MORTALITY** and **LIFESPAN** Unknown. **Status and Threats** Has a wide range, is common in many areas and is globally secure. It has declined significantly in much of its European distribution range since the 1960s, but remains widespread and numerous in its Asian range. Trapping, conversion of grassland habitats, and widespread hunting and poisoning of prey are threats, especially in E Europe, Mongolia and China. Legally hunted for fur in Russia. Red List LC, population trend Decreasing.

■ Siberian Weasel

■ Japanese Weasel

■ Steppe Polecat

Plate 84

SIBERIAN WEASEL

JAPANESE WEASEL

STEPPE
POLECAT

# WESTERN POLECAT *Mustela putorius*

EUROPEAN POLECAT, COMMON POLECAT, FERRET
HB ♀ 20.5–38.5cm, ♂ 29.5–46cm; T 7–14cm;
W ♀ 0.4–0.92kg, ♂ 0.5–1.7kg

Dark chocolate brown to near black, with buff-yellow underfur that is obvious on the sides and neck. Face is buff to silvery white, with a dark mask. The progenitor of the domestic ferret (possibly also with interbreeding from the closely related Steppe Polecat; page 180), and they hybridise, producing fertile offspring. **Distribution and Habitat** W Russia, N Scandinavia throughout W and C Europe, including Britain (absent from Ireland), and extreme N Africa (Morocco and Algeria). Inhabits lowland forest, wooded steppes, vegetated dunes, marshes, meadows and river valleys in open habitat, to 1,500m in Europe (Pyrenees and Alps) and to 2,000m in N Africa (Rif Mountains). Occurs in agricultural areas and close to human settlements. **Feeding Ecology** Eats mainly small rodents, shrews, lagomorphs, frogs and toads. Other prey includes birds, reptiles, fish, eels, invertebrates and eggs; fruits and other plant items are eaten mainly by young animals. Takes domestic poultry, occasionally becoming a serious pest. Foraging is solitary, mainly nocturno-crepuscular and terrestrial. Scavenges from carrion and occasionally from human refuse, bird feeders and food scraps, especially during winter food shortages. Caches excess food, e.g. 40–120 frogs (W Russia). **Social and Spatial Behaviour** Solitary. Male ranges overlap 1 or more smaller female ranges. Female ranges tend to be exclusive; male ranges have variable overlap and are most exclusive during the breeding season; ranges are assiduously scent-marked, especially while breeding. Range size 0.65–1.65km (♀s) and 1–3.05km (♂s; linear ranges along riverbanks, Poland), and 0.42–1.21km² (♀s) and 1.07–2.8km² (♂s; fragmented forest–agricultural mosaic, Luxembourg). **Reproduction and Demography** Seasonal. Mating March–June in most of the range, a month earlier in Britain; births April (Britain, May) to early August, peaking mid-July. Gestation 40–43 days, without delayed implantation. Litter size 2–13, averaging 4–6; large litters may be due to hybridisation with ferrets. Weaning at 5–7 weeks. MORTALITY Mostly anthropogenic, especially roadkills, trapping and domestic dogs; starvation is an important factor during severe winters, especially for newly independent subadults. LIFESPAN <5 years in the wild, 14 in captivity. **Status and Threats** Widespread and relatively common. Persecuted very heavily in the past, which, combined with loss of habitat, led to widespread and severe declines. It is still declining in parts of the range, especially where habitat conversion is advancing in W Europe, but it is recovering in many areas, e.g. Britain and Switzerland. Localised threats include roadkills, prey declines (e.g. dramatic reduction of European Rabbits in Mediterranean range) and persecution as a perceived pest. It is now largely protected from hunting and trapping in most W Europe range states; it is legally trapped in Russia, although intentional trapping pressure is low and most mortality is unintentional 'by-catch' during trapping efforts for more valuable fur species such as American Mink (page 178) and martens. Hybridisation with feral ferrets erodes genetic purity in some areas, e.g. S Britain and N Germany, although not at levels to be considered a major threat. Wild Western Polecats are captured in Algeria (and possibly Morocco) and kept for hunting rabbits, which may constitute a threat if the remaining population is small and isolated, as suspected. Red List LC, population trend Decreasing.

# EUROPEAN MINK *Mustela lutreola*

HB ♀ 32–40cm, ♂ 28–43cm; T 12–19cm;
W ♀ 0.4–0.6kg, ♂ 0.6–1.1kg

Uniformly glossy chestnut-brown to dark coffee brown with slightly paler underparts. Upper lips, chin and tip of the muzzle are white, sometimes extending down the throat and chest. Very similar in appearance to introduced American Mink, which has replaced European Mink in most of its native distribution. European Minks are slightly smaller, typically with white muzzles and upper lips, whereas white fur in American Minks is usually restricted to the chin, and is often absent entirely. Despite appearances, the 2 species are not closely related; European Mink's closest relatives are Steppe Polecat and Western Polecat. **Distribution and Habitat** W Russia, and isolated populations in Belarus, Estonia, Latvia, Ukraine, coastal Romania and the French–Spanish border. Sympatric with introduced American Mink in most of its current range; NW Russia (the Arkhangelsk region and Komi Republic) and the Northern Caucasus region may be exceptions. Rarely more than 100m from fresh water; preferred habitats are slow-flowing streams, lake shores and wetlands that do not completely freeze in winter. **Feeding Ecology** Semi-aquatic and forages for small, mainly vertebrate prey along waterways, especially small rodents such as European Water Vole, Bank Vole, Wood Mouse and introduced Muskrat. Other prey includes small fish, frogs, crustaceans, aquatic insects, and occasionally birds and reptiles. Foraging is solitary, nocturno-crepuscular, and both terrestrial and aquatic; it is also an excellent swimmer, pursuing prey underwater in dives of 5–20 seconds. Caches surplus kills. **Social and Spatial Behaviour** Solitary. Large male ranges overlap 1 or more smaller female ranges, with low to moderate overlap within sexes (especially males). Ranges expand in autumn–winter to locate unfrozen water. Linear range size 0.3–5.1km (♀s) and 2.9–11.4km (♂s). Density estimates 2–12/10km of waterway. **Reproduction and Demography** Seasonal. Mating February–April (early May in captivity); births April–June. Gestation 35–48 days, without delayed implantation (71–76 days reported from fur farms). Litter size 1–8, averaging 4–5. Weaning at 7–9 weeks, at which juveniles can capture small prey. MORTALITY Most recorded mortality is anthropogenic, mainly through trapping. LIFESPAN 10 years in captivity. **Status and Threats** Formerly distributed throughout Europe (including European Russia) west of the Ural Mountains. Overhunting for fur and habitat destruction (water pollution, damming and draining) have extirpated the species from >95% of its historic range and 18 range countries. The current distribution is now restricted to isolated fragments in Estonia (extinct on the mainland, reintroduced on Hiiumaa Island), France (possibly extinct), Romania, Russia, Spain and Ukraine. The largest numbers are in Russia (<15,000 in discontinuous populations), followed by ~1,000–1,500 in the Danube delta, Romania. All populations are threatened by ongoing habitat degradation, illegal and accidental trapping, persecution and roadkills. Introduction of the larger, competitively aggressive American Mink is thought to be an additional factor. Red List CR, population trend Decreasing.

 Western Polecat ■ European Mink

**Plate 85**

Scent-marking

**WESTERN POLECAT**

Domestic
Ferret

**EUROPEAN
MINK**

Hunting
Water Vole

# LEAST WEASEL *Mustela nivalis*

**COMMON WEASEL**

Includes **EGYPTIAN WEASEL** *M. subpalmata*, **SICHUAN WEASEL** *M. russelliana* and **TONKIN WEASEL** *M. tonkinensis*
HB 11.4–26cm; T 7–9cm; W 0.025–0.3kg

The world's smallest carnivore, tiny with a short tail without a black tip. Except in southern populations, brown fur moults to pure white in winter; transitional winter forms occur in temperate areas. Sometimes Egyptian Weasel is classified separately in Egypt, but genetic analysis indicates no species-level differences. Classification of Sichuan Weasel (known from 8 specimens from C China) and Tonkin Weasel (1 specimen from N Vietnam) is based on extremely limited data; both are treated here as Least Weasel. **Distribution and Habitat** Global, from approximately 35–40°N to the Arctic, encompassing Canada, Alaska, NE USA, Eurasia and N Africa. Introduced in New Zealand, Malta, Crete, the Azores and São Tomé. Occurs in virtually all habitats with cover and rodents, from sea-level to 4,000m. Inhabits agricultural and urban areas. **Feeding Ecology** Small rodent specialist, hunting mainly mice, rats, Meadow Vole, Field Vole, water voles, lemmings and cotton rats. Larger mammals, including lagomorphs, moles and squirrels, are also killed, especially by males. Other food includes birds, fledglings, eggs, herptiles, fish and invertebrates (mainly beetles and earthworms). Takes poultry in rare cases. Foraging is solitary and cathemeral; constantly active to maintain a very fast metabolism, making 5–10 kills/24 hours. Hunting is mostly terrestrial; its tiny tubular body enables hunting in burrows and rodent snow tunnels. Occasionally scavenges carrion during winter. Caches surplus kills in burrows. **Social and Spatial Behaviour** Solitary with aggressive territorial defence. Breeding males often abandon territories in search of females. Ranges 0.002–0.7km² (♀s) and 0.006–0.26km² (♂s). Densities fluctuate widely depending on rodent population cycles, e.g. 2.4–13/km² (Finland). **Reproduction and Demography** Aseasonal, peaking in spring to late summer. Gestation 34–37 days, without delayed implantation. Litter size 1–19, averaging 4–10. Weaning at 4–7 weeks; juveniles can kill at 6–7 weeks. Sexual maturity (both sexes) 3–4 months. **MORTALITY** Populations turn over very rapidly, with annual adult mortality of 75–97%, mainly from food shortages and predation. **LIFESPAN** Rarely >2 years in the wild, 10 in captivity. **Status and Threats** Widely distributed, with a broad habitat tolerance. Apparently naturally rare in North America and has declined locally, e.g. UK. Vulnerable to rodenticides, and persecuted intensely in some areas as a predator of game birds. Red List LC, population trend Stable.

# STOAT *Mustela erminea*

**ERMINE, SHORT-TAILED WEASEL**
HB 17–34cm; T 4.2–12cm; W 0.06–0.37kg

Small weasel, rusty-brown to chocolate brown in summer moulting to white in winter, except in southern populations. Tail has a black tip. In North America (called the Short-tailed Weasel), it is smaller with a proportionally shorter tail than sympatric Long-tailed Weasel (page 186). **Distribution and Habitat** Global, from approximately 35°N to the Arctic, throughout Eurasia, North America and Greenland. Introduced in New Zealand. Inhabits a very wide range of habitats, from Arctic tundra to semi-desert, from sea-level to 3,000m. Inhabits farmland. **Feeding Ecology** Very similar diet to Least Weasel's, but kills more larger prey, especially rabbits and squirrels. Where lagomorphs are absent, small rodents are the mainstay. Prodigious nest predator of eggs and fledglings, and also eats adult birds, herptiles, invertebrates and fruits. Takes domestic poultry. Foraging is mostly nocturnal and terrestrial, but driven by high energetic requirements that necessitate flexible foraging. Caches surplus prey. Occasionally scavenges from carrion and human refuse. **Social and Spatial Behaviour** Solitary and territorial. Male ranges overlap multiple female ranges, and adults repel same-sex intruders. Males abandon territories during breeding in search of females. Range size 0.02–1.35km² (♀s) and 0.08–3.13km² (♂s). Density estimates 3–10/km², exceptionally reaching 22/km² during rodent irruptions. **Reproduction and Demography** Seasonal. Mating June–August; births April–May (following year). Gestation 223–378 days, with delayed implantation (embryonic development 28–30 days). Litter size 4–18, averaging 6–8. Weaning 4–12 weeks. Females sexually mature at 4–6 weeks, and may be pregnant before they are weaned. **MORTALITY** Annual mortality 40–54% (3–6-month-old subadults) to 78–83% (2.25–2.5-year-old adults), mainly from prey shortages and predation. **LIFESPAN** Rarely >3 years in the wild, 10 in captivity. **Status and Threats** Widely distributed and relatively common to abundant. Legally trapped in much of its range, and persecuted as a predator of game birds and poultry, but resilient to harvest. CITES Appendix III – India; Red List LC, population trend Stable.

# ALTAI WEASEL *Mustela altaica*

**ALTAI MOUNTAIN WEASEL, ALPINE WEASEL**
HB 21.7–28.7cm; T 9–14.5cm; W ♀ 0.12–0.22kg, ♂ 0.22–0.35kg

Pale buff-brown upperparts, darkening slightly in summer, with pale cream to creamy-yellow underparts. Feet conspicuously creamy white, and no black tip to tail. **Distribution and Habitat** C and N Asia, in the Himalayan, Pamir, Altai and Tien Shan mountains, S Russia, N Mongolia, and C and E China; uncertain but likely in North Korea. Inhabits alpine meadows, grassland, steppes and rocky areas at 1,500–5,200m. Occurs in remote human habitations in sheds, barns and cellars, but avoids degraded agricultural landscapes. **Feeding Ecology** Poorly known. Small rodents and lagomorphs, especially pikas, zokors, hamsters, sousliks and voles, are probably the main prey. Also eats birds (including ptarmigans), eggs, herptiles, invertebrates and fruits. Forages diurnally, at least where potential predators such as Red Foxes (page 114) and Stone Martens (page 168) are mainly nocturnal. Caches surplus kills. **Social and Spatial Behaviour** Poorly known. Assumed to be solitary and territorial. **Reproduction and Demography** Poorly known; likely seasonal. Mating February–March (Kazakhstan). Gestation 35–40 days, apparently without delayed implantation. Litter size 2–8, exceptionally to 13. **MORTALITY** Poorly known. Populations appear to undergo large fluctuations. **LIFESPAN** Unknown. **Status and Threats** Declining across much of its range due to habitat degradation from overgrazing by livestock, and agricultural poisoning of prey. Used for folkloric charms in Nepal, where mummified carcasses are believed to prevent infant deaths. CITES Appendix III – India; Red List NT, population trend Decreasing.

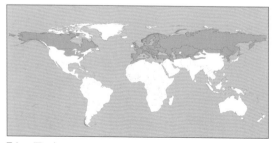

■ Least Weasel

■ Stoat ■ Altai Weasel

**Plate 86**

Summer

**LEAST WEASEL**

Winter

Summer

Winter

**STOAT**

**ALTAI WEASEL**

# COLOMBIAN WEASEL *Mustela felipei*

### FELIPE'S WEASEL

HB 21.7–22.5cm; T 11.1–12.2cm; W *c.*0.12–0.15kg

South America's smallest weasel. Very small; uniformly very dark brown, including the tail, with pale buff-orange underparts and sometimes a small dark patch on the chest. Easily confused with Long-tailed Weasel, but lacks its black-tipped tail. Natural history and ecology are almost entirely unknown. **Distribution and Habitat** Restricted to the Andes of Colombia and N Ecuador, where it is known from only 6 physical records and 5 sightings. All records are from high Andean forest at 1,525–2,700m, usually in riparian areas and river valleys (although this is probably a sampling artefact). **Feeding Ecology** Unknown. Assumed to be a rodent specialist, like other weasels. **Social and Spatial Behaviour** Unknown. All records are of single animals. **Reproduction and Demography** Unknown. **Status and Threats** Occurs in a very restricted distribution and is naturally rare, based on the relative rates it appears in surveys and museum records, e.g. compared to Long-tailed Weasel. Known only from mid- to high-elevation forest habitat, which is under intense pressure in the Andes for forestry and conversion to agriculture or pasture. Local people kill weasels for depredation on poultry and domestic guinea pigs, though it is unclear whether Colombian Weasels are involved. Red List VU, population trend Decreasing.

# LONG-TAILED WEASEL *Mustela frenata*

HB ♀ 20.3–22.8cm, ♂ 22.8–26cm; T 7.6–15.2cm;
W ♀ 0.8–0.25kg, ♂ 0.16–0.45kg

Long-bodied weasel with a proportionally long tail measuring half to two-thirds the body length. Summer coat is rich, rusty brown to chocolate brown, with creamy-white to rich yellow underparts. Northern populations moult to pure white in winter; tail always has a black tip, regardless of region and season. Southern populations do not moult to white. The species has distinctive white or yellow facial markings in Central America, Mexico and S USA. **Distribution and Habitat** S Canada, the USA, Mexico, Central America, Venezuela, Colombia, Ecuador, Peru, extreme NW Brazil and N Bolivia. Occurs in virtually all habitats, from arctic–alpine to tropical, and absent only from true desert interiors. Most abundant in open woodland, brushland, riparian grassland, meadows and marshes. Occupies modified habitats, including logged areas, fence rows, fields, cropland and pastures. **Feeding Ecology** Opportunistic generalist with a wide diet, but rodents, lagomorphs and insectivores are the mainstay. Common prey includes voles, deer mice, cotton rats, wood rats, chipmunks, shrews, moles, pikas, cottontails, Volcano Rabbit (Mexico) and Snowshoe Hare (mainly juveniles). Also takes birds, reptiles (including kingsnakes and Bullsnake), insects and eggs; an important nest predator in some areas. Occasionally preys on small carnivores, mainly other small weasels. Takes domestic poultry, and there is a credible record of predation on 3-day-old piglets. Foraging is mainly nocturno-crepuscular but flexible; diurnalism increases during winter. Does not hibernate. Hunts mainly by sight and smell, ceaselessly investigating burrows, crevices, nests and log hollows for quarry. Prey is subdued by a distinctive hold, in which it tightly entwines the victim with its body and administers a killing bite to the nape (small prey) or a suffocating bite to the throat. Adult weasels make 3–4 kills a day; a Colorado population estimated at 8,000 weasels killed an estimated 11 million prey items (mostly rodents) annually. Caches surplus prey, and scavenges from carrion and human refuse. **Social and Spatial Behaviour** Solitary, with enduring ranges that overlap, but with exclusive core areas. Adults mostly avoid each other except during the breeding season, when males seek out females and aggressively repel other males. Mixed-sex pairs occasionally associate temporarily outside the breeding season, e.g. sharing burrows. Male ranges encompass 1 or more female ranges, and males attempt to increase their range size during breeding to encounter more females. Average range size 0.52km² (♀s) and 1.8km² (♂s; fragmented agricultural habitat, Indiana) to 0.1–0.24km² (both sexes) in better-quality habitat. Density estimates 0.4–0.8/km² (agricultural habitat) to 19–38/km² (high-quality oak forest and marshland). **Reproduction and Demography** Seasonal. Mating July–August (North America); births April–May (following year). Gestation 205–337 days, with delayed implantation (embryonic development 21–28 days). Litter size 4–9, averaging 6. Kittens weaned at around 35–36 days and independent at 3 months. Females sexually mature at 9–12 weeks; males typically breed in their second year. MORTALITY Rates poorly known, but weasel populations turn over rapidly, with high mortality balanced by high reproduction. Natural mortality is mainly from predation, especially by raptors, foxes and Coyote (page 102). LIFESPAN Rarely more than 3 years in the wild. **Status and Threats** The most widespread mustelid in the western hemisphere, and it has the greatest habitat tolerance of American weasels. Populations fluctuate significantly and rapidly, depending on prey availability; abundance declines under agricultural intensification, prompting local extinctions when combined with low prey numbers. Legally trapped in its North American range, but no longer sought after for commercial trade. Red List LC, population trend Stable.

# AMAZON WEASEL *Mustela africana*

### TROPICAL WEASEL

HB 24–38cm; T 16–21cm; W *c.*0.1–0.3kg

Small weasel, uniformly red-brown to dark brown, including the tail. Underparts are pale buff to cream, bisected with a dark brown stripe running from the lower belly to the chest or throat; stripe is discontinuous in 2–3 segments in some individuals. Natural history and ecology are very poorly known. **Distribution and Habitat** Restricted to the Amazon Basin of N Bolivia, Brazil, E Ecuador and E Peru; possibly more widely distributed, e.g. S Colombia to S French Guiana, but no records. All records come from Amazonian lowland forest. **Feeding Ecology** Unknown. Assumed to be a rodent specialist, like other weasels. Foraging is possibly diurnal; 1 sighting was at 10:00. **Social and Spatial Behaviour** Unknown. Most records are of single animals, with 1 sighting of 4 animals, probably a mother–offspring group. **Reproduction and Demography** Unknown. **Status and Threats** Status largely unknown. Occurs over a wide range where much

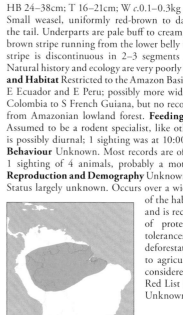

of the habitat is well preserved, and is recorded from a number of protected areas. Habitat tolerances are unknown, but deforestation and conversion to agriculture and pasture are considered the primary threats. Red List LC, population trend Unknown.

■ Colombian Weasel ■ Long-tailed Weasel ■ Amazon Weasel

**Plate 87**

COLOMBIAN
WEASEL

LONG-TAILED
WEASEL

Winter

Summer

AMAZON
WEASEL

# YELLOW-BELLIED WEASEL
## *Mustela kathiah*

HB 20–29cm; T 12.5–18cm; W *c*.0.15–0.3kg
Very small weasel, russet-brown to dark maroon-brown, with rich buff-orange or yellowish underparts and a conspicuously white lower face. Feet sometimes have white flecking or small patches. Natural history and ecology are very poorly known. **Distribution and Habitat** SE China (about 80% of its range), N and E Indochina, N Myanmar, and the Himalayas from Bhutan to Kashmir. Inhabits mainly temperate and evergreen forest from sea-level to 4,000m. Occurs in highly degraded forest patches and scrub mosaics, e.g. in Hong Kong and N Laos. **Feeding Ecology** Unknown. Assumed to prey mainly on rodents, other small vertebrates and invertebrates, similar to other weasels. Reported to raid poultry coops on Hainan Island, China. **Social and Spatial Behaviour** Unknown. All records are of single animals. **Reproduction and Demography** Unknown. **Status and Threats** Status poorly known, but the species occurs in highly degraded habitat and in areas that are under intense hunting pressure, e.g. near Phongsaly town, Laos, suggesting that it is tolerant of habitat loss and resilient to anthropogenic pressure. CITES Appendix III – India; Red List LC, population trend Stable.

# STRIPE-BACKED WEASEL
## *Mustela strigidorsa*

**Back-striped Weasel**
HB 25–32.5cm; T 13–20.5cm; W 0.7–2kg
Small weasel, dark mahogany-brown to rich russet-brown, with a fine silvery-white or creamy dorsal stripe from the crown to the base of the tail. Cheeks and throat are creamy white to rich yellow-cream, narrowing to a thin yellow line running along the belly to the groin. Natural history and ecology are very poorly known. **Distribution and Habitat** NE India, N and C Myanmar, S China, N Thailand, N and C Laos, and Vietnam. Most records are from evergreen hill and montane forests to 2,500m, and associated secondary forest, bamboo stands, scrub and grassland. **Feeding Ecology** Poorly known. One was observed attacking a bandicoot rat estimated at 3 times its size, and another was seen carrying a suspected White-bellied Rat. Local people report that it takes domestic poultry; 2 animals for sale in a Laotian wildlife market were killed apparently while raiding a chicken coop, and the only individual captured for science (NE Thailand) was baited with a live chicken. **Social and Spatial Behaviour** Unknown. All records are of single animals. Very rarely appears in wildlife surveys, including by camera-trapping, suggesting it is naturally rare, but this remains to be confirmed. **Reproduction and Demography** Unknown. **Status and Threats** Status very poorly known. Does not have especially high economic value and appears in wildlife markets moderately frequently, mainly in China, where 3,000–4,000 animals were harvested for fur

annually in the 1970s. Sometimes killed as a perceived poultry pest. Red List LC, population trend Stable.

# MALAY WEASEL *Mustela nudipes*

HB 30–36cm; T 24–26cm; W *c*.1kg
Unmistakable weasel, bright orange to reddish brown, usually with a paler orange neck and a creamy-white to pale orange head. Distal half of the tail is pale orange to white. Natural history and ecology are very poorly known. Recorded moving in a very distinctive zigzag pattern with the brightly coloured tail held high like a flag; whether this is typical or associated with fleeing the observer is unknown. **Distribution and Habitat** Sumatra, Borneo, Peninsular Malaysia and S Thailand; reports from Java are erroneous. Recorded from lowland and hill tropical forests, heath forest, swamp forest, montane forest and montane scrub from sea-level to 1,700m. Sometimes occurs in degraded habitat, including exotic plantations and peri-urban areas. **Feeding Ecology** Unknown. Diet assumed to be similar to that of other small *Mustela* weasels, i.e. small rodents, birds, eggs and herptiles. **Social and Spatial Behaviour** Unknown. Most records are of single animals, with 1 sighting of 2 animals; always on the ground or on ground-level objects such as rocks and logs. **Reproduction and Demography** Unknown. **Status and Threats** Status very poorly known. Apparently widespread within its range, but rarely recorded and difficult to see. Has been recorded in degraded habitats, including urban areas, suggesting some tolerance for anthropogenic pressures; its presence in higher-altitude forest buffers it to some extent from the extreme pressures on lowland forest in the Sundaic region. Red List LC, population trend Decreasing.

# INDONESIAN MOUNTAIN WEASEL
## *Mustela lutreolina*

HB 29.7–32.1cm; T 13.6–17cm; W 0.3–0.34kg
Small, dark weasel. Uniformly dark brown with slightly paler underparts, sometimes with inconspicuous creamy-white patches on the chin, throat, upper chest and groin. It is the only dark weasel species on Sumatra and Java. One of the least-known carnivore species; known only from 15 museum records and <5 modern sightings and camera-trap images. **Distribution and Habitat** Java and S Sumatra (uncertain elsewhere in Sumatra), where it is restricted to highlands at 1,400–3,000m. All records are from hill and montane forests, with a single sighting taking place in alpine scrub above the treeline at 3,000m (Mt Kerinci, Sumatra). **Feeding Ecology** Unknown. Diet assumed to be similar to that of other small *Mustela* weasels, i.e. small rodents, birds, eggs and herptiles. **Social and Spatial Behaviour** Unknown. All records are of single animals, except for the single confirmed wild sighting, which was of 4 animals moving in a 'train' fashion, almost certainly a female and 3 large juveniles. Extremely rare in wildlife surveys, including by camera-trapping, suggesting it is naturally scarce, although this remains to be confirmed. **Reproduction and Demography** Unknown. **Status and Threats** Status very poorly known. Its montane forest habitat is under significant pressure from illegal forestry and conversion, e.g. to coffee plantations, especially in Java. However, the species' habitat tolerances and its dependence on undisturbed forest are unclear. Not especially valued for trade, and hunting is less intense in montane habitat than in comparable lowland areas. Red List LC, population trend Stable.

■ Yellow-bellied Weasel

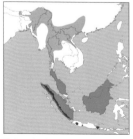
■ Stripe-backed Weasel
■ Malay Weasel
■ Indonesian Mountain Weasel

**Plate 88**

STRIPE-BACKED
WEASEL

YELLOW-BELLIED
WEASEL

MALAY WEASEL

INDONESIAN MOUNTAIN
WEASEL

# MARINE OTTER *Lontra felina*

### CHUNGUNGO

HB 53–79cm; T 30–36.2cm; W 3.2–5.8kg

Smallest South American otter, uniformly glossy, dark brown with a slightly paler muzzle, cheeks and underparts. Broad head has a short muzzle with heavy, long whiskers (for which it is sometimes called the 'sea cat'), and the tail is relatively short. **Distribution and Habitat** Restricted to the Pacific coast of South America, patchily distributed from C Peru to Tierra del Fuego and Isla de los Estados, Argentina. Found along rugged rocky coasts rarely more than 100m offshore and 50m inland; occasionally travels up coastal freshwater inlets. Occurs in wharves and groynes near urban areas. **Feeding Ecology** Feeds primarily on marine crustaceans, fish and molluscs. Also takes freshwater shrimp in coastal rivers. Large prey, e.g. Southern King Crab, is taken ashore to eat, while small prey is consumed at sea; floats on its back to eat, but does not use rock anvils as do Sea Otters (page 192). Occasionally hunts on land, primarily chicks of colonially nesting seabirds; actively excavates the burrows of Peruvian Diving Petrel to reach chicks. Foraging is cathemeral and mainly solitary; observed pairs and trios are mother–young groups. Adults congregate amicably at food patches such as fishery dumps. Sometimes scavenges from human fishing waste on shore. **Social and Spatial Behaviour** Solitary, with facultative territorial behaviour. Often found close together with entirely overlapping ranges, but resident otters do not move, forage or rest together. Adults, especially females, become more territorial and occupy exclusive core areas where food occurs in patches. Range size similar for the sexes, linearly 1.3–4.1km and <110m wide. **Reproduction and Demography** Poorly known. Pups recorded year-round, peaking September–November (C Chile), although seasonality may be more pronounced further south. Gestation 60–65 days. Litter size 1–4, averaging 2. MORTALITY Poorly known. Most documented deaths are anthropogenic; Killer Whale, sharks and large raptors (on pups) are putative predators. LIFESPAN Unknown. **Status and Threats** Reduced to an estimated 1,000–2,000 adults in a series of discontinuous populations. Declining due to human overfishing of prey, combined with illegal killing by fishermen as competitors and for fur. Also killed by entanglement in nets and by domestic dogs around docks and urban beaches. Almost extinct in Argentina. CITES Appendix I; Red List EN, population trend Decreasing.

# SOUTHERN RIVER OTTER
## *Lontra provocax*

### PATAGONIAN RIVER OTTER, HUILLIN

HB 57–80cm; T 35–43cm; W 8–14.5kg

Medium-sized otter. Mid-brown to dark brown, with a pale greyish muzzle, throat and upper chest, becoming beige on the underparts. **Distribution and Habitat** Patagonian Argentina and Chile. Occurs in freshwater lakes, rivers and wetland with dense bank vegetation, as well as marine rocky coasts, estuaries

and marshes. Avoids disturbed waterways such as canals. **Feeding Ecology** Crustacean specialist, eating mainly large freshwater crabs and crayfish; small, slow-moving fish are the second-most important food category. Also eats molluscs and, less so, amphibians and birds. Foraging is solitary and cathemeral. **Social and Spatial Behaviour** Solitary. Ranges are stable, with low overlap among males and greater overlap among females. Range size differs little between sexes, linearly 7.4–22.3km with very small core areas, usually <1.5km, centred within patches of thick vegetation for denning. Density averages 0.73/km of marine coast (S Chile). **Reproduction and Demography** Thought to be seasonal, depending on location. Pups observed year-round in southern range, but mating occurs December–March, with births thought to occur in July in C Chile. Gestation unknown; assumed to include delayed implantation. Litter size 1–4, averaging 2. MORTALITY and LIFESPAN Unknown. **Status and Threats** Now known only from 7 discontinuous populations that occupy a fraction of its former range. Serious threats include widespread habitat degradation by water pollution, wetland draining, dredging, canalisation and clearing of bank vegetation, as well as illegal hunting for fur, which is intense in some areas. CITES Appendix I; Red List EN, population trend Decreasing.

# NEOTROPICAL OTTER
## *Lontra longicaudis*

### NEOTROPICAL RIVER OTTER

HB 46–66; T 37–84cm; W 5–12kg (exceptionally to 15kg)

Very similar to Southern River Otter, but generally larger and more heavily built, and with paler fur around the cheeks and muzzle. The 2 species are separated by range. Leucism is recorded (Mexico). **Distribution and Habitat** N Mexico to Uruguay and N Argentina. Occurs mostly in clear, flowing streams, rivers and lakes in a variety of forest, woodland and scrub habitats, from sea-level usually to 1,500m, exceptionally above 3,000m. In coastal areas, occurs near fresh water such as river outlets and rain-fed lagoons. Avoids silted and sluggish waterbodies. Occurs in suitable habitat near human settlements. **Feeding Ecology** Eats mainly fish, especially catfish, characins and cichlids, as well as crustaceans, and large aquatic insects and their larvae. Molluscs, amphibians, reptiles, birds and mammals (including rats and Nutria) are opportunistically taken. Fruit is recorded in the diet, and is possibly consumed while eating frugivorous fish. Small prey is eaten in the water, while large prey is carried to shore or tree snags to consume. Foraging is solitary and mainly diurno-crepuscular; becomes nocturnal in areas of human disturbance. Scavenging is suggested by the presence of Capybara fur in scats. **Social and Spatial Behaviour** Poorly known. Solitary. Adults very actively scent-mark ('sprint') prominent features such as logs, root systems, sandbars and rocks, but ranging and territorial patterns are poorly studied. Density estimates 0.8–2.8/km of shore. **Reproduction and Demography** Semi-seasonal. Mating mainly February–May, but year-round in some areas. Gestation 56–86 days; it is unclear if a short period of delayed implantation accounts for the wide variation. Litter size 1–5, averaging 2–3. Pups start swimming at around 2.5 months. MORTALITY Predation known by anacondas, caimans, piranhas and Jaguar (page 50). LIFESPAN Unknown. **Status and Threats** Species has a wide range, but its status is poorly known. Heavily hunted for fur before 1970, leading to localised extinctions in much of its range. Continued illegal hunting remains a concern, but main threats today are habitat conversion to agriculture and ranching, combined with wetland drainage, damming and water pollution. Sometimes killed intentionally or accidentally by fishermen. CITES Appendix I; Red List NT, population trend Decreasing.

■ Marine Otter

■ Southern River Otter
■ Neotropical Otter

**Plate 89**

MARINE
OTTER

SOUTHERN RIVER
OTTER

NEOTROPICAL
OTTER

# NORTH AMERICAN OTTER
## *Lontra canadensis*

**RIVER OTTER, NEARCTIC OTTER, CANADIAN OTTER**
HB 58–73cm; T 31.7–47cm; W 3.4–15.5kg

The only otter in North America except for Sea Otter (coastal W USA and Canada). Uniform pale brown to dark brown, with a pale cream to greyish muzzle, throat and chest. **Distribution and Habitat** Canada (excluding E Ellesmere and Prince Edward islands) and USA, including most of Alaska. Occurs in all types of non-polluted fresh and coastal waterbodies with well-vegetated or rocky shorelines, including streams, rivers, ponds, lakes, estuaries, marshes, beaches and reservoirs. **Feeding Ecology** Eats mainly slow-moving, schooling and bottom-dwelling fish, especially carp, minnow, catfish, bowfin and suckers. Crustaceans, especially crayfish, are the second-most important component of the diet. Fast-swimming fish such as salmon are taken infrequently except during spawning runs. Opportunistically eats frogs, reptiles, waterbirds and mammals, mainly Muskrats, Nutria (introduced) and, rarely, North American Beavers (probably juveniles). Occasionally catches small terrestrial mammals in deep snow, including Snowshoe Hares. Foraging is mainly nocturno-crepuscular, with increased diurnalism where it is undisturbed and during winter; active through winter and forages under ice. Hunts alone or in social groups. Can swim to 11km/h and remain underwater for up to 4 minutes. Hunting success poorly known; solitary adult females catch prey in 38% (lake) to 62% (small inlet) of dives. Occasionally scavenges from carrion. **Social and Spatial Behaviour** Sociality complex and fluid. Adults are generally solitary, with the primary social unit comprising a mother and cubs, but sociality increases with food availability. Mother–cub families may include helpers, either yearlings from previous litters or unrelated young adults. Large clans of up to 18 (mainly males) form in coastal Alaska, probably linked to cooperative hunting of large pelagic fish; females sometimes join clans, but never while raising cubs. Members of social groups are gregarious and play together, e.g. 'snow-sliding'. Ranges vary from being largely exclusive to overlapping extensively. Average range sizes include 9.6km$^2$ (♀s) to 30.4km$^2$ (♂s; SE Minnesota) and 70km$^2$ (♀s) to 231km$^2$ (♂s; Alberta). **Reproduction and Demography** Seasonal. Mating December–April; births January–May (following year). Gestation 10–12 months, with delayed implantation (actual gestation 61–63 days). Litter size 1–6. Weaning at 12 weeks. Cubs can swim at 60 days. Sexual maturity at 12–18 months; first breeding rarely before 2–3 years. MORTALITY Most mortality is anthropogenic. The most important natural factor is starvation, mainly in the far north of the range. Adults are occasionally killed by predators ranging from Bald Eagle to Killer Whale. LIFESPAN 13 years in the wild, 25 in captivity. **Status and Threats** Extirpated from around 75% of its original range by the 1970s due to massive unregulated trapping and degradation of aquatic habitats. Rehabilitation of waterways and reintroduction programmes have restored it to much of its range; it is possibly extinct or very rare in about a third of its historic US distribution, and is extinct in Mexico. Remains susceptible to pollutants and habitat loss. Legally trapped for fur where populations are considered secure, in 29 US states and 11 Canadian provinces. CITES Appendix II; Red List LC, population trend Stable.

# SEA OTTER *Enhydra lutris*

HB 100–120cm; T 25–37cm; W ♀ 14.5–32.7kg, ♂ 21.8–45kg

Largest mustelid by weight. Rufous-brown to dark brown, typically with a cream or greyish head, the colour extending variably on the throat and chest. Young pups have light brown woolly fur. It is the only completely marine otter species; can live its entire life at sea. **Distribution and Habitat** Endemic to the N Pacific, in coastal NE Russia (Kamchatka Peninsula and associated islands), N Japan, British Columbia, Alaska, Washington and California. Inhabits coastal marine environments, typically within 1km of shore. **Feeding Ecology** Diet overwhelmingly dominated by marine invertebrates such as sea urchins, clams, abalones, mussels and crabs. Squid and octopus are eaten especially during episodic abundances, e.g. California. Fish comprise only occasional prey, but are important to Aleutian Islands populations. Dives up to 100m (usually 25–40m) for an average of 60–120 seconds (up to 260 seconds), and finds prey mostly by sight with its strong underwater vision or by touch. Carries prey to the surface in a fold of skin in its armpit, and breaks open hard-shelled items by smashing them against a rock held on its belly (the rock is also transported in the armpit fold). Between 63% (subadults) and 82% (adults) of foraging dives are successful. Eats 20–33% of its body weight each day to compensate for heat loss to its cold environment. Able to drink sea water. **Social and Spatial Behaviour** Basically solitary, but with wide regional and temporal variation. Adults mostly occupy enduring ranges, and either space themselves out or overlap extensively depending on food availability. High-quality food patches such as squid flushes promote overlap, and otters sometimes aggregate in large 'rafts' of up to 2,000 individuals to feed. During breeding and where females occupy small stable ranges, males establish exclusive territories and exclude other males. Rafts of non-breeding males form in some areas. Average range size 0.8–6.8km$^2$ (♀s) and 0.4–4.8km$^2$ (♂s) in California, and linear 38km (♀s) to 50km (♂s) in Washington. **Reproduction and Demography** Weakly seasonal; breeding occurs year-round, but births peak May–June (Washington and Alaska), and weakly January–March (California). Gestation 4–12 months (averaging 180–218 days), with delayed implantation. Litter size 1, exceptionally 2. Pups are born at sea, and carried and suckled by the mother at rest; they can swim at 2 months. Weaning and independence coincide at 5–9 months. MORTALITY For pups, mortality varies from 17% (Kodiak Island, Alaska) to 53% (Amchitka Island, Alaska, with limited food). Adults generally have low mortality, e.g. 4–11% (Kodiak Island), mainly from starvation and predation. LIFESPAN 15 (♂s) to 20 (♀s) in the wild, 30 in captivity. **Status and Threats** Previously very heavily exploited for its luxuriant fur, which reduced a total estimated population of 300,000 to <2,000 by 1911. Strict protection and reintroductions have restored it to an estimated 125,000, although local declines continue to occur. The main threats are oil spills and other contaminants. Elevated Killer Whale predation in response to seal declines is implicated (though not proven) in declines in the Alaskan Aleutian Islands. Also killed by entanglement in fishing nets and by disease, including exotic disease introduced to waterways by humans. CITES Appendix I California, Appendix II – elsewhere; Red List EN, population trend Decreasing.

■ North American Otter       ■ Sea Otter

**Plate 90**

Snow-sliding

**NORTH AMERICAN
OTTER**

Group at sea

Nursing
young

**SEA OTTER**

# GIANT OTTER *Pteronura brasiliensis*

HB 86.4–130cm; T 45–75cm; W ♀ 22–26kg, ♂ 26–34kg

The largest Latin American mustelid and the world's second largest (by weight, after Sea Otter; page 192). Strongly built, with a very robust, powerful skull and a long, muscular paddle-like tail. Uniformly dark chocolate brown with creamy-white markings on the chin and throat that vary from light stippling to a solid patch that extends onto the chest; markings are unique to individuals. **Distribution and Habitat** Endemic to South America, from Venezuela to E Paraguay and S Brazil; likely extinct in Argentina and Uruguay. Requires clear, slow-moving waterways or lakes in intact forest, woodland and wetland. Occasionally occupies agricultural canals and artificial reservoirs, but does not tolerate waterways in open and highly disturbed habitats. **Feeding Ecology** Primarily piscivorous; adults eat around 3kg of fish a day, mainly characins, catfish, perch and cichlids. Most fish captured measure 0.1–0.4m, but Giant Otter is capable of taking catfish measuring more than 1m. Other prey types infrequently recorded include reptiles (including anacondas to 3m, caimans to 1.5m and large turtles), small mammals, birds, crustaceans and molluscs. Hunts in family groups, but with little evidence of cooperation except in subduing large prey; group members provision cubs and large prey is sometimes shared, otherwise individuals mostly eat their own catches. Exclusively diurnal. Small prey is eaten in the water and large prey is taken to the bank or fallen trees to consume. Adults catch up to 3.2 fish/hour. **Social and Spatial Behaviour** Social and territorial. Lives in highly cohesive family groups comprising a monogamous adult pair and its offspring from 1 or more generations. Groups usually number 4–8; largest recorded groups, numbering to 20, are probably temporary associations of 2 or more families. Groups defend their territories from neighbours, largely by scent-marking and mutual avoidance, but clashes are aggressive and occasionally fatal. Group territories are linearly shaped and spaced along riverbanks or lake edges. Group territory size (linearly) 5.2–32km, averaging 9.3–11.4km. **Reproduction and Demography** Weakly seasonal. Only the alpha pair breeds in the group. Litters are born in dens in low, sloping banks with dense cover. Births occur mainly in the dry season in areas with marked seasonality, e.g. August–October (Suriname) and April–September (Brazilian Pantanal). Gestation 52–70 days. Litter size 1–5, averaging 2–3. Cubs can swim at 6 weeks and accompany the group as it forages from 3–4 months; weaning at 8–9 months. Dispersal first occurs at 10 months, but usually at 2–3 years; males thought to disperse more often than females. MORTALITY Poorly known. Adults are sometimes killed in intraspecific fights. Black and Spectacled caimans are occasional predators, largely on cubs. LIFESPAN 12.8 years (minimum estimate) in captivity. **Status and Threats** Formerly heavily hunted for fur, leading to extirpation or declines across much of its range. Hunting is rare today, but its narrow ecological needs and slow reproductive rates make it vulnerable to habitat modification, pollution of waterways by mining contaminants (e.g. mercury), agricultural run-off and overfishing. Persecuted by fishermen as perceived competitors for fish, and caught accidentally in fishing nets. Critically endangered in Ecuador and Paraguay. CITES Appendix I; Red List EN, population trend Decreasing.

# EURASIAN OTTER *Lutra lutra*

EUROPEAN OTTER, COMMON OTTER
Includes JAPANESE OTTER *L. nippon*
HB ♀ 59–70cm, ♂ 60–90cm; T 35–47cm;
W ♀ 6–12kg, ♂ 6–17kg

Medium-sized otter, uniformly dull mid-brown to dark brown with pale cream to white underparts. Population in Japan has been considered a separate species, Japanese Otter (*L. nippon*), but the evidence is equivocal. **Distribution and Habitat** Eurasia, from W and N Europe to the Russian Far East and S China; scattered populations across C and Southeast Asia, with isolated populations in S India, Sri Lanka, Sumatra and N Africa. Confirmed in Japan (Tsushima Island) in 2017 after no records since 1979. Inhabits a wide variety of aquatic habitats, always with bank vegetation, rocks or debris, including rivers, streams, lakes, wetland, swamp forest, mangroves and coastal areas, from sea-level to 4,120m. Occupies rural and urban waterbodies only if they have sufficiently intact bank cover. **Feeding Ecology** Eats principally fish, freshwater amphibians and invertebrates, especially crabs, crayfish and aquatic insects. Occasional prey items consist of birds, including seabirds such as fulmars and guillemots in coastal populations, water voles, rats, rabbits (which are killed in their burrows) and reptiles. Plant matter sometimes appears in the diet, but is probably taken incidentally while consuming prey. Rarely takes carrion. Foraging is largely nocturno-crepuscular and solitary, except for mothers with attendant cubs. Adults eat approximately 1–1.5kg of fish a day, representing around 12% (♂s) to 28% (♀s with cubs) of their body weight a day. **Social and Spatial Behaviour** Solitary and territorial. Males maintain large territories encompassing numerous female territories. Females are essentially solitary, but 2–3 adult females (probably related) may share and jointly defend a group territory – although each female maintains an exclusive core area and rarely interacts with the others. Territories are small and mostly exclusive in high-density areas, with size and overlap increasing as density declines. Average territory size (linearly) 7–18.7km (♀s) and 15–38.8km (♂s); individual males are recorded using linear areas extending up to 84km. Density estimates 1/5km (riverbank) to 1/2–3km (lakeshore). **Reproduction and Demography** Aseasonal or seasonal, depending on seasonality of food availability. Mating in W and N Europe and Russia January–April; births peak April–May. Gestation 60–63 days. Litter size 1–4, exceptionally 5 (captivity). Cubs can swim at 2 months, are weaned at around 4 months and stay with their mother until 10–12 months. Sexual maturity at 18 (♂s) to 24 (♀s) months. MORTALITY Rates poorly known, but the most important factors are roadkills, starvation and intraspecific aggression. LIFESPAN 16 years in the wild (but rarely older than 4), 22 in captivity. **Status and Threats** Has undergone significant declines in much of its range, due to a combination of overfishing, habitat loss and hunting. Highly vulnerable to canalisation of rivers, clearing of riverine vegetation, dam construction, draining of wetlands and aquaculture, and pollution associated with development. Roadkill is the main mortality factor in most of Europe. Hunted intensively, mainly for traditional medicinal use, in Asia. CITES Appendix I; Red List NT, population trend Decreasing.

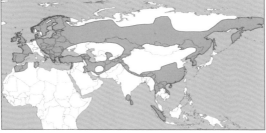
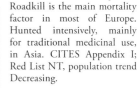

■ Giant Otter    ■ Eurasian Otter

**Plate 91**

Family group

**GIANT OTTER**

**EURASIAN OTTER**

# HAIRY-NOSED OTTER *Lutra sumatrana*

HB 57.5–82.6cm; T 35–51cm; W 5–8kg
Medium-sized otter, very dark brown with white or yellowish upper lips, chin and throat patch. Very distinctive bulbous muzzle and broad nose covered entirely with fur. The rarest and least known of Asian otters. **Distribution and Habitat** Endemic to extreme Southeast Asia, with discontinuous populations known from S Vietnam, S and E Cambodia, extreme S Thailand, S Malaysia, Borneo and Sumatra. Recorded mainly from peat swamps, flooded forest, wetland and mangroves, as well as rivers, lakes and mountain streams. **Feeding Ecology** Thought to eat mainly fish such as gouramis, climbing perch, walking catfish and snakeheads. Water snakes are frequent prey in Thailand. Also eats small numbers of crabs, insects, frogs, lizards, birds and small mammals. Camera-trap records show that it is cathemeral. Reportedly a very fast and agile swimmer that weaves in and out of mangrove roots and bank debris to capture fish. **Social and Spatial Behaviour** Virtually unknown. Usually reported as solitary, but reliable records exist of small groups numbering to 5, including an observation of 2 adults with a pup. **Reproduction and Demography** Poorly known. Limited records of pups cluster in November–February, and litters in the wild number 1–2 (based on very few observations). MORTALITY and LIFESPAN Unknown. **Status and Threats** Very rare, to the point where it was considered extinct until recent 'rediscoveries'. Now confirmed from a handful of sites, where it is seriously threatened by development and degradation of habitat, combined with widespread poaching for the illegal fur trade in China and, to a lesser degree, for meat and traditional medicine. CITES Appendix II; Red List EN, population trend Decreasing.

# ASIAN SMALL-CLAWED OTTER
## *Aonyx cinereus*

### ORIENTAL SMALL-CLAWED OTTER
HB 36–47cm; T 22.5–27.5cm; W 2.4–3.8kg
Smallest otter, uniformly dark brown, sometimes with an ashy-grey tinge. Greyish-white lower face, throat and upper chest. Claws are vestigial on all the feet. Most closely related to Smooth-coated Otter and African clawless otters (page 198); hybridisation with the former is known from Singapore. **Distribution and Habitat** S China through Indochina, Myanmar and Nepal to N India (with isolated populations in E and S India), the Philippines (Palawan), Borneo, Sumatra and Java. Inhabits freshwater bodies from sea-level to 2,000m, including rivers, mountain streams, lakes, peat swamps, mangroves and coastal wetland. Occupies anthropogenic habitats provided there is cover, e.g. rice paddies. **Feeding Ecology** Specialises in freshwater crabs, followed by small fish such as mudskippers, catfish and gouramis. Also eats snails, aquatic insects, shellfish, amphibians, snakes and small mammals. Captives leave shellfish in the sun until the heat opens them, but it is unknown if wild animals do likewise. Foraging is social and mainly diurno-crepuscular, but nocturnal when disturbed. Hunts by sight and by searching in mud and bank

debris with its very dextrous forepaws. **Social and Spatial Behaviour** Intensely social, living in extended family groups of 2–15, thought to comprise a breeding pair and its offspring of 1 or more generations. Group members inhabit a stable range and are always together, moving, foraging and resting as one. Range sizes and densities are unknown. **Reproduction and Demography** Monogamous, with breeding apparently restricted to the alpha pair, but reproduction is poorly known. Gestation 60–86 days. Litter size 2–7, averaging 4–5. Captive males help raise pups, and other group members are thought to act as helpers in the wild. MORTALITY Most documented deaths are anthropogenic. LIFESPAN 15 years in captivity. **Status and Threats** Threatened by habitat degradation, especially from damming, draining of wetlands and peat swamps, water pollution from agricultural run-off, and aquaculture. This is exacerbated by loss of prey from overfishing and pollution, combined with direct persecution; throughout the whole of Asia, all otters are killed for fur, meat and traditional medicine, and as perceived pests by fishermen and shrimp farmers. CITES Appendix II; Red List VU, population trend Decreasing.

# SMOOTH-COATED OTTER
## *Lutrogale perspicillata*

### INDIAN SMOOTH-COATED OTTER, SMOOTH OTTER
HB 59–75cm; T 37–43.2cm; W 7–11kg
Largest Asian otter. Glossy, short, very smooth fur, typically chestnut-brown to dark brown. A creamy-white or yellowish throat patch runs from the upper lips and chin to between the front legs. **Distribution and Habitat** S Asia, from SE Pakistan through India, Indochina, S China, Borneo, Sumatra and Java; isolated population in SW Iraq. Inhabits lowland and plains waterbodies, including rivers, lakes, wetland, peat swamps and mangroves. Found in rice paddies and artificial ponds. **Feeding Ecology** Eats mainly fish, often taking introduced pest species such as tilapia and European Carp. Also eats crustaceans (especially in mangroves and rice paddies), snails, insects, frogs, and occasionally birds and rodents such as Ricefield Rat. Foraging is cathemeral, with elevated diurnalism during winter. Forages in family groups, with some evidence of cooperative driving of fish into reeds, where they are caught. In parts of India and Bangladesh, it is tamed and used by fishermen to catch fish and herd them into nets. **Social and Spatial Behaviour** Highly social, living in groups of 2–11, thought to centre around a female and her offspring from multiple generations. Adult males are sometimes observed with groups, but it is unclear whether they are permanent members. Range size estimated at 7–12km of river to each family group. Density estimates (linearly) 1–1.3/km of shore. **Reproduction and Demography** Seasonal. Mating August–September; births October–February (India and Nepal); there is some evidence that it breeds year-round under high food availability. Gestation 60–63 days. Litter size 1–5. MORTALITY Poorly known, but groups mount a formidable defence against predators; a credible record exists of a family group fatally injuring an Indian fisherman who had captured a cub in his net. LIFESPAN 20 years in captivity. **Status and Threats** Fairly widely distributed, but estimated to have declined by >30% over the past 30 years. Vulnerable to the same threats as other Asian otters; being essentially a lowland species, it is particularly vulnerable to the intense development pressure on wetlands throughout S Asia. CITES Appendix II; Red List VU, population trend Decreasing.

■ Hairy-nosed Otter

■ Asian Small-clawed Otter

■ Smooth-coated Otter

**Plate 92**

HAIRY-NOSED
OTTER

Foraging in shallows

ASIAN
SMALL-CLAWED
OTTER

Family
group

SMOOTH-COATED OTTER

# SPOTTED-NECKED OTTER
## *Hydrictis maculicollis*

HB 57.5–76cm; T 38.5–44cm; W ♀ 3.5–4.7kg, ♂ 4.5–6kg
(exceptionally to 9kg)

Smallest African otter, chocolate brown, sometimes with a reddish cast. Throat, chest and sometimes belly are marked with white to creamy-white blotches, unique to individuals. Chin and upper lip are white. Formerly classified in *Lutra*, but recent genetic analyses now place it within the unique genus *Hydrictis*, most closely related to Sea Otter (page 192). **Distribution and Habitat** Sub-Saharan Africa, from Guinea to Ethiopia, south to South Africa. Inhabits unsilted and unpolluted freshwater habitats with dense bank vegetation, including lakes, streams, rivers and large swamps. Rarely found >10m from water. **Feeding Ecology** Eats mostly small fish (<20cm), especially cichlids, catfish, barbell, tilapia and introduced trout. Also eats crabs and frogs, especially in the relatively fish-poor waters of southern Africa; diet comprises almost entirely fish in the richer great lakes of C and E Africa. Opportunistically eats aquatic insects, their larvae and occasionally waterbirds. Foraging is solitary or in small social groups, and mostly diurnal with elevated nocturnalism during moonlight. Almost all fishing occurs within 10m of the shore. Around 50% of dives produce a catch, averaging 1 capture every 66 seconds. Scavenging on land not recorded, but takes dead and live fish from fishing nets. **Social and Spatial Behaviour** Sociality flexible. Adults are often solitary, and small family groups (up to 5) usually comprise a female and kittens, but non-breeding adults (especially males) often associate in larger groups numbering up to 21. Individuals and groups appear to be non-territorial, with high overlap between ranges. Range size averages 5.8km² (♀s) and 16.2km² (♂s) in KwaZulu-Natal, South Africa. **Reproduction and Demography** Apparently seasonal (Lake Victoria); mating is in July and births in September, although litters are recorded at other times elsewhere. Gestation approximately 60 days. Litter size 1–3. MORTALITY Nile Crocodile is considered the main predator, but there are no details. LIFESPAN Unknown. **Status and Threats** Widespread and numerous in good habitat, especially C and E Africa's great lakes. However, gradually declining in most of its range due to siltation and pollution. Also drowned in fishing nets, killed by fishermen and valued for traditional medicinal beliefs in many areas. CITES Appendix II; Red List NT, population trend Decreasing.

# CAPE CLAWLESS OTTER *Aonyx capensis*

AFRICAN CLAWLESS OTTER,
AFRICAN SMALL-CLAWED OTTER
HB ♀ 73–73.6cm, ♂ 76.2–88cm; T 46.5–51.5cm;
W ♀ 10.6–16.3kg, ♂ 10–21kg

Large, powerful otter, uniformly mid-brown to dark brown, with a white to pale grey muzzle, throat and upper chest. Feet are partially webbed; the hind paws have small grooming claws, while the forepaws lack claws except for vestigial 'fingernails'. **Distribution and Habitat** Most of sub-Saharan Africa; absent from the Congo

■ Spot-necked Otter

■ Cape Clawless Otter
■ Congo Clawless Otter

Basin and from arid SW and NE Africa. Inhabits lakes, rivers, streams, ponds, estuaries, mangroves and marine habitats close to fresh water, which is required for drinking. Relatively tolerant of pollution and siltation, and occupies urban streams, canals and reservoirs. **Feeding Ecology** Crustacean specialist, eating mainly crabs, crayfish and lobsters. Also eats fish, octopus, frogs and molluscs. Populations in Eastern and Western Cape provinces (South Africa) increase fish consumption during the cold winter, when fish are sluggish and easily caught. Aquatic insects, birds and small mammals (mostly riparian rodents and shrews) are occasionally consumed. Sporadically kills domestic ducks and geese on farmland. Foraging is mainly nocturno-crepuscular, with increased diurnalism where undisturbed, and solitary or in small social groups. Uses its very dextrous forepaws to find and capture prey, mostly in shallow water less than 1.5m deep. Locates and pursues fish mainly by sight. **Social and Spatial Behaviour** Females are mainly solitary, while males are either solitary or live in small groups numbering up to 5 that occupy a shared range; group members generally travel alone, but regularly meet in a 'fission-fusion' pattern, sometimes sharing large prey. Adult female ranges have relatively little overlap, while males vary from little (especially for groups) to extensive overlap. Average territory size (linearly) 17km (♀s) and 42km (♂s) in fresh water, South Africa. Density estimates 1/1.4–5km. **Reproduction and Demography** Thought to be aseasonal, with birth peaks in the rainy season. Gestation 60–63 days. Litter size 1–3. Kittens born with pale smoky-grey woolly fur. They are weaned at around 45–60 days and remain with the mother for up to 12 months. MORTALITY Most known mortality is anthropogenic; Nile Crocodile, Lion (page 46) and African Fish Eagle occasionally kill otters. LIFESPAN 13 years in captivity. **Status and Threats** Widespread and tolerant of some habitat modification, but threatened by severe degradation with associated pollution, siltation and eutrophication. Persecuted as a perceived problem on fish farms, and valued for traditional medicine. CITES Appendix I – Cameroon and Nigeria, Appendix II – elsewhere; Red List NT, population trend Decreasing.

# CONGO CLAWLESS OTTER
## *Aonyx congicus*

SWAMP OTTER, CONGO SMALL-CLAWED OTTER
HB 79–97cm; T 41–56cm; W 14–25kg

Very similar to Cape Clawless Otter and sometimes regarded as the same species, but limited genetic and morphological data indicate they are distinct. They overlap at the edges of their respective distributions in Uganda and Rwanda (and possibly elsewhere). **Distribution and Habitat** Endemic to the Congo Basin; exact range limits unknown, given confusion with Cape Clawless Otter. Inhabits rivers, wetland and swamps in undisturbed rainforest. Not known from marine habitats, but may occur in coastal lagoons and mangroves. **Feeding Ecology** Diet includes earthworms, frogs, freshwater crabs, fish and aquatic insects. Earthworms are a key component of the diet based on observations from Mbeli Bai, Republic of the Congo, where otters grub in the mud for earthworms with their dextrous forepaws, consuming up to 3 a minute. Diurno-crepuscular where undisturbed. **Social and Spatial Behaviour** Poorly known. Most sightings are of individuals or mothers with young. Small groups of up to 4 are reported. Forages close to Spotted-necked Otter without conflict (Mbeli Bai). **Reproduction and Demography** Poorly known. Probably breeds year-round given its equatorial range. Litter size 1–3. Kittens born with pale fur that darkens to adult coloration by 2 months. MORTALITY and LIFESPAN Unknown. **Status and Threats** Status poorly known. Likely occurs in suitable habitat throughout the Congo Basin, which is well preserved over vast areas. Forest loss and overhunting for bushmeat are primary threats, thought to prompt local declines near settlements. CITES Appendix II; Red List NT, population trend Decreasing.

**Plate 93**

Foraging pair

SPOTTED-NECKED
OTTER

Male coalition

CAPE
CLAWLESS
OTTER

CONGO CLAWLESS OTTER

Finding a carnivore skull in the field is a rare event, but for the very fortunate, the following section provides a guide for identification.

The Carnivora are distinguished by their unique cheek teeth. Early in carnivoran evolution, the upper last premolar and lower first molar evolved into a pair of flattened cutting shears called the carnassials. The carnassials are an unmistakable signature of the true carnivores. In most mammals that evolved carnivory, the posterior molars became the flattened carnassial form for slicing meat. In true carnivores, however, the carnassials are located in the middle of the tooth row, in front of the posterior molars. This arrangement freed up the molars in the Carnivora for different purposes. Over time, they became more robust in different species, with reduced shearing edges and greater crushing surfaces, enabling bones and insects, and seeds, fruits and other plant matter to be eaten.

The resulting dual-purpose dentition incorporates teeth that both shear (the carnassials) and crush (the molars). It is typified in dogs, and in fact most modern carnivores have elements of both tooth types. From this type of dentition, a transition to an even more herbivorous diet is possible – the carnassials themselves gradually become less blade-like and more molar-like to deal with tough vegetation. In the Giant Panda and Red Panda, the carnassial shear has disappeared entirely, and both species are completely herbivorous. In an alternative evolutionary route, the rear molars gradually shrink until there is little or no crushing ability and the dentition is all carnassial, with teeth that can only slice meat. This hyper-carnivorous dentition type is most advanced in the cats, and modern cats have lost all their rear molars or retain them only as residual, useless pegs.

The range of carnassial–molar combinations in carnivores furnished them with unique evolutionary flexibility to rise to dominance over other early mammal groups that used their rear molars for carnivory and lacked that plasticity; most of those early groups are now extinct.

Although not as uniquely carnivoran as the carnassials, the canines are the most distinctive and emblematic teeth in carnivore skulls. The canines are used primarily for securing and killing prey, and are also deployed in defensive bites, for instance during intraspecific fights. The smallest and foremost teeth in the skull are the incisors, used mainly for grooming fur as well as for some food handling, for example for plucking fur or feathers, or stripping peel from fruits.

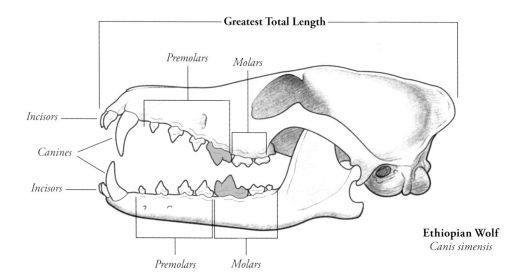

**Greatest Total Length**

Premolars

Molars

Incisors

Canines

Incisors

**Ethiopian Wolf**
*Canis simensis*

Premolars

Molars

**Skull**

*An Ethiopian Wolf skull, showing the different teeth categories present in carnivores. In the Carnivora, the unique carnassials (shaded) are made up of the upper last premolar and the lower first molar. Measurements with the illustrations that follow give skull length for each species (in scientific nomenclature known as the greatest total length, referring to the length between the two most distant points on the skull).*

## Plate 1

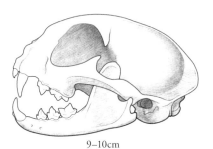

9–10cm

**Chinese Mountain Cat**
*Felis bieti*

8–11.2cm

**Wildcats**
*Felis silvestris, Felis lybica*

## Plate 2

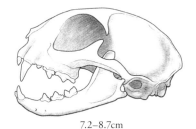

7.2–8.7cm

**Black-footed Cat**
*Felis nigripes*

8–9.5cm

**Sand Cat**
*Felis margarita*

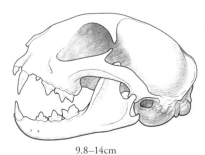

9.8–14cm

**Jungle Cat**
*Felis chaus*

## Plate 3

8.5–9.3cm

**Pallas's Cat**
*Otocolobus manul*

12.3–15.1cm

**Fishing Cat**
*Prionailurus viverrinus*

## Plate 4

7.9–10.2cm

**Leopard Cats**
*Prionailurus bengalensis, Prionailurus javanensis*

## Plate 5

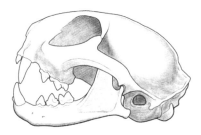

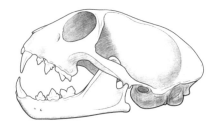

7.3–7.9cm

**Rusty-spotted Cat**
*Prionailurus rubiginosus*

9–9.8cm

**Flat-headed Cat**
*Prionailurus planiceps*

## Plate 6

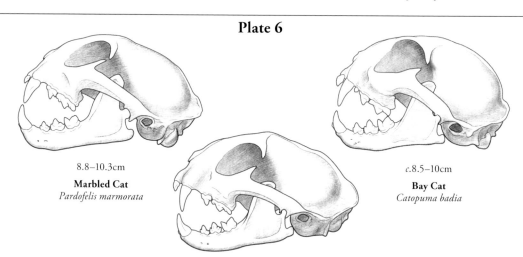

8.8–10.3cm

**Marbled Cat**
*Pardofelis marmorata*

*c.*8.5–10cm

**Bay Cat**
*Catopuma badia*

11.9–15.7cm

**Asiatic Golden Cat**
*Catopuma temminckii*

## Plate 7

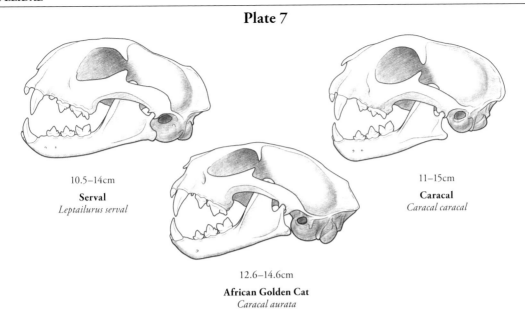

10.5–14cm
**Serval**
*Leptailurus serval*

11–15cm
**Caracal**
*Caracal caracal*

12.6–14.6cm
**African Golden Cat**
*Caracal aurata*

## Plate 8

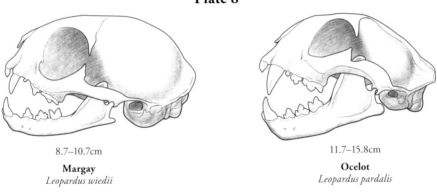

8.7–10.7cm
**Margay**
*Leopardus wiedii*

11.7–15.8cm
**Ocelot**
*Leopardus pardalis*

## Plate 9

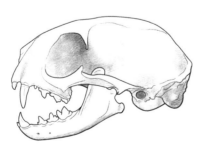

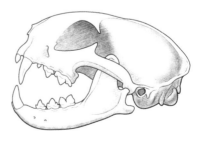

6.8–8.5cm
**Tigrinas**
*Leopardus tigrinus, Leopardus guttulus*

8.5–10.8cm
**Geoffroy's Cat**
*Leopardus geoffroyi*

## Plate 10

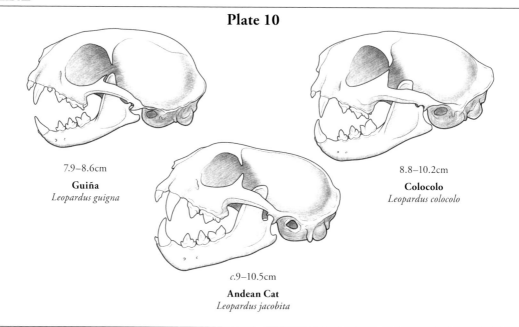

7.9–8.6cm
**Guiña**
*Leopardus guigna*

8.8–10.2cm
**Colocolo**
*Leopardus colocolo*

*c.*9–10.5cm
**Andean Cat**
*Leopardus jacobita*

## Plate 11

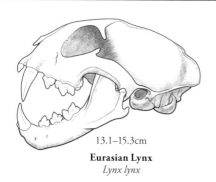

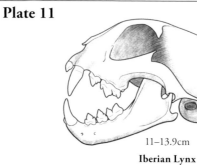

13.1–15.3cm
**Eurasian Lynx**
*Lynx lynx*

11–13.9cm
**Iberian Lynx**
*Lynx pardinus*

## Plate 12

10.6–13.7cm
**Bobcat**
*Lynx rufus*

11.7–13.9cm
**Canada Lynx**
*Lynx canadensis*

## Plate 13

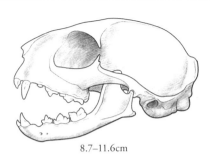

8.7–11.6cm

**Jaguarundi**
*Herpailurus yagouaroundi*

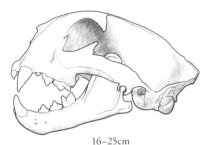

16–25cm

**Puma**
*Puma concolor*

## Plate 14

15–19.3cm

**Cheetah**
*Acinonyx jubatus*

## Plate 15

16.5–20cm

**Snow Leopard**
*Panthera uncia*

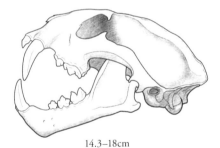

14.3–18cm

**Clouded Leopards**
*Neofelis nebulosa, Neofelis diardi*

## Plate 16

25.3–37.9cm

**Tiger**
*Panthera tigris*

## Plate 17

26.7–42cm

**Lion**
*Panthera leo*

## Plate 18

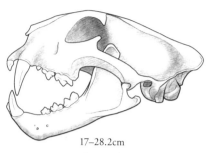

17–28.2cm

**Leopard**
*Panthera pardus*

## Plate 19

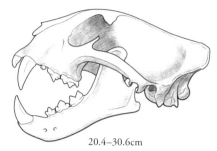

20.4–30.6cm

**Jaguar**
*Panthera onca*

## Plate 20

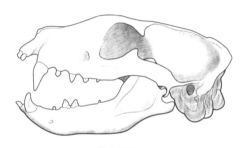

13.9–15.5cm

**Aardwolf**
*Proteles cristata*

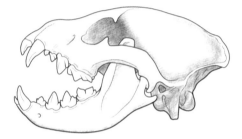

23.3–26.5cm

**Striped Hyaena**
*Hyaena hyaena*

## Plate 21

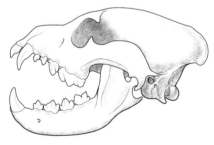

22–27.5cm

**Brown Hyaena**
*Parahyaena brunnea*

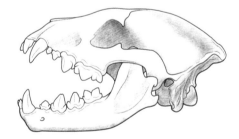

27–29.2cm

**Spotted Hyaena**
*Crocuta crocuta*

## Plate 22

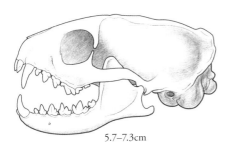

5.7–7.3cm

**Small Indian Mongoose**
*Herpestes (Urva) auropunctatus*

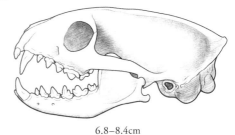

6.8–8.4cm

**Small Asian Mongoose**
*Herpestes (Urva) javanicus*

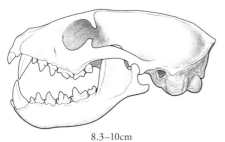

8.3–10cm

**Short-tailed Mongoose**
*Herpestes (Urva) brachyurus*

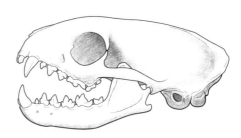

7.1–8.2cm

**Indian Grey Mongoose**
*Herpestes (Urva) edwardsii*

## Plate 23

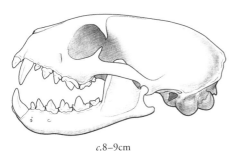

*c.*8–9cm

**Collared Mongoose**
*Herpestes (Urva) semitorquatus*

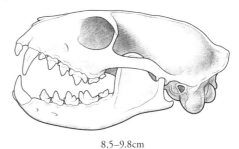

8.5–9.8cm

**Crab-eating Mongoose**
*Herpestes (Urva) urva*

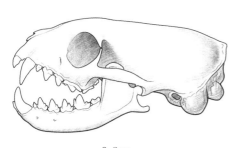

8–9cm

**Ruddy Mongoose**
*Herpestes (Urva) smithii*

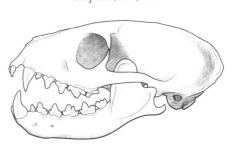

9.8–10.3cm

**Stripe-necked Mongoose**
*Herpestes (Urva) vitticollis*

## Plate 24

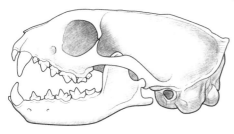

6.2–7.4cm

**Cape Grey Mongoose**
*Herpestes pulverulentus*

6.5–6.7cm

**Common Slender Mongoose**
*Herpestes sanguineus*

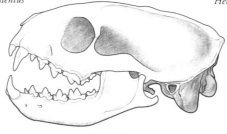

8.7–10.7cm

**Egyptian Mongoose**
*Herpestes ichneumon*

## Plate 25

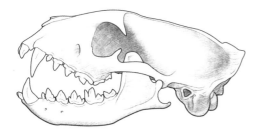

10.5–11.4cm

**Long-nosed Mongoose**
*Herpestes naso*

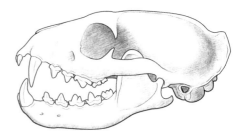

9.6–11.1cm

**Marsh Mongoose**
*Atilax paludinosus*

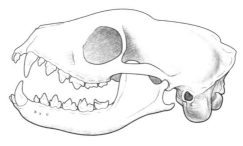

9.6–11.6cm

**White-tailed Mongoose**
*Ichneumia albicauda*

## Plate 26

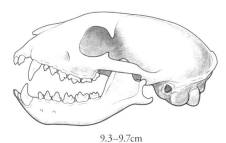

9.3–9.7cm

**Bushy-tailed Mongoose**
*Bdeogale crassicauda*

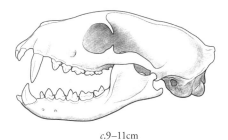

*c.*9–11cm

**Jackson's Mongoose**
*Bdeogale jacksoni*

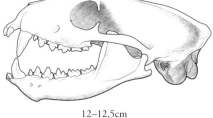

12–12.5cm

**Black-legged Mongoose**
*Bdeogale nigripes*

## Plate 27

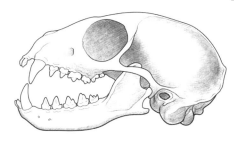

5.8–6.5cm

**Meerkat**
*Suricata suricatta*

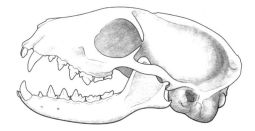

9cm

**Selous's Mongoose**
*Paracynictis selousi*

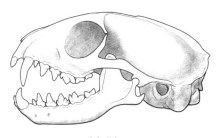

5.8–7.8cm

**Yellow Mongoose**
*Cynictis penicillata*

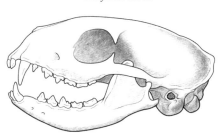

9cm

**Meller's Mongoose**
*Rhynchogale melleri*

## Plate 28

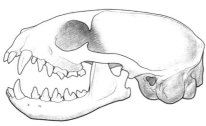

*c.*6cm

**Pousargues's Mongoose**
*Dologale dybowskii*

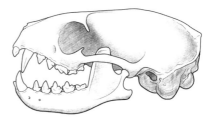

5–6cm

**Somali Dwarf Mongoose**
*Helogale hirtula*

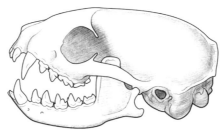

5–6cm

**Common Dwarf Mongoose**
*Helogale parvula*

## Plate 29

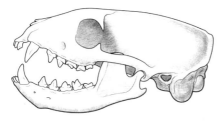

6.7–7.3cm

**Gambian Mongoose**
*Mungos gambianus*

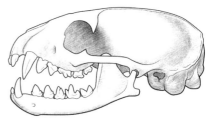

6.2–7.9cm

**Banded Mongoose**
*Mungos mungo*

9.5–10cm

**Liberian Mongoose**
*Liberiictis kuhni*

## Plate 30

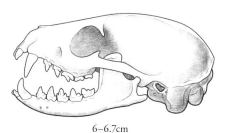

6–6.7cm

**Angolan Cusimanse**
*Crossarchus ansorgei*

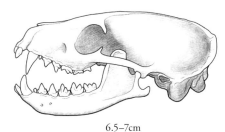

6.5–7cm

**Flat-headed Cusimanse**
*Crossarchus platycephalus*

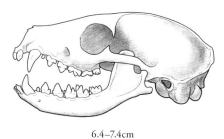

6.4–7.4cm

**Common Cusimanse**
*Crossarchus obscurus*

6.5–8cm

**Alexander's Cusimanse**
*Crossarchus alexandri*

## Plate 31

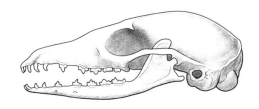

8.4–9.7cm

**Falanouc**
*Eupleres goudotii*

11.5–14cm

**Fosa**
*Cryptoprocta ferox*

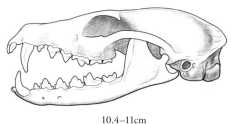

10.4–11cm

**Fanaloka**
*Fossa fossana*

# Plate 32

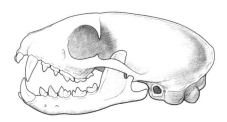

7cm

**Brown-tailed Vontsira**
*Salanoia concolor*

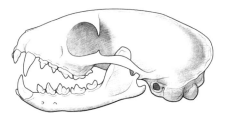

5.8–6cm

**Narrow-striped Boky**
*Mungotictis decemlineata*

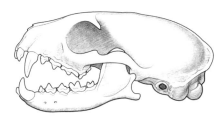

6.5–7.2cm

**Ring-tailed Vontsira**
*Galidia elegans*

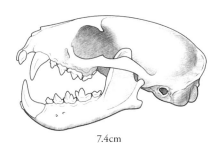

7.4cm

**Broad-striped Vontsira**
*Galidictis fasciata*

## PRIONODONTIDAE & VIVERRIDAE

# Plate 33

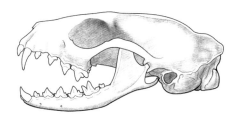

7.2–7.9 cm

**Banded Linsang**
*Prionodon linsang*

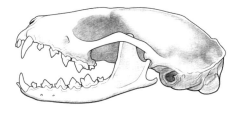

6.4–7.3cm

**Spotted Linsang**
*Prionodon pardicolor*

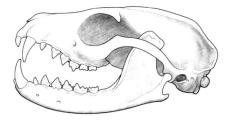

9.2–12cm

**Small-toothed Palm Civet**
*Arctogalidia trivirgata*

# Plate 34

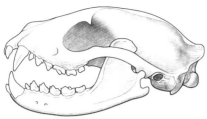

11.4–13.7cm

**Masked Palm Civet**
*Paguma larvata*

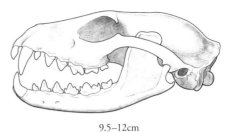

9.5–12cm

**Common Palm Civet**
*Paradoxurus hermaphroditus*

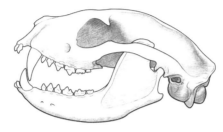

13–15.6cm

**Binturong**
*Arctictis binturong*

# Plate 35

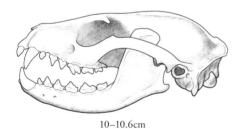

10–10.6cm

**Golden Palm Civet**
*Paradoxurus zeylonensis*

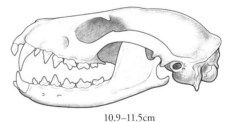

10.9–11.5cm

**Brown Palm Civet**
*Paradoxurus jerdoni*

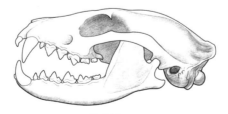

*c.*11–14.5cm

**Sulawesi Civet**
*Macrogalidia musschenbroekii*

## Plate 36

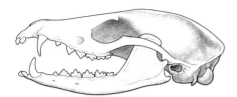

c.9.5–11.3cm

**Owston's Civet**
*Chrotogale owstoni*

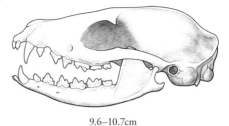

9.6–10.7cm

**Banded Civet**
*Hemigalus derbyanus*

c.9.5–10.5cm

**Hose's Civet**
*Diplogale hosei*

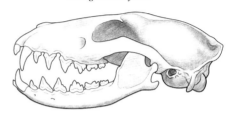

10.9–12.5cm

**Otter Civet**
*Cynogale bennettii*

## Plate 37

c.14.5cm

**Malabar Civet**
*Viverra civettina*

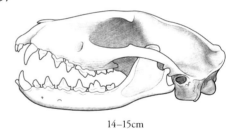

14–15cm

**Large-spotted Civet**
*Viverra megaspila*

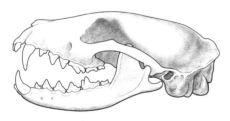

9.2–10.2cm

**Malay Civet**
*Viverra tangalunga*

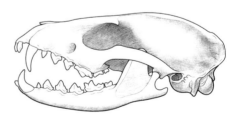

12.7–14.4cm

**Large Indian Civet**
*Viverra zibetha*

## Plate 38

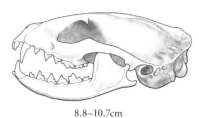

8.8–10.7cm

**Small Indian Civet**
*Viverricula indica*

11.5–15.5cm

**African Civet**
*Civettictis civetta*

## Plate 39

7.7–9cm

**Abyssinian Genet**
*Genetta abyssinica*

7.8–9.3cm

**Hausa Genet**
*Genetta thierryi*

7.7–9.8cm

**Servaline Genet**
*Genetta servalina*

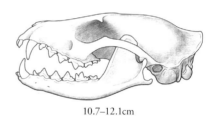

10.7–12.1cm

**Giant Genet**
*Genetta victoriae*

## Plate 40

8.4–9.2cm

**Small-spotted Genet**
*Genetta genetta*

8.7–9.4cm

**Miombo Genet**
*Genetta angolensis*

9.4–10cm

**Johnston's Genet**
*Genetta johnstoni*

9.7–11.4cm

**Aquatic Genet**
*Genetta piscivora*

# Plate 41

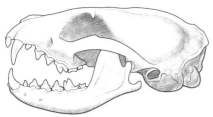

8.5–9.1cm

**Rusty-spotted Genet**
*Genetta maculata*

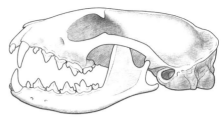

8.6–9.3cm

**Cape Genet**
*Genetta tigrina*

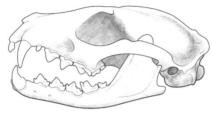

9.2–10.1cm

**Pardine Genet**
*Genetta pardina*

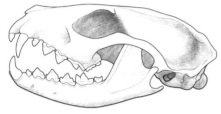

*c.*9–10cm

**King Genet**
*Genetta poensis*

9.6–10.8cm

**Bourlon's Genet**
*Genetta bourloni*

## VIVERRIDAE & NANDINIIDAE

# Plate 42

6.4–7.3cm

**Central African Oyan**
*Poiana richardsonii*

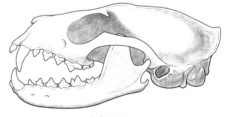

8.4–11.1cm

**African Palm-civet**
*Nandinia binotata*

## Plate 43

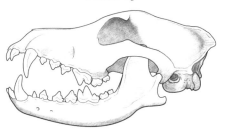

15–21cm

**Dingo**
*Canis lupus familiaris/Canis familiaris*

## Plate 44

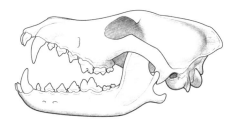

21.1–29.4cm

**Grey Wolf**
*Canis lupus*

## Plate 45

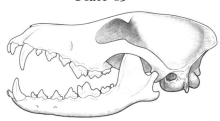

17–22cm

**Coyote**
*Canis latrans*

## Plate 46

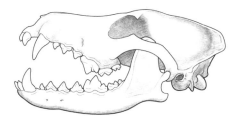

19.7–26.1cm

**Red Wolf**
*Canis 'rufus'*

## Plate 47

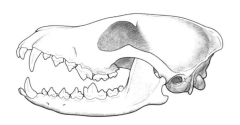

14.3–17.9cm

**Eurasian Golden Jackal**
*Canis aureus*

## Plate 48

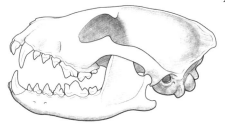

16.6–20cm

**Dhole**
*Cuon alpinus*

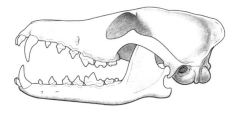

19.1–21cm

**Ethiopian Wolf**
*Canis simensis*

## Plate 49

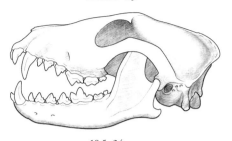

18.5–24cm

**African Wild Dog**
*Lycaon pictus*

## Plate 50

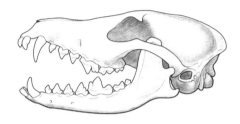

14.3–17cm

**Black-backed Jackal**
*Canis (Lupulella) mesomelas*

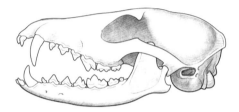

15–17.3cm

**Side-striped Jackal**
*Canis (Lupulella) adusta*

## Plate 51

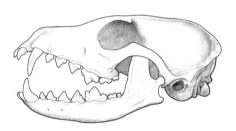

12–13.5cm

**Arctic Fox**
*Vulpes lagopus*

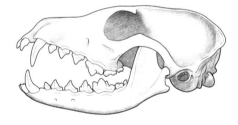

11.7–15.7cm

**Red Fox**
*Vulpes vulpes*

## Plate 52

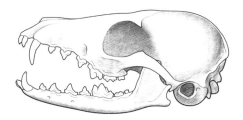

10–12cm

**Kit Fox**
*Vulpes macrotis*

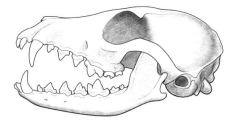

10.8–12cm

**Swift Fox**
*Vulpes velox*

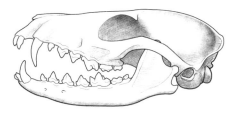

*c.*10–12.5cm

**Indian Fox**
*Vulpes bengalensis*

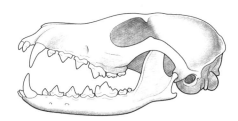

9.8–11.8cm

**Corsac Fox**
*Vulpes corsac*

## Plate 53

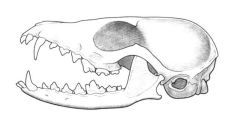

9.1–9.9cm

**Blanford's Fox**
*Vulpes cana*

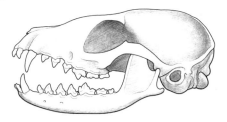

10cm

**Pale Fox**
*Vulpes pallida*

10–11.7cm

**Rüppell's Fox**
*Vulpes ruepellii*

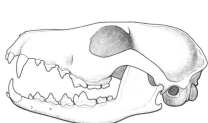

14.9–15.8cm

**Tibetan Fox**
*Vulpes ferrilata*

# Plate 54

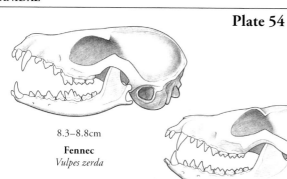

8.3–8.8cm
**Fennec**
*Vulpes zerda*

10.4–12.5cm
**Bat-eared Fox**
*Otocyon megalotis*

9.3–11.5cm
**Cape Fox**
*Vulpes chama*

# Plate 55

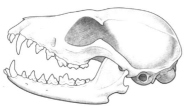

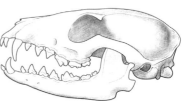

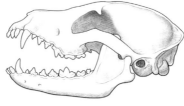

9.7–11cm
**Island Fox**
*Urocyon littoralis*

11–12.7cm
**Raccoon Dog**
*Nyctereutes procyonoides*

11.1–13.2cm
**Grey Fox**
*Urocyon cinereoargenteus*

# Plate 56

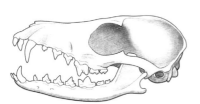

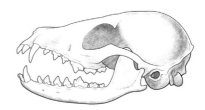

11–14cm
**Chilla**
*Lycalopex griseus*

16–18.8cm
**Culpeo**
*Lycalopex culpaeus*

*c.*11–13cm
**Sechuran Fox**
*Lycalopex sechurae*

## Plate 57

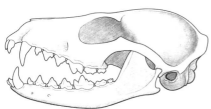

11.1–11.8cm

**Hoary Fox**
*Lycalopex vetulus*

12.9–15.4cm

**Pampas Fox**
*Pseudalopex gymnocercus*

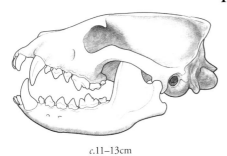

11.2–13.8cm

**Crab-eating Fox**
*Cerdocyon thous*

16.1–17.2cm

**Short-eared Dog**
*Atelocynus microtis*

## Plate 58

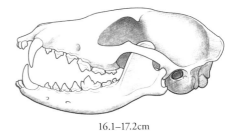

*c.*11–13cm

**Bush Dog**
*Speothos venaticus*

20–23.5cm

**Maned Wolf**
*Chrysocyon brachyurus*

## Plate 59

26.5–31.7cm

**Giant Panda**
*Ailuropoda melanoleuca*

## Plate 60

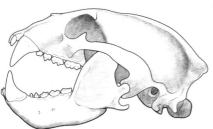

20.6–27.9cm

**Sun Bear**
*Helarctos malayanus*

26–34.5cm

**Sloth Bear**
*Melursus ursinus*

## Plate 61

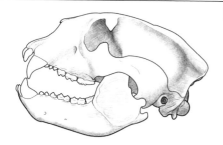

27–31cm

**Andean Bear**
*Tremarctos ornatus*

23.2–30.6cm

**Asiatic Black Bear**
*Ursus thibetanus*

## Plate 62

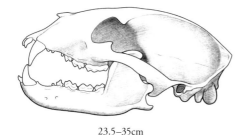

23.5–35cm

**American Black Bear**
*Ursus americanus*

## Plate 63

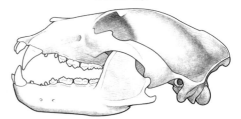

26–42.2cm

**Brown Bear**
*Ursus arctos*

## Plate 64

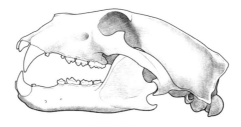

33.7–41cm

**Polar Bear**
*Ursus maritimus*

## Plate 65

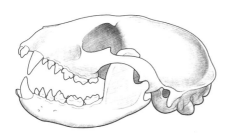

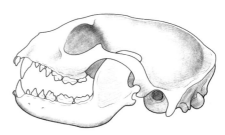

9.3–13.6cm

**Northern Raccoon**
*Procyon lotor*

12.9–14.3cm

**Crab-eating Raccoon**
*Procyon cancrivorus*

## Plate 66

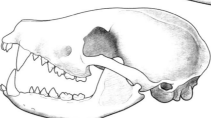

9.7–11.5cm

**Mountain Coati**
*Nasuella olivacea*

10.9–12.5cm

**South American Coati**
*Nasua nasua*

12–13.8cm

**White-nosed Coati**
*Nasua narica*

## Plate 67

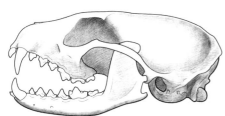

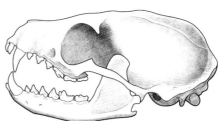

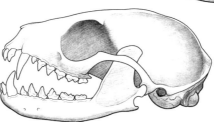

7–8.3cm

**Ringtail**
*Bassariscus astutus*

8.1–9.1cm

**Cacomistle**
*Bassariscus sumichrasti*

7.5–8.5 cm

**Northern Olingo**
*Bassaricyon gabbi*

## Plate 68

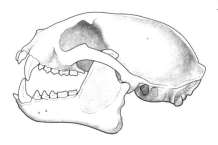

8.4–10cm

**Kinkajou**
*Potos flavus*

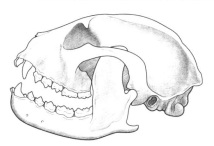

10.5–12.4cm

**Red Panda**
*Ailurus fulgens*

**MEPHITIDAE**

## Plate 69

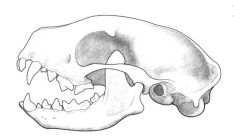

6.9–8.8cm

**Striped Skunk**
*Mephitis mephitis*

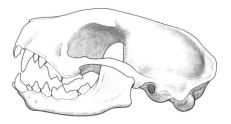

5.5–7.3cm

**Hooded Skunk**
*Mephitis macroura*

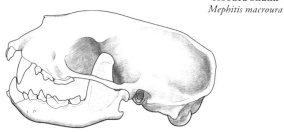

6.5–8.5cm

**American Hog-nosed Skunk**
*Conepatus leuconotus*

## Plate 70

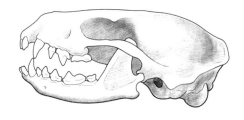

5.5–7.5cm

**Molina's Hog-nosed Skunk**
*Conepatus chinga*

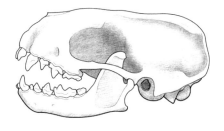

c.6.5–8.5cm

**Striped Hog-nosed Skunk**
*Conepatus semistriatus*

## Plate 71

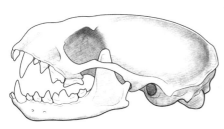

c.4.9–6.4cm

**Eastern Spotted Skunk**
*Spilogale putorius*

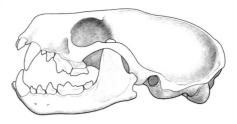

4.9–6.4cm

**Western Spotted Skunk**
*Spilogale gracilis*

## Plate 72

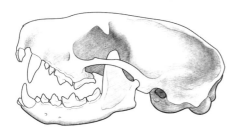

4.2–5cm

**Pygmy Spotted Skunk**
*Spilogale pygmaea*

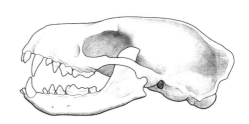

c.7cm

**Palawan Stink-badger**
*Mydaus marchei*

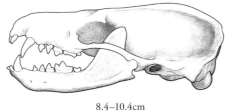

8.4–10.4cm

**Sunda Stink-badger**
*Mydaus javanensis*

## Plate 73

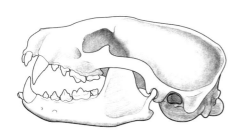

10.5–13.2cm

**American Badger**
*Taxidea taxus*

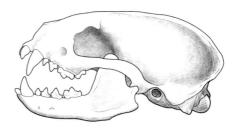

11.2–15.6cm

**Honey Badger**
*Mellivora capensis*

## Plate 74

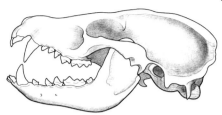

11–13.3cm

**Sumatran Hog Badger**
*Arctonyx hoevenii*

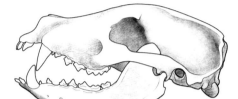

12–15.1cm

**Northern Hog Badger**
*Arctonyx albogularis*

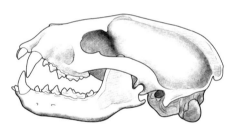

15–17.7cm

**Greater Hog Badger**
*Arctonyx collaris*

## Plate 75

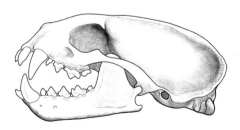

11.6–14.7cm

**European Badger**
*Meles meles*

## Plate 76

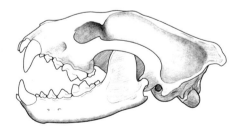

10.3–12.5cm

**Tayra**
*Eira barbara*

13.6–17.5cm

**Wolverine**
*Gulo gulo*

# Plate 77

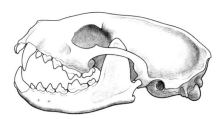

9.9–13.5cm

**Fisher**
*Pekania pennanti*

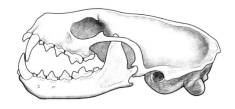

7.9–9.5cm

**Sable**
*Martes zibellina*

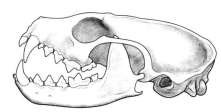

6.8–8.8cm

**American Marten**
*Martes americana*

# Plate 78

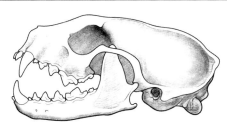

7.8–8.7cm

**Stone Marten**
*Martes foina*

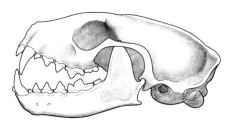

7.5–8.8cm

**Pine Marten**
*Martes martes*

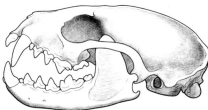

7.5–8.5cm

**Japanese Marten**
*Martes melampus*

# Plate 79

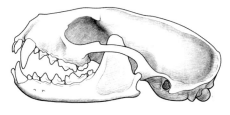

8.9–11.1cm

**Yellow-throated Marten**
*Martes flavigula*

## Plate 80

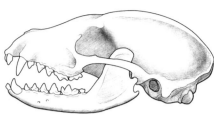

7.4–8.3cm

**Small-toothed Ferret Badger**
*Melogale moschata*

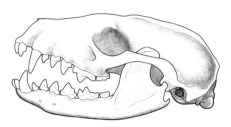

7.6–8.9cm

**Large-toothed Ferret Badger**
*Melogale personata*

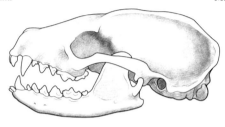

c.7.4–8.5cm

**Javan Ferret Badger**
*Melogale orientalis*

## Plate 81

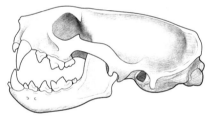

c.4.8–5.7cm

**Patagonian Weasel**
*Lyncodon patagonicus*

7–9cm

**Lesser Grison**
*Galictis cuja*

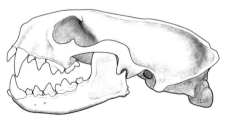

8.9–10.8cm

**Greater Grison**
*Galictis vittata*

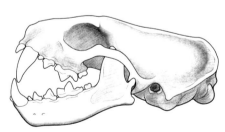

4.8–5.6cm

**Marbled Polecat**
*Vormela peregusna*

# Plate 82

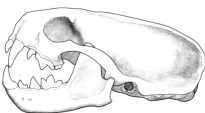

4.8–5.7cm

**Striped Weasel**
*Poecilogale albinucha*

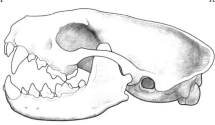

5.2–6cm

**Libyan Weasel**
*Ictonyx libycus*

5.9–6.8cm

**Zorilla**
*Ictonyx striatus*

# Plate 83

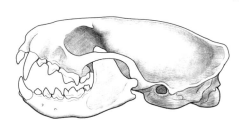

5.3–7.1cm

**American Mink**
*Neovison vison*

5.7–7cm

**Black-footed Ferret**
*Mustela nigripes*

# Plate 84

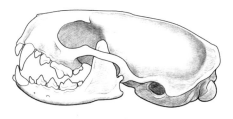

5.6–6.7cm

**Siberian Weasel**
*Mustela sibirica*

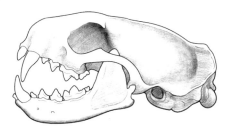

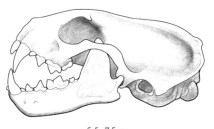

5.5–7.5cm

**Steppe Polecat**
*Mustela eversmanii*

## Plate 85

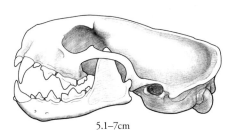

5.1–7cm

**Western Polecat**
*Mustela putorius*

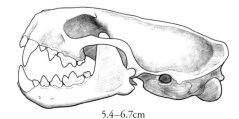

5.4–6.7cm

**European Mink**
*Mustela lutreola*

## Plate 86

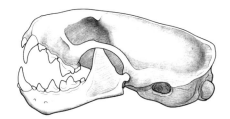

2.8–3.5cm

**Least Weasel**
*Mustela nivalis*

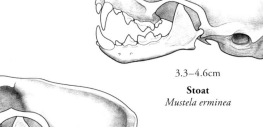

3.3–4.6cm

**Stoat**
*Mustela erminea*

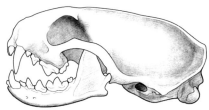

4.3–5.3cm

**Altai Weasel**
*Mustela altaica*

## Plate 87

*c.*3.8–4.5cm

**Colombian Weasel**
*Mustela felipei*

3.8–5.6cm

**Long-tailed Weasel**
*Mustela frenata*

*c.*4–5cm

**Amazon Weasel**
*Mustela africana*

**Plate 88**

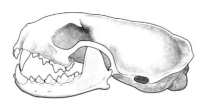

4.2–5cm

**Yellow-bellied Weasel**
*Mustela kathiah*

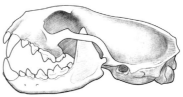

5.4–6.6cm

**Stripe-backed Weasel**
*Mustela strigidorsa*

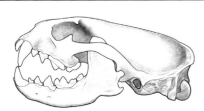

5–5.3cm

**Malay Weasel**
*Mustela nudipes*

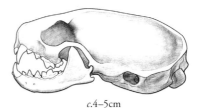

*c.*4–5cm

**Indonesian Mountain Weasel**
*Mustela lutreolina*

**Plate 89**

9–11.2cm

**Marine Otter**
*Lontra felina*

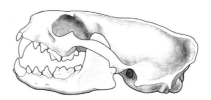

10.3–11.8cm

**Southern River Otter**
*Lontra provocax*

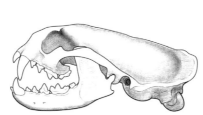

9.4–12cm

**Neotropical Otter**
*Lontra longicaudis*

**Plate 90**

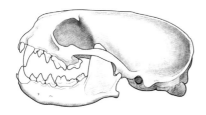

10–13cm

**North American Otter**
*Lontra canadensis*

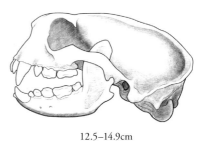

12.5–14.9cm

**Sea Otter**
*Enhydra lutris*

## Plate 91

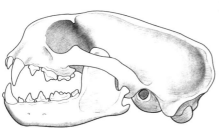

15.5–17.5cm

**Giant Otter**
*Pteronura brasiliensis*

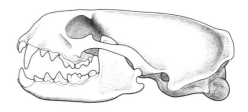

10–13cm

**Eurasian Otter**
*Lutra lutra*

## Plate 92

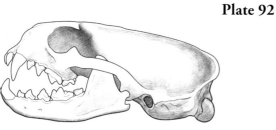

10–12cm

**Hairy-nosed Otter**
*Lutra sumatrana*

8.5–9.5cm

**Asian Small-clawed Otter**
*Aonyx cinereus*

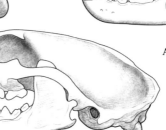

11–13.2cm

**Smooth-coated Otter**
*Lutrogale perspicillata*

## Plate 93

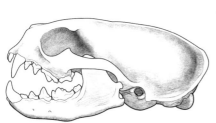

9.4–11.2cm

**Spotted-necked Otter**
*Lutra maculicollis*

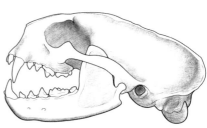

12.5–14.5cm

**Cape Clawless Otter**
*Aonyx capensis*

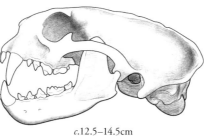

*c.*12.5–14.5cm

**Congo Clawless Otter**
*Aonyx congicus*

# FOOTPRINTS

Far more so than skulls (pages 200–232), carnivores are likely to leave their footprints behind. Indeed, in many cases it is much more possible to find carnivore tracks than the animal itself. This section includes tracks from a variety of carnivores. For many species, reliable tracks have never been recorded in the field, but all families except Nandiniidae are represented here.

Carnivores are either digitigrade, in which they stand on the tips of the toes (as in felids, genets and canids); or plantigrade, in which they stand on the entire foot, including the heel (as in bears and raccoons). These two types produce distinct footprints:

- Tracks of digitigrade species typically show only the toe pads, including claws when non-protractile, and the plantar pad, which is analogous to the fleshy pads at the base of the fingers on a human palm. In most feliform carnivores, the plantar pad has three lobes, compared to two lobes in caniform species (although there are exceptions in both cases).
- Tracks of plantigrade species show a metacarpal or metatarsal pad underlying the wrist or the heel respectively, which is often entirely or partially fused with the plantar pad, producing one large pad print with the toes, similar to the impression of human feet (compare with the bear footprints on the pages that follow).

Most feliform carnivores and canids have five toes on the front foot and four toes on the hind foot. In digitigrade species such as felids, hyaenids, canids, some herpestids and some viverrids, the fifth toe on the front foot (the 'dewclaw') does not touch the ground and is absent from tracks. In some species, this digit has been lost entirely; the African Wild Dog (page 110) is unique among canids for lacking this toe. Most caniform carnivores and most eupleridae have five toes on both the front and hind feet.

Claw impressions typically appear for species that lack the ability to protract their claws – the majority of caniform species, hyaenids, and many viverrids, herpestids and euplerids. The tracks of cats (except for the Cheetah; page 40), genets, oyans and ringtails (Procyonidae) generally do not show claw marks except in deep substrate such as mud or snow, or when the animal is running.

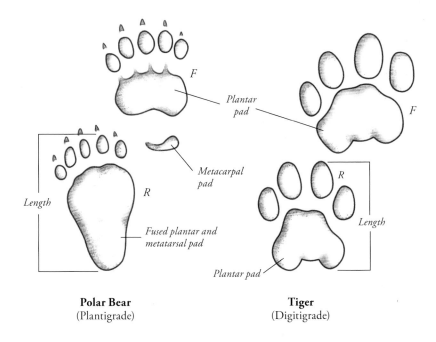

**Polar Bear**
(Plantigrade)

**Tiger**
(Digitigrade)

*Footprints*
*Typical plantigrade (Polar Bear; page 140) and digitigrade (Tiger; page 44) carnivore footprints, showing both fore (F) and rear (R) impressions. The length measurements provided in the following section are taken from the front tips of the middle toe pads to the back of the plantar or metatarsal pad; generally, measurements are provided only for the front print (annotated F); where they appear, rear print measurements are annotated R.*

## Plate 1

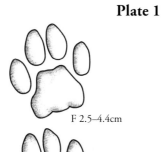

F 2.5–4.4cm

**African Wildcat**
*Felis lybica*

F 2.5–4.4cm

**European Wildcat**
*Felis silvestris*

## Plate 2

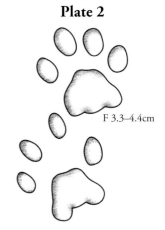

F 3.3–4.4cm

**Jungle Cat**
*Felis chaus*

## Plate 3

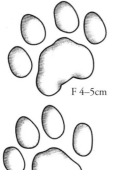

F 4–5cm

**Fishing Cat**
*Prionailurus viverrinus*

## Plate 4

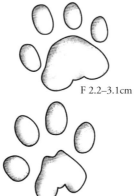

F 2.2–3.1cm

**Leopard Cats**
*Prionailurus bengalensis,*
*P. javanensis*

## Plate 5

F 2.1–2.7cm

**Flat-headed Cat**
*Prionailurus planiceps*

## Plate 6

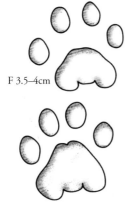

F 3.5–4cm

**Marbled Cat**
*Pardofelis marmorata*

F 4–5.4cm

**Asiatic Golden Cat**
*Pardofelis temminckii*

## Plate 7

F 4–5.1cm

**Serval**
*Leptailurus serval*

F 4.5–5.5cm

**Caracal**
*Caracal caracal*

## Plate 8

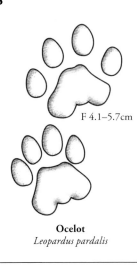

F 2.3–3.2cm

F 4.1–5.7cm

**Margay**
*Leopardus wiedii*

**Ocelot**
*Leopardus pardalis*

## Plate 11

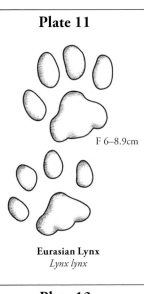

F 6–8.9cm

**Eurasian Lynx**
*Lynx lynx*

## Plate 12

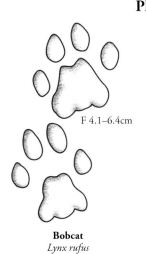

F 4.1–6.4cm

F 5.6–8.7cm

**Bobcat**
*Lynx rufus*

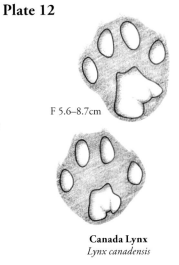

**Canada Lynx**
*Lynx canadensis*

## Plate 13

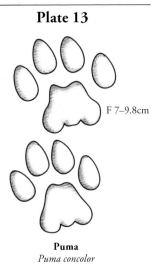

F 7–9.8cm

**Puma**
*Puma concolor*

## Plate 14

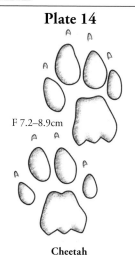

F 7.2–8.9cm

**Cheetah**
*Acinonyx jubatus*

## Plate 15

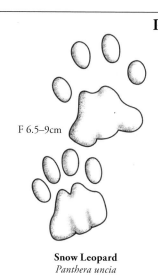

F 6.5–9cm

**Snow Leopard**
*Panthera uncia*

F 6.3–7.8cm

**Clouded Leopards**
*Neofelis nebulosa, N. diardi*

## Plate 16

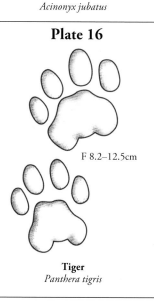

F 8.2–12.5cm

**Tiger**
*Panthera tigris*

## Plate 17

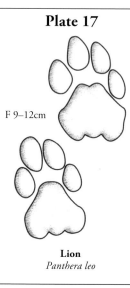

F 9–12cm

**Lion**
*Panthera leo*

## Plate 18

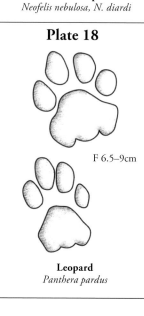

F 6.5–9cm

**Leopard**
*Panthera pardus*

## Plate 19

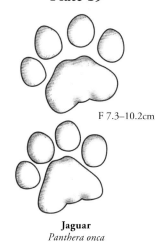

F 7.3–10.2cm

**Jaguar**
*Panthera onca*

# HYAENIDAE

## Plate 20

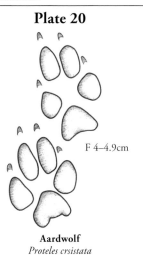

F 4–4.9cm

**Aardwolf**
*Proteles crsistata*

## Plate 21

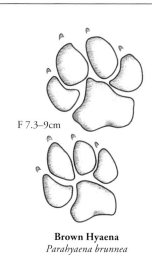

F 7.3–9cm

**Brown Hyaena**
*Parahyaena brunnea*

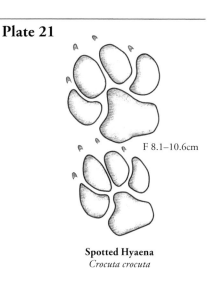

F 8.1–10.6cm

**Spotted Hyaena**
*Crocuta crocuta*

# HERPESTIDAE

## Plate 22

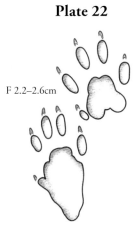

F 2.2–2.6cm

**Small Indian Mongoose**
*Herpestes (Urva) auropunctatus*

## Plate 23

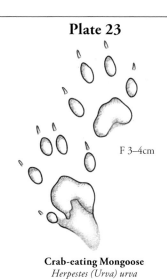

F 3–4cm

**Crab-eating Mongoose**
*Herpestes (Urva) urva*

## Plate 24

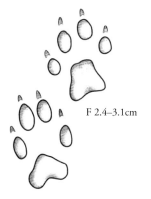

F 2.4–3.1cm

**Cape Grey Mongoose**
*Herpestes pulverulentus*

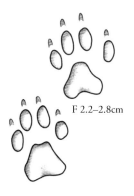

F 2.2–2.8cm

**Common Slender Mongoose**
*Herpestes sanguineus*

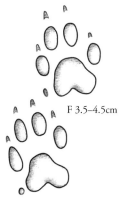

F 3.5–4.5cm

**Egyptian Mongoose**
*Herpestes ichneumon*

## Plate 25

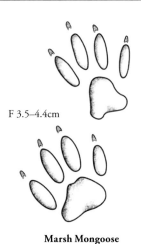

F 3.5–4.4cm

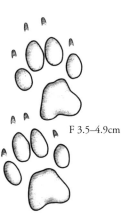

F 3.5–4.9cm

**Marsh Mongoose**
*Atilax paludinosus*

**White-tailed Mongoose**
*Ichneumia albicauda*

## Plate 27

F 2–2.9cm

**Yellow Mongoose**
*Cynictis penicillata*

## Plate 28

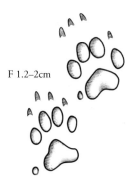

F 1.2–2cm

**Common Dwarf Mongoose**
*Helogale parvula*

## Plate 29

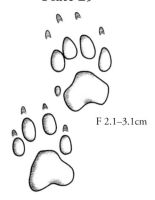

F 2.1–3.1cm

**Banded Mongoose**
*Mungos mungo*

## Plate 31

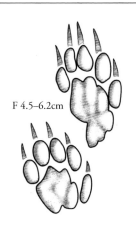

F 4.5–6.2cm

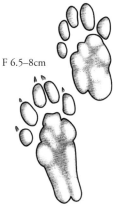

F 6.5–8cm

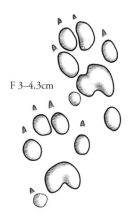

F 3–4.3cm

**Falanouc**
*Eupleres goudotii*

**Fosa**
*Cryptoprocta ferox*

**Fanaloka**
*Fossa fossana*

## Plate 32

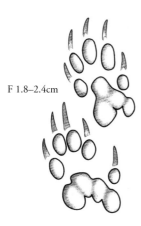

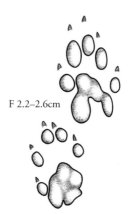

F 1.8–2.4cm

F 2.2–2.6cm

**Narrow-striped Boky**
*Mungotictis decemlineata*

**Ring-tailed Vontsira**
*Galidia elegans*

## PRIONODONTIDAE & VIVERRIDAE

## Plate 33

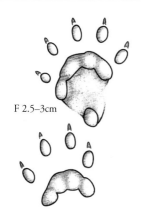

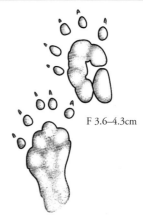

F 2.5–3cm

F 3.6–4.3cm

**Banded Linsang** *Prionodon linsang*
**Spotted Linsang** *Prionodon pardicolor*

**Small-toothed Palm Civet**
*Arctogalidia trivirgata*

## Plate 34

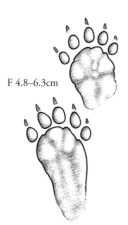

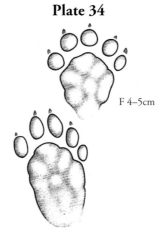

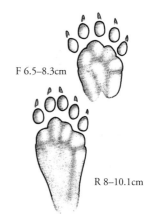

F 4.8–6.3cm

F 4–5cm

F 6.5–8.3cm

R 8–10.1cm

**Masked Palm Civet**
*Paguma larvata*

**Common Palm Civet**
*Paradoxurus hermaphroditus*

**Binturong**
*Arctictis binturong*

## Plate 36

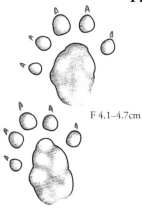

F 4.1–4.7cm

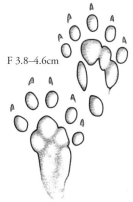

F 3.8–4.6cm

**Owston's Civet** *Chrotogale owstoni*
**Banded Civet** *Hemigalus derbyanus*

**Otter Civet**
*Cynogale bennettii*

## Plate 37

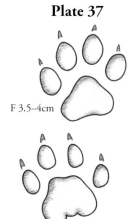

F 3.5–4cm

**Large Indian Civet**
*Viverra zibetha*

## Plate 38

F 2.5–3.2cm

**Small Indian Civet**
*Viverricula indica*

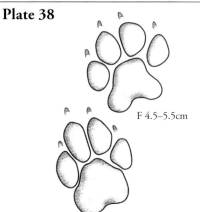

F 4.5–5.5cm

**African Civet**
*Civettictis civetta*

## Plate 41

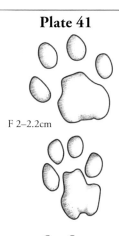

F 2–2.2cm

**Cape Genet**
*Genetta tigrina*

# CANIDAE

## Plate 44

F 7–14cm

**Grey Wolf**
*Canis lupus*

## Plate 45

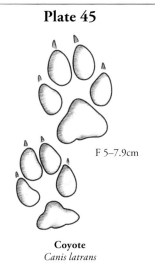

F 5–7.9cm

**Coyote**
*Canis latrans*

## Plate 46

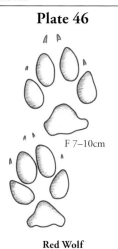

F 7–10cm

**Red Wolf**
*Canis 'rufus'*

## Plate 47

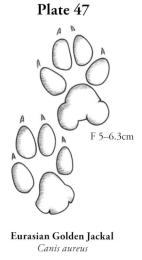

F 5–6.3cm

**Eurasian Golden Jackal**
*Canis aureus*

## Plate 48

F 5.5–7.3cm

**Dhole**
*Cuon alpinus*

## Plate 49

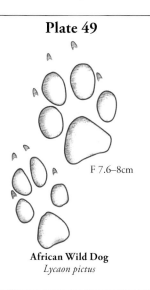

F 7.6–8cm

**African Wild Dog**
*Lycaon pictus*

## Plate 50

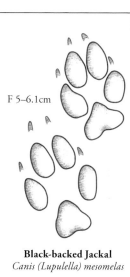

F 5–6.1cm

**Black-backed Jackal**
*Canis (Lupulella) mesomelas*

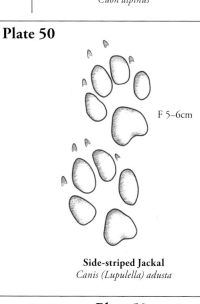

F 5–6cm

**Side-striped Jackal**
*Canis (Lupulella) adusta*

## Plate 51

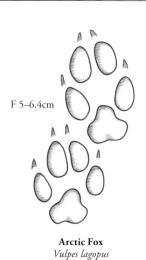

F 5–6.4cm

**Arctic Fox**
*Vulpes lagopus*

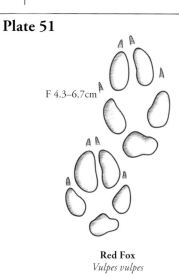

F 4.3–6.7cm

**Red Fox**
*Vulpes vulpes*

## Plate 52

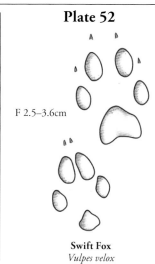

F 2.5–3.6cm

**Swift Fox**
*Vulpes velox*

## Plate 54

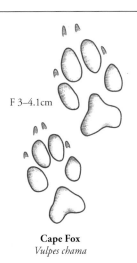

F 3–4.1cm

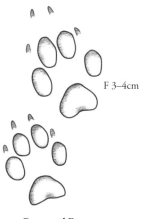

F 3–4cm

**Cape Fox**
*Vulpes chama*

**Bat-eared Fox**
*Otocyon megalotis*

## Plate 55

## Plate 58

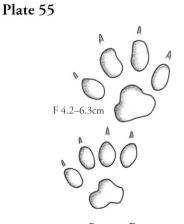

F 3–4.2cm

F 4.2–6.3cm

F 4.3–6.2cm

**Grey Fox**
*Urocyon cinereoargenteus*

**Raccoon Dog**
*Nyctereutes procyonoides*

**Bush Dog**
*Speothos venaticus*

URSIDAE

## Plate 59

## Plate 60

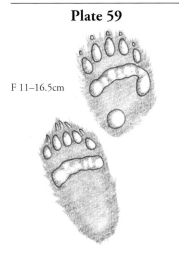

F 11–16.5cm

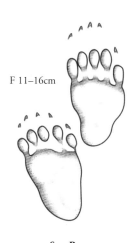

F 11–16cm

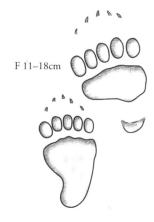

F 11–18cm

**Giant Panda**
*Ailuropoda melanoleuca*

**Sun Bear**
*Helarctos malayanus*

**Sloth Bear**
*Melursus ursinus*

# URSIDAE

## Plate 61

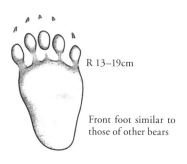

R 13–19cm

Front foot similar to those of other bears

**Asiatic Black Bear**
*Ursus thibetanus*

## Plate 62

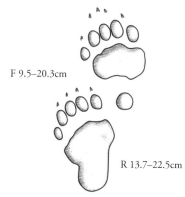

F 9.5–20.3cm

R 13.7–22.5cm

**American Black Bear**
*Ursus americanus*

## Plate 63

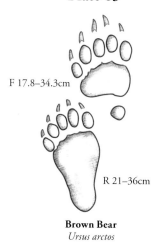

F 17.8–34.3cm

R 21–36cm

**Brown Bear**
*Ursus arctos*

## Plate 64

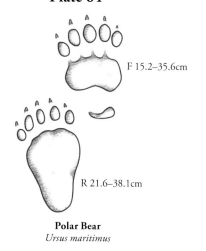

F 15.2–35.6cm

R 21.6–38.1cm

**Polar Bear**
*Ursus maritimus*

# PROCYONIDAE

## Plate 65

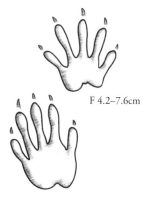

F 4.2–7.6cm

**Northern Raccoon**
*Procyon lotor*

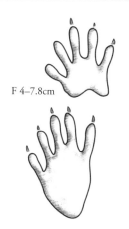

F 4–7.8cm

**Crab-eating Raccoon**
*Procyon cancrivorus*

## Plate 66

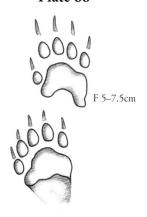

F 5–7.5cm

**White-nosed Coati**
*Nasua narica*

## Plate 67

## Plate 68

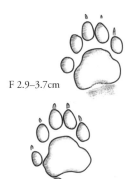

F 2.9–3.7cm

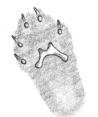

F 4.9–6.5cm

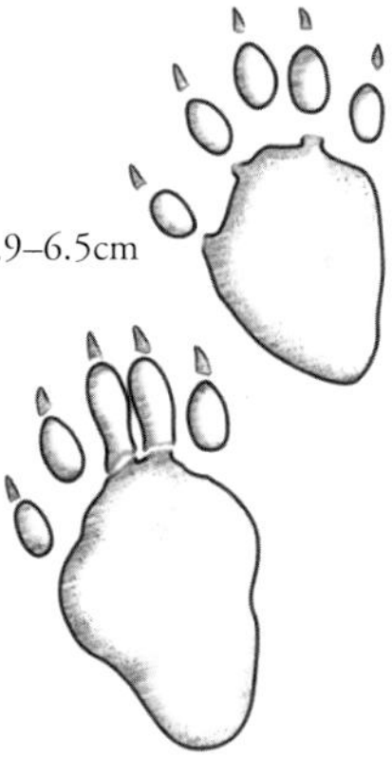

F 5–7cm

**Ringtail**
*Bassariscus astutus*

**Kinkajou**
*Potos flavus*

**Red Panda**
*Ailurus fulgens*

MEPHITIDAE

## Plate 69

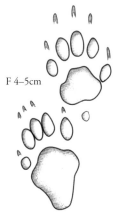

F 4–5cm

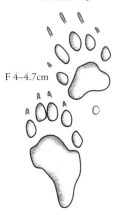

F 4–4.7cm

F 4.3–6.6cm

**Striped Skunk**
*Mephitis mephitis*

**Hooded Skunk**
*Mephitis macroura*

**American Hog-nosed Skunk**
*Conepatus leuconotus*

## Plate 71

## Plate 72

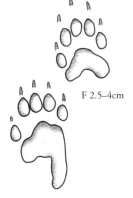

F 2.5–4cm

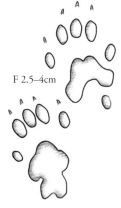

F 2.5–4cm

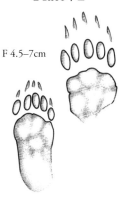

F 4.5–7cm

**Eastern Spotted Skunk**
*Spilogale putorius*

**Western Spotted Skunk**
*Spilogale gracilis*

**Sunda Stink-badger**
*Mydaus javanensis*

## Plate 73

F 7–8.8cm

F 7.5–9.5cm

**American Badger**
*Taxidea taxus*

**Honey Badger**
*Mellivora capensis*

## Plate 74

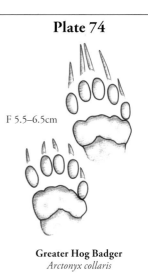

F 5.5–6.5cm

**Greater Hog Badger**
*Arctonyx collaris*

## Plate 75

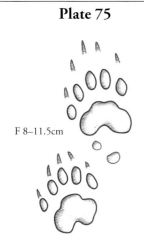

F 8–11.5cm

**European Badger**
*Meles meles*

## Plate 76

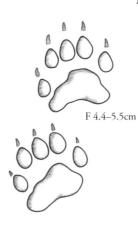

F 4.4–5.5cm

**Tayra**
*Eira barbara*

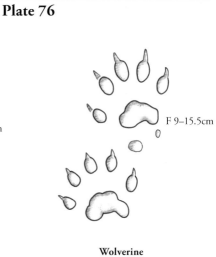

F 9–15.5cm

**Wolverine**
*Gulo gulo*

## Plate 77

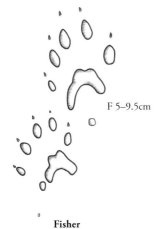

F 5–9.5cm

**Fisher**
*Pekania pennanti*

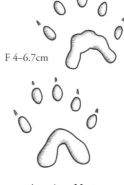

F 4–6.7cm

**American Marten**
*Martes americana*

## Plate 78

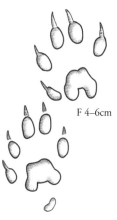

F 4–6cm

F 3.7–5.5cm

**Stone Marten**
*Martes foina*

**Pine Marten**
*Martes martes*

## Plate 79

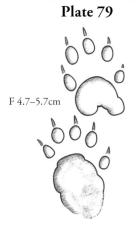

F 4.7–5.7cm

**Yellow-throated Marten**
*Martes flavigula*

## Plate 80

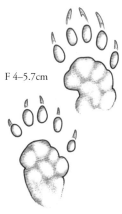

F 4–5.7cm

**Bornean Ferret Badger**
*Melogale everetti*

## Plate 81

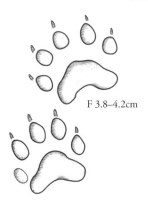

F 3.8–4.2cm

**Greater Grison**
*Galictis vittata*

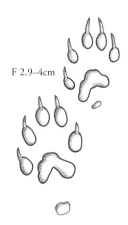

F 2.9–4cm

**Marbled Polecat**
*Vormela peregusna*

## Plate 83

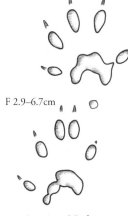

F 2.9–6.7cm

**American Mink**
*Neovison vison*

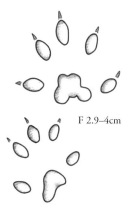

F 2.9–4cm

**Black-footed Ferret**
*Mustela nigripes*

### Plate 85

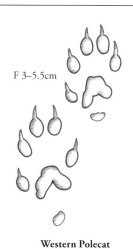

F 3–5.5cm

**Western Polecat**
*Mustela putorius*

F 2.6–5.5cm

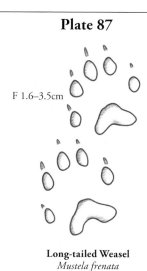

**European Mink**
*Mustela lutreola*

### Plate 86

F 0.8–1.6cm

F 1.1–2.7cm

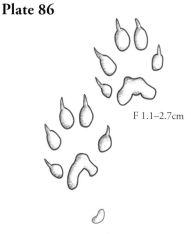

**Least Weasel**
*Mustela nivalis*

**Stoat**
*Mustela erminea*

### Plate 87

F 1.6–3.5cm

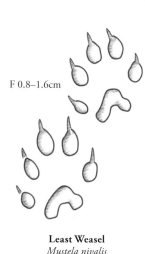

**Long-tailed Weasel**
*Mustela frenata*

### Plate 88

F 1.8–2.5cm

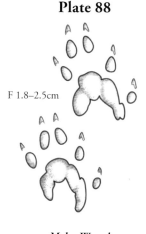

**Malay Weasel**
*Mustela nudipes*

### Plate 89

F 4–7.3cm

**Neotropical Otter**
*Lontra longicaudis*

### Plate 90

F 5.4–8.3cm

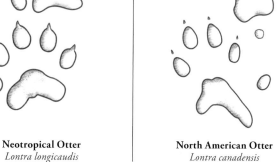

**North American Otter**
*Lontra canadensis*

## Plate 91

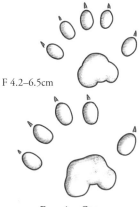

F 4.2–6.5cm

**Eurasian Otter**
*Lutra lutra*

## Plate 92

F 4.6–5.5cm

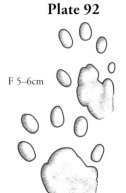

F 5–6cm

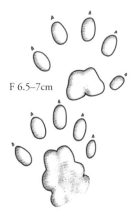

F 6.5–7cm

**Hairy-nosed Otter**
*Lutra sumatrana*

**Asian Small-clawed Otter**
*Aonyx cinereus*

**Smooth-coated Otter**
*Lutrogale perspicillata*

## Plate 93

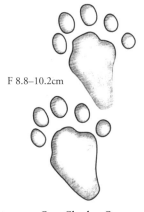

F 8.8–10.2cm

**Cape Clawless Otter**
*Aonyx capensis*

# GLOSSARY

**albinism** Complete or partial absence of pigment in the skin, feathers, hair and eyes due to a reduced ability to produce the pigment melanin, usually inherited as a recessive genetic trait. Albino individuals have white hair with pink eyes and skin.

**altiplano** High plateau in west-central South America where the Andes are at their widest; dominated by cold, dry desert and grasslands.

**anthropogenic** Any effect, process or material derived from human activities, e.g. anthropogenic threats are those created by people.

**aposematism** Referring to adaptations to deter predation, typically in which striking warning coloration signals the unprofitability of a prey item to potential predators, e.g. the black-and-white markings of skunks.

**arachnid** Member of the invertebrate arthropod class Arachnida, characterised by having eight legs (in some species the front pair converts to a sensory function). Includes spiders, scorpions, mites, ticks and solifuges.

**arboreal** Living predominantly or entirely in trees.

**arthropod** Invertebrate animal with an external skeleton (exoskeleton), a segmented body and jointed appendages. Includes insects, spiders, scorpions and crustaceans.

**caatinga** Arid scrubland and dry forest biome of northeastern Brazil.

**caching (of food)** Storing food for future consumption, usually for the lean season, e.g. the northern winter.

**camera-trap** Automated camera used to capture photographs of wild animals, typically for inventory and monitoring efforts.

**caniform** Referring to the carnivore suborder Caniformia, comprising the 'dog-like' families Canidae, Ursidae, Otariidae, Phocidae, Odobenidae, Procyonidae, Ailuridae, Mephitidae and Mustelidae (and the extinct family Amphicyonidae). Caniform species tend to have non-protractile claws and are plantigrade (with the exception of the Canidae).

**canine (teeth)** (also called cuspids, fangs or, in the case of those of the upper jaw, eye teeth) Relatively long, pointed teeth located at the front of the jaw, and often the largest teeth in a mammal's mouth. The canines are used primarily for killing prey, holding or processing food, and occasionally as weapons in fights between conspecifics or in defence against attack.

**carnassial** In the Carnivora, the modified last (fourth) upper premolar and first lower molar teeth, which are used in concert for shearing tissue with a scissor-like action (the 'carnassial shear').

**carnivore** Organism that eats mainly animal tissue, whether through predation or scavenging. In scientific terminology, a carnivore is a mammal within the order Carnivora.

**cathemeral** Active at any time during the day or night, without any distinct pattern.

**caudal** Pertaining to the tail.

**cerrado** Tropical dry savannah of Brazil, mainly located in the states of Goiás and Minas Gerais.

**Chaco** Semi-arid ecoregion dominated by dry savannah and thorn forest, found from western Paraguay to southeastern Bolivia and northwestern Argentina.

**clade** Taxonomic group of organisms classified together on the basis of shared similar features traced to a common ancestor. Not a formal taxonomic classification level (as, e.g., species), but indicates closer relatedness of any two or more taxa compared with other taxa.

**conspecific** Of the same species.

**crepuscular** Active primarily during twilight, i.e. at dawn and dusk.

**crustacean** Large group of arthropod invertebrates usually treated as a subphylum, Crustacea; includes lobsters, crayfish, crabs, barnacles, shrimp and krill.

**cyclical abundance** 'Boom–bust' cycles in which some species reproduce rapidly during periods of food abundance, with a corresponding very rapid population growth that declines equally as rapidly during lean periods, resulting in a population crash. A natural feature of many species' population cycles, most famously the Snowshoe Hare.

**deciduous** In reference to plants losing their foliage seasonally.

**delayed implantation (embryonic diapause)** In which development of the embryo is postponed shortly after conception by delaying implantation in the uterus. The embryo is maintained in a state of dormancy as long as it remains unattached to the uterine lining, extending the normal gestation period for up to a year. Thought to optimise reproductive success by timing mating and birth to avoid severe lean periods such as northern winters and prolonged drought.

**dewclaw** Fifth innermost digit of the foot of many mammals (and some other vertebrates), equivalent in position to the human thumb. In digitigrade species, it does not make contact with the ground when the animal is standing. Vestigial, with no function, in many species.

**digitigrade** In terrestrial mammalian locomotion, an animal that stands or walks on the tips of its digits, technically on its distal and intermediate phalanges ('finger bones'), e.g. in felids and canids.

**disperser** Cohort of an animal population that leaves its natal range to seek out unoccupied habitat in which to settle and establish a home range. In carnivores, dispersers tend to be young adults that have been evicted from their natal range or social group.

**distal** Usually of appendages, meaning the part of an organ furthest from the point of attachment to the body, e.g. the distal vertebra of the tail is the tip.

**disturbed forest** Forest that has significant areas of anthropogenic disturbance, caused by, e.g., clearing, logging and fires.

**diurnal** Active primarily during the day.

**dorsal** Upper side of animals that run, fly or swim in a horizontal position.

**erythristism** Overproduction of red (or orange) pigment, giving animals red-coloured fur or skin.

**evergreen** With regard to plants having foliage in all seasons.

**feliform** Referring to the carnivore suborder Feliformia, comprising the 'cat-like' families Felidae, Hyaenidae, Herpestidae, Eupleridae, Prionodontidae, Viverridae and Nandiniidae (and the extinct family Nimravidae). Protractile claws and digitigrade locomotion are more widespread among feliform species than in caniform species.

**feral** A feral organism is one that has escaped from domestication and returned, partly or wholly, to a wild state.

**frugivore** Organism in which fruit is the preferred food, e.g. the Kinkajou (page 148).

**fynbos** Afrikaans for 'fine bush'. Unique, highly diverse heathland vegetation occurring in a small belt of the Western Cape province of South Africa.

**genus** (pl. genera) Low-level taxonomic rank (a taxon) used in the classification of living and fossil organisms.

**haul out** Behaviour associated mainly with pinnipeds of temporarily leaving the water between periods of foraging for rest sites on land or ice.

**herbivore** Organism that eats plants.

**herptile** Collective term for reptiles (class Reptilia) and amphibians (class Amphibia).

**hibernation** State of inactivity and metabolic depression in animals, characterised by lowered body temperature, reduced breathing rate and reduced metabolic rate. Enables animals to survive lean-season (usually winter) food shortages by slowly metabolising fat reserves.

**home range** Area occupied by an individual, pair or group of animals required to satisfy the basic requirements for surviving and reproducing. Home range and territory are essentially equivalent, but the term 'home range' carries no implication of active defence against intruders.

**hypercarnivore** Usually defined as a species in which more than 70 per cent of the diet is tissue from animals, with non-animal foods such as fungi, fruits and other plant material making up the remainder.

**hyperphagia** Meaning 'excessive eating'. In biology, occurs during the period prior to hibernation in which animals prepare for winter by constant foraging to lay down fat reserves.

**incisor** Frontmost type of tooth in heterodont mammals (those with different types of teeth). Used primarily for processing food, grooming and defensive biting.

**invertebrate** Animal without a backbone (vertebral column). Ninety-five per cent of all animal species are invertebrates, ranging from simple organisms such as sea sponges and flatworms to complex animals such as arthropods and molluscs.

**keratin** Key structural material making up the outer layer of vertebrate skin, as well as hair, horn, feathers, hoofs, nails, claws and bills.

**kleptoparasitism** Form of feeding in which one animal takes prey or other food from another that has caught, collected or otherwise prepared it, including food that has been stored.

**kopje** Isolated rock hill, knob, ridge or small mountain that rises abruptly from a surrounding level plain.

**lagomorph** Members of the order Lagomorpha (meaning 'hare form'), made up of two living families, the Leporidae (hares and rabbits) and Ochotonidae (pikas).

**leucism** Genetic condition characterised by reduced pigmentation in animals and humans. Unlike albinism (a defect in pigment production), leucism renders the skin unable to support pigment cells. Leucistic animals are white or pale in colour, and have pigmented eyes (unlike albinos), e.g. so-called white Lions (page 46).

**Llanos** Seasonally flooded open savannah habitat in Colombia and Venezuela.

**melanism** Elevated dark pigmentation of skin, feathers, hair and eyes due to an excess of the pigment melanin, usually inherited as a recessive genetic trait. Melanistic individuals are black or near black, and occur in many carnivores, especially felids, viverrids, herpestids and canids.

**mesic** Characterised by having a moderate water supply, e.g. mesic habitats are moderately well watered.

**mesocarnivore** Mid-sized carnivores, broadly occupying the middle trophic level in an ecosystem, competitively subdominant to large carnivores and dominant to small species, e.g. Bobcats (page 19) and Coyotes (page 102) in North America.

**miombo** Mesic to semi-arid woodland characterised by *Brachystegia* trees, found across south-central Africa.

**molar** Rearmost and often most complex tooth type in the majority of mammals. In carnivores, typically employed to grind or crush food items ranging from nuts to bone.

**mollusc** Phylum (Mollusca) of invertebrate animals that includes snails, slugs, squid, octopus, cuttlefish, clams, oysters, scallops and mussels.

**morph** In biology, occurs when two or more clearly different phenotypes exist in the same population of a species.

**myrmecophagy** Feeding behaviour defined by consumption of termites and/or ants.

**natal range** Same as 'birth' range: the area in which an animal is born and raised until it disperses.

**nocturnal** Active primarily during the night.

**nocturno-crepuscular** Active primarily during dusk, night and dawn.

**obligate carnivore** Animal depending solely on the nutrients found in animal flesh for survival. Lacks the physiology required for efficient digestion of plant material; any vegetation consumed is typically as an emetic rather than for nutritional gain.

**oestrus** Stage during a female animal's reproductive cycle in which she is receptive to the male for mating, and ovulates (sometimes stimulated by copulation).

**Pantanal** Seasonally inundated open woodland–wetland biome in western Brazil, Paraguay and Bolivia.

***páramo*** Neotropical, largely Andean ecosystem of glacier-formed valleys and wet grasslands interspersed with lakes, peat bogs, shrublands and forest patches.

**plantigrade** In terrestrial mammalian locomotion, an animal that stands or walks with the metacarpals or metatarsals flat on the ground, so that the entire foot makes contact with the ground, e.g. humans and ursids.

**primary forest** Forest of native species with little or no evidence of human activities and where ecological processes are not significantly disturbed.

**protractile** Of claws, the ability to extend the claws deliberately from a relaxed, withdrawn position, as in felids and genets. This is often incorrectly termed 'retractile', which is in fact the relaxed state of the claws.

**proximal** Usually referring to appendages, meaning the part of an organ closest to the point of attachment to the body, e.g. the proximal vertebra of the tail is the base.

**riparian** Habitat occurring at the interface between land and a freshwater waterway such as a river or stream.

**scavenging** Behaviour in which a predator consumes carcasses or carrion not killed by itself or members of its social group.

**scent-marking** Behaviour used by animals to demarcate their territory, usually carried out by depositing strong-smelling secretions such as urine at prominent locations within the range.

**secondary forest** Forest or woodland that has regrown or is in the process of regrowing after a major natural or anthropogenic disturbance such as fire or logging. It is younger than primary forest and lacks its old-growth structure, and is typified by a denser and more 'weedy' subcanopy.

**species** Often defined as a group of organisms capable of interbreeding and producing fertile offspring. While in many cases this definition is adequate, more precise or differing measures are often used, such as similarity of DNA, morphology or ecological niche.

**subspecies** (abbreviated to subsp. or ssp.) Either a taxonomic rank subordinate to species, or a taxonomic unit in that rank. A subspecies cannot be recognised in isolation: a species will either be recognised as having no subspecies at all, or two or more, but never just one.

**sympatric** Of two or more species occurring in the same area or range.

**Terai** Lowland region in southern Nepal and northern India characterised by dense floodplain grassland.

**termitaria** Termite mound, also often called an 'anthill'.

**terpenes** Defensive organic compounds produced by a wide variety of plants and some insects, such as termites and swallowtail butterflies, to deter predation.

**terrestrial** Living predominantly or entirely on land.

**territory** Area occupied by an individual, pair or group of animals which is demarcated and defended against other members of the same species. A territory can also be viewed as an actively defended home range.

**ungulate** Several groups of mammals traditionally grouped together due to the fact that they use the tips of their toes, usually hoofed, to support their whole body weight. Includes all hoofed mammals such as deer, antelopes, horses, cattle, giraffes, camels, llamas, tapirs, rhinoceroses, hippopotamuses and elephants.

**vertebrate** Animals of the subphylum Vertebrata, having a backbone (vertebral column). Includes fish, amphibians, reptiles, birds and mammals.

**vocalisation** Production of sound by the passage of air across the vocal chords, and used by animals to communicate to conspecifics and other species.

# ACKNOWLEDGEMENTS

This book has relied heavily on numerous people for comments, data, publications and reference material. Many people provided images or assisted in locating them for the preparation of the plates, in some cases to illustrate species or forms that had never been accurately depicted. For this, particular thanks go to: Francesco Angelici, Sixto Angulo, Rosario Arispe, Jane Ashley-Edmonds, Christos Astaras, Guy Balme, Eyal Bartov, Jerry Belant, Abelardo Rodriguez Bolaños, Jeffrey P. Bonner, Adam Britt, Milo Burcham, Duncan Butchart, Marcelo Carrera, Erika Cuellar, Rogerio Cunha de Paula, Daniela DeLuca, James Eaton, Mohammad Farhadinia, Charles Foley, Nick Garbutt, Oscar E. Murillo García, Arash Ghoddousi, Anthony Giordano, Varad B. Giri, Helle Goldman and Jon Winther-Hansen, Lon Grassman, Andy Hearn, Philipp Henschel, Rafael Hoogesteijn, Bob and Kris Inman, Andy Jennings, Jaime Jimenez, Arlyne Johnson, Calvin Jones, Roland Kays, Marcella Kelly, Barney Long, Leo Maffei, Sean Matthews, Divya Mudappa, Andy Noss, Andres Novaro, Stephane Ostrowski, Antonio Rossano Mendes Pontes, Ingrid Porton, Shankar Raman, Justina Ray, Scott Roberton, Jo Ross, Chris Roche, Brian Rode, Carlos A. Saavedra Rodríguez, Fabio Rohe, Steve Ross, Ricardo Sampaio, Jim Sanderson, Kevin Schafer, Alex Sliwa, SOMASPA (Panama), Rob Steinmetz, Simon Stobbs, Chris and Tilde Stuart, Narong Suannarong, Tim Tetzlaff, Fernando Tortato, Marcos Tortato, Sara Tromp and Joe Walston.

I am similarly indebted to the following colleagues, who reviewed sections of the text and commented on plates: Ben Allen, Arturo Caso, Natalie Dawson, Andrew Derocher, Philippe Gaubert, John Goodrich, Andy Hearn, Kris Helgen, Marna Herbst, Jan Kamler, Carlos Behur Kasper, Roland Kays, Tom McCarthy, David MacDonald, Sean Matthews, Dale Miquelle, Divya Mudappa, Tadeu de Oliveira, Alan Rabinowitz, Alan Root and Howard Quigley. For addressing specific queries and providing publications, unpublished data and other comments, I thank Ben Allen, Guy Balme, Nick Brickle, Vincent Burke, Sasha Carvaja, Armando X. Castellanos, Jerry Dragoo, Colin Groves, Lauren Harrington, Frank Hawkins, Roland Kays, Klaus-Peter Koepfli, Erin McCloskey, David Macdonald, Kate McFadden, Javier Pereira, Miguel Pinto, Pamela Racobs, Juan Repucci, Jo Ross, Steve Ross, Tainara Venturini Sobroza and Cintia Tellaeche.

I am grateful to Darrin Lunde and Eileen Westwig (American Museum of Natural History, New York) and to Bill Stanley (Field Museum, Chicago) for making available their carnivore skull specimens, and to Sarah Arnoff, Joanna Cagan and Graeme Patterson for photographing them. Sarah also compiled additional reference material for carnivore skulls and footprints. A special thanks to Sally McClarty for executing the wonderful illustrations for these sections. Thank you to the IUCN Red List Unit for material to prepare distribution maps, in particular Craig Hilton-Taylor for permission to use the unit's spatial data, and Jemma Window and Max Fancourt for assistance in providing those data. Special thanks to Ben Allen, Carlos Benhur Kasper, Peter West and CENAP/ICMBio (Brazil) for assisting with new mapping data.

I am especially grateful to Philippe Gaubert, who provided photographs, publications, unpublished data and invaluable comments on little-known genets, and Geraldine Veron who did likewise for viverrids and herpestids. Kris Helgen very kindly made available his team's revised classification of hog badgers before it was published and, with Roland Kays, he assisted similarly with his ongoing effort to revise olingo taxonomy. Eduardo Eizirk generously previewed his ongoing analysis of hog-nosed skunk phylogeography. Will Duckworth and Andrew Kitchener commented extensively on the nomenclature and taxonomy of all species. Mike Hoffmann provided a constant stream of new information, publications and contact details from his extensive network. I am very grateful to Olaf Bininda-Emonds, who provided his raw data on carnivore phylogenies. At Panthera, I thank David Katz for compiling measural data and the glossary, Erin Archuleta for double-checking many details during the preparation of the first edition, and Lisanne Petracca for preparing the maps in the second edition.

# INDEX

Scientific names of all non-carnivore species mentioned in the text can be accessed at www.researchgate.net/profile/Luke_Hunter3

Numbers in **bold** refer to plate numbers. Numbers in roman are page numbers.

Aardwolf **20**, 52, 206, 237
Abyssinian Genet **39**, 90, 215
Abyssinian Wolf *see* Ethiopian Wolf
*Acinonyx jubatus* **14**, 40, 205, 236
Afghan Fox *see* Blanford's Fox
African Civet **38**, 88, 215, 240
African Clawless Otter *see* Cape Clawless Otter
African Golden Cat **7**, 26, 203
African Golden Wolf *see* African Wolf
African Linsang *see* Central African Oyan
African Palm-civet **42**, 96, 216
African Sand Fox *see* Pale Fox
African Small-clawed Otter *see* Cape Clawless Otter
African Striped Weasel *see* Striped Weasel
African Wildcat **1**, 14, 201, 234
African Wild Dog **49**, 110, 218, 241
African Wolf **47**, 106
Ailuridae 10, 148, 124, 244
*Ailuropoda melanoleuca* **59**, 130, 221, 242
*Ailurus fulgens* **68**, 148, 224, 244
Alexander's Cusimanse **30**, 72, 211
Alpine Weasel *see* Altai Weasel
Altai Mountain Weasel *see* Altai Weasel
Altai Weasel **86**, 184, 230
Amazon Weasel **87**, 186, 230
American Badger **73**, 158, 225, 245
American Black Bear **62**, 136, 222, 243
American Hog-nosed Skunk **69**, 150, 224, 244
American Marten **77**, 166, 227, 245
American Mink **83**, 178, 229, 246
*Anaguma see* Japanese Badger
Andean Bear **61**, 134, 222
Andean Cat **10**, 32, 204
Andean Fox *see* Culpeo
Andean Hog-nosed Skunk *see* Molina's Hog-nosed Skunk
Andean Mountain Cat *see* Andean Cat
Angolan Cusimanse **30**, 72, 211
Angolan Genet *see* Miombo Genet
Angolan Slender Mongoose *see* Kaokoveld Slender Mongoose
Ansorge's Cusimanse *see* Angolan Cusimanse
*Aonyx capensis* **93**, 198, 232, 248
*Aonyx cinereus* **92**, 196, 232, 248
*Aonyx congicus* **93**, 198, 232
Aquatic Genet **40**, 92, 215
Arctic Fox **51**, 114, 218, 241
Arctic Wolf *see* Grey Wolf
*Arctictis binturong* **34**, 80, 213, 239
*Arctictis whitei* 80
*Arctogalidia trivirgata* **33**, 78, 212, 239
*Arctonyx albogularis* **74**, 160, 226
*Arctonyx collaris* **74**, 160, 226, 245
*Arctonyx hoevenii* **74**, 160, 226

Argentine Grey Fox *see* Chilla
Asian Badger **75**, 162
Asian Small-clawed Otter **92**, 196, 232, 248
Asiatic Black Bear **61**, 134, 222, 243
Asiatic Golden Cat **6**, 24, 202, 234
Asiatic Jackal *see* Eurasian Golden Jackal
Asiatic Wild Dog *see* Dhole
*Atelocynus microtis* **57**, 126, 221
*Atilax paludinosus* **25**, 62, 208, 238
Azara's Fox *see* Pampas Fox

Back-striped Weasel *see* Stripe-backed Weasel
Bahamas Raccoon 142
Banded Civet **36**, 84, 214, 240
Banded Linsang **33**, 78, 212, 239
Banded Mongoose **29**, 70, 210, 238
Banded Palm Civet *see* Banded Civet
Barbados Raccoon 142
*Bassaricyon alleni* **67**, 146
*Bassaricyon gabbii* **67**, 146, 223
*Bassaricyon medius* **67**, 146
*Bassaricyon neblina* **67**, 146
*Bassariscus astutus* **67**, 146, 223, 244
*Bassariscus sumichrasti* **67**, 146, 223
Bat-eared Fox **54**, 120, 220, 242
Bay Cat **6**, 24, 202
Bay Lynx *see* Bobcat
*Bdeogale crassicauda* **26**, 64, 209
*Bdeogale jacksoni* **26**, 64, 209
*Bdeogale nigripes* **26**, 64, 209
*Bdeogale omnivora* 64
Bearcat *see* Binturong
Beech Marten *see* Stone Marten
Bengal Fox *see* Indian Fox
Binturong **34**, 80, 213, 239
Black-backed Jackal **50**, 112, 218, 241
Black-footed Cat **2**, 16, 201
Black-footed Ferret **83**, 178, 229, 246
Black-footed Mongoose *see* Black-legged Mongoose
Black-legged Mongoose **26**, 64, 209
Black Mongoose 60
Black Slender Mongoose *see* Kaokoveld Slender Mongoose
Black-tipped Mongoose *see* Common Slender Mongoose
Blanford's Fox **53**, 118, 219
Blue Fox *see* Arctic Fox
Bobcat **12**, 36, 204, 235
Bokiboky *see* Narrow-striped Boky
Bornean Ferret Badger **80**, 172, 246
Bourlon's Genet **41**, 94, 216
Broad-striped Malagasy Mongoose *see* Broad-striped Vontsira
Broad-striped Vontsira **32**, 76, 212
Brown Bear **63**, 138, 222, 243
Brown Hyaena **21**, 54, 206, 237
Brown Mongoose **23**, 58
Brown-nosed Coati *see* South American Coati
Brown Palm Civet **35**, 82, 213
Brown-tailed Mongoose *see* Brown-tailed Vontsira
Brown-tailed Vontsira **32**, 76, 212

Brush Wolf *see* Coyote
Burmese Ferret Badger *see* Large-toothed Ferret Badger
Bush Dog **58**, 128, 221, 242
Bushy-tailed Mongoose **26**, 64, 209

Cacomistle **67**, 146, 223
Cameroon Cusimanse *see* Flat-headed Cusimanse
Canada Lynx **12**, 36, 204, 235
Canadian Lynx *see* Canada Lynx
Canadian Otter *see* North American Otter
Canidae 9–10, 98–128, 217–21, 240–2
*Canis adusta* **50**, 112, 218, 241
*Canis anthus see Canis lupaster*
*Canis aureus* **47**, 106, 217, 241
*Canis dingo* 98
*Canis dingo hallstromi* **43**, 98
*Canis familiaris* **43**, 98, 217
*Canis hallstromi* **43**, 98
*Canis himalayensis* 100
*Canis latrans* **45**, 102, 217, 240
*Canis latrans* var. (*Canis 'oriens'*) **46**, 104
*Canis lupaster* **47**, 106
*Canis lupus* **44**, 100, 217, 240
*Canis lupus dingo* 98
*Canis lupus familiaris* **43**, 98, 217
*Canis lupus* var. (*Canis 'lycaon'*) **46**, 104
*Canis 'lycaon' see Canis lupus*
*Canis mesomelas* **50**, 112, 218, 241
*Canis 'oriens' see Canis latrans*
*Canis 'rufus'* **46**, 104, 217, 241
*Canis simensis* **48**, 108, 200, 217
Cape Clawless Otter **93**, 198, 232, 248
Cape Fox **54**, 120, 220, 242
Cape Genet **41**, 94, 216, 240
Cape Grey Mongoose **24**, 60, 208, 237
Cape Hunting Dog *see* African Wild Dog
Caracal **7**, 26, 203, 235
*Caracal aurata* **7**, 26, 203
*Caracal caracal* **7**, 26, 203, 235
Celebes Palm Civet *see* Sulawesi Civet
Central African Large-spotted Genet *see* Rusty-spotted Genet
Central African Oyan **42**, 96, 216
Central American Cacomistle *see* Cacomistle
Central American Spotted Skunk *see* Southern Spotted Skunk
*Cerdocyon thous* **57**, 126, 221
Channel Islands Fox *see* Island Fox
Cheetah **14**, 40, 205, 236
Chilla **56**, 124, 220
Chinese Desert Cat *see* Chinese Mountain Cat
Chinese Ferret Badger *see* Small-toothed Ferret Badger
Chinese Hog Badger *see* Northern Hog Badger
Chinese Mountain Cat **1**, 14, 201
Chinese Steppe Cat *see* Chinese Mountain Cat
*Chrotogale owstoni* **36**, 84, 214, 240
*Chrysocyon brachyurus* **58**, 128, 221
Chungungo *see* Marine Otter

*Civettictis civetta* **38**, 88, 215, 240
Coatimundi *see* White-nosed Coati
Collared Mongoose **23**, 58, 207
Colocolo **10**, 32, 204
Colombian Weasel **87**, 186, 230
Common Cusimanse **30**, 72, 211
Common Dwarf Mongoose **28**, 68, 210, 238
Common Fox *see* Red Fox
Common Genet *see* Small-spotted Genet
Common Grey Mongoose *see* Indian Grey Mongoose
Common Hog-nosed Skunk *see* American Hog-nosed Skunk
Common Jackal *see* Eurasian Golden Jackal
Common Otter *see* Eurasian Otter
Common Palm Civet **34**, 80, 213, 239
Common Polecat *see* Western Polecat
Common Raccoon *see* Northern Raccoon
Common Slender Mongoose **24**, 60, 208, 237
Common Weasel *see* Least Weasel
Conepatus chinga **70**, 152, 224
*Conepatus humboldtii* 152
*Conepatus leuconotus* **69**, 150, 224, 244
*Conepatus mesoleucus* 150
*Conepatus semistriatus* **70**, 152, 224
Congo Clawless Otter **93**, 198, 232
Congo Small-clawed Otter *see* Congo Clawless Otter
Corsac *see* Corsac Fox
Corsac Fox **52**, 116, 219
Cougar *see* Puma
Coyote **45**, 102, 217, 240
Cozumel Raccoon *see* Pygmy Raccoon
Crab-eating Fox **57**, 126, 221
Crab-eating Mongoose **23**, 58, 207, 237
Crab-eating Raccoon **65**, 142, 223, 243
Crab-eating Zorro *see* Crab-eating Fox
Crested Genet **39**, 90
Crested Servaline Genet *see* Crested Genet
*Crocuta crocuta* **21**, 54, 206, 237
Cross Fox *see* Red Fox
*Crossarchus alexandri* **30**, 72, 211
*Crossarchus ansorgei* **30**, 72, 211
*Crossarchus obscurus* **30**, 72, 211
*Crossarchus platycephalus* **30**, 72, 211
*Cryptoprocta ferox* **31**, 74, 211, 238
Cuc Phuong Ferret Badger **80**, 172
Culpeo **56**, 124, 220
*Cuon alpinus* **48**, 108, 217, 241
*Cynictis penicillata* **27**, 66, 209, 238
*Cynogale bennettii* **36**, 84, 214, 240
*Cynogale lowei* 84

Darwin's Fox **56**, 124
Desert Dwarf Mongoose *see* Somali Dwarf Mongoose
Dhole **48**, 108, 217, 241
Dingo **43**, 98, 217
*Diplogale hosei* **36**, 84, 214
*Dologale dybowskii* **28**, 68, 210
Durrell's Vontsira *see* Brown-tailed Vontsira

Dwarf Mongoose *see* Common Dwarf Mongoose

Eastern Coyote **46**, 104
Eastern Lowland Olingo **67**, 146
Eastern Mountain Coati 144
Eastern Spotted Skunk **71**, 154, 225, 244
Eastern Wolf **46**, 104
Egyptian Mongoose **24**, 60, 208, 237
Egyptian Weasel 184
Eira *see* Tayra
*Eira barbara* **76**, 164, 226, 245
*Enhydra lutris* **90**, 192, 231
Ermine *see* Stoat
Ethiopian Dwarf Mongoose *see* Somali Dwarf Mongoose
Ethiopian Genet *see* Abyssinian Genet
Ethiopian Wolf **48**, 108, 200, 217
*Eupleres goudotii* **31**, 74, 211, 238
Eupleridae 8, 74–6, 211–12, 238–9
Eurasian Golden Jackal **47**, 106, 217, 241
Eurasian Lynx **11**, 34, 204, 235
Eurasian Otter **91**, 194, 232, 248
Eurasian Pine Marten *see* Pine Marten
European Badger **75**, 162, 226, 245
European Mink **85**, 182, 230, 247
European Otter *see* Eurasian Otter
European Pine Marten *see* Pine Marten
European Polecat *see* Western Polecat
European Wildcat **1**, 14, 201, 234
Everett's Ferret Badger *see* Bornean Ferret Badger
Eyra *see* Jaguarundi

Falanouc **31**, 74, 211, 238
Fanaloka **31**, 74, 211, 238
Felidae 7–8, 14–50, 201–206, 234–6
Feline Genet 92
*Felis bieti* **1**, 14, 201
*Felis chaus* **2**, 16, 201, 234
*Felis lybica* **1**, 14, 201, 234
*Felis margarita* **2**, 16, 201
*Felis nigripes* **2**, 16, 201
*Felis silvestris* **1**, 14, 201, 234
Fennec **54**, 120, 220
Fennec Fox *see* Fennec
Ferret *see* Western Polecat
Fisher **77**, 166, 227, 245
Fishing Cat **3**, 18, 201, 234
Fishing Genet *see* Aquatic Genet
Flat-headed Cat **5**, 22, 202, 234
Flat-headed Cusimanse **30**, 72, 211
Fosa **31**, 74, 211, 238
Fossa *see* Fosa
*Fossa fossana* **31**, 74, 211, 238

*Galictis cuja* **81**, 174, 228
*Galictis vittata* **81**, 174, 228, 246
*Galidia elegans* **32**, 76, 212, 239
*Galidictis fasciata* **32**, 76, 212
*Galidictis fasciata grandidieri* **32**, 76
Gambian Mongoose **29**, 70, 210
*Genetta abyssinica* **39**, 90, 215
*Genetta angolensis* **40**, 92, 215
*Genetta bourloni* **41**, 94, 216

*Genetta cristata* **39**, 90
*Genetta felina* 92
*Genetta genetta* **40**, 92, 215
*Genetta johnstoni* **40**, 92, 215
*Genetta maculata* **41**, 94, 216
*Genetta pardina* **41**, 94, 216
*Genetta piscivora* **40**, 92, 215
*Genetta poensis* **41**, 94, 216
*Genetta servalina* **39**, 90, 215
*Genetta thierryi* **39**, 90, 215
*Genetta tigrina* **41**, 94, 216, 240
*Genetta victoriae* **39**, 90, 215
Geoffroy's Cat **9**, 30, 203
Giant Genet **39**, 90, 215
Giant Otter **91**, 194, 232
Giant Panda **59**, 130, 221, 242
Glutton *see* Wolverine
Golden Jackal *see* Eurasian Golden Jackal
Golden Palm Civet **35**, 82, 213
Golden Wolf *see* African Wolf
Grandidier's Vontsira **32**, 76
Greater Grison **81**, 174, 228, 246
Greater Hog Badger **74**, 160, 226, 245
Grey Fox **55**, 122, 220, 242
Grey-headed Tayra *see* Tayra
Grey Wolf **44**, 100, 217, 240
Grey Wolf-Coyote hybrids **46**, 104
Grizzly Bear *see* Brown Bear
Guadeloupe Raccoon 142
Guigna *see* Guiña
Guiña **10**, 32, 204
*Gulo gulo* **76**, 164, 226, 245

Hairy-nosed Otter **92**, 196, 232, 248
Hausa Genet **39**, 90, 215
*Helarctos malayanus* **60**, 132, 222, 242
*Helogale hirtula* **28**, 68, 210
*Helogale parvula* **28**, 68, 210, 238
*Hemigalus derbyanus* **36**, 84, 214, 240
*Herpailurus yagouaroundi* **13**, 38, 205
*Herpestes auropunctatus* **22**, 56, 207, 237
*Herpestes brachyurus* **22**, 56, 207
*Herpestes edwardsii* **22**, 56, 207
*Herpestes flavescens* **24**, 60
*Herpestes fuscus* **23**, 58
*Herpestes hosei* 56
*Herpestes ichneumon* **24**, 60, 208, 237
*Herpestes javanicus* **22**, 56, 207
*Herpestes naso* **25**, 62, 208
*Herpestes nigrata* 60
*Herpestes pulverulentus* **24**, 60, 208, 237
*Herpestes sanguineus* **24**, 60, 208, 237
*Herpestes semitorquatus* **23**, 58, 207
*Herpestes smithii* **23**, 58, 207
*Herpestes urva* **23**, 58, 207, 237
*Herpestes vitticollis* **23**, 58, 207
Herpestidae 8, 56–72, 207–11, 237–8
Himalayan Black Bear *see* Asiatic Black Bear
Himalayan Weasel *see* Siberian Weasel
Himalayan Yellow-throated Marten *see* Yellow-throated Marten
Hoary Fox **57**, 126, 221
Hoary Zorro *see* Hoary Fox
Honey Badger **73**, 158, 225, 245
Honey Bear *see* Sun Bear

Hooded Skunk **69**, 150, 224, 244
Hose's Civet **36**, 84, 214
Hose's Mongoose 56
Huillin *see* Southern River Otter
Humboldt's Hog-nosed Skunk 152
Huroncito *see* Patagonian Weasel
*Hyaena hyaena* **20**, 52, 206
Hyaenidae 8, 52–4, 206, 237
*Hydrictis maculicollis* **93**, 198, 232

Iberian Lynx **11**, 34, 204
*Ichneumia albicauda* **25**, 62, 208, 238
Ichneumon *see* Egyptian Mongoose
*Ictonyx libycus* **82**, 176, 229
*Ictonyx striatus* **82**, 176, 229
Indian Brown Mongoose *see* Brown
   Mongoose
Indian Fox **52**, 116, 219
Indian Grey Mongoose **22**, 56, 207
Indian Jackal *see* Eurasian Golden Jackal
Indian Smooth-coated Otter *see* Smooth-
   coated Otter
Indochinese Leopard Cat *see* Mainland
   Leopard Cat
Indonesian Mountain Weasel **88**, 188,
   231
Indonesian Stink-badger *see* Sunda Stink
   badger
Island Fox **55**, 122, 220
Island Grey Fox *see* Island Fox

Jackson's Mongoose **26**, 64, 209
Jaguar **17**, 50, 206, 236
Jaguarundi **13**, 38, 205
Japanese Badger **75**, 162
Japanese Marten **78**, 168, 227
Japanese Otter 194
Japanese Weasel **84**, 180
Javan Ferret Badger **80**, 172, 228
Javan Mongoose *see* Small Asian Mongoose
Javan Small-toothed Palm Civet *see* Small-
   toothed Palm Civet
Jerdon's Palm Civet *see* Brown Palm Civet
Johnston's Genet **40**, 92, 215
Jungle Cat **2**, 16, 201, 234

Kaokoveld Slender Mongoose **24**, 60
Kharza *see* Yellow-throated Marten
Kinabalu Ferret Badger *see* Bornean Ferret
   Badger
King Fox *see* Blanford's Fox
King Genet **41**, 94, 216
Kinkajou **68**, 148, 224, 244
Kit Fox **52**, 116, 219
Kodkod *see* Guiña
Kolinsky *see* Siberian Weasel

Large Grey Mongoose *see* Egyptian
   Mongoose
Large Indian Civet **37**, 86, 214, 240
Large-spotted Civet **37**, 86, 214
Large-spotted Genet *see* Cape Genet
Large-toothed Ferret Badger **80**, 172, 228
Least Weasel **86**, 184, 230, 247
Leighton's Linsang *see* Leighton's Oyan
Leighton's Oyan **42**, 96

Leopard **18**, 48, 206, 236
*Leopardus colocolo* **10**, 32, 204
*Leopardus geoffroyi* **9**, 30, 203
*Leopardus guigna* **10**, 32, 204
*Leopardus guttulus* **9**, 30, 203
*Leopardus jacobita* **10**, 32, 204
*Leopardus oncilla* 30
*Leopardus pardalis* **8**, 28, 203, 235
*Leopardus pardinoides* 30
*Leopardus tigrinus* **9**, 30, 203
*Leopardus wiedii* **8**, 28, 203, 235
*Leptailurus serval* **7**, 26, 203, 235
Lesser Grison **81**, 174, 228
Lesser Oriental Civet *see* Small Indian
   Civet
Lesser Panda *see* Red Panda
Liberian Mongoose **29**, 70, 210
*Liberiictis kuhni* **29**, 70, 210
Libyan Weasel **82**, 176, 229
Lion **17**, 46, 205, 236
Little-spotted Cat *see* Northern Tigrina
Long-nosed Cusimanse *see* Common
   Cusimanse
Long-nosed Mongoose **25**, 62, 208
Long-snouted Mongoose *see* Long-nosed
   Mongoose
Long-tailed Weasel **87**, 186, 230, 247
*Lontra canadensis* **90**, 192, 231, 247
*Lontra felina* **89**, 190, 231
*Lontra longicaudis* **89**, 190, 231, 247
*Lontra provocax* **89**, 190, 231
Lowe's Otter Civet 84
*Lupulella adusta see Canis adusta*
*Lupulella mesomelas see Canis mesomelas*
*Lutra lutra* **91**, 194, 232, 248
*Lutra nippon* 194
*Lutra sumatrana* **92**, 196, 232, 248
*Lutrogale perspicillata* **92**, 196, 232, 248
*Lycalopex culpaeus* **56**, 124, 220
*Lycalopex fulvipes* **56**, 124
*Lycalopex griseus* **56**, 124, 220
*Lycalopex gymnocercus* **57**, 126, 221
*Lycalopex sechurae* **56**, 124, 220
*Lycalopex vetulus* **57**, 126, 221
*Lycaon pictus* **49**, 110, 218, 241
*Lyncodon patagonicus* **81**, 174, 228
*Lynx canadensis* **12**, 36, 204, 235
*Lynx lynx* **11**, 34, 204, 235
*Lynx pardinus* **11**, 34, 204
*Lynx rufus* **12**, 36, 204, 235

*Macrogalidia musschenbroekii* **35**, 82, 213
Mainland Clouded Leopard **15**, 42, 205,
   236
Mainland Leopard Cat **4**, 20, 202, 234
Malabar Civet **37**, 86, 214
Malagasy Civet *see* Fanaloka
Malay Civet **37**, 86, 214
Malay Weasel **88**, 188, 231, 247
Malayan Stink-badger *see* Sunda Stink-
   badger
Malayan Sun Bear *see* Sun Bear
Maned Wolf **58**, 128, 221
Manul *see* Pallas's Cat
Marbled Cat **6**, 24, 202, 234
Marbled Polecat **81**, 174, 228, 246

Margay **8**, 28, 203, 235
Marine Otter **89**, 190, 231
Marsh Mongoose **25**, 62, 208, 238
*Martes americana* **77**, 166, 227, 245
*Martes caurina* **77**, 166
*Martes flavigula* **79**, 170, 227, 246
*Martes foina* **78**, 168, 227, 246
*Martes gwatkinsii* **79**, 170
*Martes martes* **78**, 168, 227, 246
*Martes melampus* **78**, 168, 227
*Martes zibellina* **77**, 166, 227
Masked Palm Civet **34**, 80, 213, 239
Meerkat **27**, 66, 209
*Meles anakuma* **75**, 162
*Meles leucurus* **75**, 162
*Meles meles* **75**, 162, 226, 245
Meller's Mongoose **27**, 66, 209
*Mellivora capensis* **73**, 158, 225, 245
*Melogale cucphuongensis* **80**, 172
*Melogale everetti* **80**, 172, 246
*Melogale moschata* **80**, 172, 228
*Melogale orientalis* **80**, 172, 228
*Melogale personata* **80**, 172, 228
*Melursus ursinus* **60**, 132, 222, 242
Mephitidae 10–11, 150–6, 224–5, 244
*Mephitis macroura* **69**, 150, 224, 244
*Mephitis mephitis* **69**, 150, 224, 244
Miombo Genet **40**, 92, 215
Molina's Hog-nosed Skunk **70**, 152, 224
Moon Bear *see* Asiatic Black Bear
Mountain Coati **66**, 144, 223
Mountain Lion *see* Puma
*Mungos gambianus* **29**, 70, 210
*Mungos mungo* **29**, 70, 210, 238
*Mungotictis decemlineata* **32**, 76, 212, 239
Musang *see* Common Palm Civet
*Mustela africana* **87**, 186, 230
*Mustela altaica* **86**, 184, 230
*Mustela erminea* **86**, 184, 230, 247
*Mustela eversmanii* **84**, 180, 229
*Mustela felipei* **87**, 186, 230
*Mustela frenata* **87**, 186, 230, 247
*Mustela itatsi* **84**, 180
*Mustela kathiah* **88**, 188, 231
*Mustela lutreola* **85**, 182, 230, 247
*Mustela lutreolina* **88**, 188, 231
*Mustela nigripes* **83**, 178, 229, 246
*Mustela nivalis* **86**, 184, 230, 247
*Mustela nudipes* **88**, 188, 231, 247
*Mustela putorius* **85**, 182, 230, 247
*Mustela russelliana* 184
*Mustela sibirica* **84**, 180, 229
*Mustela strigidorsa* **88**, 188, 231
*Mustela subpalmata* 184
*Mustela tonkinensis* 184
Mustelidae 11, 158–98, 225–32, 245–8
*Mydaus javanensis* **72**, 156, 225, 244
*Mydaus marchei* **72**, 156, 225

Nandinia *see* African Palm-civet
*Nandinia binotata* **42**, 96, 216
Nandiniidae 9, 96
Narrow-striped Boky **32**, 76, 212, 239
Narrow-striped Mongoose *see* Narrow-
   striped Boky
*Nasua narica* **66**, 144, 223, 243

*Nasua nasua* **66**, 144, 223
*Nasuella meridensis* 144
*Nasuella olivacea* **66**, 144, 223
Nearctic Otter *see* North American Otter
*Neofelis diardi* **15**, 42, 205, 236
*Neofelis nebulosa* **15**, 42, 205, 236
Neotropical Otter **89**, 190, 231, 247
Neotropical River Otter *see* Neotropical Otter
*Neovison vison* **83**, 178, 229, 246
New Guinea Highland Wild Dog *see* New Guinea Singing Dog
New Guinea Singing Dog **43**, 98
Nilgiri Marten **79**, 170
North African Striped Weasel *see* Libyan Weasel
North American Otter **90**, 192, 231, 247
North American Red Fox 114
North-west Asian Badger *see* Asian Badger
Northern Grey Fox *see* Grey Fox
Northern Hog Badger **74**, 160, 226
Northern Olingo **67**, 146, 223
Northern Raccoon **65**, 142, 223, 243
Northern Tigrina **9**, 30, 203
*Nyctereutes procyonoides* **55**, 122, 220, 242

Ocelot **8**, 28, 203, 235
Olingos **67**, 146
Olinguito **67**, 146
Oncilla *see* Northern Tigrina
Oriental Civet *see* Malay Civet
Oriental Small-clawed Otter *see* Asian Small-clawed Otter
*Otocolobus manul* **3**, 18, 201
*Otocyon megalotis* **54**, 120, 220, 242
Otter Civet **36**, 84, 214, 240
Ounce *see* Snow Leopard
Owston's Civet **36**, 84, 214, 240
Owston's Palm Civet *see* Owston's Civet

Pacific Marten **77**, 166
*Paguma larvata* **34**, 80, 213, 239
Painted Dog *see* African Wild Dog
Palawan Binturong 80
Palawan Stink-badger **72**, 156, 225
Pale Fox **53**, 118, 219
Pallas's Cat **3**, 18, 201
Pallid Fox *see* Pale Fox
Pampas Cat *see* Colocolo
Pampas Fox **57**, 126, 221
Panamanian Olingo *see* Western Lowland Olingo
Panther *see* Leopard
Panther (Florida) *see* Puma
*Panthera leo* **17**, 46, 205, 236
*Panthera onca* **19**, 50, 206, 236
*Panthera pardus* **18**, 48, 206, 236
*Panthera tigris* **16**, 44, 205, 233, 236
*Panthera uncia* **15**, 42, 205, 236
Pantot *see* Palawan Stink-badger
*Paracynictis selousi* **27**, 66, 209
*Paradoxurus hermaphroditus* **34**, 80, 213, 239
*Paradoxurus jerdoni* **35**, 82, 213

*Paradoxurus zeylonensis* **35**, 82, 213
*Parahyaena brunnea* **21**, 54, 206, 237
Pardel Lynx *see* Iberian Lynx
Pardine Genet **41**, 94, 216
*Pardofelis marmorata* **6**, 24, 202, 234
Patagonian Hog-nosed Skunk *see* Humboldt's Hog-nosed Skunk
Patagonian River Otter *see* Southern River Otter
Patagonian Weasel **81**, 174, 228
*Pekania pennanti* **77**, 166, 227, 245
Philippine Stink-badger *see* Palawan Stink-badger
Pine Marten **78**, 168, 227, 246
*Poecilogale albinucha* **82**, 176, 229
*Poiana leightoni* **42**, 96
*Poiana richardsonii* **42**, 96, 216
Polar Bear **64**, 140, 222, 233, 243
Polar Fox *see* Arctic Fox
Potos flavus **68**, 148, 224, 244
Pousargues's Mongoose **28**, 68, 210
Prairie Wolf *see* Coyote
*Prionailurus bengalensis* **4**, 20, 202, 234
*Prionailurus javanensis* **4**, 20, 202, 234
*Prionailurus planiceps* **5**, 22, 202, 234
*Prionailurus rubiginosus* **5**, 22, 202
*Prionailurus viverrinus* **3**, 18, 201, 234
*Prionodon linsang* **33**, 78, 212, 239
*Prionodon pardicolor* **33**, 78, 212, 239
Prionodontidae **8**, 78, 212, 239
*Procyon cancrivorus* **65**, 142, 223, 243
*Procyon gloveralleni* 142
*Procyon lotor* **65**, 142, 223, 243
*Procyon maynardi* 142
*Procyon minor* 142
*Procyon pygmaeus* **65**, 142
Procyonidae 10, 142–8, 223–4, 243–4
*Proteles cristata* **20**, 52, 206, 237
*Pteronura brasiliensis* **91**, 194, 232
Puma **13**, 38, 205, 235
*Puma concolor* **13**, 38, 205, 235
Pygmy Raccoon **65**, 142
Pygmy Skunk *see* Pygmy Spotted Skunk
Pygmy Spotted Skunk **72**, 156, 225

Raccoon Dog **55**, 122, 220, 242
Rasse *see* Small Indian Civet
Ratel *see* Honey Badger
Red Fox **51**, 114, 218, 241
Red Lynx *see* Bobcat
Red Panda **68**, 148, 224, 244
Red Wolf **46**, 104, 217, 241
Reed Cat *see* Jungle Cat
*Rhynchogale melleri* **27**, 66, 209
Richardson's Linsang *see* Central African Oyan
Ringtail **67**, 146, 223, 244
Ring-tailed Coati *see* South American Coati
Ring-tailed Mongoose *see* Ring-tailed Mongoose
Ring-tailed Vontsira **32**, 76, 212, 239
River Otter *see* North American Otter
Royal Fox *see* Blanford's Fox
Ruddy Mongoose **23**, 58, 207
Rüppell's Fox **53**, 118, 219

Rusty-spotted Cat **5**, 22, 202
Rusty-spotted Genet **41**, 94, 216

Sable **77**, 166, 227
Saharan Striped Polecat *see* Libyan Weasel
Salano *see* Brown-tailed Vontsira
*Salanoia concolor* **32**, 76, 212
*Salanoia durrelli see Salanoia concolor*
Sand Cat **2**, 16, 201
Sand Fox *see* Rüppell's Fox and Tibetan Fox
Savannah Mongoose *see* Pousargues's Mongoose
Sea Otter **90**, 192, 231
Sechura Desert Fox *see* Sechuran Fox
Sechura Fox *see* Sechuran Fox
Sechuran Fox **56**, 124, 220
Selous's Mongoose **27**, 66, 209
Serval **7**, 26, 203, 235
Servaline Genet **39**, 90, 215
Short-eared Dog **57**, 126, 221
Short-tailed Mongoose **22**, 56, 207
Short-tailed Weasel *see* Stoat
Siberian Polecat *see* Siberian Weasel
Siberian Weasel **84**, 180, 229
Sichuan Weasel 184
Side-striped Jackal **50**, 112, 218, 241
Silver-backed Jackal *see* Black-backed Jackal
Silver Fox *see* Red Fox
Simien Fox *see* Ethiopian Wolf
Simien Jackal *see* Ethiopian Wolf
Skunk-bear *see* Wolverine
Slender Mongoose *see* Common Slender Mongoose
Slender-tailed Meerkat *see* Meerkat
Sloth Bear **60**, 132, 222, 242
Small Asian Mongoose **22**, 56, 207
Small-eared Dog *see* Short-eared Dog
Small Grey Mongoose *see* Cape Grey Mongoose
Small Indian Civet **38**, 88, 215, 240
Small Indian Mongoose **22**, 56, 207, 237
Small-spotted Cat *see* Black-footed Cat
Small-spotted Genet **40**, 92, 215
Small-toothed Dog *see* Hoary Fox
Small-toothed Ferret Badger **80**, 172, 228
Small-toothed Palm Civet **33**, 78, 212, 239
Smooth-coated Otter **92**, 196, 232, 248
Smooth Otter *see* Smooth-coated Otter
Snow Leopard **15**, 42, 205, 236
Sokoke Bushy-tailed Mongoose 64
Somali Dwarf Mongoose **28**, 68, 210
Somali Slender Mongoose **24**, 60
Somalian Slender Mongoose *see* Somali Slender Mongoose
South African Small-Spotted Genet *see* Feline Genet
South American Coati **66**, 144, 223
Southern Grey Fox *see* Chilla
Southern River Otter **89**, 190, 231
Southern Spotted Skunk **71**, 154
Southern Tigrina **9**, 30, 203
Spanish Lynx *see* Iberian Lynx
Spectacled Bear *see* Andean Bear

*Speothos venaticus* **58**, 128, 221, 242
*Spilogale angustifrons* **71**, 154
*Spilogale gracilis* **71**, 154, 225, 244
*Spilogale putorius* **71**, 154, 225, 244
*Spilogale pygmaea* **72**, 156, 225
Spotted Fanaloka *see* Fanaloka
Spotted Hyaena **21**, 54, 206, 237
Spotted Linsang **33**, 78, 212, 239
Spotted-necked Otter **93**, 198, 232
Steppe Cat *see* Pallas's Cat
Steppe Fox *see* Corsac Fox
Steppe Polecat **84**, 180, 229
Steppe Weasel *see* Steppe Polecat
Stoat **86**, 184, 230, 247
Stone Marten **78**, 168, 227, 246
Stripe-backed Weasel **88**, 188, 231
Stripe-necked Mongoose **23**, 58, 207
Striped Hog-nosed Skunk **70**, 152, 224
Striped Hyaena **20**, 52, 206
Striped Mongoose *see* Banded Mongoose
Striped Polecat *see* Zorilla
Striped Skunk **69**, 150, 224, 244
Striped Weasel **82**, 176, 229
Sulawesi Civet **35**, 82, 213
Sulawesi Palm Civet *see* Sulawesi Civet
Sumatran Hog Badger **74**, 160, 226
Sun Bear **60**, 132, 222, 242
Sunda Clouded Leopard **15**, 42, 205, 236
Sunda Leopard Cat **4**, 20, 202, 234
Sunda Otter Civet *see* Otter Civet
Sunda Stink-badger **72**, 156, 225, 244
*Suricata suricatta* **27**, 66, 209
Suricate *see* Meerkat
Swamp Cat *see* Jungle Cat
Swamp Otter *see* Congo Clawless Otter
Swift Fox **52**, 116, 219, 241

Tanuki *see* Raccoon Dog
*Taxidea taxus* **73**, 158, 225, 245
Tayra **76**, 164, 226, 245
Teledu *see* Sunda Stink-badger
Temminck's Golden Cat *see* Asiatic Golden Cat
Thierry's Genet *see* Hausa Genet

Three-striped Palm Civet *see* Small-toothed Palm Civet
Tibetan Black Bear *see* Asiatic Black Bear
Tibetan Fox **53**, 118, 219
Tibetan Sand Fox *see* Tibetan Fox
Tiger **16**, 44, 205, 233, 236
Tiger Cat *see* Northern Tigrina
Timber Wolf *see* Grey Wolf
Toddy Cat *see* Common Palm Civet
Tonkin Weasel 184
Tree Fox *see* Grey Fox
Tree Ocelot *see* Margay
*Tremarctos ornatus* **61**, 134, 222
Tres Marias Raccoon 142
Tropical Weasel *see* Amazon Weasel
Tsushima Island Marten *see* Japanese Marten
Tundra Wolf *see* Grey Wolf
Two-spotted Palm-civet *see* African Palm-civet

*Urocyon cinereoargenteus* **55**, 122, 220, 242
*Urocyon littoralis* **55**, 122, 220
Ursidae 10, 130–40, 221–2, 242–3
*Ursus americanus* **62**, 136, 222, 243
*Ursus arctos* **63**, 138, 222, 243
*Ursus maritimus* **64**, 140, 222, 233, 243
*Ursus thibetanus* **61**, 134, 222, 243
*Urva auropunctatus see Herpestes auropunctatus*
*Urva brachyurus see Herpestes brachyurus*
*Urva edwardsii see Herpestes edwardsii*
*Urva fuscus see Herpestes fuscus*
*Urva javanicus see Herpestes javanicus*
*Urva semitorquatus see Herpestes semitorquatus*
*Urva smithii see Herpestes smithii*
*Urva urva see Herpestes urva*
*Urva vitticollis see Herpestes vitticollis*

Vietnam Ferret Badger *see* Cuc Phuong Ferret Badger
*Viverra civettina* **37**, 86, 214
*Viverra megaspila* **37**, 86, 214

*Viverra tangalunga* **37**, 86, 214
*Viverra zibetha* **37**, 86, 214, 240
*Viverricula indica* **38**, 88, 215, 240
Viverridae 9, 78–96, 212–16, 239–40
*Vormela peregusna* **81**, 174, 228, 246
*Vulpes bengalensis* **52**, 116, 219
*Vulpes cana* **53**, 118, 219
*Vulpes chama* **54**, 120, 220, 242
*Vulpes corsac* **52**, 116, 219
*Vulpes ferrilata* **53**, 118, 219
*Vulpes fulva* 114
*Vulpes lagopus* **51**, 114, 218, 241
*Vulpes macrotis* **52**, 116, 219
*Vulpes pallida* **53**, 118, 219
*Vulpes rueppellii* **53**, 118, 219
*Vulpes velox* **52**, 116, 219, 241
*Vulpes vulpes* **51**, 114, 218, 241
*Vulpes zerda* **54**, 120, 220

Water Mongoose *see* Marsh Mongoose
West African Cusimanse *see* Common Cusimanse
West African Large-spotted Genet *see* Pardine Genet
West African Linsang *see* Leighton's Oyan
Western Hog-nosed Skunk 150
Western Lowland Olingo **67**, 146
Western Mountain Coati *see* Mountain Coati
Western Polecat **85**, 182, 230, 247
Western Spotted Skunk **71**, 154, 225, 244
White Fox *see* Arctic Fox
White-naped Weasel *see* Striped Weasel
White-nosed Coati **66**, 144, 223, 243
White-tailed Mongoose **25**, 62, 208, 238
Wolverine **76**, 164, 226, 245

Xenogale 62

Yellow-bellied Weasel **88**, 188, 231
Yellow Marten *see* Japanese Marten
Yellow Mongoose **27**, 66, 209, 238
Yellow-throated Marten **79**, 170, 227, 246

Zorilla **82**, 176, 229